The Society of Text

The Society of Text
Hypertext, Hypermedia, and the Social Construction of Information

edited by
Edward Barrett

The MIT Press
Cambridge, Massachusetts
London, England

Publisher's Note

This format is intended to reduce the cost of publishing certain works in book form and to shorten the gap between editorial preparation and final publication. Detailed editing and composition have been avoided by photographing the text of this book directly from the authors' prepared copy.

Second printing, 1991

© 1989 Massachusetts Institute of Technology

This book was printed and bound in the United States of America.

Library of Congress Cataloging-in-Publication Data

The Society of text / edited by Edward Barrett.
    p.   cm. -- (Information systems)
   Includes index.
   ISBN 0-262-02291-5
   1. Hypertext (Computer system) 2. Technical
writing--Data processing. I. Barrett, Edward.
II. Series: Information systems (Cambridge, Mass.)
QA76.76.H94S65   1989
005.75'4--dc20   89-31898
                                                 CIP

Contents

Acknowledgments

Versions of some chapters in this book were first presented at the fifth annual *Conference on Writing for the Computer Industry* which I direct each summer at MIT. For their support of this conference I wish to thank Frederick J. McGarry, Director of the Office of the Summer Session at MIT, Maria Murphy, Assistant-Director, and their staff. In addition, I would also like to thank John Kirsch, Philip Rubens, and Muriel Zimmerman for their help in organizing this conference.

I am especially grateful to James Paradis of the MIT Writing Program for our many discussions about computing technology and documentation as part of our collaborative work on the *Educational Online System.* My thanks also to David Custer and Bruce Lewis for our discussions about computers and education.

From the MIT Press, I wish to thank Frank Satlow and especially Terry Ehling for their support and assistance in bringing this volume to print.

Finally, I am most pleased to express my gratitude to Kenneth R. Manning, Head of the Writing Program, for his encouragement and generous support of my work on writing and computers at MIT. With respect I dedicate this volume to him.

Introduction

Thought and Language in a Virtual Environment

The Society of Text continues an examination of online information and net-worked systems that I began in *Text, ConText, and HyperText* (Barrett, 1988). As in my first book, this volume asserts a synthesis of three related areas of activity within the computer industry: writing, management, and engineering--and this synthesis implies a revisioning of the roles of writer and manager and engineer in systems development. In addition, *The Society of Text* also presents for examination an alternative model for thinking about the design and use of hypertext and hypermedia systems and their role in the creation of "text." In essence, this new model is based on the social construction of knowledge and rejects traditional cognitive terminology. The contributors to *The Society of Text* are leading researchers in writing and computing within industry and the academy. Working versions of many of the chapters in this book were first presented at the annual conference on "Writing for the Computer Industry" which I direct each summer at MIT.

Modeling "mind" in the computer

The title of this volume is, obviously, a response to Marvin Minsky's *The Society of Mind* (1986). Minsky's canny book develops a way of thinking about the mind that may also be productive of a way of thinking about a computer. Of course, "develops" is too strong a word since *The Society of Mind* unfolds like a prose sonnet sequence, each essay building toward a unified theory, yet restricted by the contingency of a self-imposed form, in this case the most obvious for a writer--the end of the page. Minsky seems to be using a particular style of writing that is representative of the cognitive model he is invoking: just as "mind" is created out of the actions of hypothetical, un-thinking subagencies and agents, his "theory" is constructed out of an alignment of meanings conveyed by his brief, seemingly atomistic essays.

In Minsky's model, "mind" is an epiphenomenon of *subagencies* that work in various administrative alliances to accomplish goals. Attainment of these goals is a sign of "development" or "growth," of "understanding" or "reason." Mind, therefore, is reduced to that which is in itself essentially mindless, an organization, a structure along which connections are made and ends attained, although larger questions involving the values of those ends and how one assesses those values or draws motives for wanting to attain these ends are not fully addressed. Cognition moves along, and is created by, branching *K-lines* of Boolean chasteness.

I assume Minsky develops this model of the mind because he feels it maps so well to the computer. If mind, or intelligence, is really a network of innumerable, mindless internal connections, it should be possible to personify them in the design of a computer system. Thus, Minsky sketches a theory of mind as part of an established tradition for thinking about computer design, one that seeks to model the mind in the machine.

The Society of Text, therefore, alludes to this tradition in computer science, but only to suggest another model for system use and development, a model that eschews cognitive terminology for an emphasis upon the social construction of knowledge. Certainly, the beginnings of hypertext are steeped in cognitive theory. Vannevar Bush (1945) specifically states that his prototype hypertext system, *Memex*, works the way the human mind does, and the particular psychology of mind he brings in to defend his design principle is *associationalism*, the concept that mind functions by means of associative leaps from one thing to another. Douglas Engelbart (1963), another pioneer in hypertext development, also asserts that his system, *NLS/Augment*, enlarges the scope of human thought. Finally, Ted Nelson (1980), who coined the word "hypertext," conceived of the *Xanadu* project as an empowerment of human memory, allowing an individual to draw interconnections between disparate texts stored online for the purpose, presumably, of showing deeper structure and meaning. The Coleridgean reference in the naming of his system is no mere grace note. Nelson's conception of hypertext is highly Romantic: the computer tracks the mind as it interlinks seemingly disparate text objects and facilitates that motion of mind through highly developed annotation features; programming, in other words, permits the sculpting of imaginative insights. But what are the effects of modeling cognitive theory in computing technology?

Knowledge representations

Any system founded upon a particular conception of mind will be partially constrained by the limitations of that initial conception. The least effective application of computing technology in the development of information systems is the sort that results in the production of static knowledge representation systems, rather than adequate tools for the construction of meaning and knowledge. By "knowledge representation" I mean a closed system that objectifies a theory of how the mind works, or how knowledge looks when it is developed. Such systems have the seeming-virtue of completeness: a *view of things* is coherently and completely expressed, and this internal machine perspective leads the user to incorporate that perspective in the completion of a task. I have discussed the behaviorism implied in this design approach in the introduction to *Text, ConText, and HyperText* (see also, Barrett and Paradis, 1988). Skinnerianism in computer design is superbly suited to a limited perspective of machine use: most commonly a single-user single-machine dynamic with the computer often relegated to an environment other than the one in which active knowledge construction takes place.

Certainly, hypertext, on one level, offers representations of closed knowledge systems: some sort of database will exist as a ground for further manipulation. This database will be structured by the initial programming effort to help the user navigate in new ways through the mass of information stored online. The primary question, then, is the degree to which a hypertext system preserves authorial (that is, programming) imperatives. If the internal structure is too highly constrained by the initial programming input, the user is relegated to the position of merely manipulating text-objects through an *a priori* associative web. A collage of conceptual or factual blocks may be achieved, but a deeper structuring of imaginative insights may not be possible.

However, hypertext systems, following Nelson, should also permit context-free annotation functions. In general, I take this concept of online annotation in hypertexts to be something more than a mere establishment of a link between two objects. After all, the drawing of an arrow from one point to another silently implies paragraphs of meaning. What is a gesture for if not to imply further language about the thing pointed at? What bothers me in the concept of hypertext linking is the minimalism of these pointing gestures. To know that one programming line will take me from *a* to *b* constrains my ability to overlook the obvious (of course, if the *a-b* polarity is obvious but overlooked by the initial hardwired linking we have a whole other set of problems to contend with). And if "annotation" is merely the mechanical fastening of two nodes together without the ability to comment upon this new connection (to set it up for further manipulation, or to help the user be reminded of the essence of this connection, or to explain the nature of this connection to someone else), then the hypertext silently orbits around true meaning and understanding like a cold, although bright, moon around the real core of living thought and action.

What, after all, are we trying to do when we annotate or comment upon something? Except for the most basic procedural operations, information is called up, and comments exchanged, to help someone reconstruct a text--if by "text" we mean not only words in some rhetorical format, but also *any kind of work*: a discussion of alternatives, the attempt at understanding something, the development of an agenda for a meeting, as well as the drafting of a report. At other times we reconstruct a "text" for the purpose of changing someone else's understanding of something--in other words, we are asserting control over another's text, deconstructing it in order to recompose it. At the core of all of these different manipulations of "text" is a *communicative function*, between ourselves and others, or within the private arena of the self. Language is being used to construct meaning, and that meaning is being communicated to others or back to the individual.

In essence, then, text is a social construct, and "hypertext" a paradigm for the social construction of meaning or alternate "texts." The highly touted *non-linearity* of hypertext should be taken in its most complete sense: an a-cyclic, asynchronous sharing of language around central topics of concern--a communicative function for the creation of new texts, new scripts for the understanding of the individual and the group. And this communication, and that creation of new understanding, imply a *pointing at* more than text-objects; it entails the use of language to criticize, analyze, and compose anew the social justifications for holding this or that text or way of thinking and understanding as central.

The most supple hypertext, therefore, would be one that does more than provide mere navigational guides through an already chartered database of text-objects with some minor reconfigurations of content possible. A true hypertext, in my interpretation, would not necessarily imply a conceptual level already ingrained by the programmer because this sort of structure preserves authorial imperatives and may permit only facile shuffling of conceptual blocks--a mechanical associationalism dealing only with surface meaning. Instead, a muscular hypertext, an active system rather than a passive one, would support the social construction of meaning that characterizes understanding and communication in the larger world beyond the computer screen. Real objects, intellectual and affective orderings of meaning in the individual and the group, supplant the miniaturism of mere object-oriented programming through a system that facilitates the creation, annotation, and exchange of new "texts" within the community of users. Hypertext, in this view, escapes from the collapsed inner world of the machine and enters history. But to do this requires a shift from the paradigm that seeks to model the mind in the machine--a de-emphasis upon the "smart machine" that Zuboff (1988) claims has "textualized" the workplace. Instead, we need to textualize the computer itself.

From society of "mind" to society of "text"

The alternative model that I propose here has already been applied to a range of fields (see Bruffee, 1986 for a complete bibliography), but not to research into the design and implementation of computing technology (but see Winograd and Flores, 1986). In essence, the social construction model places emphasis on the primacy of language and all of the social processes by which language develops and is used. Those things we call "knowledge," "reality," or "facts," are viewed as community-generated linguistic entities that are constitutive of the communities that generate them. Such a model questions traditional epistemological assumptions behind a cognitive theory of knowledge: it asks us to think of such presumably internal and individualistic possessions as thought or knowledge as essentially social in origin.

The broad outlines of this model certainly map well to my experiences as educator, writer, and member of a development team that has produced the *Educational Online System* for writing instruction and document production at MIT. As an educator I am well aware of the social, collaborative dynamics that go into writing instruction, indeed, instruction in all subject areas. While I may not go as far as

Bruffee in asserting that my main goal is to explore a social justification for belief (Bruffee, 1982), I certainly do participate in analyzing and communicating the ideas my students have about certain texts (their own and others), and this analysis is achieved through social, linguistic interactions in-class and out-of-class. As a writer--and as a writer who tends to stress pragmatism in the production of a text, rather than hewing strictly to one approach or another--I know that *writing is thinking* and that I seem to recognize what I know and don't know as I am writing. In other words, writing allows me to externalize certain inchoate ideas for my own inspection. Furthermore, when I am writing I am cognizant of the fact that I am frequently riding the crest of language in performance: that is, I rely upon the structure of my language to create meaning for me--the grammar of a thought.

But my work on the development of the *Educational Online System* (EOS) at MIT demonstrated most fully the value of a social construction perspective in the design and implementation of advanced computing technology for instructional and conferencing uses. For several years, development of a system for teaching writing (and other subjects) that took advantage of the Athena-supported network at MIT languished in discussions about the application of AI to writing instruction and document creation. Various cognitive process theories of writing and development, derived from Piaget and others, were suggested as models for a machine prototype, but members of the Writing Program never felt quite at ease with software built on these theories. Or perhaps it might be more correct to say that we never could accept wholesale the pedagogical theories these systems implied. Furthermore, it was difficult to see how certain programs could be worked into the real-time activities of classroom instructors which we sought to support.

It was not until members of the Writing Program asserted control over the design process and simply wrote down what kinds of instructional activities they usually performed in and out of class that specifications for a system were produced. Implementation of a working system was achieved within four months. Instead of attempting to define a hypothetical model of the human mind which we would personify in the computer, we defined the actions that took place when that mind was engaged in a process of creating, analyzing, and sharing texts. Thus, the internal workings of mind were not mapped to the machine; instead, we conceived of the classroom as a "mechanism" for interaction and collaboration and mapped those social processes to the computer. In essence, we textualized the computer: we made it enter, and used it to support, the historical, social processes that we felt defined the production of texts in any instructional or conferencing environment.

As a result of this experience, it was clear that the writer's role in the development of computing technology was enhanced by the rejection of the cognitive process model for system design. As Bruffee (1986) says, since social construction identifies knowledge with language use, the problems presented by this model are the sort writers are well equipped to solve. With the computer seen as a means for supporting the linguistic dynamics implied by this theory, writers as well as engineers are crucial to the design procedure.

Hypertext and social construction

A hypertext is ideally a sort of topography of social construction. After all, a hypertext is fundamentally a linguistic entity that exists to be manipulated, transformed through a series of collaborative acts either between just one user and the original database (that is, the original programmed structure), or among many users performing various operations upon a central core of texts. These operations (drawing new links or annotating existing blocks of text) imply a community of individual users each with a different set of assumptions, a different level of conceptual understanding, and different experiences. Yet the hypertext focuses their interactions and initiates a new historical projection of their understanding and beliefs. In this view, hypertext is seen outside of any particular cognitive model of design or use. The programming structures underlying, indeed, giving rise to the hypertext merely support the larger *hyper-context* of social construction: a matrix of knowledgeable peers defining what they think through the medium of language. *How* the mind works is, therefore, relatively unimportant since focus is now upon computer support for the conversation of knowledgeable peers--the *social content of the interface* is predominant; we need not theorize about how our personal, inner mental environments work (whether by associative leaps or divine inspiration or Boolean operations) because the *virtual environment* of the hypertext permits us to objectify our ideas in the writing of new texts.

Moreover, this virtual environment of the hypertext is most completely evoked within the larger context of a networked, online environment. When I think of an individual working at a stand-alone hypertext or hypermedia system, I feel the same shock St. Augustine reports he felt the first time he saw someone reading silently to himself beneath a tree. What is the point of an *ideal* text that can be infinitely reshaped and communicated anew if the dynamic of use is locked into a primarily personal environment? The actual power of a hypertext derives from its geographic as well as its ideational extensions--from its social content as well as its intellectual status as a document. The online environment allows an individual to draw into the hypertext conversation disparate others because the physical forms of space are made more plastic. Yet even the "forms" or categories of textual apprehension are made more malleable in the online environment because networked systems should, ideally, permit one operation (such as composing a text) to be instantly transformed into the exchange and annotation of that text by others; as space melts away, the collaborative operations of review and re-visioning are expanded.

Vygotsky's Thought and Language *in a virtual environment*

Social construction draws strength from the work of the early twentieth-century Soviet psychologist, Lev Vygotsky. His posthumous book, *Thought and Language* (1962) remains a tonic response to the work of Jean Piaget whose theories of cognitive development form one element in Minsky's *Society of Mind*. Vygotsky postulated a relationship between thought and speech, rather than an absolute identification, and it is his analysis of this relationship in *Thought and Language* that is especially relevant to any discussion of computing technology and information systems.

For Vygotsky the development of thought, of intellect in general, was determined by language use: "intellectual growth is contingent upon mastering the social means of thought, that is, language" (51). He, therefore, stressed the historical character of verbal thought and insisted that "concept formation" (clearly a concern for hypertext development) was a creative rather than mechanistic activity; it could not be reduced to mere associative thinking. The long middle chapter in *Thought and Language*, "An Experimental Study of Concept Formation," should be required reading by developers of hypertext systems. In that chapter, Vygotsky traces the stages in the development of conceptual thinking and contrasts the advanced concept to the more primitive complex of the associative type, which he calls "a concrete grouping of *objects* connected by factual bonds" (62, italics mine). Any factually present connection may lead to the inclusion of a given element into a complex.

It is this conception of the "complex" that seems to me relevant to the assessment of hypertext systems. Each link, once included in a complex, is as important, says Vygotsky, as the first and may become the magnet for a series of other objects (64). Thus, without a hierarchical organization all attributes are functionally equal. Such a complex fails to rise above its elements, in contrast to an advanced concept; a complex merges with the objects that compose it (65). It is a fusion of objects, rather than a synthesis and analysis of them. For Vygotsky, an advanced concept emerges "only when the abstracted traits are synthesized anew and the resulting abstract synthesis becomes the main instrument of thought" (78). And the vehicle for this synthesis is language use.

Clearly, according to this model of development two things stand out: advanced thinking is more than the sum of its parts. We cannot merely collage strings of objects together to attain a richer meaning or understanding. In fact, doing so threatens the accumulating links at any point since each one is as important as the next--each one can potentially magnetize a whole other set of objects to be strung together as part of the whole. Unified thought is absent; we are left with the mere appearance of cohesive thinking. A menu. Secondly, language is more than a representation of knowledge in this scheme; it is the instrument for achieving it since language allows us to synthesize and analyze the parts of the temporary whole we are considering, no matter what the context happens to be: figuring out a procedure for operating a machine, or operating a machine to help us figure out something else.

Therefore, a hypertext that merely allows a user to string together disparate objects of cognition without supporting the analysis and synthesis of these objects in effect exiles us to a realm outside of thought, indeed, outside of language itself. Instead, we merely recompose a picture of how things would appear to someone who already possesses understanding of them. As Vygotsky says in *Mind in Society* (1978), "all the higher functions originate as actual relations between human individuals" (57)--a change from an "object-oriented movement" to a movement "aimed at another person, a means of establishing relations" (56) through communication and language. It is this paradigmatic relationship that hypertext must eventually support.

Within this brief introduction we have moved from Minsky's *Society of Mind* to Vygotsky's *Mind in Society*, from a cognitive perspective to social construction, in an attempt to suggest a workable model for assessing information systems, specifically hypertext and hypermedia. Text itself--its creation, exchange, and annotation--offers a way of modeling the operations of a mind, a way of mapping the individual to the computer.

Cambridge, Massachusetts

1988

References

Barrett, E. *Text, ConText, and HyperText: Writing with and for the Computer*. Cambridge, MA: MIT Press, 1988

Barrett, E. and J. Paradis. "Teaching Writing in an On-line Classroom." *Harvard Educational Review* 58 (1988): 154-171.

Bruffee, K. A. "Liberal Education and the Social Justification of Belief." *Liberal Education*. 68 (1982): 95-114.

_____. "Social Construction, Language, and the Authority of Knowledge: A Bibliographical Essay." *College English* 48 (1986): 773-790.

Bush, V. "As We May Think." *Atlantic Monthly* 7 (1945): 101-108.

Engelbart, D.C. "A Conceptual Framework for the Augmentation of Man's Intellect." In *Vistas in Information Handling*. London: Spartan Books, 1963.

Minsky, Marvin. *The Society of Mind*. New York: Simon and Schuster, 1986.

Nelson, T.H. "Replacing the Printed Word: A Complete Literary System." *IFIP Proceedings*. October 1980: 1013-1023.

Vygotsky, L. S. *Mind in Society*. Ed. Michael Cole. Cambridge, MA: Harvard UP, 1978.

_____. *Thought and Language*. Ed. and trans. Eugenia Hanfmann and Gertrude Vakar. Cambridge, MA: MIT Press, 1962. Rev. ed. 1986.

Winograd, T. and Fernando Flores. *Understanding Computers and Cognition: A New Foundation for Design*. Reading, MA: Addison-Wesley, 1986.

Zuboff, S. *In the Age of the Smart Machine: The Future of Work and Power*. New York: Basic Books, 1988.

Part I
Hypertext and Hypermedia: Designing Systems for the Online User

In Part I Philip Rubens examines the genealogy of recent innovations in online information and hypermedia and offers an assessment of these advances. Rubens situates his discussion in the context of the workplace and training. Roger Grice continues this assessment of "new horizons for technical communications" in light of his analysis of the wants and needs of online users. David Herrstrom and David Massey place hypertext development in the context of the "world of action," stressing the work environment itself over technology, and sketch a hypertext design to satisfy the demands of this context for use. Finally, Patricia Ann Carlson offers an illustration of how to integrate several forms of "intelligence" into a hypertext application.

Online Information, Hypermedia, and the Idea of Literacy

Philip Rubens

Communication Research Laboratory
Rensselaer Polytechnic Institute
Troy, New York 12180-3590

This essay examines the genealogy of recent innovations in online information and hypermedia. In doing so it provides an overview of the more important developments and the applications of these advances. While the essay celebrates those successes that are clearly exceptional, it also assesses the more typical, and sometimes equally useful, techniques found in less dramatic and innovative environments. Finally, the essay asks the reader to consider some of the more optimistic scenarios for the future of online information and hypermedia in relation to the concept of literacy.

In previous essays I have argued that online information makes unusual demands on users of computing equipment, both in terms of their practices as users of machinery and as consumers of information (Rubens, 1987; Rubens, 1988). When we operate machinery we want that machine to be as transparent as possible to our work. Typewriters and automobiles are good examples of the kinds of human-machine interactions that have been successful. Once one sets the default parameters of a typewriter they can effectively ignore the machine and concentrate, instead, on the writing task. Similarly, automobiles require very little attention to their operation; we do not need to know much information beyond what the gauges and the ambient conditions provide.

What characteristics make the computer so difficult to comprehend or use? First, the computer possesses a mystique that makes it appear deceptively human. That is, for the most part, the work we see it perform is more associated with human activities than a machine, which performs labor. The computer, instead, performs tasks more often associated with human reasoning activities. Thus, we feel as though we are interacting with an active intelligence. This human quality makes us both expectant and impatient with anything associated with computing. We expect it to operate with a human rationale and it does not; we expect it to interact with us in a human manner and it does not.

The primary culprit in this uneasy relationship seems to be the interface, the level at which we interact with machines. The interface includes, but is not limited to, the interactions possible, the "language" — either verbal or graphic — of the interaction, and the ways in which these two characteristics interact themselves. The remainder of this chapter will explore the nature of these interactions and relationships. In doing so it will examine the characteristics of information, the strategies used to access information, and the historical development of online information and hypermedia.

1. Online versus Other Information Sources

What kinds of information do humans use in resolving tasks? Obviously, we access information through some sensory channel or combination of channels. But, on a more elemental level, how do we gather information that supports tasks? Such information comes from two (2) primary sources: informants, and manuals or books.

Human Informants

Informants are people, usually supposed or acknowledged experts, to whom people turn when trying to learn a new activity. It would be improbable that we would select an informant at random to help us learn some new activity. Usually we seek out the best source we can locate.

Using informants as information sources creates several unusual problems. First, if the informant possesses expert knowledge in a particular task domain, they have likely formulated a "fast path" for performing the kinds of tasks typical of that domain. However, that path may have little correspondence to the ways in which "typical" interactions occur in this same domain. For example, an expert may know how to salvage damaged data files by prowling through memory with octal codes. Learning this procedure would be categorically different from other task resolutions in the same domain if the typical interaction is based on command strings. Thus, the new user would have a set of operations that can resolve a particular problem, but that resolution is different from typical interactions and unlikely to add little to their operational knowledge of the machine.

Although most ethnographic research relies on informants for specific cultural information, field researchers must always assume the additional responsibility of learning the "language" in which the informant speaks. At first glance that statement probably seems trivial, especially since computing tasks assume adult users learning and using processes in the same domain. However, when one considers the many ways in which a process can be discussed, programmed, or constructed, as well as regional anomalies in programming, then this responsibility becomes far more important.

Electronic Informants

Thus far we have assumed that an informant refers to a human being who possesses exceptional expertise in a specialized field and agrees to share that background. Online information, especially since it resides within the computer itself, shares many of the characteristics of an informant. It can offer assistance to the user who seeks the resolution to a problem. However, all of the difficulties outlined thus far increase with online information. In this instance, if the user cannot successfully formulate their own problem statement then the online information may not be sufficient to the task of problem resolution.

For instance, if users try to locate specific information about the maintenance of a mechanical device, they will have to know the assembly (at the macro level) that contains relevant information for resolving problems in sub-assemblies. If users do not have that information in their memory, then the online information could be of little help. In contrast to a human informant, the computer can only offer exactly the information requested.

Perhaps more sophisticated hypermedia can resolve such a dilemma. However, I intend to argue later that the metaphor of a "seamless" information, or data, pool has its own flaws. During that discussion, I also intend to examine a variety of hypermedia styles and interactions.

Manuals as Informants

Beyond informants, human or electronic, users must depend on written manuals. At present, the trend is to present information in a linear fashion based on some dominant organizing principle. Following such a procedure allows writers and product manufacturers to capitalize on the deeply sedimented reading behaviors common in our culture. That is, one can reasonably expect readers to know something about locating tools (tables of contents and indexes), something about text structure (headers and specialized typography), and something about the relationship between text and illustrations. While these capabilities appear relatively simplistic and straightforward, they represent powerful behaviors that allow readers to use an incredible variety of texts with success.

But readers also exhibit impatience with texts that treat them meanly. A poorly indexed text, for instance, will frustrate readers. Using too many layout conventions (many indiscriminable headers or numerous type variations) will have a similar effect. Regardless of the manual feature that introduces the difficulty, the reader usually reacts in the same manner. Readers will either reject or distrust the text. This behavior offers an analog to the way in which a person reacts to an unreliable informant: flawed information encourages the interrogator to distrust a source (Kantrowitz, 1984).

Poor presentation characteristics particularly disadvantage books. Books cannot offer additional information beyond their "silent" text, and they provide only a limited number of entry points; nothing can be added to a printed text. Thus, users who have difficulty with texts have little recourse to resolve their difficulties. The nature of the activities that computer users attempt to support with a text exacerbate these problems. These people want to find information that will support their work and get on with it. They want quick entry points, identifiable information targets, and multiple support where necessary. They do not want to spend time reading long or complex blocks of text.

Human and electronic informants can supplement books. However, users must realize that multiple and idiosyncratic interpretations of "texts" exist and that such interpretations often contain elemental flaws. Human informants, for instance, have the capability of adding information to texts that emanates from specialized knowledge rather than from any information the product manufacturer or writer provided. An electronic informant can only add its own version of the same static reality the text describes. One could argue that electronic information provides additional entry points, especially in hypermedia; however, an authorial algorithm establishes the links in most information pools and, as such, renders these pools subject to the same kinds of difficulties introduced by any expert opinion.

The key premise of this discussion thus far has been that humans, electronic information, and paper documents play a key role as "informant" in providing information for users. Each of these informants can make their own claims concerning how well they achieve their mission. Each, however, still possesses its own peculiar shortcomings as well. The remainder of this paper explores the ways in which people try to use electronic information as a reference source and the impact that has on the development of information content and presentation strategies.

2. Online versus Other Information Strategies

Thus far we have considered the ways in which people try to discover information to support computer tasks. That process has lead us to consider the nature of human, paper, and electronic information. However, the single most common interaction behavior still relies on "guessing." Humans will try to apply previous knowledge to any situation before they will seek assistance of any kind. In driving a new model automobile, for instance, people will simply take a few moments to familiarize themselves with the unique features of the controls and then they will drive. In computing a similar situation occurs.

For example, a new user will try an action or use a command string from a previous release of a product before they will examine the supporting documentation for changes. This behavior has created an entire class of "read me first" documents generally included with new product releases. It would be interesting to know how many of these documents users actually read. People guess primarily because they do not want to be bothered with learning some new interaction style or technique. They want to get on with their work and to do so quickly.

When pressed to discover how something operates or why they cannot succeed in performing a task, users will actually read. However, they read to perform a task and not simply to acquire knowledge. Thus, this reading depends on discriminable targets and ease of entry to succeed. The current wave of graphic interfaces and the ease of including illustrations in referential texts has introduced a significant interaction difficulty: a concurrent need for readers to know how to read visual information and to establish links between the verbal and the visual. At present, we seem to take visual literacy as a given despite the fact that our entire educational process aims at verbal literacy at the expense of the visual. Probably, users will not understand complex graphic symbology or intuit the underlying "grammar" of that symbology with ease. I realize that, given the excellent performance of graphic interfaces, this statement seems to defy current anecdotal wisdom. I do not maintain that such interfaces do not facilitate performance; I do assert that the grammar, the ways in which we combine graphical information, may not be as intuitive as we believe. I make this point because it seems to me that the development of graphic interfaces has assumed considerable importance in the computing industry and the lack of specific visual (as opposed to verbal) literacy has the potential to become a pressing educational issue.

Relationships in information data pools

An additional problem centers on the nature of information and the ways in which people want to interact with that information. I said earlier that I took issue with the idea of "seamless" information. Let me explain why that concept troubles me.

In searching for information in a paper-based environment, users employ many of the text-based processes I outlined earlier (identifiable visual targets, specialized typographic conventions, referential entry points, etc.). These processes, based on learned reading behaviors, provide readers with the basis for obtaining text-based information in fairly sophisticated ways. For example, readers can both "flag" and/or annotate text very simply and easily. This basic tracking technique allows readers to perform additive tasks, the kinds of tasks most common in computing, with relative ease. Thus, learned behaviors can provide a powerful basis for retrieving information from paper.

The major shortcoming of seamless information focuses on the ability of readers to identify relevant information. In tests of user performance with paper text, the most common difficulty centered on the readers' inability to understand when they had located the correct response to resolve their problem (Rubens and Rubens, 1988). For example, if the user had to construct a command string to list several lines in an editing file, they should have proceeded to the editing functions and located the listing command. However, many users located the listing command in the telecommunication function of the program. They did so chiefly because the list command in the index had multiple entries for all major functions. In addition, they did consider the correct command in the editing function but rejected it primarily because the product, a telecommunication package, coincidentally had an editor. This example typifies the problem formulation difficulties users encounter. Since the majority of users do not possess the specific knowledge of subject area specialists, the expert informants discussed earlier, they find it difficult to separate irrelevant from relevant information for the successful completion of their tasks.

This problem is not confined to computing either. In aviation, for instance, new technicians and maintenance personnel, many of whom must retrieve information from electronic sources, must know the location of subassemblies in the larger assemblies on an aircraft. Seamless information provides no "parsing" rules for discovering where in the available "universe" or pool of information the correct path lies.

The volume of information presented by a seamless information data pool implies that more information is better or more inclusive. In reality, more information simply requires the user to consider and process more information that may be indiscriminable. The path to a useful response may, in fact, be even more obscure in such data pools. Having said that what would I propose as alternatives?

First, I suggest data retrieval methods in which the underlying program sorts the user's reaction in fairly sophisticated ways. For instance, if the user initiates a search for a particular item, the response should include all of those items that represent true "hits" on the specified search condition. However, the program should continue to monitor the user's response to the hits offered and delete those records from the hits associated with those the user seems to be discarding and bring in more hits associated with those the user seems apt to retain. In addition, the system should offer the user a real-time account of this operation and the option to browse the hits the program acts upon (Salton, 1975). By using such a system, hits on a search for a sub-assembly or sub-system would be allowed initially to embrace all incidences of a search term(s) across a product but could eventually be narrowed to one incidence of the term(s) in the correct assembly. In the previous list command example, for instance, the index provided a full range of all incidences of the list command but did not distinguish among the various list commands. The electronic version of this same search would eliminate the user's rejects until only the list command associated with the editor remained. This procedure helps the user envision future searches better and helps with problem definition.

Second, I suggest that related functions be captured by data retrieval methods. That is, if someone needs help with setting parameters for a specific set of functions, the retrieval program also provides information about how these actions will interact with other functions. While this may be seen as a fairly typical cross-reference, in actuality it functions as an advisor (acting as an expert informant). A typical scenario might be found in the telecommunication industry: switch setting on large computing systems. When an operator sets one switch how does that action impact other switches? At present, such a problem can only be resolved with very large switch tables that often occupy entire books. An online information system could replace these texts and their somewhat inadequate functionality by providing cross-reference linkages.

Dealing with electronic informants

Electronic informants possess a set of capabilities somewhere between those of humans and a book. That is, they can be queried for additional information or clarification as a human can, though not in the same level of detail; they are not as static as a book and can still emulate some of the characteristics of texts readers find useful.

The primary difficulty in communicating with an electronic informant resides in the conflict between expectations and deliverables. Humans expect the interface to provide reliable information of the same quality and character as another human informant; when that expectation cannot be achieved, humans tend to distrust the computer.

3. Online Historical Development

Online information seems to have developed for two reasons. First, industry had a felt need to reduce the quantity of paper documentation they produced. Second, presenting information within the context of the same system or product being used had the potential to make the information appear integral to the product. In its earliest form, online information consisted of octal codes presented on the screen to denote error conditions. Users had either to know what the code meant or be able to find its meaning in a large document set.

The first major improvement on this situation occurred when natural language error messages appeared directly on the screen. The second major development occurred with the introduction of online help itself. In this instance, fairly well developed screens could be accessed that explained particular difficulties in some detail. However, both of these earlier innovations still expected the user to rely on a printed manual for the bulk of their information needs.

The actual turning point occurred when product and information developers embraced two ideas. First, the information had to be thought of as part of the product. Second, the users' work situation had to present a feeling of unity. Both of these could be achieved with online information. However, little agreement existed in terms of program philosophy about the sophistication needed for online information; as a consequence, three distinct lines of online information development evolved: isolated, co-resident, and interactive.

Isolated online information

Isolated online information operates on the same device that the user employs for their task but requires the user to leave that task to access the online information and this event, in itself, creates several difficulties. First, it imposes a formidable memory task on the user. The user must remember the problem and its location in order to return to her task. The same memory tasks remain after consulting the online information. Thus, the user has to maintain information related to both task and location throughout the life cycle of the information enquiry.

Second, the user must formulate the problem before leaving the task with its attendant application which may be rich in problem resolution clues. This situation is less than desirable because the problem formulated in the midst of task completion may not be expressed in precisely the same terms as those found in the data pool. For example, graphing values from a spread sheet may require opening a new file before a graph can be created. In the task context the user wants to know how to create a graph; in the online information context, that may be embedded within the procedures for opening a file. Thus, while retaining location information in the task domain, the user must restructure the problem in terms the online information finds useful rather than in relation to the original task domain context or any internal representation of the original problem.

Third, the user must return to the task domain and complete or initiate a successful activity. Isolated online information requires yet a third level of memory processing on the user's part: the retention of additive command strings constructed from one or more sources in the data pool. Since most computing tasks require additive solutions (i.e.: How do I do something unique with a typical command?), the user must often consult more than one source (some of which are unproductive, some of which are incorrect search paths, and some of which are correct searches but misunderstood). Now the user must construct a response in her head (or on paper) and return to the task domain. At this point several options occur. One, the response is correct, adequately understood, and correctly entered (in which case the information enquiry succeeds). Two, the response is correct, inadequately understood, and correctly entered (in which case the enquiry succeeds but the potential for future failures increases). Three, the response is correct, adequately understood, and incorrectly entered (in which case the enquiry fails). As you can see, the possibilities for failure are much more common and viable than those that ensure success.

A final difficulty with isolated online information is that it retains the flavor of the book's best interactions without offering the best features of the book's ability to support tasks. Isolated online information often occurs when a company wants to reduce its commitment to paper without making any commitment to the needs of the user. Thus, books, that already exist as electronic signals, are simply ported over into the online environment and called online information (rather than text online). To use this information the user employs exactly the same behaviors and operations as she would if she were using a hard copy printed document. One interaction — the ability to refer to a book while interacting with a task — is significantly lacking. That is , the user, the task, and the information (the book) operate in a co-resident, not isolated, environment. I will examine the potential of this latter situation in the following discussion of co-resident online information.

Co-resident Online Information

The second major innovation in online information centers on the introduction of systems in which the user retains the task domain as an active process on the screen contemporaneous with the online information. Windows, the programming innovation that fostered this capability, can be displayed in various ways: overlays, tiling, and split screens.

Overlays. The least helpful of these techniques seems to be overlays. An overlay window covers part of the screen whenever the user accesses online information. Behind this overlay window the task domain resides in view, though the user can take no direct action in that domain as long as the online information window remains active. In at least one sense this situation offers some improvement over isolated online information: the user can still see the general task context which elicited the problem she is attempting to resolve in the online information window.

With the introduction of co-residency, online information acquired some extremely useful features: scrolling, dynamic positioning and selectivity, better context-sensitivity, and interactive passbacks. Scrolling operates in much the same manner as the same feature on typical word processing programs. Some idiosyncratic keystroke(s), dedicated paging key(s), or pointing device action(s) have the ability to move the text (or graphic) by specified increments, potentially both vertically and horizontally, around the display screen. Including this feature in the online information window allows the information developer to include significantly larger information sets in a smaller dedicated screen area.

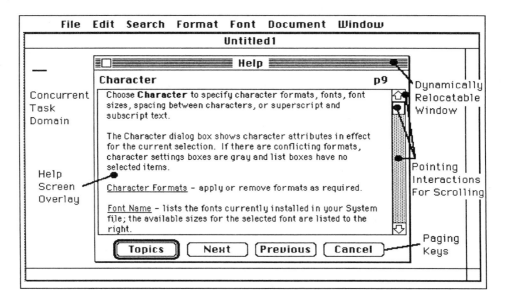
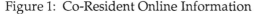

Figure 1: Co-Resident Online Information

Dynamic window positioning physically allows the user to move, and, in some instances, influence the size of the information window. In addition, selectivity provides the user with the ability to "toggle" between the task domain and the online information. This feature allows the user to initiate an information query with the task domain active and to move the task domain in front of the information window to reconsider the problem at will. More recent innovations allow multiple applications to operate simultaneously on the same screen and this versatility continues to influence the ways in which supporting online information can be offered.

Context-sensitivity moves the user from the immediate task domain to information relevant for that domain. Thus, if a user attempts to configure a program to add a coating to a run in a paper production plant and does not know the code for superfine clay coating, he can find that code by placing the cursor in the field for "coating applications" and activate the online information. The interface program will examine the screen for the cursor location and display information relevant to that field. Closely related to context-sensitivity is the concept of a passback feature. In contrast to isolated online information, passbacks allow interaction between the task domain and the online information. This feature also presents the possibility, in some controlled circumstances, of users creating their own specific mini-manuals. That is, users can copy frequently accessed information from the online information data pool into their own short versions. I intend to discuss custom online information in more detail later.

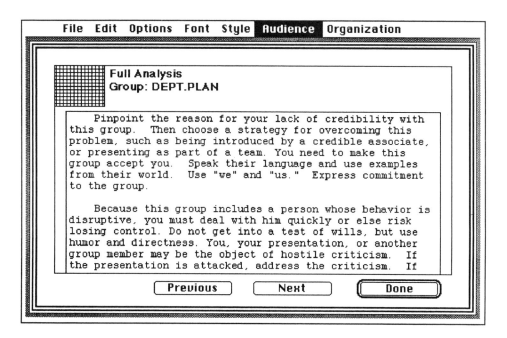

Figure 2: Context-Sensitive Help

Tiling. Specific screen areas dedicated to particular kinds of activities or purposes characterize tiling. For example, in Figure 3, the upper few lines of the screen contain location and navigation information, the bottom few lines contain interaction information, the left quadrant contains the major information area (with an action entry line at the bottom left), and the right third quadrant secondary information areas elicited by interaction keys. None of these areas overlap. In this example the task domain and the supporting information reside contemporaneously on the same screen.

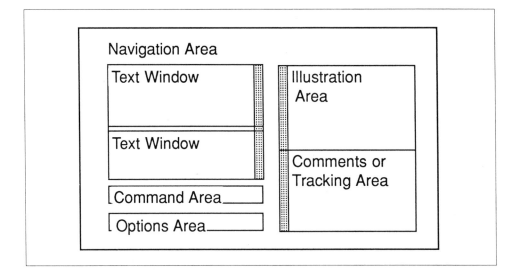

Figure 3: Dedicated Screen Areas

Tiling does not necessarily represent an advance in online design because the windows must remain static. However, the degree of access to both the online information and the task domain, as well as navigation, placement, and interaction information has proven extremely useful. Tiling also obviates a problem observed in more dynamic windowing programs in that these latter programs often create the so-called "crowded" desktop. Opening many applications and their associated online information simulta-neously leaves the user with a crowded screen with little indication about the location of specific information pieces or the relationships among the pieces depicted. This situation creates additional memory overhead on the user's part and often leads to loss of productivity in the task domain.

Split Screens. Simply displaying split screens offers yet another method for arranging screen "real estate." In this type of online information, the task domain remains active on one half of the screen and supporting information appears on the remaining display surface. For the most part, these screens share many of the characteristics of tiled screens in that they lack dynamic direct manipulation techniques: the user can neither re-size nor move the half screens.

Of course, one could also create a variety of hybrid screens. One program, for example, splits the screen vertically, offering the task domain on the left and supporting information on the right. However, the right half of the screen also has two halves: one offering information and the other cata-loging the user's path through the information pool. In addition, the cataloging feature allows the user to develop macros — custom online information — for storing useful, and perhaps repetitive, search paths for subsequent reference (or for less expert users to solve similar problems without direct human intervention). It should also be noted that most of these programs offer scrolling and some offer passback features. Thus, it is difficult to categorize these techniques in too restrictive a sense.

Interactive Online Information

Interactive online represents the most recent stage in innovation. It can generally be characterized by the introduction of direct manipulation, by the presence of graphic elements, by the incorporation of interactive media, and by the use of hypermedia programming techniques.

Direct Manipulation. Direct manipulation interfaces allow the user to move objects on the screen to perform computing functions. At present, the dominant metaphor for direct manipulation interfaces remains the "desktop" which employs the kinds of objects one normally finds in the office. In addition, several professions have begun to develop similar interfaces. Engineering, for example, has already deployed systems that reflect the actions of robotic assembly lines. Scientists have created a simulation system that allows them to observe computerized objects in action. They can, for instance, test aircraft models in simulated wind tunnels. This innovation somewhat obviates the aura of the computer as an analog to the brain in that it focuses on the control of mechanical processes. Similar developments in this area are proceeding with considerable rapidity.

Graphic Interface. A significant portion of direct manipulation interfaces relies on some type of graphic or iconic "vocabulary" to achieve its success. In the example cited earlier, the desktop, icons representing paper documents and file folders facilitate the move from handling paper files to using electronic files. Users perform actions on these objects by simply moving or selecting them and issuing highly truncated commands from either the keyboard or via dynamic menuing systems (i.e. pull-down or pop-up menus).

Despite the success of these graphic elements several issues remain unresolved that can compromise future graphic interface design. The major issue is the size of the graphic "vocabulary." In any one product it may become difficult to create discriminable icons for every function. While I am aware that some very large products have developed equally large, and supposedly successful, iconic sets, I continue to remain skeptical. I am skeptical primarily because these sets always offer the icon and a natural language label for the icon. It remains unclear which of these elements — graphic or language — provides the most powerful search target in the task domain. I am not suggesting that an icon fails if it cannot stand alone. In fact, several studies have indicated that comprehension improves with redundant text and illustrations (Duchastel, 1980; Bernard, 1981). Thus, the systems I am examining have the potential to be extremely supportive in the task domain. I am suggesting, that the switch from graphic with supporting text label to graphics alone will be as fraught with difficulties as any iconic signage.

Elsewhere I have argued that iconic representations need to be codified (Rubens and Krull, 1988). Such a code offers a sensible and possible solution. When one examines an existing iconic system, such as Bliss symbolics, one finds that it can be employed to create an iconic vocabulary and grammar that possesses sufficient vitality to not only represent objects but actions performed on objects. In general, the ability to account for actions performed on objects is presently lacking (perhaps with the exception of completion bars) in graphic interfaces. Future movements towards standards in the computing industry should consider the creation of iconic vocabularies and grammars, perhaps based on the already extant iconography developed by the International Standards Organization, as a primary concern.

The problems prompted by iconic interfaces represent a particularly compelling issue primarily because it impacts basic education and the education of information developers. In terms of basic education it means that academia must reconsider the concept of literacy to add visual literacy. They must consider how this new field will impact curricula, how this new literacy will be defined, the relationship of visual and verbal literacy, and how literacy will be evaluated. In this one single, and very important area, computing is exerting new pressures on our society and its educational activities.

Interactive Media. As early as the mid-1960's many educational theorists had already successfully mated video to computers. In one demonstration project, a science course was converted to computer assisted instruction and keyed to a video tape. The CAI program monitored students by a system called item analysis, which counts failures and successes and contains a number of branching routines to send students to work appropriate for their level. If the student could not grasp a particular concept after having moved through a prescribed regimen, then the videotape would wind to the correct location and the student would view either a demonstration of the principle under study or hear a lecture on the same topic. The links between video and the computer, however, have been unreliable, difficult, and expensive.

The recent advances in CD-ROM (compact disk read only memory) and laserographic media holds promise for interactive media. Many CD-ROM-based information systems are already in routine use to replace both paper- and film-based information. They provide many of the interactions that capitalize on the more sophisticated text usage behaviors discussed above and add many new dimensions. The most powerful of these interactions is the ability retrieve associated information in clever and useful ways.

Hypermedia Programming. The powerful retrieval methods alluded to in the previous paragraph developed out of the innovation called hypermedia. Hypertext, the parent of hypermedia, is a programming methodology that provides sophisticated relational activities in data sets. Originally thought of as "non-sequential" writing (Nelson, 1988), hypermedia interacts with other media and computing functions — video and sound — and comfortably resides in the graphics and direct manipulation interface. For all of its power and sophistication, however, this tool does have some potential difficulties that have been neither addressed nor assessed.

In the earlier discussion of movement from the task domain to the online information supporting tasks, I outlined a series of difficulties layered onto the memory demands of the reader. One demand that I discussed was the problems readers have in separating relevant and irrelevant information. A good illustration of this difficulty can be seen in the number of search patterns in which users move through a text to resolve a problem, find several incorrect responses, find a likely response, find more incorrect responses, and then realize that the first likely response was the answer they sought. Two events must now occur. First the reader must back-up through referential information (most likely in a random rather than linear fashion). Second, they must perform these actions from memory. My point here is that readers — in the midst of an enquiry based on their own, often flawed, formulation of the problem (which they revise often during their search) — find it difficult to ascertain when they have found the correct answer (Conklin, 1987).

Hypermedia's response to this difficulty is to offer what has generally been described as "seamless information." That is, the enriched links among various parts of the data set provide as much information as possible on any one topic. While I believe this concept is powerful, and I would not reject such assistance in online information, I suggest that the potential here is to simply offer someone, who is already under stress, more information to process, whether or not that information relates directly to the tasks at hand.

Without reviewing all of the potential varieties of hypermedia, I would like to explore some of the responses to the difficulty outlined above. Consider, for example, the concept of "links." To behave in a rational manner links, usually a term in text or a "hot" button in a graphic, must have three characteristics. First, any links provided by the developer must describe an error-free path for the program to follow. Second, the links must be capable of quickly transporting the user to useful information. Third, some indication of the relationships among parent, sibling, and context-sensitive information must be established for the user.

Since the developer, in all but a few hypermedia systems, creates the links, users still must trust the rational approach, as well as the mindset, of the developer. To avoid the all-to-frequent programming dilemma of GIGO (garbage in, garbage out), some intelligent structuring must occur early in the development cycle. Hypermedia requires a good data model. That is, the shape of the underlying data files has to possess enough vitality to be amenable to many uses. Hypermedia also requires a governing rationale for links. Employing one linking rationale in one section of a product and shifting to another rationale later asks users to remember too much detail. In addition, it creates the possibility that revisions or enhancements to the product will be difficult to perform. At present, global editing functions for hypermedia programs are limited.

GIGO also has implications for users. Hypermedia nodes, the basic presentational unit (usually limited to a screen), and their associations still do not provide enough guidance for users. Some applications do offer graphic browsers, bookmarks, or tree diagrams. However, the inter-relationship of nodes is not as obvious as it is in a textually interwoven book.

Despite these difficulties, the most powerful of these programs can perform quick and powerful retrievals. One of the more useful of these interactions is the ability to create custom or personal paths through data sets. In such a scenario the user moves through the data set and logs a particularly useful path to resolve the problem under consideration. Once the path's efficacy has been validated, the user creates a macro that will reconstruct the same path in the future. This function is especially useful when an expert constructs a macro for a difficult problem that can be employed by less knowledgeable users to resolve that problem. Notably, such paths can incorporate sophisticated alternative media, such as sound and motion, unavailable in paper-based information.

Some hypermedia interfaces have been mated to CD-ROM, some possess graphic and direct manipulation interfaces as well, and some add expert level boolean search capabilities and a command mode for those users who want to type in command strings. While these combinations and hybrids are, indeed, powerful innovations in online information, they raise important issues for training users to employ these sophisticated systems.

4. Future Directions in Online Information

At present two very different streams of development seem to be emerging in terms of electronic information development. On the one hand, online information, typically associated with task support, continues to evolve, while, on the other hand, hypermedia continues to search for a specific purpose and audience.

Conventional online information continues to support basic tasks in the workplace. This information is usually composed of text ported into the online information data set from existing electronic word processing signals. In a few instances, some graphics are also available. Finally, a select few of the more sophisticated online information systems interact with alternative media such as CD-ROM. In these systems the data sets write to both paper and the screen by manipulating the single data set to fit the output medium. For the most part, however, online information does not provide as much user support as either paper documentation or an expert informant.

Hypermedia seems to be moving away from supporting tasks to the manipulation of extremely large data sets. The more optimistic scenarios for hypermedia envision a worldwide network of hypermedia nodes which will allow users to research topics in various intellectual domains. The intent seems to be to create a platform that allows researchers to work together regardless of distances. To implement such a system would require a complete reconception of the technologies, the controlling programs, and the nature of human and human-machine interaction.

In less ambitious scenarios hypermedia is seen as a method for controlling and manipulating large document sets to support tasks. The most frequent line of development relies on the ability of hypermedia to present various information forms -- text and graphics -- with equal facility. Several large projects have already proven the efficacy of such an approach.

Hypermedia, then, is viewed in two ways in the online information community. In one sense it represents the logical continuation of developments in online information. In a more creative sense, however, it offers some intriguing possibilities for interactions not currently available.

I want to conclude by offering some observations on the future of online information. In doing so I will discuss the impact of online information technologies on the workplace, the worker, and education.

Impact on the Workplace

In the contemporary workplace workers commonly share large pools of information, collaborate on tasks, and control remote mechanical processes. Information moves across continents as easily as across the street. Finally, the very style and character of the workplace has the potential for considerable change. People no longer need to drive long distances or to congregate in specific locations. The capabilities of computing equipment, its developing support for various tasks, and the ease of accessibility all create the potential for new working conditions. Much of the credit goes to the new interfaces and their ease of use. The key difficulty now is to ensure some measure of standardization of these interfaces and interaction techniques across products and product lines.

Impact on the Worker

Workers find the newest generation of interfaces easier to learn and easier to use. Reductions in training time, reductions in time-to-productivity, fewer errors in typing commands, and easier recognition of the nature of documents illustrate but a few of the changes in the ways in which users have reacted to these new innovations. However, the ease of use has also enticed the user into attempting more sophisticated computing tasks, many of which she is neither trained nor qualified to perform. Thus, honesty on the part of product manufacturers is needed, as well as more training to incorporate these more sophisticated tasks into an information developer's repertoire.

Impact on Education

The impact on education is actually two-fold. First, I believe we must re-evaluate the concept of literacy in an increasingly visual world. We have never undertaken such a task; and it, indeed, reverses the popular concept of literacy as related to words. Visual literacy alone will be a massive task. It will require not only learning visual vocabularies and grammars (not to mention developing them), but also new ways of considering the structure of texts and the behaviors needed to work with these electronic texts. Second, it will require new, specialized courses for information developers who will be the prime movers in the movement from paper to electronic information. This education will influence their course work with more concentration on human-computer interaction, graphics, programming, and the like. Both of these changes offer educators an exciting opportunity, one as exciting as the invention of movable type itself.

References

Bernard, Robert, et al. "Can images provide contextual support for prose?" *Educational Communication and Technology Journal* 29 (1981): 101-108.

Conklin, J. *A Survey of Hypertext.* MCC Technical Report STP-356-86, Rev. 2. Austin, TX: Microelectronics and Computer Technology Corporation, 1987.

Duchastel, P. C. "Research on illustrations in text." *Educational Communication and Technology Journal* 28 (1980): 283-287.

Kantrowitz, Michael. "Editorial Economics: Consequences of Policy Alternatives," Unpublished Ph. D. dissertation, Rensselaer Polytechnic Institute, Troy, NY, 1985.

Nelson, Theodor H. "Managing Immense Storage." *BYTE* January 1988.

Rubens, Philip and Brenda Knowles Rubens. "Usability and Format Design." In *Effective Documentation: What We Have Learned from Research*. Stephen Doheny-Farina, ed. Cambridge, MA: MIT Press, 1988.

Rubens, Philip. "The Impact of Innovative Communication Technologies: Online Documentation, the Reader, and the Writer." *Iowa Journal of Business and Technical Communication*, Vol. 1, #2 (September 1987): 5-20.

_____. "Online Information and the Electronic Discourse Community." In *Discourse Communities and Their Relationship to Writing Instruction*. Carolyn Matelene, ed. NY: Random House, 1988.

_____ and Robert Krull. "Communicative Function of Icons as Computer Commands." In *Proceedings of the 1988 ACM-SIGDOC*. In press, 1988.

Salton, G. *Dynamic Information and Library Processing*. Englewood Cliffs, NJ: Prentice-Hall, 1975.

Online Information: What Do People Want? What Do People Need?

Roger A. Grice
IBM Corporation
Kingston, NY

Because we have grown up using printed information, we all have definite opinions about what we want and need from printed information. By extension, we can often predict what others may want or need. But what of online information? To many, it is so new that it is treated as a novelty; to others it is a mysterious unknown, more to be held in awe (or, perhaps, in contempt) than used. What then is the developer of online information to do to ensure that the online information meets the needs of its users? Through observation, surveys, and extrapolation we can determine those characteristics that are effective aids to using the information and those that are detractors and inhibitors.

Some factors that affect online information's ease of use (and, hence, acceptability by users) are: familiarity, support of users' tasks, ease of learning and first use, navigability, ease of modification, and appearance. When designing online information, we can best meet the needs of users by first focusing on those users, not on the information itself, and then developing the online information to meet their needs.

New Horizons for Technical Communicators

Technology has opened new horizons for technical communicators. Not that many years ago, the only medium generally available for presenting technical information was the printed page—almost invariably an 8 1/2 x 11 white page printed with black ink. Look at where we are today.

- Hypermedia systems allow people to access information in the sequence, volume, and format that best suits their needs at the time they access the information; they can change their access strategy each time they need to refer to the information.

- CD ROM gives people quick, direct access to vast quantities of information. An entire encyclopedia can be put on one compact disk, and people can retrieve information sequentially, by topic, or by selected key words.

- The rapid growth and acceptance of online information leads some observers to believe that we are rapidly move towards a "paperless society," one in which it will no longer be necessary to have any printed information at all.

- Computer-based training, satellite broadcasting, and videotapes have enabled education to move out of a structured, centralized classroom and into people's working environments and individualized schedules.

As our increased use of and dependance on information grows and our society evolves from an agrarian and manufacturing society to an "information society," (Porat 1978) the movement is not *only* in the direction of increased use of information but, more specifically, in the direction of computer information—so much so that it has been claimed that we have become not an "information society" but a "cybernetic society" (Porush 1985, p.1). The major theme of this volume, "the society of text," reaffirms not only the importance of computer information but, perhaps more importantly, the degree to which information for and about computers has permeated the very fabric of our society. Producing information is no longer an isolated literary act; it is a social act, requiring the orchestrated skills of many, and the information affects, to varying degrees, the work and lives of the many people who use it.

Thus, when the contributors to *Text, ConText, and HyperText: Writing with and for the Computer* (Barrett 1988) discuss issues facing today's technical communicators, their contributions are no longer divided into the simple, familiar categories of the past decades (writing, editing, and illustration, for example), but into "Artificial Intelligence, Document Processing, and Hypertext," "Management, Training, and Corporate Culture," and "Designing Online Information." Certainly the emphasis has shifted over the past several years—providing more opportunities to better meet the needs of the readers and users of our information and yet, at the same time, placing greater demands on those who produce the information.

If, then, we are moving toward an even greater use of, and reliance on, computers and information about computers, it is even more important than before that technical communicators not only document what exists but also serve as user advocates, lobbying within their organizations for the needs of those who will use the products and information that is produced (Casey 1980). Exploiting the powers of hypermedia systems and online information presentation systems may be, in the long run, less an exploitation of technology than it is a socially conscious act designed to meet to the fullest the needs of an audience. For what are improved facilities for presenting online information, hypermedia delivery systems, and fast, efficient means of storing and retrieving data if not the tools we need to best meet the information needs of our audience?

But we must temper our actions with a note of caution. We must resist the ever-present temptation to use blindly all the new tools that technology presents to us. We must remember that tools are there to help us achieve goals; the use of tools is not the end we are seeking.

Getting off to a Good Start

Before designing any collection of online information, two basic questions must be answered:

1. What do users really **want**?

2. What do users really **need**?

Asking these two questions presumes that the answer to an even more basic question is known:

   Who are the users whose wants and needs are to be met?

But, unfortunately, the presumption of an answer does not always mean that the question has been answered or, if answered, that it has been answered as well or as completely as it should be. A knowledge of users—their background, abilities, and working habits— is key to making effective online information (Krull and Rubens 1986).

People generally need to be provided with some information before they can use a computer or a computer application. This information is made available from several sources:

1. The computer tells about itself (switches and labels).
2. Programs produce online information on the computer's screen.
3. Books associated with the computer tell about both the computer and the computer programs—and also about the books themselves (and sometimes about the authors of those books).

To produce information that is truly useful, we need to find out what people want and need, understand some characteristics of online information that affect its usefulness, and then determine how to match information characteristics to people's requirements.

First Things First

Finding out about users for a product (and the information that is part of the product or that is associated with it) may not be easy, but it is a most important activity. It is surely one of the first things that must be done in planning any information package. Information about an audience may be available from those responsible for marketing the product or from those who will plan for the product's design, development, and distribution.

If you've ever worked on developing a new product, finding out who the audience is for the product is an obvious step, so I won't belabor the point. If this is a new activity for you, you might want to read up on the subject before starting so that you don't overlook important steps. (See, for example, Caernarven-Smith 1983, 1988, Alberty 1987, and Burton 1988.)

But having found out *who* the audience is, how do we find out what people want and need? There are several ways available.

1. Ask people what they want.
2. Determine what they need.
3. Find out what products and what types of information are currently available and learn from their apparent strengths and weaknesses.
4. Conduct tests on early versions of the product or on currently available products to measure users' performance and attitudes.

Ask People What They Want

Take advantage of every opportunity to find out what kind of information people really want and in what form they want it. If you are producing information for a known group of customers, ask them. If you have the opportunity to meet with a group of information users, ask them. At the 32nd International Technical Communication Conference, for example, a group of attenders was asked for their opinions about online information (Fisher, Grice, Ramey, and Ridgway 1987). Respondents gave their views on a wide range of topics; the major conclusions of their responses were:

1. They were more concerned with the format of the online information and
   their ability to move through it than they were with textual characteristics
   and color.
2. Color was not particularly important to them and was not really considered
   to be a worthwhile research subject.
3. They believed consistency was very important.
4. They believed that online Help should serve as a quick reference, not as a
   replacement for printed information, and that it should be specific and
   context sensitive.
5. They thought that online information was best suited for procedures that
   were to be followed.

Some of these results were expected; others were not. It was expected that
consistency would be considered to be important, but color, for all its novelty (to
some) and prominence in advertisements and demonstrations, was not considered
to be. For all the talk and predictions about a "paperless society," respondents
to the above survey did not want online information to serve as a complete
replacement for printed information. The implication is fairly obvious: not
everything that *can* be put online *should* be put online; people prefer some ties to
forms and practices with which they are familiar. And the tie may be not only
one of familiarity; if people have used printed versions of information and know
that those versions work, they may worry that online versions will not work and
thus resist trying them.

Determine What People Need

Determining what people actually need is not as easy as finding out what they
want or what they like. Wants and preferences can be learned from
questionnaires and surveys. Actual needs must be determined by studying the
kinds of work people do and how they go about doing it. To determine what
types of online information people really need, those responsible for designing
and developing the information must observe the people at work. They must
analyze the tasks that the people perform to do their work; they must learn their
requirements.

Determining actual needs may involve developing several radically different
versions of the same set of online information and learning which one is most
effective in a user's actual working environment. It may well involve an
extensive iterative design, development, and testing process. But without this
sort of activity, users' needs will not be known and will not be readily satisfied.

Find Out What's Available

When we set out to produce printed information—books, manuals, or brochures—we need not always start from scratch. We can use existing works as models or samples and build from there. We can note strong features and weak features of what we see, adopt or adapt the good, and correct the deficient. We can then be off to a good start. However, maybe because of the relative newness of online information, efforts to produce new online information are often seen as new situations, with few, if any, ties to earlier efforts and products. To take this approach is to lose much of what could have been learned and used. To take this approach requires the person developing the online information to spend much time "reinventing the wheel," leaving less time for innovation and improvement.

What then can developers of online information do to help ensure the success of their information, to ensure that it truly meets the needs of its users? They can find out what is available:

- **To see**—Look at the best (and the worst) that is available. See if you can spot trends and preferences; learn what seems to be effective, what is well received by users or potential users, and what seems suitable for the types of applications in which you are interested. You can perform competitive evaluations on related information products to see how features and functions compare.

- **To use**—What do you have available to work with? Do you have the proper tools to work with. If you do, use the tools to your best advantage. But if the tools you need are not available in your organization, lobby for them; you need to have the proper tools to satisfy your own requirements and meet the needs of your users. Make sure that you investigate and test the tools before you tie your work effort to them; selecting the wrong tool can make your work harder and your results less effective than they should be.

- **To read, hear, and study**—Look around at conferences and trade shows, at computer stores, in journals and magazines, and even around your own place of work. You may be surprised at how much you can find.

Conduct Tests

Testing is one way to observe and measure how well people like online information and how well they can use it (often two separate issues). There are many ways to go about testing depending on time, resources, goals of testing, and availability of products, people, and testing facilities. The tests can be as formal or informal as your situation requires, but remember that the quality of the tests will, in large measure, determine the quality of the results you obtain.

Testing can be expensive, and the fear of this expense often stops people from incorporating testing into their development and verification plans. But you can always find ways to cut corners and economize—often without affecting the validity of the testing. Careful thought to the nature of the tests can give a good payback in the types of tests that can be conducted and the types of test results that can be expected.

Testing can be made an integral part of the process you use to develop online information. You don't have to wait until you're finished to start testing. Informal tests of prototypes and early draft versions of the online information can be conducted to test and improve the information in an iterative fashion so that changes and improvements can be made *during* the testing-and-development cycle and the online information changed to incorporate test results as soon as those results are known.

Iterative testing during development need not aim for statistical results; its purpose is to improve, not to evaluate and rate. Anecdotal test results can be invaluable; they can be used to make needed changes that meet the needs of users. Informal tests of early prototypes can also be less expensive to conduct than full-scale tests of completed information. "User surrogates" from within your own organization can be used for the tests rather than hiring persons from outside. And because the tests can be conducted earlier in the information-development cycle, there is more time to incorporate the changes suggested by the tests and observe their effect.

Often you can benefit by using results that others have obtained and applying them to your own projects. You can get results of tests performed by others and adapt them, if necessary, to meet the unique features of the online information you are developing. Check around within your own organization; someone may have done a test very similar to the one you would conduct yourself. Check around outside your organization; testing results are often available in conference proceedings, as university reports, or reports from research centers. Of course, not all test results are made generally available; they may well contain proprietary information. But if test results don't contain proprietary information, people are often happy to share the results they have obtained.

How Do We Find out What Users Want?

The best starting point for finding out what users want is to find out who the users are (or will be) and what they do now. People will use the information so they can get work done, most often work associated with their jobs. So before starting we must learn and understand what types of people we are producing information for, what kinds of work they will be doing, and how the information will support them in getting the work done. It is also important to understand what they are doing *now*. If the information will describe or support a new way of working, writers must take a different approach than when developing information that describes a task that will be familiar to most people. Writers must also consider how people currently obtain the information they need to get their work done. If, for example, they already use online information, writers need not provide as much tutorial and explanatory information on how to use the online information. If, on the other hand, people are not familiar with using online information or perhaps not even familiar with finding information themselves (relying on training courses or help from co-workers, for example), writers will have to provide the necessary lead-in information and may even need to alert people to the existence of the information and the uses they can make of it.

Choice of a proper starting point is very important. All too often people starting out to design and develop online information start with the "technological givens"—the colors and type fonts available for display, the available screen size, and the amount of available storage—or the "subject-matter givens"—what must be said about the product or what information is available to start working with. While these starting points may be useful for the writer, they may not be useful for the user (the analogy from composition research is the difference between *writer-based prose* and *reader-based prose*). Thus to make a good start in producing effective online information, don't focus on the technology or the information itself; focus on the people who will use the information, the tasks that they will perform, and the information that they will need to perform those tasks. Then take action.

Focus on People

Consider who will use the information you will produce. Learn about them, the tasks that they will do using the information you provide, and how your information will support those tasks. Who are the potential customers for the product? Those responsible for marketing and planning the product can be a good source of information. Do an audience analysis; find out as many things as you can about the audience and then determine how your findings will affect the information you produce. The information should respond to every point raised in your analysis (Caernarven-Smith 1983). If you have the opportunity to mail surveys to your customers or survey them by phone, take advantage of the opportunity. Better yet is the opportunity to visit customers at their place of work, see their working environment and how they work in it, and talk to them about their work and their information needs.

Focus on People's Tasks

Ward's task-analysis approach to developing information (1987) starts with defining the characteristics of the audience for the information and the tasks they will perform, the audience's starting point or background, the environment in which they will work, the goal or end point of their work, and the information they will need to perform their work and reach their goals.

See and Woestendiek (1987) recommend an analogous procedure for designing an interactive interface. Their procedure starts with defining the audience, their previous experience, and how use of this interface differs from that experience and then defines the tasks to be performed, the function, or goal, associated with the interface, and the breadth and depth of the interface.

These approaches are well grounded in prior methodologies, such as Mager's goal analysis for preparing instructional objectives (Mager 1972).

Focus on People's Information Needs and Preferences

Get feedback from those who use the information you have developed. Conduct surveys to find out how they use the information, what they like and dislike, what changes or additions they would like made to it, and what they want or expect in the future. Follow up the surveys, if at all possible, with in-depth examination of topics of special interest or concern. The follow-up can take the form of telephone surveys, customer council meetings, or visits to customers' offices to see how they work and how the information you provide is really used.

Take advantage of every opportunity to see how they use the information and try to determine how well it meets their needs.

Take Action!

Use what you learn about the customers to build composite customer profiles that you and others in your organization can use. These profiles capture what you have learned and can serve as an excellent base for developing, or modifying, information to meet customers' needs; they consolidate and preserve what you have learned. They can get you off to a great start in your information-development activities.

At the same time, you can develop profiles of the products on which you work, noting those features that customers find useful and attractive and others that are less desirable. This information, too, can serve as a useful base for subsequent activities, enabling you and your organization to build on past successes and avoid repeating prior mistakes.

See where the best matches of people and products occur, and use this information. Producing effective and success information requires the skillful application of product analysis, audience analysis, task analysis, and project analysis (Caernarven-Smith 1988).

Don't Force People to Fit the Interface—Design it to Fit Them!

Information properly designed to be used by its intended audience will be easy for them to use. They will be able to use it naturally. In *Mindstorms*, Papert explains how by putting children in control of computers (rather than under control of the computers), the children are able to explore, learn about, and master use of computers. Computer systems, online information, and even printed information can be designed so that people are confident and in control. It should be designed correctly from the start; adaptation and modification should not be steps that users are forced to go through. (If they *choose* to make modifications to the information so that their needs are better met, that is fine. But the choice should be theirs; it should not be mandated.)

As an example of adaptation, consider this error message[1]; it's one I receive quite often; you may have seen in once or twice yourself.

```
┌─────────────────────────────────────────────────┐
│                                                   │
│                                                   │
│         ILLEGAL ENTRY                             │
│                                                   │
│                                                   │
└─────────────────────────────────────────────────┘
```

Usually, when I get this message, the situation is something like this:

```
┌─────────────────────────────────────────────────┐
│         My Favorite Text Editor                   │
│                                                   │
│   00152  lines of my wonderful prose.             │
│   00153  The next line needs text inserted after it. │
│   00j*m  Here's where I try to insert lines.      │
│                                                   │
│         ILLEGAL ENTRY                             │
│                                                   │
└─────────────────────────────────────────────────┘
```

The message is telling me I hit the wrong keys, and I know from experience what I need to do before going on. But consider this example:

```
┌─────────────────────────────────────────────────┐
│         Police Inquiry System                     │
│                                                   │
│   1987 convictions for J. Doe:                    │
│                                                   │
│         ILLEGAL ENTRY                             │
│                                                   │
└─────────────────────────────────────────────────┘
```

Or this one:

> **Generic Adventure Game**
>
> Attempt made to enter cave through locked door:
>
> ILLEGAL ENTRY

The same message appearing in each example has the same wording but conveys (or should convey) very different meaning. The moral is this: the messages all made sense to the person who designed them, and they **may**, in fact, make sense to the person who receives them (these examples were pretty obvious, so there probably wasn't too much confusion). But they all ignore the **context** in which a person receives the message. They are product centered, not user centered. If the user is aware of the context and understands the context, all will be well. But this may be a rather large gamble to take.

Consider this analogy. Sometime in your life you have probably had to deal with a clock or a watch with hands that were a little loose or "off." While this may have been a nuisance or inconvenience, you were probably able to figure out about what time it was because of the context supplied by the clock—the numbers ranged sequentially, clockwise around the face of the clock. You may have had trouble telling if it was twenty or twenty five minutes to five, but you probably would not have been too late for supper. But what of the more recent digital clocks with LED (light-emitting diodes) to display the time? If two of the diodes stop working, you might have no idea if the number displayed should be 0, 2, 5, 6, 8, or 9. There is no context to help you figure out what, if anything, is missing from the display, and without that context, you may have no way of determining the answer.

The "Illegal Entry" examples may have drawn a laugh or a smile as you read them, but if you received them while stuck trying to figure out what to do next, I'm sure they would seem far less humorous. (Again, the context in which you would receive them is different from the context in which you are now reading about them.)

Will People Read the Online Information We Produce?

People don't always read the books and manuals we've been writing. We know that. Should we expect them to read online information? Possible answers to that question are:

1. Probably not.
2. Yes, but only to get a job done.
3. Maybe, but only as a last resort.

If we expect people to use the online information we produce, the information must be:

1. **Useful**—to those who will use it. It must support their work and be the type of information they need in the format they want it.
2. **Easy to use**—by those who will use it. This means that it must be developed based on what was learned from analyzing the audience for the information and the tasks that they will perform. Once the information is developed, it must be reviewed and tested, revised based on the reviews and tests, and tested again to ensure that it is accurate and suitable.
3. **Possibly attractive and enjoyable**—but function and usability must not be sacrificed for the sake of appearance alone. Of course, online information can, and should, be designed to be attractive as well as useful.

Online information can be designed so that it is useful and enjoyable to be used :

> without being silly
> without being insulting to its users
> without wasting users' time.

Some Factors that Affect Whether People Will Use the Information

Designers of online information can make choices that will affect the ultimate success of the information. Some topics that must be considered are:

1. Familiarity of the subject matter, the presentation, and the conventions used.
2. Support of users' tasks, so that they can get their work done.

3. Ease of learning and first use to get started and be productive with a minimum amount of confusion and frustration.
4. Navigability so that users can move from one piece of information to another.
5. Ease of modification, so that they can customize, adapt, and personalize.
6. Appearance.

Let's examine each of these factors briefly.

Familiarity

For centuries, people have used the printed page as a major source of information. Moving to a computer's display screen as a source of information is, for many, a major change, one with which they may not be comfortable. To ease and simplify their transition, those who develop online information can use conventions and traditions of printed information to give users a sense of familiarity, so they will feel as if they are in control, a feature that Papert has shown to be of vital importance.

The attempt to present a familiar image may or may not work, depending on the technology's ability to mirror printed information. On the other hand, tying too closely to an old analogy may hinder—new concepts don't map well, and people may be tied to the old and never learn or exploit new features. For example, those who look upon a word processor as a typewriter will be slow to use and exploit the new features of the word processor. Their mental model will lock them into old, familiar use patterns.

For those users who may be somewhat familiar with online information, similarity of an online information package to those that they have already seen can be an aid to using the new package. If the conventions used are the same as those used earlier, the online information will seem familiar to users because they will respond in ways they are used to. And if the online information is similar to their expectations, not presenting "surprises" or causing confusion, they will be more comfortable and more productive than they might otherwise be.

The old saw tells us that familiarity breeds contempt. But when assessing the effectiveness of online information, familiarity breeds ease of use. (Of course, well designed information will require less familiarity to appear easy to use than will poorly designed information.)

Achieving Familiarity Through Consistency—IBM's Common User Access

One aid to achieving consistency, familiarity, and ease of navigation is for all panels for related products to look the same and work the same. In March 1987, IBM Corporation announced Systems Application Architecture (SAA), a software direction that provides the framework for developing consistent applications across major computing environments. One component of SAA that is germane to our discussion is Common User Access (CUA), a set of guidelines and specifications for creating online panels (IBM Corp. 1987). The goal of CUA is to help users develop a proper conceptual model quickly through consistent use of panel elements and panel design.

One of the biggest obstacles that people encounter when using computer products is the wide variety of standards, conventions, and practices that are in general use. People who are used to seeing system messages displayed at the top of a display screen suddenly encounter them on the bottom when they use a new application program. The function key that usually saves a file may erase the file in a new application or when using a familiar application in a different environment. Users never get a chance to become comfortable and familiar with a set of conventions because the conventions keep changing.

IBM's Common User Access (CUA) provides a consistent set of conventions that designers of application programs can use to create programs that will present users with a consistent, familiar interface. Berry states that CUA provides "a transfer of users' conceptual-level learning across different and evolving technologies" (1988, p. 281) and provides a framework for application designers, programming developers, and tools designers to use in their work. It "standardize[s] the look and feel of the user's view of of an application. It redefines and expands the role of technical communicators—writers, editor, and graphic artists—who help design and document software" (Szydlik 1988, p. 183).

This CUA format, which applies to all types of online panels (menu, entry, information, list, or logo), has three major components:

1. **Action bar**—which gives users access to the group of actions that the application supports
2. **Panel body**—which gives users a place to enter commands and data and to receive output and status information
3. **Function key area**—which displays the function keys available for users to select for actions.

These three components, in turn, can be made up of the nine panel elements defined for CUA: panel body area separators, panel ID, panel title, instructions on use, column and group headings, field prompts, scrolling information, message area, and command area. The layout of a typical panel is:

```
Action Bar and Pull Downs
------------------------------------------



            Panel Body



------------------------------------------
Function Key Area
```

Support of Users' Tasks

It is imperative that the online information support users' tasks. Because the use of online information is more closely associated with using a computer product than printed information is, this degree of support is even more critical in online information than in printed. The tasks described must match the tasks that users perform (and in the order that they perform them or when they request the task-supportive information).

There should be as little "overhead" as possible associated with the online information; it should be easy for people get the information, read it, and get away from it. The online information can, unfortunately, place unnecessary burdens on people and prevent them from performing their tasks. If the panel that a user is working on is completely replaced by a panel full of Help information, it may be difficult for the user to remember why the Help was needed or to return to the work. The way that the information is presented to users has the potential for being as important as the information itself (Cherry, Fryer, Steckham, and Fischer 1988). Thus, the help provided must be context sensitive and nondisruptive. It must provide the information that the user needs when the help is requested and must not interfere (or should interfere as little as possible) with the work that the user is doing.

The online information should give users feedback so they know how they are doing, and the feedback should be given at frequent enough intervals that users do not have a sense of being "lost" or out of touch with the work they are doing.

Ease of Learning and First Use

The first impression that people have of online information can often be a lasting one. The ease with which people can learn from the information and, through it, start using the product may affect the way they will always think of the information and the product. And the range can be quite wide: from walk-up-and-use products to those that require long, extensive training. Poorly designed information may, in fact, scare people away from a product; they may use only a portion of it or not use it at all

Factors to consider are:

- How well the tasks to be done match the user's expectations and cognitive framework (way of thinking and viewing the problem at hand).
- The amount of guidance offered to the user.
- The complexity of the tasks that must be performed.
- As discussed earlier, the degree to which conventions are familiar and consistent.

Navigability

Given a new book to read or look at, most of us feel comfortable examining it. We know how to leaf through it (forwards or backwards), how to place our fingers between pages to mark places we may want to return to, how to read it completely, and how to put it down when we no longer want to look at it. Navigating through a book rarely presents a serious problem.

But what about information presented online? We are often puzzled or lost and ask:

- Where am I?
- Where have I been?
- Where do I go next?
- How do I get out of here?

Some of this puzzlement is caused by the relative newness of online information, but it can be lessened, or eliminated, by exploiting the capabilities of online media, such as the consistent use of appropriate navigation aids to help users keep track of their position. For example,

- Guideposts, such as "screen 5," "screen 1 of 8," or a "thermometer" that marks the relative position in the information, the percentage completed.
- Actions that can be taken ("push key x to do this" or "push key y to do that").
- Identification of keys that can be used to take action, such as ESCAPE, END, QUIT, RETURN, or HELP.
- Identification of the overall context (such as a structure diagram or stack map).
- Consideration of most appropriate use of disruptive versus nondisruptive functions (such as Help).

While some of these navigation aids are very "unbooklike," they do enable users to maneuver as comfortably and as easily as they can with printed information. The advent of hypermedia, however, raises a host of new questions about navigability. In a system where individual users chose their paths through the information, the concept of "a place in the information" starts to fall apart. Users may well have arrived at the same location from very different starting points and thus have very different perceptions of their relative place in an information package.

Ease of Modification

Giving users the ability to modify the information to suit their individual needs and preferences can make them feel more involved and more comfortable. Such actions as changing colors on display panels, rearranging the order of items on a menu or list, changing the names or abbreviations of commands, or modifying the text of messages does not cause a major change to the online information, but the change can have a large effect on how well users perceive and use the information.

Major modification of the online information may not, however, be desirable. While changing colors or adding synonyms may not present problems, major changes made to command formats or order of items on a menu may, in fact, make other forms of information, such as context-sensitive Help more difficult to use or less useful when used.

Appearance

Perhaps more research has been done on the appearance of online information than on any other aspect. This may be because appearance is easier to test and measure than other factors, or it may be a carry-over from printed material where appearance is a more dominant factor than in online information. Appearance of online information may not be as important as we might at first think, but it does count. Factors to be considered are:

1. Effects of type font and size
2. Effects of text density
3. Effects of color
4. "Special effects"

Effects of Type Font and Size

The choice of type size seems not to be a major factor; indeed, there is sometimes no choice of available fonts or type sizes. Within limits, however, smaller type can be read faster if the information is formatted to reduce the need for eye motion. As with printed information, mixed case is preferred to all-upper or all-lower case (Fryser and Stirling 1984). Within limits, line length is not a major factor. Krull and Rubens, for example, conclude "that there may be only a small advantage to short versus long lines when one examines reading speed" (Krull and Rubens 1984, p. 14).

Effects of Text Density

Because information on display screens is presented as projected light rather than the reflected light that readers are used to seeing on printed pages, users' perception of text density may be be different for online information than for printed information.

Little systematic research has been done, but screens with text-character densities as low as 15-25% (Danchak 1976) have been recommended, while others found no significant differences in performance with densities ranging from 25% to 50% (Krull and Rubens 1985). As with traditional printed information, very dense text on screens slows the reading of online information. (If the densities cited seem low to you, keep in mind that the text density of many printed pages in the range of 40% to 50%.)

Effects of Color

Opinions on use of color vary. Use of color may aid in initial learning by making the information more distinctive or memorable. But use, actually misuse, of color can be a distraction, and the color may get in the way of use and understanding. As with traditional printed information users seem to like "color for a reason" and find it helpful, but random color or too much color distracts. If color is used with no apparent reason, users may spend time and energy trying to figure out meanings for the colors, wasting their time and possibly misinterpreting the information in their attempt to derive a reason for the uses of colors.

Because online information about computers and computer use generally makes greater use of color than printed information for the same subjects, it is important to remember the impact that color blindness can have on use of the information. Screen displays that depend on the user distinguishing between red and green, for example, may be useless to many people. Similarly, color schemes with little distinction between foreground and background colors may "hide" information from people who can not distinguish colors clearly. On the other hand, color schemes with too great a distinction or with too many vivid colors may be perceived as pictures to be viewed rather than information to be read and understood.

And, as always happens with color, we must remember that many people are partial to, or have aversions to, various colors; we must not allow our personal color preferences to dominate the information to the point that it becomes ineffective for many users.

"Special Effects"

Online presentation of information offers technical communicators options not available with traditional printed information. For example, sound, animation, blinking, color changes, and interaction with the information are available to involve people in the information, to make them active users rather than passive readers. Rather than presenting finished diagrams to be seen and absorbed as a whole, the online information can be designed so that a diagram is presented in pieces and "built up" as it is explained or as users ask for more information. Thus the components and workings of a mechanical object can be presented as an integral part of an illustration rather than as a separate topic.

As with most new features and capabilities, however, there can be a strong tendency to want to overuse these capabilities. While it is entirely possible to present large blocks of information as blinking text, it should not take much thought to realize the disastrous effect this blinking could have on someone trying to read the text. And while animation can be a great aid to showing how something operates or how data is moved through a process, the overuse of animation can cause confusion and hide the principles that the technical communicator wants to present.

Some Concluding Thoughts

As we examine the social construction of information, trying to use newly available technologies to best meet the needs of our audiences, some things are quite clear.

To start with, we don't have all the answers that we want or need. In many cases, we don't even have all the questions. We are now in the mode of trying to "catch up with technology," learning how to use it and to avoid misusing it. Standing on the threshold of great new advances, we must study our position and evaluate our options.

These options are probably best studied through systematic research. We, as technical communicators, must support and encourage research so that we will be able to get the answers that we need. We can do some of the research ourselves; we can collaborate with others to do some more. That which is beyond our means or capabilities should not be written off. Rather, we must find ways and means to ensure that it is done, and done well.

We must make certain that we don't let the medium overpower the message. Hypermedia may be an excellent solution to some communication problems; it may be an overpowering solution to others. The availability of CD ROMs and their ability to store and retrieve vast quantities of information does not mean that there are not still cases in which a simple pocket reference card is the best solution.

We must always keep in mind that the first concern of a technical communicator is the audience. To meet the audience's wants and needs, we must first know them **well**. We must remember that users may not be as familiar with the subject, the medium, or the conventions as we are. They may not even care! It's up to us—technical communicators—to make use of the information as easy and productive as possible for them.

Note

1. This example grew out of a discussion of interactive interfaces with with Lenore Ridgway and Edward See in November 1987. I thank them for allowing me to use it here.

References

1. Alberty, Catherine A. 1987. "A Step Beyond Audience Analysis: A Writer's Awareness of Audience While Composing," *Proceedings of 34th International Technical Communication Conference*, Denver, Colorado. Washington, DC: Society for Technical Communication, ʀᴇᴛ-26—ʀᴇᴛ-29.
2. Barrett, Edward. 1988. *Text, ConText, and HyperText: Writing with and for the Computer*. Cambridge, MA: The MIT Press.
3. Berry, R.E. 1988. "Common User Access—A Consistent and Usable Human-Computer Interface for the SAA Environments," *IBM Systems Journal*, Vol. 27, No. 3. Armonk, NY: IBM Corporation. pp. 281-300.
4. Burton, Sarah K. 1988. "Doing the Impossible: Documenting for the Elusive 'Everybody' Audience," *Proceedings of 35th International Technical Communication Conference*, Philadelphia, Pennsylvania. Washington, DC: Society for Technical Communication, ᴡᴇ-174—ᴡᴇ-175.
5. Caernarven-Smith, Patricia. 1983. *Audience Analysis & Response* Pembroke, MA: Firman Technical Publications, Inc.
6. Caernarven-Smith, Patricia. 1988. "You Need More Than an Audience To Do Audience Analysis," *Proceedings of the 36th Annual Technical Writers' Institute*, June 7-10, 1988, Rensselaer Polytechnic Institute, Troy, NY: pp. 165-173.
7. Casey, Bernice. 1980. "Lobbying for the Software User." *Proceedings of 27th International Technical Communication Conference*, Minneapolis, Minnesota. Washington, DC: Society for Technical Communication, R-171—R-175.
8. Cherry, Joan, Barbara Fryer, Melanie Steckham, and Michael Fischer. "Do Formats for Presenting Online Help Affect User Performance and Attitudes?" *Proceedings of the 35th International Technical Communication Conference*, Philadelphia, Pennsylvania. Washington, DC: Society for Technical Communication: pp. ʀᴇᴛ-87—ʀᴇᴛ-89.
9. Danchak, M. M. 1976. "CRT Displays for Power Plants." *Instrumental Technology* Vol. 23, No. 10. pp. 29-36.
10. Fisher, Lou, Roger Grice, Judy Ramey, and Lee Ridgway. 1987. "Online Information: What Conference Attenders Expect (A Report of a Survey)."

Technical Communication Vol. 34, No. 3. Washington, DC: Society for
Technical Communication. pp. 150-155.

11. Fryser, Benjamin S. and Keith H. Stirling. 1984. "The Effect of Spatial
    Arrangement, Upper-Lower Case Letter Combinations, and Reverse Video on
    Patron Response to CRT Displayed Catalog Records," *Journal of the
    American Society for Information Science* Vol. 35, No. 6. pp. 344—350.

12. Krull, Robert and Philip Rubens. 1984. "An Eye Motion Study of Online
    Information," *Proceedings of the 1984 Annual USER-bility Symposium*,
    Kingston, NY, IBM Corporation. pp. 9-17.

13. Krull, Robert and Philip Rubens. 1985. "Online Information Layout and
    User Input Systems." unpublished report, Rensselaer Polytechnic Institute.

14. Krull, Robert and Philip Rubens. 1986. "Online Information Content and
    Navigation," *Linking Technology and Users*, Conference Record of The
    International Professional Communication Conference, Charlotte, North
    Caroline. New York. Institute of Electrical and Electronics Engineers. pp.
    23-28.

15. IBM Corp. 1987. *Systems Application Architecture: Common User Access
    Panel Design and User Interaction*, SC26-4351. Boca Raton, Florida.

16. Mager, Robert F. 1972. *Goal Analysis,.* Belmont, California: Fearon
    Publishers.

17. Papert, Seymour. 1980. *Mindstorms: Children, Computers, and Powerful
    Ideas.* New York: Basic Books.

18. Porat, Marc Uri. 1978. "Global Implications of the Information Society."
    Journal of Communication, Winter 1978. Philadelphia: University of
    Pennsylvania Press: pp. 70-80.

19. Porush, David. 1985. *The Soft Machine: Cybernetic Fiction.* London and
    New York: Methuen & Co.

20. See, Edward J. and Douglas C. Woestendiek.   1987. "Effective User
    Interfaces: Some Common Sense Guidelines," *Proceedings of the Fifth
    International Conference on Systems Documentation* June 8-11 1986, Toronto,
    Canada. NY: The Association for Computing Machinery. pp. 87-94.

21. Szydlik, Frederick P. 1988. "The Interface Defined: IBM's Common User
    Access and Technical Communication," *Proceedings of the 36th Annual
    Technical Writers' Institute*, June 7-10, 1988, Rensselaer Polytechnic Institute,
    Troy, NY: pp. 183-193.

22. Ward, Robert A. 1984. "A Task Analysis Primer for Technical
    Communicators," *Proceedings of the 31st International Technical
    Communication Conference*, Seattle, Washington. Washington, DC: Society
    for Technical Communication: we-86—we-88.

Hypertext in Context

David S. Herrstrom, Ph.D.
David G. Massey, Ph.D.

Human Performance Associates
Mendham, New Jersey 07945

We propose here a hypertext design to solve problems common to documentation for end-users of computer systems. By "documentation" we mean instructions and reference materials that enable users of computer systems to accomplish specific tasks. The "context" of our title suggests the problem to which our hypertext design offers a solution. Often hypertext seems to be a solution searching for a problem; consequently, many hypertext designs appear to be driven by technology rather than by the needs of users. Our solution arises from real problems encountered in the world of action where users must learn and apply computer systems to get a job done. Our approach to hypertext, then, is to place it squarely in the context of user needs; and this context makes us skeptical of recent hypertext hype.

The user is part of a system that includes the tool for accomplishing work — the computer — and the work environment itself, which defines task demands and thus user needs. The hypertext enthusiast focuses on its power to present users with myriad nodes of information from which to choose according to their desire for information. The skeptic, on the other hand, emphasizes the "confusing web of alternatives" that hides relevant information from the user, who will "pursue links of no relevance and arrive at relevant information without having first viewed prerequisite, supporting information" [1]. Though we recognize the power of hypertext, our enthusiasm is tempered by the limitations of one part of the system — the user. We can improve the tool, the computing machine itself, as well as the working environment, but we cannot escape the constraints of human information processing. And this limitation is most apparent in the world of action where users, under the pressure of difficult jobs, must suddenly master a new computer tool to accomplish their work objectives.

In this article, we first provide an overview and propose an "engineering" approach to the design of user documentation implemented through hypertext. Second, we further define the context — the world of action — for documentation design and the user needs that arise from it. And third, we sketch our hypertext design — a hierarchical array — that satisfies the user's information needs. Our design has proven successful in print documentation, and we see it as transferable to a hypertext medium. But the design gains in transfer, since a powerful search-and-retrieval engine such as hypertext adds the advantages of fast access speed and instantaneous juxtaposition of related information.

1. Overview

User Needs

Hypertext, with its ability to provide easy access to a large amount of data, holds great promise for improving user documentation. Taking advantage of hypertext's powerful links and discrete nodes, we can begin to exploit the rich possibilities for users of what Jeff Conklin calls the "structured browsing" members of the hypertext family [2]. The promise for improving user documentation can only be fulfilled, however, if hypertext is developed in the context of well-defined user groups who approach varied, complex tasks with different levels of knowledge and skill. Task-driven users browse on weekends, not when they need to find, under time pressure, a specific command or procedure to achieve a computer-related objective.

General web structures of information that invite unguided exploration, as a result, do not fill the bill. Systems such as *Hyperties*, for example, are limited only by the cost of data entry and the curiosity of the museum browser [3]. These admirably satisfy a general audience's curiosity, their desire to know more about an intriguing subject. But such systems cannot meet the specific user's need to "find and do." In effective user documentation, designers focus specific users on <u>only</u> the information they need to accomplish well-defined computer tasks, given their level of knowledge and skill.

This context of users in a world of action means we must shift our focus from user interests to user needs. We must strategically narrow the possibilities of the hypertext web, if we are to exploit hypertext technology for designing better user documentation. In short, for the task-driven, impatient user, we must trade the fascinating webs of information now offered by most hypertext systems for efficient nets or what we term **hierarchical arrays** of information.

"Engineering" Approach

To deliver computer systems that people can use, we must engineer the "user support" every bit as carefully as the computer tool itself. In designing user documentation that employs hypertext systems, this means that we accept the responsibility as designers for providing the right information nodes and links, rather than burdening users with a plethora of choices with only a few relevant to their needs. We must enable users to access easily all needed information while hiding from view extraneous information not related to the task at hand.

To engineer user documentation through hypertext that meets these objectives, the designer must address two primary concerns from the user's standpoint: 1) accessibility and 2) relevance. Information is accessible if users can find it both when they know what they are looking for and when they do not. Information is relevant if it is the appropriate type and size of information module, both comprehensible and useful. The key to accessibility and relevance for specific user groups is a carefully engineered matrix of information, an array that enables users to move efficiently on clearly mapped paths through nodes of information, typed and sized according to their needs.

2. The Context

World of Action

The principle user motive in what we are calling the "world of action" is to find a piece of information (e.g., procedural instructions) and use it to perform a job-related computer task. (By contrast, a task such as database search for information, per se, consists solely in finding and retrieving the information.) At its simplest, we can imagine a single type of user, whom we can define precisely, and a single kind of task, with standard procedures that we can match exactly with the user. The information design problem in this case is easily solved. We custom design a document explicitly for one known user performing a standardized task.

In the real world of action, however, we know that the problem is more complex. In developing user documentation for the computer industry, we must meet the needs of disparate users required to perform complex tasks. We cannot in this world develop a customized document for each user, of course, because the range of users is too great and their various tasks too complex.

To define the world of action, then, is to define the range of our users and the nature of their tasks. The range of users is determined primarily by their levels of knowledge and skill, though attitude is often critical. We can classify them accordingly from "novice" to "expert" as M. L. Schneider does [4]. And we must in the same document often provide information for the novice, the expert, levels in between, and the casual user, who may become an expert for a week in a narrow area, but six months later must relearn those same procedures. To discover the nature of their tasks, we must investigate complexity and frequency of each task and the circumstances under which it is performed. Most often we encounter not only a range of users whom we must address in a single document, but a range of task complexity as well.

User Needs

Defining user needs, then, requires profiling the user groups, analyzing their tasks, and then comparing what the user brings to the task (knowledge and skill) with what the task requires. The discrepancy between user capabilities and task requirements yields the necessary support that must be "engineered" for the user. Since we cannot develop a customized document for each user, we have to find ways of providing the necessary information that will be accessible to a range of users performing a variety of tasks. We must support them in formulating the complex task required; we must enable them to access information that supports their task; and we must provide them with relevant information once accessed.

We can only answer the question of how much support to provide within the context of the user's capabilities and objectives. Clearly, not every user within a task domain will formulate the task in the same way. The novice user, of course, will define the task differently than the expert. Similarly, the novice will need different types of information (e.g., tutorial) and level of detail than the expert.

The four basic types of information required to support the user are: 1) overview, 2) tutorial, 3) procedural, and 4) reference. Overview and tutorial information are needed prior to performing the task itself, while procedural and reference information provide step-by-step instructions and related "support," respectively, within the task arena.

Overview information is general and serves to orient the user, providing the "big picture." Tutorials teach prerequisite knowledge and skills for using the computer. By contrast, both procedural and reference information provide specifics on how to do a particular task. Given their range of skill and knowledge, as well as a range of task complexity, users will take different paths through these types of information to satisfy their needs. The novice, for example, would most likely proceed from overview to tutorial, then to procedural and reference information. On the other hand, the expert may go directly to the reference information, occasionally needing procedural instructions. Other users take different paths, which document designers can map in detail.

Design Solutions

Over the last decade, a number of print-based mechanisms have evolved to make the designer's job of satisfying information support needs easier. We have learned to:

- Layer documents in tiers or types of information for different users
- Design these layers and page formats for quick access
- Provide more than one level of detail as required
- Include access tools such as task indexes.

To accommodate the user's need for an appropriate procedural sequence and step size, we have separated the checklist of "what to do" from the details of "how to do" information. In short, we have designed information types and access paths that accommodate a specific set of user needs within the world of action.

The task-driven user, of course, wants faster access to only relevant information. This user's fundamental need is for **explicit procedural and reference information accessed in predictable ways**. The access mechanisms and information designs we have developed over the last few years for print documentation have satisfied this need.

But despite better access tools and better methods of segregating and highlighting types of information, users under time pressure often find themselves flipping from one section of a printed manual to another in a number of time-consuming iterations and, at the same time, trying to keep a finger in four different sections at once. This is very costly in terms of cognitive overhead, and the pressure of the task domain points up the need for a better solution that yields faster access and juxtaposition of related information, such as procedural instructions and reference detail.

We need, then, a mechanism to realize proven documentation design with greater speed and less user overhead. Hypertext applications, as superb access-and-retrieval engines, suggest that mechanism. Hypertext does not, however, inherently provide a design solution. We have proven design solutions in print documentation. But hypertext enables us to implement in certain work environments these design solutions more efficiently than ever before.

3. Hypertext Strategy

Hierarchical Array

Achieving our objectives of explicitness and predictability narrows down the kinds of hypertext that are appropriate. Hypertext systems are most often designed as webs, which allow users to move virtually from anywhere to anywhere by association. As a consequence, webs allow deep exploration, in that the only limit to successive branchings, once a user enters the web, is the time and patience of the information developer and programmer. By the same token, access is unpredictable and the type of information in the node may be unknown. This is a recipe for user frustration.

Instead of an associative web, therefore, we propose a purposive net (Figure 1). This net, which enables us to satisfy the needs of the task-driven user, we term a **hierarchical array** of information. Our design contains a finite set of clearly typed information modules, according to explicit conventions, accessed by a few strategic, well-defined paths. Our hypertext net is hierarchical in that its information modules, the nodes of the system, are tiered according to level of detail. Procedural and reference information are designed in separate tiers, from general to specific. Each tier follows a well-defined level of detail targeting a

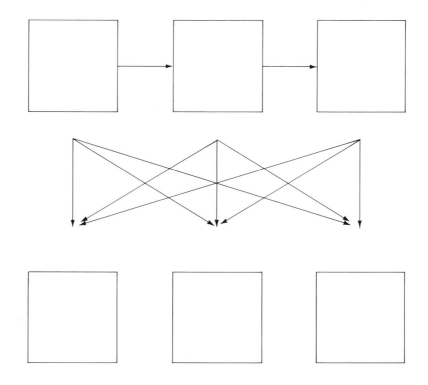

Figure 1 — Hierarchical Array

specific group of users. And the relationship of procedural to reference information is hierarchical by priority of access. For example, access priorities may be:

1. Overall purpose of the task
2. Main steps in the task
3. Detailed, step-by-step instructions for completing the task (sized according to the user's experience)
4. Related specifications, conditional variants, command arguments, and so forth required to complete the task.

If the hierarchical levels of detail constitute the linear aspect of our "hierarchical array," the wholly accessible modules of information constitute its non-linear aspect. Here an electronic medium, and specifically hypertext, offers a qualitatively different approach from print. The speed of hypertext is not just quantitatively faster than print, but reaches a point of instant juxtaposition. It provides a simultaneity that makes a qualitative difference in the user's processing of information. The user can move directionally "up" and "down" levels of detail, but the user can also move to any intersection of the hierarchy, skipping levels or jumping across from one level to another. Access links, that is, between information nodes provide paths to all information.

But not all paths can be equal and open for all users. For our hypertext design to work, designers must type and size information nodes and clearly map the paths to them according to user needs. Designers must circumscribe the user's movement, making choices about what will be accessible and what will not. This opposes a strategy that leaves these choices in the user's hands. Under time pressure, users need to be guided by what they expect, both in ways of access and in what information will be accessed.

In designing a hierarchical array, the designer devises **predictable paths to expected information.** The array reveals its structure (say, through maps and icons), aiding the user in creating an accurate mental model of the system's knowledge space. And the model becomes reinforced in the user's mind through repeated, predictable use.

Accessible Information

Predictable access in a task-driven context must enable the user, first, to formulate the task required to accomplish a work objective and, second, branch to procedural and reference information that supports the task. Because the user does not know initially where to branch, the links in formulating the task must be implicit, that is, defined in the system.

Formulating the task, from the user's point of view, raises the problem of defining the task in the way that the system designer, based on task analysis, has defined it. Task formulation can be aided by a form of keyword search that begins with the user's guess. The designer supplies implicit links from the guess to its variants, in effect making a wrong guess impossible (Figure 2). The guess, for example, could be the plural form where the system recognizes the singular; a synonym; or a main task which the system handles as a subtask [5]. Once users identify their task with the aid of the hypertext system, they can move via explicit links to relevant procedural and reference information nodes.

Relevant Information

Under time pressure, user needs are satisfied by the proper balance and juxtaposition of procedural and reference information. To emphasize the hierarchical relationship between these information types, which is made explicit in our hypertext design, we call them, respectively, "directive" and "supportive."

Each of these types has a hierarchy of levels of detail according to the range of users — novice to expert. For illustration here, we define three levels of detail for each, though the designer may define greater or fewer depending on the user's needs. Levels of directive information are: 1) checklist, a list of "what" to do for the expert; 2) high-level procedures or "how" to do for the intermediate user; and 3) low-level procedures, a detailed "how" to do for the novice. Levels of supportive information are: 1) summary or general explanation; 2) examples or detailed explanation; and 3) options, variables, or tables of values, and so forth. In a real application, the hierarchy of nodes for both types of information would be defined in answer to the question: "Exactly what type and level of information will each user group need to perform this

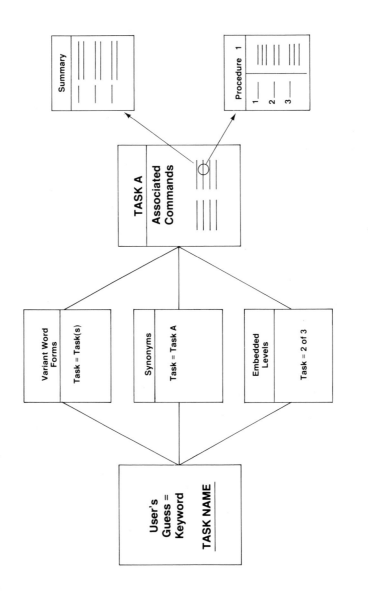

Figure 2 — Access Links

well-defined task?"

Keying these directive and supportive nodes, with their carefully designed
levels of detail, to the range of respective user needs results in our hierarchical
array (Figure 3). The information nodes are thus explicit and conventionalized,
with icons and maps to aid the user's choice and juxtaposition of nodes based on

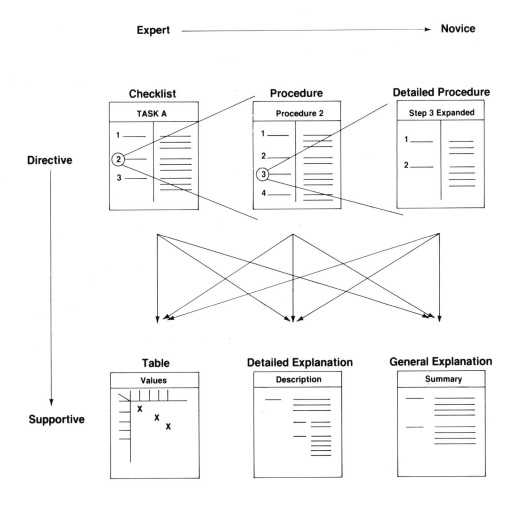

Figure 3 — Information Nodes

"typical" need. The user knows exactly what kind of information will be at each intersection of the array. And each contains expected and relevant information for performing a specific task, given a certain level of knowledge and skill.

Once users define the task (via implicit links within the system), they move along a predictable, explicit link to, say, a checklist for the task (Figure 4). With hypertext a key stroke leads there. The user then moves to the appropriate level of directive information (e.g., step-by-step procedure). Needing to know the meaning of a word or the required command at a certain point, the user then moves to the appropriate supportive information. The expert, of course, may not need to be reminded of procedures at all and may go directly to supportive detail. The hierarchical array enables the user to do this, because all nodes of the array are accessible, though circumscribed by explicit conventions that keep users from proceeding down irrelevant paths.

The Payoff

Thus, hypertext has enabled us to implement predictable paths to expected information with low user overhead. Providing expected information means that the user will not be forced to access irrelevant detail. Providing clear paths means that the user will not become disoriented. Explicit information nodes, combined with predictable links in a hierarchical array, provide users with what they need to perform a specific task without the necessity of interpreting the structure itself.

Task-driven users welcome faster paths to the right information, but not at the expense of cognitive overhead. Providing them with efficient links along a hierarchical array solves this dilemma. Such an array limits the possible paths through information nodes, virtually unlimited in an associative web structure. What it loses, however, in reducing browsers' opportunities, it gains in targeting users' needs. Stressed computer users do not browse. They are generally happy to perform a computer-related task with a single keystroke. We believe the hypertext design presented here will bring documentation designers a step closer to delivering what computer users want.

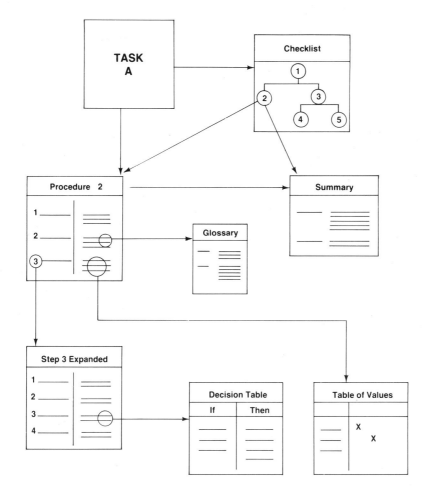

Figure 4 — Information Paths

Notes

[1] William P. Jones, "A Critical Assessment of Hypertext Systems," ACM CHI Proceedings (1988), pp. 224-225.

[2] Jeff Conklin, "Hypertext: An Introduction and Survey," IEEE Computer (September 1987), pp. 26 ff.

[3] Gary Marchionini and Ben Schneiderman, "Finding Facts vs. Browsing Knowledge in Hypertext Systems," IEEE Computer (January 1988), pp. 74 ff.

[4] M. L. Schneider, "Models for the Design of Static Software User Assistance," in Directions in Human/Computer Interaction, eds. A. Badre and B. Schneiderman (Norwood, NJ: Ablex, 1982), p. 138.

[5] Marchionini and Schneiderman, p. 76.

Hypertext and Intelligent Interfaces for Text Retrieval

Patricia Ann Carlson

Department of Humanities
Rose-Hulman Institute of Technology
Terre Haute, Indiana 47803

Any successful electronic publishing system must provide access to text and graphics in a timely and meaningful fashion. This study identifies three categories of retrieval facilities and considers their efficacy when combined with hypertext. Because of its structure and connectivity, a hypergraph (hypertext web) incorporates intelligence, perhaps more than is possible with most current, static database storage representations. The purpose of this study is to suggest retrieval facilities that will squeeze as much functionality out of the hypergraph as possible.

The hypertext concept considers a body of knowledge as a database -- potentially a highly organized, compressed structure of richly interconnected "chunks" -- and allows for flexible indexing and retrieval by implementing a "smart" interface (a programmable "idea processing" mechanism). Hypertext, as the backbone for development philosophy, permits advanced design features -- such as enhanced functionality, customized views, and improved knowledge synthesis and representation -- which, in turn, increase the user's ability to interact productively with information.

1. Introduction

Since 1985, a significant hypertext community has emerged. The number of conferences and application products announced over the last few months reflects the intensity of industry and academic interest. However, the field is still new and lacks a record of experience and a systematic assessment.

Activities in the field appear to be clustered around two central areas: ideal hypertext and applied hypertext. Dan Shafer, in "Hypermedia and Expert Systems: A Marriage Made in Hyper Heaven" (HyperAge, 1988), explains the difference through an analogy. Suppose a teacher gave each student in a class an extremely large collection of 3 x 5 index cards containing the contents of the course and told the class to browse through the information in any order that suited them. Since each student would undoubtedly take a different path through the body of information, how could the teacher then give a common examination? Each student would have a different view of the body of information, and the transfer of knowledge would be uneven.

The opposite approach is for the teacher to give the class rigorous instructions concerning which cards to read and which to bypass -- thereby ensuring that all pupils have been exposed to the same information. Such an approach obviously produces a rigid procedure which might not accommodate individual learning styles. Perhaps more important, this canonical view impoverishes the idea of a textbase (the collection of cards) because it provides only one view of the data.

Clearly many applications of threaded text fall somewhere between absolute freedom and rigorous structure, and thus could benefit from an interface which facilitates information retrieval. Useful (but relatively simple) automated features to help users traverse a body of information include string and keyword search capability, cross-referencing, and indexing. More powerful navigational devices -- whether we call them embedded expert systems, smart filters, or interactive interfaces -- can guide readers through a textbase and increase the user's ability to interact productively with information.

This paper discusses the use of intelligent access mechanisms for large, complex textbases which have been designed and stored online in a hypertext format. Large, complex paper textbases exist in most professions (medicine, law, academic disciplines) and in most business and industrial settings (corporate records, training materials, maintenance manuals). This article uses air craft maintenance manuals as an illustration of how to integrate several forms of "intelligence" into a hypertext application.

Smart interfaces, embedded expert systems, and intelligent filters when applied to a hypertext all share a common purpose: *to help the user select a path through the textbase that is tailored for a particular application or purpose.* One example of an intelligent access mechanism for an air craft maintenance manual is an online troubleshooting tree. In other words, a fully automated diagnostic system guides the technician to the most likely fault and then, on request, displays the manual text for the appropriate rectification procedure. In a sense, the automated troubleshooting tree becomes a filter for the textbase. However, this intelligent interface would be inadequate and perhaps even an impediment to accessing information if the user were motivated by a different information need -- say, for example, the need to use the text for reference purposes only.

As they currently exist, air craft maintenance manuals represent a paper textbase (usually multi-volumed, complex, and highly interconnected). Typically, a technician accesses the material in search of instructions to perform a specific maintenance or repair task. Her success in finding the information in a timely fashion depends, in part, upon an understanding of the organization of the document(s) and on the amount of experience she has had with the system. In short, users of traditional manuals develop an expertise for finding information in the paper system. Encapsulating user expertise and providing ease-of-access to electronic information are priority items for online information development.

Traditionally, information retrieval systems have consisted of relatively structured databases (such as legal citations, library card catalogs, scientific or medical journal abstracts) which are searched by using keywords, inverted indexing, cross-referencing, string searches, and pattern matching. These methods can be refined through Boolean logic connections (AND, OR, NOT), by designating a proximity (a numerical boundary within which the combination of query terms must appear), and by indicating scope (the set of entries over which the search will take place). Clearly, for large, full-text databases blind search is not feasible. Currently, meaningfully narrowing the search may require the services of a skilled researcher, who -- in consultation with the end user

-- formulates a search strategy based on preplanning, use of thesauri, and successive iterations.

Low-cost, high-capacity storage devices (particularly CD ROM) have increased interest in information retrieval (IR) and the notion of documents as databases or, more specifically, textbases. Vannevar Bush's 1945 call for automated, global libraries of text and graphics was refined thirty years later by Alan Kay into the "dynabook." Today, various disciplines of information sciences have pushed these concepts near the realm of reality. Examples of large textbases now or soon-to-be available on CD ROM include the Oxford English Dictionary, Bowker's Books in Print, and Grolier's Encyclopedia. However, any electronic information delivery system must be able to -- at the very minimum -- duplicate the capabilities provided by the combination of an experienced reader and a well-designed paper text. Anything less degrades the system: leaving at best, an electronic page-turner; at worse, even less than the paper version. Furthermore, in order to justify abandoning the conventional method and medium, an electronic system should offer improvements, such as increased flexibility, reduction in storage, and convenient document development and maintenance.

This study assumes that paper manuals containing operations and maintenance instructions will be automated using the concept of hypertext. Documents stored in hypertext have active cross-references. Each entry in the textbase is called a node; the combination of the nodes and their connecting links form a hypertext network (hypergraph). Both nodes and links can be typed (that is, tagged in a specific way which allows them to be identified individually or as members of a set). Given these features of hypertext, online information can be characterized by structure and by connectivity. The focus of this paper is to determine how the innate features of a hypertext can augment traditional search techniques -- such as those used in database management systems (DBMS) -- as well as facilitate the integration of more advanced search procedures now being developed in Artificial Intelligence (AI) research. Figure 1 delineates the specific area of my interest -- the intersection of three research domains:

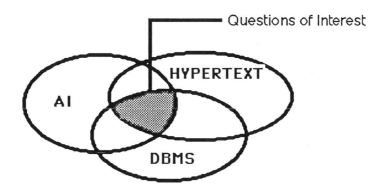

Figure 1:   Study Domain

2. Four Issues Central to the Hypertext Concept

Detractors point out that much of the interest in hypertext is on a theoretical level. They charge that few fully specified systems exist, and many of the commercial products which pose as hypertext are not (Raskin, 1987). Since hypertext systems have a brief history of application, we have sparse evidence for their effectiveness, let alone proven principles to guide design. The newness of the idea is reflected in the proliferation of suggested applications and in the enthusiasm of the participants in the dialogue. Four major issues being debated in the literature are central to the implementation of a hypertext document database.

Authoring versus Browsing

A major issue of debate concerns whether or not -- in order to be genuine -- a hypertext system must support user-initiated links. Purists contend that unless the user can make bi-directional links -- or chart new paths through the information space -- the system is not truly hypertext. This camp sees hypertext *not* as a tool for information management, but as an environment for knowledge development and open-ended problem exploration. In their view, constructing the web -- or graph of links -- which conjoins the fragmented chunks represents learning, creativity, and collaboration. Viewing hypertext as a convenience for storing and accessing huge bodies of text, they charge, reduces the concept to database management system (DBMS) technology.

Mental Model and Metaphor

The two interrelated concepts of mental model and metaphor are crucial to user interface aspects of system design. The goal of each is to accommodate the user's preconceptions and to increase ease-of-use. Users normally approach a task with some concept of how to proceed. This model, or image, comes either from knowledge or experience with the task domain. When the domain is unknown, the user may develop a mental model through an analogy with a familiar domain.

Proponents of hypertext contend that non-linear information processing mirrors two natural patterns of human information processing -- association networks and hierarchies. Furthermore, hypertext systems are more malleable and can mold themselves to user expectations more easily than paper or early electronic text storage formats. However, it is important to note that hypertext is not a form of artificial intelligence. AI tries to encapsulate human knowledge in a paradigm which can then be used by a machine. Hypertext, on the other hand, is intended to augment human thinking by providing a dynamic platform for processing and presenting data.

Search and Navigation

Just as any database, a hypertext information retrieval system has two central components:

o <u>a document database</u>: which can be -- (1) a large, loosely structured library of documents which have been placed online directly from hardcopy, (2) a highly organized, compressed, structure of richly interconnected "chunks," which have meaningful boundaries between sets and subsets and logical relationships among elements, (3) a variation of organization somewhere between these two extremes.

o an assistance processor: a retrieval mechanism (or a collection of retrieval mechanisms) for effective access to and management of the database.

As a rule-of-thumb, one can say that there is a reciprocity between the amount of design put into each element. Relatively unformatted libraries require more complicated software in the retrieval mechanisms or -- lacking such software support -- the assistance of a knowledgeable research specialist, if the user requires fine-grained applications. On the other hand, text which has been specifically preprocessed for the system requires less complicated software. A hypertext-flavored maintenance manual should be a symbiotic relationship between the intelligence built into the web and the capabilities of a smart interface.

Data Preparation -- Translating Text in Hypertext

The written word -- as it exists today -- has been molded to suit a paper delivery system. While in some applications, it may be feasible to construct text especially for a hypertext representation, most implementations will only be cost-effective if documents authored for paper can be modified for a hypertext environment (Raymond and Tampa, 1987). This translation process raises questions of rhetoric and knowledge structures.

These are not trivial problems. Extracting a workable hypertext representation from an existing document can be difficult. In most cases, the author(s) are not available for consultation, so answers to questions of meaning and form may have to be inferred from the paper representation. In many cases, form does not reflect logic because the requisites of paper and typesetting exert powerful influences on text formatting. [For example, the original paper Oxford English Dictionary was restricted to a fixed number of pages by the publishing contract. Therefore, every effort was made to conserve space -- hence the dense typesetting, use of abbreviations and symbols, and limited use of meaningful white space (Raymon and Tompa, 1987)].

Additionally, not all texts are suitable for hypertext representation. Hypertext makes the deep structure of a knowledge domain explicit (Raymon and Tompa, 1987). Although there is no universal model for hypertext implementation, experience suggests that if the document is closely interwoven through rhetorical devices, then decomposition into chunks and links will be difficult, with lose of information and confusion of meaning a potential result. For some documents, this conversion is either impossible or not desirable because it destroys the subtle interconnections of theme, argument, metaphor, and word choice.

3. Heuristic Search Techniques

Because brute force or blind search through all nodes in a database produces a combinatorial explosion, almost all research into automated information extraction focuses on ways to more fruitfully direct the search algorithm.   Attempts to produce a "superbook" have merged the forces of IR, DBMS, Hypertext, and AI to focus on the single crucial issue of implementation: *how to provide search procedures which are accurate, complete, and comfortable for the end user.*

The remainder of this paper suggests approaches to "smart" interfaces for a hypertext-based maintenance manual. These examples are divided into three categories, based on relative degree of "newness" and the extent to which they approximately an expert system. Examples in the first category have their roots in traditional DBMS techniques. Examples in the second category draw heavily upon recent research in cognitive science. Examples from the third category model intelligence using AI practices.

All hypertext systems are characterized as a collection of nodes (modules) and links (webs), allowing for three-dimensional navigation through a body of data.

o Modules: pools of information collected in one anthology, labeled or typed, and electronically stored as nodes in a database.

o Webs: the pattern of links among the nodes. The links can be predefined by the hypertext system designer or the user(s) can establish the links as part of walking through the information space.

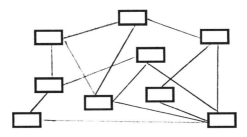

Figure 2:   3-D Information Processing

Since the intent of my paper is to demonstrate how hypertext design (or the presence of a hypergraph) enhances retrieval mechanisms, each of the following three categories is illustrated by a variation of Figure 2, showing how the interface is grafted onto the concept of a hyperweb.

Category 1

Until recently, large textual databases involved mainframes, magnetic storage, and complex user interfaces operated by trained researchers and skilled librarians. Because of the expense, such systems were found only in large corporations, universities, or research institutions . Smaller organizations could purchase time through several online services. Typical retrieval devices in such systems are based on keyword search techniques. Speed is enhanced through inverted indexing and query language which supports Boolean operations. Unfortunately, these methods do not produce ideal rates for completeness or accuracy. A typical query hits only about 50 percent of the relevant texts and returns about the same percentage of irrelevant texts (Colvin, 1986).

Using an inquiry-based interface has been the dominant concept in IR since the 1950s. However, improvements to the query form have been made over time. Methods to improve completeness and accuracy include enhancements to the basic search algorithms of the system. Areas of intensive research today include natural language query, vector and probabilistic models, use of a "seed" (statistical profiling of a sample which is then used as a query template), weighted keyword searches, and layered information structures (as represented by embedded menus). The latter two are explained in more detail.

Weighted Keyword Search

Keyword search is known to be flawed. Imprecision and incompleteness can be attributed to choice of search terms by users, lack of semantic analysis of texts, and the fact that relevance is difficult to represent as a bi-modal choice. Weighted keyword search offers improvements. Coupling weighted keyword search with hypertext links can improve performance in two ways. First, if links joining related concepts are part of the system, finding only a subset of nodes through algorithmic search would suffice since the user could then follow links to other semantically related nodes. Second, because the links indicate other related nodes which were not part of the "hit" list, the user can overcome the false impression of completeness which is a danger of full-text search (Oren, 1987).

Embedded Menus

The advantages of menu systems over command-driven systems have been adequately documented. In general, menus reduce cognitive overhead by limiting the need to memorize commands, by reducing training time, and by providing a structure for decision making in a computer session.

An alternative to explicit menus is to embed the menu choices within the information being displayed. With this approach, the user is less likely to be confused by menu labels because contextuality is not lost. The user is able to make an informed choice about whether she wishes to pursue a particular path. Embedded menus naturally lead to a kind of layered approach, where detail is hidden unless specifically requested. For a textbase, however, the danger is that the user is not given specific guidance as to which selections to pursue. This could be partially overcome by careful layering of the text, or by having only subsets of keywords highlighted during a given session. But these concepts require considerable time and skill in designing the knowledge structure of the textbase, and may prove inefficient in all but the smallest and perhaps simplest domains, or in domains which can be easily partitioned.

Figure 3 shows the paradigm for the search techniques of Category I. In essence,
the user is guided toward a node or subset of nodes which, in turn, provide an entry
point for traversing the web in a meaningful fashion. Though slightly different in final
implementation, each facilitates access to the database, thereby positioning the user to
make use of the knowledge structure built into the hypergraph. Some representations of
this category (vectors and query-by-example, for instance) involve sophisticated
calculations and complex algorithms.

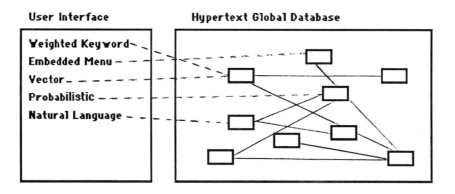

Figure 3: Category I Search Techniques

Category II

Category I search techniques help the user to enter the hypergraph at an appropriate
point; after that, navigation is a function of the hyperweb rather than the interface. As
such, these access mechanisms are analogous to indexing and cross referencing in
conventional paper texts. Category II search techniques help the user to visualize the
knowledge structure of the textbase; as such, they are analogous to various location
signals in paper text (for instance, running headers and footers, chapter titles, section
headings, type fonts, indentation, proximity, and physical features such as number of
pages and binding).

Location is one of the most difficult problems in hypertext. Electronic presentation
of text removes most of the visuo-spatial cues available in paper. Adding to the
confusion, hypertext encourages fragmentation and the proliferation of small nodes.
The result can create chaos for the end user. Adopting some form of visualization vastly
improves system usability. Three candidate methods include (1) an iconic interface, (2)
a filtered view based on one or more specific criteria, such as proximity, (3) a contiguity
or logic map.

Spatial Data Management Systems (SDMS)

User overload is a major human factors concern in any information integration system. Both common sense and scientific evidence supports the contention that visuo-spatial (e.g. use of icons) representation and retrieval are easier than symbolic (words and numbers), and the success of workplace metaphors in commercial systems warrants considering spatial management devices in a textbase interface. Huge portions of our brains are dedicated to processing visual-spatial data. Additionally, people retain a cognitive image of information contained in a fixed area, for example in an office or in a book.

The Illustrated Parts Breakdown (IPB) segment of an Air Force maintenance manual lends itself to spatial data management.   In its paper form, the IPB typically consists of hierarchical graphics and alphanumeric tables which are keyed to the graphics by callouts. The tables contain such information as the system's model number, a vendor-supplied part number, the inventory or supply category number, a brief description, the number of parts per assembly, and the applicable aircraft tail numbers.

In a hypertext version of an IPB, the user moves from a global view of the system, down levels of specificity by clicking on segments of the visual representation.   An information entry screen asks the user to select (from visual representations) the part category, the system number, the tail number, and a more specific indication of location in the aircraft. From this information, the software generates a list of "hits." By clicking on an item in the list, the user goes to a close-up graphic of the specific part. Clicking on a specific callout at this point produces all stock information, and instructions for installation. (See Figure 4.)

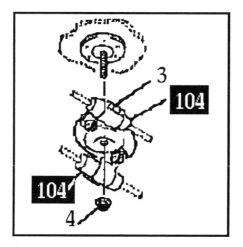

Figure 4: Graphical Interface -- Illustrated Parts Breakdown

Advantages of such direct manipulation interfaces have been outline by Ben Shneiderman (1984). Succinctly, spatial management cuts down on cognitive overload because the user approaches the system with a familiar, high-level problem domain view. Computer-dictated concepts (e.g. command language syntax) are minimized. Actions create immediate and comprehensible reactions. Stress is reduced, especially for individuals whose preferred method of working is visual/concrete rather than language/abstract.

Fisheye or Distorted View Filters

This approach -- as its name indicates -- is based on a metaphor. Researchers have noticed that humans represent information/knowledge using a prioritizing scheme. If this perceived relevance were represented visually, the picture would resemble the view from a wide angle lens. In other words, things of greater attention would be at the center, while items of lesser attention would be on the periphery -- and the image would become increasingly blurred as one moved away from the focal point.

George W. Furnas of Bell Communications Research has suggested an algorithm to simulate this purposeful distortion (Furnas, 1986). The program generates a "neighborhood" image by computing a relationship between a priori importance of an element in a knowledge structure and the distance between that element and the current position in the body of information. Empirical evidence suggests that such filters are valuable information-handling aids. For example, holophrastic viewing techniques (or hiding designated levels) have been used to help debug complex segments of computer code (Koved and Shneiderman, 1986).

Graphical Browsers

While direct manipulation tries to use a real world, physical model, graphic browsers may use a more synoptic approach. The idea of overview displays for bodies of information also appears in traditional text design, where the table of contents serves as a map for the organizational structure of a document. Graphic browsers are also visual methods of information compression: thus, they resemble in function such hardcopy devices as charts, diagrams, graphs, decision tables, and taxonomies.

Content-oriented search mechanisms have received much attention. However, hypertext systems, because of the web-like structure of connectivity, lends itself to a less well-known search mechanism -- that of structure search. If both nodes and links are typed, a user could ask for a diagram of all subnetworks that match a given pattern.

The three representatives illustrated in Figure 5 demonstrate a central feature of Category II interfaces -- they are holistic or synoptic in nature. They provide a higher-level view of the information structure and, thus, should improve ease-of-use. They conform to natural models and metaphors, making information access and manipulation easier. They minimize the impediments an electronic delivery system may have, and they allow the user to maximize whatever expertise she may have. For example, this type of interface fosters intuition and discovery. Additionally, users may follow up on hunches and educated guesses more readily.

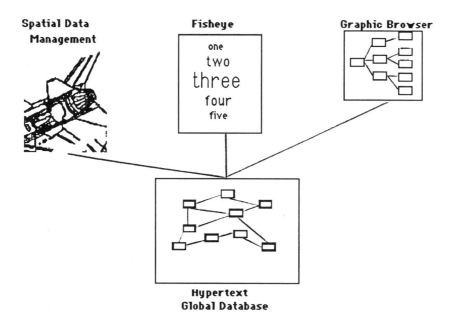

Figure 5:   Category II Search Techniques

Category III

Conjoining certain AI models with information retrieval research has produced intriguing hybrid systems.   Of particular interest are expert systems which constitute intelligent interfaces to a document database. Several efforts attempt to capture the expertise of search intermediaries in online systems. More ambitious efforts integrate browsing and automated retrieval, even to the point that the system has rudimentary models of categories of users and can select search strategies based upon a specific situation (Fox, 1986).

In many cases, the end user may not be able to tell if an application is an expert system, a decision support system, or a database management program. The latter two use conventional algorithmic approaches to problem-solving, while the former uses heuristic, symbolic, or high-order processing.   An expert system has two major components, the database and the retrieval mechanism. Adding the intelligence of an expert system requires the use of additional components -- a knowledge base and an inference engine. The expert system embodies the facts, information, knowledge, and rules-of-thumb, and other elements of heuristic expertise. The user may tap this expertise as an expert advisor or a consultant to solve problems or make decisions. At least three approaches to conjoining expert systems and hypertext are possible.

Separate Knowledge Base and Hypergraph

This configuration uses the knowledge base an an interactive interface to filter the information-rich chunks of information in the hypergraph. In this case, the expert system and the hypertext are separate components, as represented in Figure 6. After a consultation, the system automatically calls up the appropriate segment of the manual. This selection can be as generic as an entire subnet or as fine-grained as a single chunk.

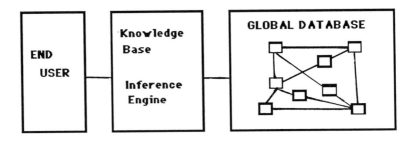

Figure 6:   Separate Expert System and Hypergraph

The automated fault diagnostic system mentioned in the introduction to this paper is a good example of an expert system which sits outside the hypergraph and acts as an intelligent interface to point the user to relevant documentation. Such a tool replaces the troubleshooting section of the maintenance manual with a sophisticated software model which advises a technician on fault isolation by taking into account availability of parts and test equipment, mission criticality of components, time to perform tasks, and component failure rates.

Merge Knowledge Base with the Hypergraph

Critics of expert systems charge that most systems are too brittle; that the user is led, lock-step, through a series of information-extracting questions without adequate opportunity to interject intuition or to adapt the system to the particular situation. Eventually, the user begins to feel like a slave. In fact, the educational value of an expert system is limited if the user cannot understand the rationale behind the various steps in the consultation session.

One approach to overcome some of these limitations is to *design the knowledge base as a hypertext* . In other words, at any point in the consultation, the user may ask for additional information on domain concepts, on particulars of the problem, or on the operation of the expert system.

For example, KnowledgePro[tm] (from Knowledge Garden, Inc.) is a software platform for building expert systems, although it is not, strictly speaking, an expert shell. The software combines an expert system, a programming language, and a hypertext product into one seamless and highly modular environment (Shafer, 1988). The expert builds text blocks in a manner similar to how she would sit down and tell someone what she knows. The expert also links these chunks of knowledge to others. Eventually, the expert adds rules and an inference engine to boost the intelligence of the system. Figure 7 represents the basic structure of this potentially important new trend in expert development tools.

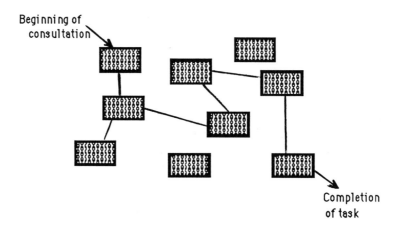

Figure 7: Merged Expert System and Hypergraph

Embed or Distribute Expert Systems within the Hypergraph

This approach is something of a combination of the previous two. The hypergraph retains its integrity, but the user is able to call up search aids at given choice points in the textbase or the search aids may acts as demons which awaken given a particular set of circumstances.

This configuration has many intriguing possibilities. Since nodes in a hypergraph can be anything from text to procedures, small knowledge bases can be stored and threaded like any other module in the web. (In other words, expert systems can call other expert systems.) Additionally, this conjunction of hypergraphs and smart interfaces may be appealing to users if the intelligent filters can be viewed as a collection of selectable information extraction tools.

Figure 8 represents a hypothetical web with embedded expert systems. Advocates of a "new-generation retrieval system" describe a multi-faceted system which accommodates individual users and specific situations. Edward A. Fox delineates the system of the future as "having multiple experts, each with private rule bases, as well as blackboard-based strategists for both analysis and access of documents, that can run as separate processes on multiple machines" (1986). While embedded expert systems may not deliver all these capabilities, they do provide more flexibility and functionality than traditional search techniques.

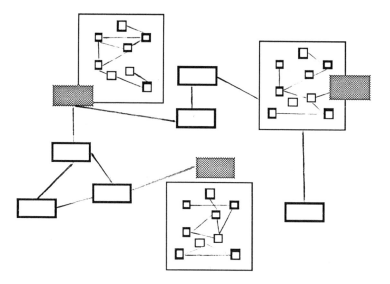

Figure 8: Embedded or Distributed Expert Systems

4. Implications

The future for document databases looks bright. The availability of CD ROM will bring down the cost of storage. An added push in the information sciences will increase research into such design issues as data models, user interface, and authoring systems. Lower costs of hardware and increased availability of object-oriented programming software will bring hypertext capabilities within the reach of the general public. Before the next decade is out, the information environment conceptualized by Vannever Bush and prototyped by pioneers such as Doug Engelbart, Ted Nelson, and Alan Kay could be a reality.

But mapping out the future for hypertext is not a matter for glib speculations. The truth of the matter is that *hypertext* is a collective term covering different instantiations -- analogous to the term *book* -- whose manifestations are numerous and varied.

For a parallel picture of what has happened to the notion of hypertext over its brief forty-three year history, consider the history of the book as technology. In its earliest form, a "book" might have been a collection of clay tablets containing cuneiform, or it might have been a bundle of notched sticks. Later versions of "books" included papyrus rolled into scrolls and tree bark bound with leather thongs. (The English word *book* is derived from the Old German work for birch.) Parchment, the fervor of monks in medieval monasteries, and advancements in calligraphy and illumination turned books into both a form of devotion and an art. Gutenberg's serendipitous connection between the mechanism of a wine press and the function of a signet ring produced movable type, and the world was on the road to the Information Age. Certainly similar variations driven by human ingenuity, improved technical capabilities, and user demands will determine the future of hypertext.

Examining the technology of text in retrospect, we can see that changes in medium have brought with them increasingly complex means of information representation. For example, several historians of ideas -- notably Father Walter Ong -- have written eloquently on the interrelations of text technology and the growth of knowledge in human culture. James Burke, in *The Day the Universe Changed*, points out that the invention of cross-referencing accelerated the accumulation of knowledge because old concepts could then be connected in new ways (Burke, 1986). Similarly, studies of the technology of text point out that changed in medium precipitate different habits of mind. Hypertext may be the beginnings of a paradigm shift in human information processing.

Previous shifts took place in an unplanned fashion, frequently over vast amounts of time. In many cases the utility (or perhaps dysfunction) of patterns and practices was understood only in hindsight. Certainly no one would argue against the benefits of serendipity in the unfolding of human history. However, with the combined wisdom of what we now understand about the workings of the human mind, text processing, and knowledge structures, it may be both advantageous and possible to guide the hypertext revolution in a meaningful fashion.

Bic and Gilbert, in "Learning from AI: New Trends in Database Technology" (1986) point out that classic DBMS and AI research have significant differences.

> In the former, representations tend to be biased toward a large number of instances of a small number of formatted data types. Knowledge representations in AI, on the other hand, are designed to deal with a small number of instances of a much larger variety of types and classes. This implies that knowledge bases tend to be rather amorphous, while databases are highly structured. Another significant difference is in the amount of implicit information. Knowledge base queries must often use inferential information inherent in the structure of the data to produce a result. In databases, such capabilities either have a very rudimentary form or, more typically, are not present at all. Finally, knowledge bases are usually special-purpose systems, aimed at a particular application, while databases are often constructed to facilitate the needs of a community of users whose requirements may be quite diverse.

Higher level models of databases (including the entity-relationship concept developed by Chen, the idea of aggregation, generalization, and deconstruction propounded by Smith and Smith, and Hammer and McLeod's semantic data model), do not depend upon statically structured records stored in a machine -oriented form. These models see a database as a highly flexible, dynamic entity supporting multiple views, allowing for object- rather than record-orientation, and encouraging inferential patterns of processing through semantic networks. The end result is a modern-day database theory whose attributes closely resemble the functionality and the flexibility of hypertext.

Undoubtedly, the future of interactive text design will exploit AI concepts. Already, the organization of hypertext more closely resembles AI knowledge representations (for example, semantic networks and procedural frames) than it does classic, static database organizations. However, the heart of any successful interactive system is a powerful, yet transparent user interface. The intelligence stored in the hyperweb must augment the intelligence of the user. The non-procedural interfaces indicated in this paper's three categories of retrieval mechanisms represent current thought and somewhat traditional models. As text becomes more interactive, novel ways of representing information will present themselves. Aiding in the emergence and accurately describing this "new rhetoric" is one of the most important jobs facing the various disciplines contributing to modern text technology.

Acknowledgments. This work was supported by a grant from the Air Force Office of Scientific Research, Contract No. F49620-87-R-0004. The research was carried out at the Human Resources Laboratory, Logistics and Human Factors Division, Wright-Patterson Air Force Base, Ohio.

REFERENCES

Bic, Lubomir and Jonathan P. Gilbert. "Learning from AI: New Trends in Database Technology." *IEEE Computer* (March 1986):44-54.

Brant, Craig M., et al. "Training Technology Scenarios for an Integrated Automated Job Aiding/Training System." Draft Version, 1986. Systems Exploration, Inc. Contract No. F33615-85-C-0010.

Burke, James. *The Day the Universe Changed.* Boston: Little, Brown and Company, 1986.

Chen, P. "The Entity-Relationship Model: Toward a Unified View of Data." *ACM Trans. Database Systems* 1 (March 1976):9-36.

Colvin, Gregory. "The Current State of Text Retrieval." *CD ROM: The New Papyrus.* Microsoft Press, 1986, pp. 131-136.

Duffy, Thomas. "Preparing Technical Manuals: Specifications and Guidelines." in *The Technology of Text: Principles for Structuring, Designing, and Displaying Text.* Vol. 2. David H. Jonassen, ed. Englewood Cliffs, N.J., Educational Technology Publications, 1985, pp. 370-392.

Fox, Edward A. "Information Retrieval: Research into New Capabilities." *CD ROM: The New Papyrus.* Microsoft Press, 1986, pp. 143-174.

Frenzel, Louis E., Jr. *Understanding Expert Systems.* Indianapolis: Howard W. Sams, 1987.

Frisse, Mark Edwin. "Searching for Information in a Hypertext Medical Handbook." *Proceedings of Hypertext '87*, University of North Carolina, Chapel Hill, pp. 57-66.

Furnas, George W. "Generalized Fisheye Views." *Proceedings CHI'86*, Boston, Massachusetts, April 13-17, pp. 16-23.

Gill, Jock and Toby Woll, "Full Text Management." *CD ROM: The New Papyrus.* Microsoft Press, 1986, pp. 137-141.

Halasz, Frank G. "Reflections on NoteCards: Seven Issues for the Next Generation of Hypermedia Systems." *Proceedings of Hypertext '87*, University of North Carolina, Chapel Hill, pp. 345-365.

Hammer, M. and D. J. McLeod. "Database Description with SDM: A Semantic Data Model." *ACM Trans. Database Systems* 6 (September 1982): 351-386.

Herot, Christopher. "Graphical User Interfaces." in *Human Factors and Interactive Computer Systems: Proceedings of the NYU Symposium on User Interfaces.* Y. Vassiliou, ed. Norwood, N.J.: Ablex Publishing Corporation, 1984, pp. 83-103.

"IMIS: Integrated Maintenance Information System -- A Maintenance Information Delivery Concept." unpublished paper, AFHRL/LRC, Wright-Patterson AFB, August 1986.

James, Geoffrey. "Artificial Intelligence and Automated Publishing Systems." *Text, ConText, and HyperText.*. Cambridge: MIT Press, 1988, pp. 15-24.

Koved, Larry and Ben Shneiderman. "Embedded Menus: Selecting Items in Context." *Communications of the ACM* 29 (April 1986):312-318.

Marchionini, Gary and Ben Shneiderman. "Finding Facts vs. Browsing Knowledge in Hypertext Systems." *IEEE Computer* January 1988, pp. 70-80.

Monarch, Ira and Jaime Carbonell, "CoalSORT: A Knowledge-Based Interface" *IEEE Expert* 2 (1): 39-53.

Oren, Tim. "The Architecture of Static Hypertexts." *Proceedings of Hypertext '87*, University of North Carolina, Chapel Hill, pp. 291-306.

Raskin, Jef. "The Hype in Hypertext." *Proceedings of Hypertext '87*, University of North Carolina, Chapel Hill, pp. 325-330.

Raymond, Darrell R. and Frank Wm. Tompa, "Hypertext and the 'New Oxford English Dictionary.'" *Proceedings of Hypertext '87*, University of North Carolina, Chapel Hill, pp. 143-153.

Remde, Joel R., Louis M. Gomez, Thomas K. Landauer. "SuperBook: An Automatic Tool for Information Exploration -- Hypertext?" *Proceedings of Hypertext '87*, University of North Carolina, Chapel Hill, pp. 175-188.

Shafer, Dan. "Hypermedia and Expert Systems: A Marriage Made in Hyper Heaven." *HyperAge: The Journal of HyperThinking* May-June 1988, pp. 26 - 33.

Shneiderman, Ben. "User Interface Design for the Hyperties Electronic Encyclopedia." *Proceedings of Hypertext '87*, University of North Carolina, Chapel Hill, pp. 189-194.

_____. "the Future of Interactive Systems and the Emergence of Direct Manipulation." in *Human Factors and Interactive Computer Systems: Proceedings of the NYU Symposium on User Interfaces.* Y. Vassiliou, ed. Norwood, N.J.: Ablex Publishing Corporation, 1984, pp. 1-27.

Smith, J. M. and D. C. P. Smith. "Database Abstractions: Aggregation and Generalization." *ACM Trans. Database Systems* 4 (December 1979):105-133.

Part II
Multimedia and Nonlinear Information Architectures

Part II presents discussions of several different and paradigmatic hypertext designs. Matthew Hodges, Ben Davis, and Russell Sasnett offer their analysis of the hypermedia *Athena Muse* system as a design document vehicle. Peggy Irish and Randall Trigg analyze several hypermedia systems as tools for collaborative work and discuss problems and promises for this application of hypermedia. Norman Meyrowitz discusses why the advanced functionality of hypertext has been slow to catch on and he presents the *Intermedia* system as a model for development. Ben Shneiderman reflects on his own experience developing *Hyperties* and discusses design issues for potential authors of hypertext documents. Janet Walker demonstrates how complexity management in software engineering is a supple design metaphor for building complex online document sets. Joseph Jaynes, however, suggests that the traditional linear approach to text presentation is a more valid design choice for online information retrieval, at least as far as instructional text in a networked environment is concerned. And John Brockmann, William Horton, and Kevin Brock conclude Part II with a description of their information odyssey from database to hypertext.

Investigations in Multimedia Design Documentation

Matthew E. Hodges, Digital Equipment Corporation
Ben H. Davis, Massachusetts Institute of Technology
Russell M. Sasnett, GTE Laboratories

Large scale, collaborative projects need detailed documentation of their design processes. Workstations are now able to provide photographic imagery, full motion digital video, and audio recordings in addition to text and graphic data. The question arises as to whether this technology can be used effectively for the management, storage, and delivery of design and process documentation. This article reports on the development of a multimedia workstation at MIT Project Athena and its experimental use as a design documentation vehicle.

Introduction

The process of designing and building a complex system, such as a car or a computer chip, entails an enormous problem of communication. Efforts of this kind may involve hundreds of people working together across great distances of space and time.

One of the bottlenecks in such an undertaking is the flow of information among the various participants. There is resistance to creating and organizing design information; there is resistance to accessing it. Engineers don't like to spend time recording the details and rationale behind design decisions even though they realize the importance of doing so. Managers prefer to see engineers working on design issues rather than writing. The result is loss of critical design information that can adversely effect not only the outcome of a particular project but the successive designs that depend on its history. Product design histories are the starting point for innovation in the information/industrial economy.

This chapter describes some initial explorations using a multimedia workstation for preparing and accessing design documentation in the context of a software engineering project. The goal of the project was to supplement written documentation with audio and video materials collected in the course of the design process. The work was undertaken at MIT using the Project Athena Visual Workstation.

The chapter is broken into two sections. The first addresses some of the technical factors involved in producing multimedia design documentation. The second addresses some of the practical issues involved in making such a technical platform work in the context of an organization.

Technical Factors

The first problems in developing a system for multimedia design documentation are technical ones having to do with the acquisition, storage, transmission, display, and dynamic management of the multimedia information. Dynamic means that multimedia design documents need to be referenced and correlated in a variety of modes, ie. chronologically, topically, formally, functionally, etc. None of these problems are simple. Our platform is quite modest in certain respects, but it gives us entry into the practical issues involved in using such a system, which appear to be at least as challenging as the technical ones.

In this section we begin with a description of the Project Athena Visual Workstation, which serves as the base system for storage, transmission, and display of information. Following this is a description of the Athena Muse authoring system which is the user-level software environment for the dynamic management of the information, and also the subject of the design documentation effort that served as our test.

The Athena Visual Workstation

Project Athena is an eight-year research and development program sponsored primarily by Digital Equipment Corporation and IBM. Project Athena's goal is to explore new, innovative uses of computing in the MIT curriculum. The project as a whole has been highly successful in developing a coherent computing environment of networked workstations.

As part of this effort, the Visual Computing Group (VCG) was started to experiment with the use of still and full-motion imagery. The VCG supports faculty members in the design of educational software involving audio and video materials as part of the content. The group offers expertise in both production of the audio-visual content and in development of the controlling software.

As an experimental delivery system, the group modified a standard Athena workstation to support 256 color graphics as well as full-motion digitized video. The

'Visual Workstation' uses either an IBM RT-PC or DEC MicroVax II workstation as a base with a Parallax Graphics board added as the display subsystem.

The Parallax Graphics board digitizes a standard NTSC video signal at 30 frames per second. The video images are presented on the display under the control of the X Window System. Video windows can be moved, scaled and clipped as any other X window. The system currently allows one window of full motion digital video. However, it is possible to create hundreds of windows containing still images grabbed from the video source. This facility is capable of supporting sophisticated multi-image displays of visual databases.

Normally, the video images are drawn from an optical videodisc player, but they can also be received from the campus cable television network, a video tape recorder, or directly from a video camera. For design documentation experiments, we use a Panasonic OMDR write-once optical disc. This device allows us to record up to 13 minutes of full motion video or 24,000 still frames and two channels of audio on an optical disc. With a simple VHS video camera we can record meetings, explanations, interviews, presentations, site visits, or "design diaries" of individuals. With a 35MM camera and an inexpensive video transfer device, documents, illustrations, overheads, photographs, etc. can be moved to the optical disc and made immediately available on the workstation.

The Athena Muse Authoring System

After developing the multimedia workstation with its basic capacities for handling text, graphics, video, and audio, we realized the system was not easy to use. Without any high level information processing tools, the only access to the machine's potential was through layers of Unix, C, X, and the X Toolkit interface.

The system had been designed for MIT faculty to develop complex educational software. After a survey of available authoring systems it was quickly apparent that no suitable application development tools were available for this purpose. In June, 1987, the VCG began to design a "construction set" for multimedia applications that would make it easy to implement the software proposed by the MIT faculty.

Over the course of the following year we developed a prototype authoring system called *Athena Muse*. Muse provides information processing support for text, graphics, video, and audio. It allows one to create structured documents that combine all of these different kinds of information. Further, one can build these documents into complex fabrics of information, using the dynamic configurations found in hypermedia or other "low structure" systems, and also draw on more highly structured information found in conventional databases.

From an educational standpoint, the purpose of the system was to provide support for three principal types of software: interactive presentations, simulations, and reference facilities. Presentations, either linear or branching, form the basis of expository teaching materials. Simulations give students control over dynamic system models based on graphic or video images; this is the most popular use of the workstations among MIT faculty. Reference facilities are used to make large bodies of information accessible to student researchers, with embedded tools that allow them to draw from these resources and integrate materials into their own notes and presentations. In the Muse architecture, all of these capabilities are integrated into a coherent environment, so that an author can freely mix the different pedagogic approaches in a single application.

Athena Muse not only provides a rich foundation for creating educational materials but also has other uses, including design documentation. Design documentation is not the primary purpose of the system as implemented at MIT, so we have not fully developed its capabilities in this area. However, our experience to date has led us to some insights on the nature of video documentation and how it can be used in design documenation.

Video in Muse

Video is a form of document that both extends in time and carries internal ''picture data''. To use it effectively, the first requirement is to be able to simply move through such a document easily. With Muse, one of the most fundamental features of the system is the use of dimensions to organize information. In the case of video, it is quite simple to create a dimension of *time* and use it to control the video.

Figure 1 shows a typical arrangement for a video document on the workstation screen, with a set of control buttons to make the video stop or play in forward or reverse at various speeds (in this case determined by the videodisc player).

Directly under the video is a slide bar which acts as a representation of time. The position of the slide bar marker indicates the current position of the video document, with the bar as a whole representing the entire length of the material. The slide bar also serves as a control on the video; one can use the mouse to drag the marker forward or back. This will cause the video to jump to the appropriate point immediately. With this kind of control, it is easy to move through the video document, searching for specific points of interest, repeating segments rapidly or holding an image still.

A second problem with using video as information in a computing environment is the difficulty of searching it. It cannot be searched for specific patterns in the way we

Figure 1: Interface for a video document

are accustomed to searching text or numeric databases. It is not easy to instruct the computer to find a point in the video where "Dan stands up" or "George finishes his introductory remarks".

As a partial solution to this difficulty, we can build on the notion of the timeline. The timeline is actually separate from the video, even though the video is dependent on it. The system is designed so that one can just as easily assign text or graphic material to the same timeline. The result is a compound document combining text, graphics, and video, all coordinated by the dimension of time. Moving the timeline forward or back will not only cause the video to change, but also the text or graphics, according to how the connections have been made between the data and the controlling dimension.

The Muse dimensions provide a mechanism for adding annotations to moving and still video. Text annotations can be used to overcome some of the difficulties of searching the video by itself. A user can mark specific points in the video scene, or add a complete textual transcript that can appear on the screen synchronized with the speakers in the video.

This facility was originally designed for adding subtitles to foreign language materials prepared for MIT undergraduate courses. In this context, students can stop the video document at any time to read the subtitles which appear in a separate window below the video. Using the mouse, students can highlight any word or phrase within the subtitle stream and have the expression looked up in a dictionary displayed on a separate part of the screen.

Conversely, students can pick out a word or phrase from some other text and then search through the subtitles to find a specific point in the video where that expression occurs. With this capability, it *is* possible to find a point in a video sequence where "Dan stands up", provided of course that such points have been annotated previously.

In Muse, any number of these streams of annotation can be added to a dimension. Different viewers can add their own annotations or the video can be searched according to different sets of annotations. An example of this would be to annotate the video in more than one language.

Using the temporal framework, editing the video becomes a process of snipping segments out of the timeline and moving them around. It is possible to open up several video documents and cut and paste from one to the other in a manner similar to cutting and pasting text in a word processor. In the context of design documentation, where speed is at a premium, this approach seems adequate, even though it is quite simple.

Cutting the motion video into meaningful pieces is only part of the problem of video editing. Equally important is to provide some means for managing the individual cuts once they have been selected. Here we use the metaphor of a photo album. The photo album provides space for a number of images to be organized on a page. Figure 2 shows the appearance of such a page, with the entire configuration displayed on the left and a magnified view shown on the right. Users have control to view any portion of the page, focusing on a single image or a group of images, which will appear on the magnification screen.

Figure 2: An electronic photo album

One of the differences with this page is that the images are not limited to still images but can be motion sequences as well. The pages of the photo album can contain text and graphics; this includes control devices such as the slide bars that control movement through the document at any level of magnification. The result is that one can use the video editor to select pieces of video and then save them in miniature in a personal photo album, where they can be organized and annotated. Later, they can be picked up and included in other documents or applications.

This suite of tools outlines the basic methods for handling video documents in Muse. As an authoring system, Muse also contains the underlying mechanisms for combining these documents into the networks of topical information that make up a design process history.

The System In Use

For our own project (the development of Muse), we wanted to generate and organize design documentation as an integral part of the development process. Since we were working on a multimedia system, naturally we wondered whether the system itself could be of use in this activity. This was the start of our experiments in using the documentation of the Muse development as a test application of the system itself.

With the prototype partially functioning from a technical viewpoint, we began to explore some of the "human factors" involved in actually putting the system to use. These had to do with first generating data, then organizing and maintaining it, and finally of accessing the material for later use. Each of these phases presents certain problems from the standpoint of using the system. The following section treats only the first phase: video data collection. Work on the latter phases depends on further refinement of the available tools.

Creating Video Data

In our experiments, the problem was to document the design of a complex piece of software, namely, the Muse construction set. The project has so far gone through three waves of design work, and one cycle of prototype development. Some of the material generated has to do with specific implementation details; some is directed toward broader design issues. The entire body of data represents a flux, with issues appearing, reappearing, and disappearing over time. The project has involved the efforts of 15 people over a period of two years.

In terms of collecting data, and in particular video data, three points stand out. The first of these relates to the mechanics of collecting video data. The other two have to do with individual skills that affect this process.

The first observation is simply that the process of creating design documentation materials must be minimized. This was one of the original reasons for experimenting with video, based on the hope that video recording could be faster than writing. Our experience has been that in order for this to work the management of the physical equipment must become as unobtrusive as turning on a small audio tape recorder. This is why the choice of VHS or 8MM video is significant. Lighting and acoustics are spontaneous in most cases and attempting to manipulate them would be disruptive. Compact video generates usable information at low cost and with a low profile. This type of equipment usually provides some in-camera annotation features like time and date so that footage can be minimally coded during capture. The equipment must be immediately accessible in order to be useful.

The second issue has to do with the selection of what data to record. Choosing the right information and recording it in the right way is the essence of successful documentation; in this respect the success of the system depends on the people using it. And it happens that the selection of material suitable for video documentation is in some ways different from that suitable for documentation in text. In some cases, with the ability to speak, gesture, and use illustrations, we found it possible to document ideas that we would not have taken the time to document in writing. Video supplies the ambient context in which information is imparted. An engineer on site pointing out design problems on an engine might refer to its sound, a difficult task for text.

The skill of selecting *what* to record is somewhat different from that of knowing *how* to present it; our third major observation is that presenting ideas effectively with video is a separate skill that has a large impact on the utility of the information. The core of the problem is not so much the polish of the presentation, but the content. Here, presentation skill refers to the ability to compact ideas into succinct expressions. The results become more refined, more precise, as understanding of the computational use of video develops.

The reason that compact presentation is so important is that video must be viewed in real time. Whereas one can scan a page of text quite rapidly, it is much more difficult to do so with video, even with powerful browsing tools described above. *Compacting* the data becomes a premium, otherwise it is not useful.

We make a trade-off in creating video documentation; for the sake of speed and minimizing the process overhead, we sacrifice of the production polish that goes into broadcast quality video. In documentation, the content is more important than the style, but this means that the content must be of high quality. In our experience, this means it must be quite compact.

A major part of our experiment was finding ways of gathering video data quickly, yet with enough precision and compactness that it proved useful later. We worked with three different approaches; a one-person presentation, a two-person interview, and a design review meeting.

For the personal presentation format a camera was focused on an illustration board. An example of how we used this arrangement in the Muse project is the documentation for a complicated timing system controlling the display of annotated video material. The designer drew some simple block diagrams to illustrate the mechanics of the system. The camera was fixed on these diagrams while the designer gave a brief verbal explanation of the workings of the system, using the diagrams to organize the presentation. The whole recording, including the preparation of the drawings, took about 10 minutes.

In another situation, where the topic was a general overview of the Muse system, we used a two-person interview format. In this situation, the chief engineers of the Muse prototype were interviewed by a peer who was unfamiliar with the project. The result is a reasonable overview of the project that was recorded without scripting or rehearsal. Certain parts of this interview are better than others; these portions were later selected in editing and combined with materials recorded on other occasions to replace the less focused parts.

This approach is effective because the interviewer draws out information very quickly in a way that is directed toward a single listener. However, the interviewer must use judgement in when to pursue specific details, and the designer must concentrate the discourse more than may be normal for him or her in one-to-one interchange. The ability to tune these skills seems to develop with practice.

The third approach that we tried was to videotape design review meetings, when the Muse design team met to discuss issues and proposals. This approach suffered two problems. One problem was the diffuse flow of information in the context of the meeting; presentation of ideas was less focused and the discussion around them tended to be more diffracted than in the two-person interview. The second problem was that the awareness that the meeting was being recorded caused the participants to be more restrained in their expressions. We found the two person interview after the design meeting to be more effective, though we continue to explore ideas for developing group interaction skills in this context.

Summary

One of the underlying questions of this experiment was whether video recordings contribute something of value to the design communication stream, as compared to written documentation. Our initial experiences have not answered this question satisfactorily, but have at least highlighted several characteristic differences between the two that will certainly have some bearing on the answer.

First, video offers the differences between spoken and written language. These two forms of communication have quite different expressive characteristics. Under certain circumstances, in creating certain descriptions, it is easier to produce spoken language than written. In the case of video, spoken language is supplemented by gesture and expressive qualities of voice. In some cases, this difference translates into a difference of speed, where video explanations can be recorded faster than textual descriptions can be written.

Second, video provides a way to present images of all kinds, a way to reveal information that cannot be represented in text. This aspect of design visualization is unique. No other medium can so quickly describe and playback ambient information. The physical context of design information, whether it is a single speaker in a remote location, the interface of human and product, or the motion of machines, can be encapsulated by video. The ability to manipulate moving imagery by slowing it down, moving it at three times normal speed, or freezing frames creates a realm of information unique to video.

Third, while video may be faster to produce than text, and allow for greater (or at least different) forms of expression, it will generally take longer to review because it is time dependent. This limitation affects the utility of such information and implies constraints on the nature and structure of its content. In a computational environment, however, in the face of rapidly advancing hardware and software technology, this limitation will be quickly diminished, if not completely eliminated. This is evident from the speed of access and browsing capabilities we are able to provide with the current visual workstation compared with prior video technology.

Fourth, we are currently working with similar limitations in our ability to index and cross reference video. A stream of video images cannot be searched easily for patterns, as one searches text. We have partially addressed this issue with the techniques for binding text and video together, giving a foothold for ''borrowing'' search strategies from the world of text. In addition, we have provided mechanisms for identifying regions of an image by means of geometric tags such as points and bounding polygons overlaid on the image. In this way we can also ''borrow'' techniques from the world of graphics. Soon we will see a merger of image processing techniques and video display technology; as this happens, more powerful techniques will become available for integrating video data into the computing environment.

Finally, we have found that successful video documentation depends both upon an understanding of the video medium and on individual skills of presentation. Of course, preparing effective text and graphic documentation also requires specialized skills; the question is how easily are the skills of one or the other domain acquired, and to what extent does the availability of a broader range of options result in better documentation.

Our initial experiments have lead to a number of matters which clearly go beyond questions of media. These issues are linked to broader questions about the nature of collaborative work and of design documentation in general. Indeed these are the larger questions; but without a platform to work from, it is not clear that they can be addressed at all. As our work with Muse continues, we will be better equipped to explore some of these broader issues.

Supporting Collaboration in Hypermedia: Issues and Experiences[1]

Peggy M. Irish and Randall H. Trigg

System Sciences Laboratory
Xerox Palo Alto Research Center
3333 Coyote Hill Road
Palo Alto, CA 94304

Hypermedia is potentially an ideal medium for supporting collaborative work, as it can capture the work, discussions about the work, and discussions about the shared use of the medium. This chapter begins with a brief description of general hypermedia systems and the NoteCards hypermedia system in particular. It presents experiences of collaborating users as they jointly develop conventions and routines and focusses on two tools resulting from such user-designed conventions. Finally, problems discovered while using NoteCards for collaboration are discussed, as well as future directions for the tools.

1. Introduction

Two "fields" in computer science, hypermedia[2] and computer supported cooperative work, have only recently and independently attracted attention in the popular media though both have been around for some time. Furthermore, there is a sense among some researchers that these two areas are or should be connected, that is, that hypermedia should be an especially appropriate technology for supporting collaborative work. The presence of several hypermedia papers at the recent conference on Computer Supported Cooperative Work (CSCW, 1986) can be taken as evidence for this perceived connection.

In many ways, the notion of supporting users working together is an old idea in the hypermedia community. Vannevar Bush's "memex" (Bush, 1945) was meant to be shared among people interested in similar subject areas. Doug Engelbart's NLS system was perhaps the first working implementation of hypermedia supporting collaboration. One important component was the Journal, a means for supporting long-term group collaboration in which interlinked designs, notes, etc. were stored and accessed by multiple authors (Englebart, 1975). Similarly, Nelson's Xanadu project is intended to provide online libraries to which people can add their own links and annotations on others' work as well as their own new papers (Nelson, 1981). In general, annotations are placed in separate objects (or nodes in the hypermedia network) and linked to the documents being annotated. Furthermore, link types (e.g. comment, response, query) can be used to capture relationships between linked objects. Trigg (1983) argues for a primitive set of link types to support online critiquing within the scientific community.

For some of the applications of hypermedia to collaborative work, the use of the system is fairly structured, e.g. software engineering in Neptune (Delisle & Schwartz, 1986) and design rationale in gIBIS (Conklin & Begeman, 1987). There are kinds of collaborative work, however, which can be both tightly-coupled and unstructured. Perhaps the primary example is co-authoring a paper (Fish et al, 1988). Because there are no universally agreed-upon conventions for co-authoring, people tend to negotiate them on the fly during the collaboration. Trigg, Suchman and Halasz (1986) argue that hypermedia is particularly appropriate for representing both the work and discussion *about* the work and about the shared use of the medium. An open question, however, is why the medium itself should support such negotiations. Can't people communicate face-to-face or by telephone or electronic mail to arrive at conventions of use? Collaborators normally manage to agree on their preferred text editor, on the logistics of draft-passing and annotation, etc. without requiring the computer environment (the text editor, say) to directly support such meta-discussion. We believe, however, that such a capability may in fact be useful. First, if the medium is hypermedia-based, then the discussion can be grounded by linking from the meta-discussion to the work itself. Second, by recording such discussion explicitly in the medium, the rationale for the decisions taken is preserved for historical purposes. In some cases, such discussions lead to proposals for tailored tools to support a particular adopted convention. The recorded discussion may prove useful to tool designers interested in the context of system use that lead to the proposal.

In this paper we present experience with one hypermedia system, NoteCards, used to support collaborative work. Following a brief overview of the system, we discuss experiences within the community of collaborative NoteCards users before, during and after the introduction of special tools to support collaboration. In particular, we describe two tools which resulted from the convention adoption process outlined above. We also discuss problems discovered while using NoteCards for collaboration, as well as future directions of the tools.

2. Overview of Hypertext and NoteCards

The core construct in hypermedia systems is a semantic network, which is a medium in which users can represent collections of related information. Hypermedia systems also provide a structure for organizing, storing, and retrieving information. Such systems provide tools to manage and display the underlying structure of the network, as well as a set of methods and protocols for tailoring the manipulation of information in the network. Most hypermedia systems have several distinguishing features in common (Conklin, 1987). In this section, we enumerate these features and explain how they have been implemented in NoteCards.

Nodes

A hypermedia system supports a database of nodes whose contents are represented using a variety of media including at least text and graphics. In addition to its contents, a node often includes a name or title among other properties. Nodes are typically displayed in separate windows, labeled with the node's title.

A node in a NoteCards database is called a *notecard*. The notecard is an electronic generalization of a 3x5 paper note card. Each notecard has a title, a user-accessible attribute-value list, and an arbitrary amount of some editable "substance," such as a piece of text, a structured drawing, or a running animation. A notecard can be "edited," i.e., retrieved from the database and displayed on the screen in an editor window that allows the user to modify the card's substance. Multiple notecards can be displayed and edited simultaneously. Several notecards displayed in their editing windows are shown in Figure 1.

Types of notecards are distinguished by the nature of their content and the operations that can be performed on them. Standard types include text cards (containing text with embedded graphics), sketch cards (containing structured drawings), and graph cards (containing network structure diagrams). There is also a facility for adding new types of cards ranging from minor variations of existing card types to types based on entirely new substances.

Links

A hypermedia system supports links which interconnect individual nodes and represent the semantic interdependencies among these nodes. Links may be depicted in many ways, from highlighted text to button-like objects. They appear in the windows of nodes and represent pointers to other nodes in the database. A mechanism exists whereby links may be followed to their destination nodes. Links of different types are supported in some systems. A link may be anchored in only its source node, or in both its source and destination nodes.

In NoteCards, each link is a typed, directed connection between a source card and a destination card. The link type is a label chosen by the user to explicitly specify the relationship between the two cards. In general, links are anchored at a specific location in the substance of their source card, but point to the entire destination card. The link between two cards is

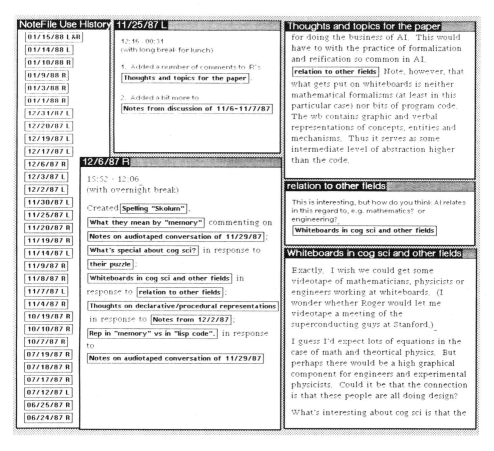

Figure 1: History and annotation cards.

represented by a *link icon*, which appears as a rectangular box in the source card. The box optionally displays various information about the link and its destination card, but usually includes at least the title of the destination card. If the user moves the mouse so that the cursor is over the icon and clicks the mouse button, the system "traverses" the link by retrieving the destination card of the link and displaying it on the screen in a window to be read or edited. Examples of link icons appear in the notecards in Figure 1.

Network storage

The database containing a hypermedia network can be stored in a variety of ways, such as: individual nodes in separate files, the entire network in one file, or the network distributed across multiple files.

A NoteCards database consists of a network of notecards and links stored in a structured file called a *notefile*. The system manages these files, transparent to the user. Users can access any number of notefiles at one time, and can create *cross-file links* that connect cards in different notefiles. Such links make it possible to relate information that is distributed across areas of research. (As we will discuss later, simultaneous access of multiple notefiles and cross-file links have not always been available in NoteCards.)

Hierarchies

In addition to a general linking mechanism, hierarchical structures are often specifically supported.

Hierarchies are supported in NoteCards through the *filebox* card type. Fileboxes are specialized cards that can be used to organize or classify groupings of notecards. A filebox is a card in which other cards, including other fileboxes, can be *filed.* Textual annotations can also appear in the filebox. In general, any card or filebox can be filed in more than one filebox, thus allowing the creation of arbitrary hierarchies of information and multiple structures over the same information.

Browsing

Hypermedia systems support one or more of the following mechanisms for browsing the database: following links to nodes to examine their contents, searching the database for some string, keyword, or attribute value, or navigating around the network using a graphical display.

Navigation is the primary means for accessing information in NoteCards. The user traverses the network by following links from card to card, choosing at each step which link(s) to traverse next. Alternatively, the user can create a *browser* card containing a structural diagram, or graph, of a network of notecards. The nodes of the graph are link icons representing cards in the network. These link icons are active in the usual sense; "clicking" on the link icon retrieves the referenced card. The edges of the graph are lines representing links between cards. Different dashing styles along these edges distinguish different types of links. An example of a browser card appears in Figure 2.

Browsers serve several functions in NoteCards. They provide the user with maps or overviews of the structure and content of a network of cards and links. Moreover, they allow the user to construct alternative views of the network by creating browsers that start from different places and/or follow different link types. Finally, browsers provide a direct manipulation editor with which the user can modify a network. (See the editor menu attached to the lower right corner of Figure 2.)

Tailorability

As part of a larger design goal to make NoteCards extensible or tailorable, the system allows users to create new card types. It also contains a

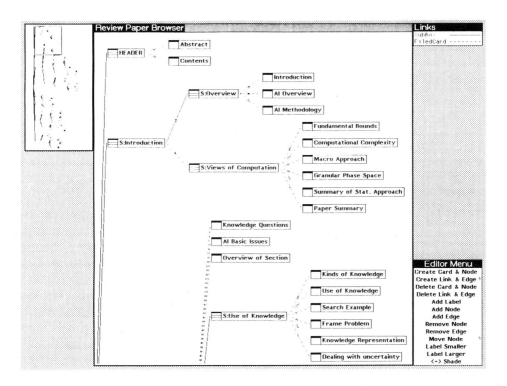

Figure 2: A browser card.

programmer's interface of more than 150 lisp function which can be used to modify the characteristics of individual cards and links, as well as to build new structures. The NoteCards programmer's interface is designed to support both minor modifications and large application developments. Using customized card types as well as these tailoring tools, users can specialize NoteCards for their applications and personal styles (Trigg, Moran & Halasz, 1987).

3. Early collaborative use of NoteCards

The NoteCards project began with an attempt to build a computer-based tool that would aid the individual in performing complex argumentation and inference tasks. One critical lesson learned from the shortcomings of this initial attempt was that complex argumentation and inference tasks depend heavily on the ability to easily capture and represent large amounts of loosely structured textual, graphical, and numerical information. With this lesson learned, the prototype of NoteCards became an extensible hypertext environment designed to help people formulate, structure, compare, and manage information (Halasz, Moran & Trigg, 1987).

As it developed, the prototype of NoteCards was transformed into a useable system which was released to a user community. Observing how the system was used for various information management and analysis tasks by the user community enabled the implementors to modify the system to better suit the needs of its users. As Halasz (1987) states, "This user community has provided invaluable feedback on the strengths and weaknesses of NoteCards as applied to a variety of tasks including document authoring, legal, scientific, and public-policy argumentation, design and development of instructional materials, design and analysis of copier parts, and competitive market analysis."

Since the NoteCards system was originally designed to support individuals working in a single notefile, collaboration had to occur outside of the NoteCards environment, e.g., through face-to-face conversations, electronic mail, or hardcopy documents. In the NoteCards user community, however, many idea processing and information management tasks are inherently collaborative. Groups of varying size, from approximately two to ten people, often work in the same area or on the same project (Halasz, 1987). Moreover, collaboration frequently involves sharing common information, whether in a notefile, a set of standard computer files, a whiteboard, or a set of hardcopy drafts. If individual users are doing their information processing in NoteCards, the tendency is for them to want to share notefiles with their collaborators. Initially, NoteCards did not support such notefile sharing.

Extending NoteCards to support collaborative work required changes in two areas: supporting the social interactions inherent in collaborative activity and supporting shared NoteCards networks. The mechanics of sharing notefiles was, and still is, limited because NoteCards does not allow multiple users to simultaneously access a common notefile. (But, see section 5.3 for a discussion of the work in progress on simultaneous sharing of notefiles.) Thus, notefile sharing is carried out using some form of "draft passing" in which collaborators take turns using a notefile. The length of time a turn may take varies from several hours to several days. Collaborators coordinate the transfer of control through electronic mail or face-to-face interactions, and the physical transfer of the actual notefile is accomplished by copying files between file servers and individual workstations.

This draft passing is surprisingly successful in allowing collaborative use of a notefile, although it has several inherent limitations. First, as mentioned above, collaborators cannot work on the shared notefile simultaneously, even in disjoint sections. Second, draft passing requires the users to manage turn taking logistics, including keeping track of the "true" version of the notefile as it is copied from one place to another. Turn taking is usually straightforward in collaborations consisting of two or three people working closely together, but becomes troublesome in larger, less tightly coupled groups. Third, collaboration sometimes requires real-time interactions between the participants, including conversations and monitoring of other collaborators' activity. Originally, NoteCards did not support such interaction, though collaborators sometimes gathered physically around the single workstation on which a notefile resided.

One early application for collaborative use of NoteCards was project management. The style of use tended to be top-down in that one person functioned as central project coordinator maintaining a notefile of materials relevant to running and monitoring the project. In one case, when organizing a project report, the various members of the project wrote sections of the report in their own personal notefiles, moved them to standard files, and passed them to the project leader. The leader then brought the files into the central notefile, merged them to form a draft, and passed the draft back to the project members for comments.

Two other collaborators used NoteCards to write a large paper together. They developed a turn-taking style that included making changes on paper copies of sections of the paper. The first collaborator made changes on his paper copy of a section, and then entered the notefile to add those changes. In parallel, the second collaborator made changes on another copy of the same section. The first collaborator then passed the notefile to his colleague, along with the revised paper copy. These documents served as histories of the changes made to the notefile. The collaborators occasionally made sweeping changes to the notefile's organization, at which time they worked together at a single workstation.

4. General NoteCards tools

Several mechanisms introduced into NoteCards to facilitate general use have proven particularly valuable for collaborators. In particular, these mechanisms have enhanced a loosely-coupled style of collaboration, in which collaborators work together, but not closely. They may be writing separate papers on a subject of mutual interest, or working on different parts of a large project. Often they don't need to be in direct communication or share the same sections of a notefile. In particular, this style of collaboration has benefited from the introduction into NoteCards of two features: multiple open notefiles and cross-file links.

4.1 Multiple open notefiles

NoteCards was built around the concept of the notefile as a "container" for a single network of related notecards. A given user could access only one notefile at a time. This restriction made it difficult (though not impossible) to merge information from two notefiles. One obvious way to organize one's work is to keep a notefile on each major topic or research category. However, NoteCards did not provide mechanisms for sharing information among such notefiles, forcing most users to work in large, cumbersome, and isolated notefiles. The initial implementation of NoteCards supported collaborative use only through a manual notefile "check-out" mechanism. A group of users could share a notefile by passing around the entire notefile. However, when one user "had" the notefile, other users were prevented from accessing any information on that notefile. Because such notefiles were large, copying them from one user's workstation to another's was a tedious process.

Large notefiles can be divided into smaller ones by using a copy/move facility. Cards and structures can be moved and copied from one notefile to another. A *structure* is a subnetwork of cards and links defined by a root card and a specification for traversing the links starting at that root card. A good example of a structure is the contents of a browser card. Browser displays are built by following the links emanating from a root card according to a set of traversal specifications. A user defines a structure by choosing a root card, the types of links to recursively follow in building the structure, and the maximum path length to be included in the structure.

The problem of oversized notefiles has been mostly solved by providing the capability for users to have multiple notefiles open simultaneously on a single workstation. This feature allows collaborators to break a notefile into pieces that each individual can access. They can work at the same time on a project, and the speed of copying notefiles across machines is greatly improved. Collaborators can maintain their network of relationships across the smaller notefiles with cross-file links (see below). In the future, effective collaborative use of NoteCards will be based on simultaneous access by multiple users to any (public) notefile. In the meantime, collaboration is greatly enhanced by the additional ability to share information in smaller units.

4.2 Cross-file links

A further restriction on collaborative use arose from the difficulty of referencing (much less accessing) information stored in one notefile from another notefile. In particular, NoteCards did not permit links between cards in different notefiles. If a user wanted to reference information in a collaborator's notefile, he had to either go outside of the normal NoteCards linking mechanism and develop some naming or addressing scheme of his own, or copy and move cards between notefiles.

To allow the creation of links that cross notefile boundaries, cross-file links were implemented in NoteCards. Users now create links between cards residing in different notefiles if the cards are both open on the screen simultaneously. Thus, for example, it is possible to file a notecard from one notefile in a filebox from another notefile. Users can create links from their own work to that of their collaborators, giving them easy access to each other's work. As the contents of cards in one notefile change, cross-file links from another notefile continue to point at the most recent versions.

One group of collaborators working on instructional design for copiers[3] has developed notefiles for each of the machines for which they offer training materials. They have discovered many common sub-systems among these machines, and have pulled material relevant to these sub-systems into a generic sub-system notefile. They used cross-file links to point from the original notefiles to the generic notefile. As they develop training for new machines, they plan to use cross-file links to point from each machine's notefile to the appropriate sub-system in the generic sub-system notefile.

5. Collaboration-specific tools

In the absence of specific support for annotation and meta-discussion in an early version of NoteCards, one set of users developed their own conventions and techniques for collaborative use of NoteCards. These conventions and techniques, among others, led to the current set of collaboration-specific tools supported in NoteCards. These tools support a closely-coupled style of collaboration, in which collaborators work together on a paper or project, and require frequent communication and close monitoring of each other's work.

5.1 Collaborator-specific behavior

The most common annotative activity is commenting on a collaborator's work. Initially, users inserted comments directly into the cards being critiqued. In order to distinguish comment from substance, they used different fonts. In the limit, however, this scheme leads to proliferating fonts as well as confusion over the historical order of annotations. They therefore adopted the convention of placing annotations in separate cards and linking to them from the cards being annotated, with the link icon at the appropriate place. Figure 1 shows annotation cards along with the cards being annotated.

Fonts were still used to distinguish between cards created by each of the collaborators. The cards on the right side of Figure 1 contain different fonts, determined according to their author. In addition, individuals found that they preferred other customizations of their sessions in a collaborative notefile. For example, they chose to set up the default properties used by the text editor in different ways. These conventions led to the development of a general tool which supports the specification of different behaviors by collaborators.

To allow a notefile to distinguish between collaborators, the Collaborator card type was created. A card of this type is created for each person or set of persons working in a notefile. The collaborator card contains information, such as the user's name, initials, preferred font, and text editor properties. An example of a collaborator card appears at the top of Figure 3,

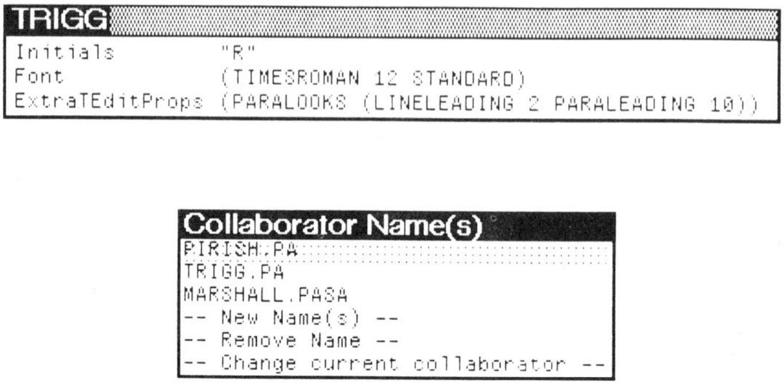

```
TRIGG
Initials          "R"
Font              (TIMESROMAN 12 STANDARD)
ExtraTEditProps (PARALOOKS (LINELEADING 2 PARALEADING 10))
```

```
Collaborator Name(s)
PIRISH.PA
TRIGG.PA
MARSHALL.PASA
-- New Name(s) --
-- Remove Name --
-- Change current collaborator --
```

Figure 3: A collaborator card and a menu of collaborators.

along with a menu showing how a collaborator is chosen for a notefile. The initials are used by History cards, which are described below. The font is automatically installed and used to display text in cards created by the collaborator. When each collaborator or set of collaborators chooses a different font, it is easy to tell at a glance what work each person has contributed to a notefile's text. A collaborator card may also be created for multiple users, in the case where several people are working on a notefile together and want to claim group ownership of their contributions. When a collaborator (or set of collaborators) opens a "collaboratized" notefile, they are asked to identify themselves. NoteCards then installs the appropriate collaborator properties by searching for their collaborator card, and appling these properties to the working session.

5.2 Record keeping

Collaborators using NoteCards recognized the need to keep a record of additions, changes, deletions, etc. made during a single session in a notefile. They found that mutual intelligibility depended on the ability of one collaborator to quickly learn what changes were made during the previous session by his or her colleague (Trigg, Suchman & Halasz, 1986). In fact, record keeping functions in several ways:

For mutual monitoring. This is especially important when the collaborators are taking turns in the shared medium. By accessing the record, one collaborator can learn what was done by the other during an earlier session.

To provide a historical record. In this form, the record can be used to answer questions like "Who did what when?"

To preserve rationale. Here, the record is used to answer questions like "Why did they choose that procedure?" That is, the record captures (or points to) the rationale for decisions made during the project. Note that these decisions can concern work process as well as work content, e.g., "How did they decide who would do the writing?"

To support chronology-based information retrieval. If properly indexed, the record can provide answers to questions like, "Show me the material I was working on two weeks ago," or "Show me the object I was working on at the same time as object A."

Normally the technology that supports such record keeping is separate from the work itself. However, because hypertext supports interlinked objects, it becomes possible for the objects comprising the records to be linked directly to the objects comprising the work. By linking directly to the work itself, the records act like an index into the database making up the work content and therefore afford easy access for collaborators monitoring one another's progress as well as for later readers curious about the history of the project.

One set of collaborators developed conventions for keeping such records. When using the notefile, each collaborator creates a special history card. They title the card with the date and the initials of the particular collaborator (or the initials of more than one, if the session is joint). The collaborator then places text in this card describing the work done in that session. They also insert links to the cards that were created or modified. All history cards are filed in a history filebox in chronological order. This allows one collaborator to quickly find and review the work done by others and follow links to the affected cards (Trigg, Suchman & Halasz, 1986).

The problem with this routine is that it requires a great deal of overhead. Users must expend the extra effort to create these histories, file them, and keep them current. The solution was to create a tool, called History cards, which automates the routine. It creates links directly to relevant cards and semi-automates the record creation process. That is, with minimal user interaction, the tool can create first approximations of records of the work done during a session. The user can then modify these records as desired.

Automated History cards provide a user-tailorable interface to a logging facility which records the various events that take place over the course of a session, such as creating and deleting cards and links, editing cards, changing card titles, etc. The user has the ability to select the types of NoteCards events to be recorded. Figure 4 shows a menu from which events can be chosen. When a collaborator chooses to compute a record of his or her work, appropriate text and "pointers" to cards representing events are automatically inserted into the history card, along with appropriate time stamps. Figure 5 shows a history card containing such computed events. Once the history has been computed and filled in, the user may modify it so as to adequately reflect the work done during the session. These modifications may include commentary, questions and links to other cards.

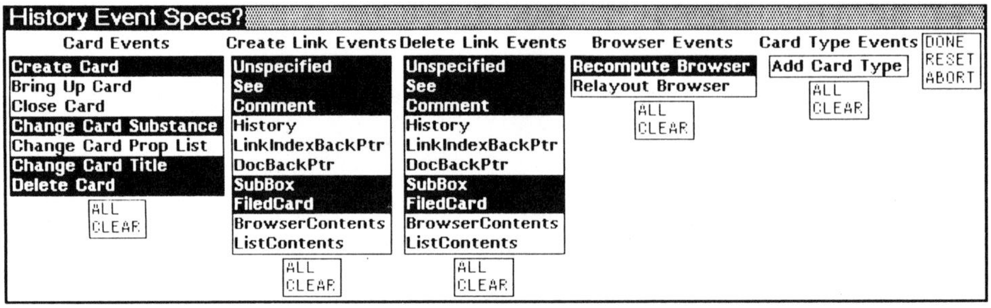

Figure 4: Specifying events to be recorded in a history card.

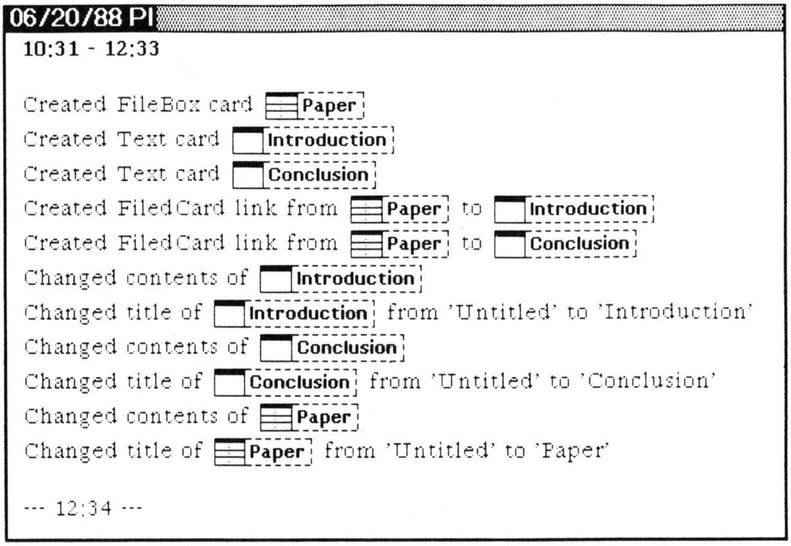

Figure 5: A semi-automated history card containing text and pointers.

The aforementioned "pointers" are pseudo-links; clicking one causes the card it represents to be opened. Note that the destination cards do not keep a record of the fact that they are being pointed to; as in Hypercard (Goodman, 1987), these pointers are not true Hypermedia links since they are "one-way." The advantage is that the user has quick access to these cards without incurring the overhead of creating regular links which include back pointers to the history card. Single pointers as well as sets of pointers can be turned into real links at the user's discretion.

Every history card is automatically filed in a "Notefile Use History" filebox, so that subsequent collaborators can quickly access all history cards in the notefile. Each user thus has the ability to view changes made by other collaborators by opening history cards created and filed during their working sessions. Because the history cards are linked to the work they represent, these later users can immediately access the database at the referenced location.

Problems

Automated history cards need improvements in the area of tying events together to make a coherent story. For example, several operations performed on one card will each appear as separate, disjoint events in the history card. Some groups of operations are frequently performed together, and should be reported together, possibly in an abbreviated format. For example, the operations of creating a card, changing its title from "Untitled" to "Introduction," and creating a filing link from it to filebox "Paper" could be summarized as "Created card 'Introduction' and filed it in filebox 'Paper'".

   Also, it is up to the collaborators to further improve on the contents of the history card. They will often need to take the time to delete extraneous information, add additional commentary, and insert other links, rather than leave it up to the next person in the notefile to make sense out of it.

5.3 Simultaneous sharing

The NoteCards system is in the process of being modified to make it possible for users to share a notefile at the same time (Trigg, Suchman & Halasz, 1986). Users will in fact have simultaneous shared access from their workstations to the notefiles residing on any machine attached to the same local-area network. Support for shared NoteCards networks, known as the NoteCards Server, will be a network citizen on which notefiles reside and which receives requests from remote users for operations on those notefiles. Since the new functionality to be obtained from the Server implementation is the ability for several different users to access the same notefile simultaneously, it must be able to handle the problems inherent to multiple-user systems. Here, we are following in the footsteps of systems like Intermedia (Garrett, Smith & Meyrowitz, 1986) and ZOG/KMS (Akscyn, McCracken & Yoder, 1987) which have for some time incorporated hypermedia databases that are simultaneously accessible by multiple users.

6. Future developments

Future developments will include additional History card facilities to help the user add a rationale of work as well as general annotations to the histories. In particular, we recognize the need to provide ways to tie events together, thus forming a more coherent story about the changes made to a notefile. In addition, we plan to integrate History cards with the Guided Tours facility recently made available in NoteCards (Trigg, 1988). Guided tours provide the means for a notefile's authors to represent and manipulate branching paths through the network for the purpose of helping future first-time readers of the notefile. In some sense, History cards also capture an intended path through a portion of the network. A proper integration of the two tools will allow History cards to be "followed" by readers in the same way that Guided Tours are followed today.

We also intend to observe the NoteCards Server in use to discover what kinds of tools are needed to help collaborators perform tasks in a simultaneous, real-time manner. These tools may include extensions of the draft-passing tools, as well as new tools specific to shared-access notefiles.

We are currently observing how cross-file links are being used, especially by collaborators; accordingly, we expect to revise the facility in the near future.

7. Conclusion

Designing a computer environment to support collaborative work requires much more than providing users with shared access to an information structuring tool. The environment needs to support meta-discussion, i.e. discussion among collaborators about the work and about the use of the medium. Meta-discussion occurring through electronic mail or some other medium separate from the medium of substantive work is not as useful. Hypermedia is likely to be a good medium for supporting such discussion for two reasons: (1) meta-discussion often needs to refer directly to portions of the work and (2) a record of the meta-discussion preserved in context can be valuable for historical and chronology-based access. Tools like History cards make possible the recording of both work, annotation, and meta-discussion. In addition, these records are active in the sense that one can gain immediate access to the work itself from within the record.

More generally, we have been continually surprised by the ingenuity with which people adapt technology to their personal applications and styles given the slightest help from the system (say, through generality, flexibility, or tailorability). This argues for systems that respect the user, giving him or her control over the environment yet also providing libraries of application-specific tools to get started. (For example, tools like Collaborator cards support different styles of working by making aspects of those styles explicit.) Recognizing people's innate adaptive abilities also argues for providing support for the convention adoption process, i.e. discussion about the medium (usually problems with it), coming to agreement on a convention, and occasionally building automated support for the convention once it becomes a burdensome routine.

Acknowledgments

We would like to thank Randy Gobbel, Frank Halasz, Cathy Marshall, and Lucy Suchman for their contributions over the years to the NoteCards collaboration project.

Notes

1. A slightly modified version of this chapter appeared in *Journal of the American Society for Information Science*, New York: Wiley, March 1989.

2. Both "hypertext" and "hypermedia" are used to refer to systems which support manipulation of and access to structured information. We use the term "hypermedia" in this paper as it is more recent and emphasizes the multi-media nature of today's systems.

3. This group is using the Instructional Design Environment, or IDE. Further information on IDE may be found in (Russell, Moran & Jordan, 1987).

References

Akscyn, R., McCracken, D. and Yoder, E. (1987). KMS: A Distributed Hypermedia System for Managing Knowledge in Organizations. *Hypertext '87 Papers*, 1-20. Chapel Hill, NC.

Bush, V. (1945, August). As We May Think. *The Atlantic Monthly*, 101-108.

Conklin, J. (1987). Hypertext: An Introduction and Survey. *Computer*, 20, 9, 17-41.

Conklin, J. and Begeman, M.L. (1987). gIBIS: A Hypertext Tool for Team Design Deliberation. *Hypertext '87 Papers*, 247-251. Chapel Hill, NC.

CSCW (1986). *Computer-Supported Cooperative Work (CSCW '86) Proceedings*, 147-174. Austin, TX.

Delisle, N. and Schwartz, M. (1986). Contexts - A Partitioning Concept for Hypertext. *Computer-Supported Cooperative Work (CSCW '86) Proceedings*, 147-152. Austin, TX.

Engelbart, D.C. (1975). NLS Teleconferencing Features: The Journal, and Shared-Screen Telephoning. *Digest of papers, IEEE Computer Society Conference (CompCon75)*, 173-176.

Fish, R., Kraut, R., Leland, M. and Cohen, M. (1988). Quilt: A Collaborative Tool for Cooperative Writing. *Proceedings of the ACM Conference on Office Automation Systems*, 30-37. Palo Alto, CA.

Garrett, L.N., Smith, K. and Meyrowitz, N. (1986). "Intermedia: Issues, Strategies, and Tactics in the Design of a Hypermedia Document System." *Computer-Supported Cooperative Work (CSCW '86) Proceedings,* 163-174. Austin, TX.

Goodman, D. (1987). *The Complete HyperCard Handbook.* New York: Bantam Books.

Halasz, F. G. (1987). Reflections on NoteCards: Seven Issues for the Next Generation of Hypermedia Systems. *Hypertext '87 Papers,* 345-365. Chapel Hill, NC.

Halasz, F. G., Moran, T. P. and Trigg, R. H. (1987). NoteCards in a Nutshell. *Proceedings of the ACM CHI + GI Conference,* 45-52. Toronto, Ontario.

Nelson, T. (1981). *Literary machines.* Swarthmore, PA 19081: T. Nelson, P.O. Box 128.

Russell, D. M., Moran T. P. and Jordan, D. S. (1987) The Instructional Design Environment. In J. Psotka, L. D. Massey, and S. A. Mutter (Eds.), *Intelligent Tutoring Systems: Lessons Learned,* 203-228. Hillsdale, NJ:Lawrence Erlbaum Associates, Inc.

Trigg, R. H. (1983). *A Network-based Approach to Text Handling for the Online Scientific Community.* PhD. Thesis, University of Maryland.

Trigg, R. H. (1988). Guided Tours and Tabletops: Tools for Communicating in a Hypertext Environment. *Computer-Supported Cooperative Work (CSCW '88) Proceedings,* 216-227. Portland, OR.

Trigg, R. H., Suchman, L. and Halasz, F. G. (1986). Supporting Collaboration in NoteCards. *Computer-Supported Cooperative Work (CSCW '86) Proceedings,* 153-162. Austin, TX.

Trigg, R. H., Moran, T. P. and Halasz, F. G. (1987). Adaptability and Tailorability in NoteCards. In H.-J. Bullinger and B. Xhackel (Eds.), *Human-Computer Interaction - INTERACT '87,* 723-728. North-Holland:Elsevier Science Publishers B.V.

The Missing Link:
Why We're All Doing Hypertext Wrong

Norman Meyrowitz

Institute for Research in Information and Scholarship (IRIS)
Brown University
155 George Street
Box 1946
Providence, RI 02912

1. Introduction

Despite over a quarter century of history, hypertext/hypermedia has not yet caught on as a **fundamental tool** for daily knowledge work. In the 60s and 70s, Engelbart's NLS [Engelbart and English, 1968] possessed extremely advanced functionality, while Brown's FRESS [van Dam, 1971] provided rich word processing combined with sophisticated linking capability. In the 80s, Xerox's Notecards [Halasz, Moran, and Trigg, 1987] and Brown's Intermedia [Meyrowitz, 1986; Yankelovich, Haan, Meyrowitz, and Drucker, 1988; Yankelovich, Smith, Garrett, and Meyrowitz, 1988], to name two, have been research successes but have not yet been widely accepted outside of the lab. Even Owl's Guide [Owl International, 1987], with fairly good penetration in both the Macintosh and IBM PC markets, and Apple's ubiquitous HyperCard [Apple Computer, Inc., 1987] are used typically not for daily knowledge work, but as a special-purpose tools to create online-help or specialized corpuses for a particular problem domain.

Carefully examining the systems created to date, uncovers a single common thread that explains why hypertext/hypermedia systems have not caught on: virtually all systems have been **insular, monolithic packages** that demand the user disown his or her present computing environment to use the functions of hypertext and hypermedia.

2. Where We Have Been

NLS, though probably a more powerful and integrated hypermedia package than any that have since been created, still made it difficult for the user to use the other non-NLS applications upon which he or she depended. Rather than use those applications within the NLS environment, the user was forced to exit or suspend NLS to operate non-NLS programs. Likewise in FRESS, one operated within a word processing/hypertext program that was launched from the CP/CMS environment on an IBM 360/67. To move to a compiler or a statistics package, one needed to exit the FRESS environment and return to the CP/CMS environment. This certainly was a chore if one needed to read the source code or the statistics in order to create a hypertext document, and an impossibility if one wanted to actually link to the statistics or code into the hypertext corpus.

3. Where We Are Now

Even in today's technology, the same barrier exists. In Notecards, which runs in the very rich InterLisp-D environment, Notecards "takes over" and provides a monolithic environment. If one wants to create hypertext documentation, for, let's say, an expert system written in the InterLisp-D programming environment, it would be difficult to do so using Notecards; when Notecards is operational, the other environments are largely unreachable. On the Macintosh and under Microsoft Windows, Guide affords a similarly insular environment. Rather than allowing users to link a Microsoft Word document to an Excel document to a MacDraw document, Guide forces the user to "import" all of those documents into the Guide system. Once in Guide, the word processing features of Word are no longer available for further editing, the drawing facilities of MacDraw are no longer available for further drawing, and the calculation facilities of Excel are no longer available for further refinement. With HyperCard, one can essentially suspend HyperCard and launch one of the existing Mac desktop applications like Excel or MacDraw, exit those, and return to the launching point in HyperCard, but it is impossible to link into HyperCard from any of those desktop applications.

4. A Glimpse of the Future

Our own Intermedia system is an attempt to prototype the future. Three years ago, Brown's Institute for Research in Information and Scholarship (IRIS) undertook the research and development of the Intermedia system, a user-level framework for creating exploratory contexts of educational and research materials for students and faculty. The underlying user-level paradigm of Intermedia is that of the *navigational link*. The link adds an additional level of integration to the normal desktop environment represented by the Macintosh Toolbox or the Microsoft Windows environments. Where previously, one could simply copy information from one desktop document to another, with Intermedia, one can create links between any selected information in one document and any selected information in another document. These ties are persistent: they survive for the lifetime of the document, both in memory and on disk. One can follow these trails of links to explore a corpus of knowledge in the same way in which one might explore an encyclopedia. At the end of each link one can find not only text, but graphic diagrams, digitized images, timelines, three-dimensional manipulable models, animation, and even video or audio. Intermedia is a tool for both the author and the reader, for both the student and the scholar — it provides a way to connect information in sophisticated and complex ways.

The endpoint of a link — also called a *block* or *link anchor* — can be any entity that the user can select in that particular application. In text, a link anchor can be an insertion point, a character, a sequence of characters, a word, a sequence of words, a paragraph or the entire document. In graphics, the link anchor can be a single graphics object or a multiple-selection of graphics objects. In a spreadsheet, for instance, the link anchor could be a cell, a range of cells, a row, a column, or a set of rows and/or columns.

To make link creation as simple an operation as possible, Intermedia uses the same interface paradigm as the now familiar cut and paste operation. The user first selects the source anchor of the link and issues the "Start Link" command from the menu (see Fig. 1). This is analogous to selecting an item and choosing "cut" or "copy," with the exception that the selection from the "Start Link" command is remembered in the *linkboard*, the hypertext equivalent of the clipboard. The user is then free to do anything that is desired, including opening other documents, creating new documents, editing existing documents, etc.

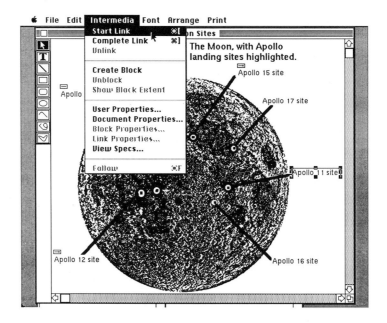

Fig. 1: The "Start Link" operation

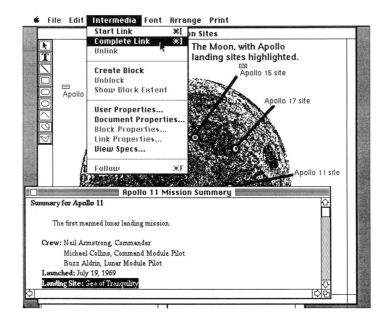

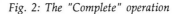

Fig. 2: The "Complete" operation

When the user finds an appropriate destination anchor for the link, he/she simply selects that anchor and issues the "Complete Link" command from the menu (See Fig. 2). This is analogous to selecting an item and choosing the "paste" command. When "Complete Link" is issued, a persistent tie is made from the anchor that is currently referenced in the linkboard to the anchor that the user just selected. This persistent tie will last eternally, unless a user explicitly deletes that link. Since links are bi-directional, a marker appears near the both source and destination anchors to indicate that a link exists and may be traversed. Following the link is as easy as selecting the link marker and issuing the "Follow" command from the menu (See Fig. 3). As a shortcut, the user can simply point at the link marker and "double-click" the mouse to traverse a link. The result of the follow operation is a traversal back to the other endpoint of the link, with that endpoint highlighted in gray (see Fig. 4).

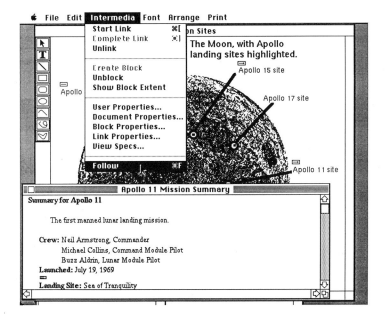

Fig. 3: The "Follow" operation

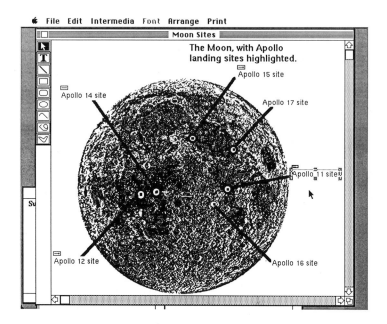

Fig. 4: Result of the "Follow" operation

5. Where We Could Be

The user view above can work only if developers can easily incorporate linking functionality into their applications. With Intermedia, we **have** designed and built a linking protocol architecture [Coombs, Gold, Haan, Riley, Meyrowitz, in press 1989] that allows new applications, if they implement a small linking protocol, to be full-fledged Intermedia documents and therefore the source or destination of links.

Yet our Intermedia applications base consists entirely of those that we write ourselves. We, unfortunately, do not have the market impact and persuasive power to convince third-party developers to create scores of new applications that adhere to a linking protocol. Who does?

Five years ago, with the exception of people at Xerox PARC and a few pioneers using Smalltalk and Lisp in research laboratories and academia, the paradigm of "cut, copy, and paste" was virtually unknown. Now, with the advent of the Lisa and Mac toolboxes, and more recently, of Microsoft Windows, that paradigm is a familiar one, even to five-year-olds using MacPaint. This paradigm caught on for four reasons: 1) powerful things could be done with this paradigm; 2) the paradigm was extremely easy to motivate and teach to end-users; 3) the toolbox vendors touted the copy and paste protocol as an important integrating factor that all software developers should include in their applications; and 4) most importantly, the toolbox supporters provided the framework for copy and paste deep in the system software and provided developers the protocols that enabled them to incorporate the paradigm into their software with relative ease. The paradigm is so widely-accepted that consumers regularly sneer at and ignore software that does not provide full cut, copy, and paste support.

Hypertext/hypermedia has the same potential for making fundamental improvements to people's daily work. Like "cut, copy, and paste," making and following links fulfills factors one and two above — it provides a powerful integrating ability and it is reasonably easy to motivate and teach to idea workers. Yet hypertext/hypermedia will only catch on as a fundamentally integrating paradigm when factors three and four can be fulfilled. Linking functionality must be incorporated, as a fundamental advance in application integration, into the heart of the standard computing toolboxes — the Macintosh desktop, Microsoft Windows, Presentation Manager [14], NextStep [15], etc. — and application developers must be provided with the tools that enable applications to "link up" in a standard manner. Only when the paradigm is positioned as an integrating factor for **all** third-party applications, and not as a special attribute of a limited few, will knowledge workers accept and integrate hypertext and hypermedia into their daily work process.

ACKNOWLEDGEMENTS

The development of the Intermedia system was a team effort of a large number of people, including Paulette Bush, Tim Catlin, Helen DeAndrade, Steve Drucker, Page Elmore, Charlie Evett, Matt Evett, George Fitzmaurice, Nan Garrett, Allan Gold, Ed Grossman, Bernard Haan, Larry Larrivee, Katie Livingston, Norman Meyrowitz, Marty Michel, Muru Palaniappan, Victor Riley, Bill Shipp, Karen Smith, Tom Stambaugh, Ken Utting, Todd VanderDoes, and Nicole Yankelovich.

Figures in this document were taken from a Lunar Geology corpus developed by Katie Livingston.

This work has been sponsored in part by Apple Computer, Inc., IBM, the Annenberg/CPB Project, and US West Advanced Technologies.

REFERENCES

Apple Computer, Inc., *Hypercard User's Guide*, Cupertino, CA, 1987.

Coombs, James H., Gold, Allan N., Haan, Bernard J., Riley, Victor A., and Meyrowitz, Norman, *The Architecture and Design of an Application-Independent Hypermedia Linking Protocol*, 1989, in press.

Engelbart, Douglas C. and English, William, "A Research Center for Augmenting Human Intellect," *Proceedings of FJCC*, Vol. 33, No. 1, AFIPS Press, Montvale, NJ, Fall 1968, pp. 395-410.

Halasz, Frank, Moran, T. P., and Trigg, Randall H., "NoteCards in a Nutshell," *Proceedings of CHI+GI 1987*, April 1987.

Meyrowitz, Norman, "Intermedia: The Architecture and Construction of an Object-Oriented Hypertext/Hypermedia System and Applications Framework," *Proceedings of OOPSLA '86*, Portland, OR, September, 1986.

Owl International, *Guide 2.0*, Bellevue, WA, 1987.

van Dam, Andries, FRESS (File Retrieval and Editing System), Barrington, RI: Text Systems, July 1971.

Yankelovich, Nicole, Bernard Haan, Norman Meyrowitz, and Steven Drucker, "Intermedia: The Concept and the Construction of a Seamless Information Environment." *IEEE Computer*, January 1988.

Yankelovich, Nicole, Karen E. Smith, L. Nancy Garrett, and Norman Meyrowitz, "Issues in Designing a Hypermedia Document System," in *Interactive Multimedia*, Redmond, WA: Microsoft Press, 1988, pp. 33-85.

Reflections on
Authoring, Editing, and Managing Hypertext

Ben Shneiderman
Head, Human-Computer Interaction Laboratory

Department of Computer Science
University of Maryland
College Park, MD 20742

This chapter offers recommendations for potential authors of hypertext documents based on the experience of designing a hypertext system and of creating a series of substantial hypertext databases on personal computers and larger workstations. Advice on choosing projects, identifying useful author tool features, and structuring knowledge is presented. Additional issues such as the design of the root document, article size, and conversion from existing databases are covered. While hypertext has exciting potentials, the dangers of poor design must be overcome to create attractive and effective products.

Introduction

Technological improvements can empower people, enabling them to accomplish tasks that once seemed impossible. Potent computer-based technologies are increasingly reshaping our expectations and "serving human needs" (Mumford, 1934). The user interface is increasingly recognized as a key factor in unleashing user creativity and productivity. Spreadsheets, word processing, desktop publishing, graphics editors, and now hypertext are all grand successes in large part because of the user interface.

Hypertext systems offer a substantially more powerful user interface to enable rapid and convenient access to large volumes of textual, graphic, video, audio, etc. databases (Conklin, 1987; Shneiderman, 1987a, 1987b). However, just because hypertext is used for an application does not ensure that the user's needs are served. Inspired writing, careful editing, and diligent managing are necessary for hypertext just as they are for any media. Key attributes of hypertext projects, which we'll call the **Golden Rules of Hypertext**, are that:

- there is a large body of information organized into numerous fragments,
- thefragments relate to each other, and
- the user needs only a small fraction at any time.

The hypertext approach supports traversal of the non-linear database of text and graphic fragments by merely pointing at phrases, link icons, link menus, or graphic image components. The embedded menu style of interaction (as opposed to menu trees) has proven to be an effective means for people to locate required information in large and complex text and graphic databases (Koved and Shneiderman, 1987). This paper explores some of the strategies in authoring or editing effective hypertext documents. Potential hypertext projects include:

  Product catalogs & advertisements
  Organizational charts & policy manuals
  Annual reports & orientation guides
  Resumes & biographies
  Contracts & wills
  Newsletters & news magazines
  Software documentation & code

  Encyclopedias, glossaries & dictionaries
  Medical & legal reference books
  Religious & literary annotations
  College catalogs & departmental guides
  Travel & restaurant guides
  Scientific journals, abstracts & indexes

  Instruction & exploration
  Repair & maintenance manuals
  Time lines & geographical maps
  Online help & technical documentation
  Cookbooks & home repair manuals
  Mysteries, fantasies & jokebooks

    Hypertext can be helpful, but there is a real danger that it can also lead to hyperchaos. The dual dangers are that hypertext may be inappropriate for some projects and that the design of the hypertext may be poor (e.g. too many links, confusing structure). Inappropriate applications would violate the Golden Rules of Hypertext. For example, a traditional novel is written as a linear form and the reader is expected to read the entire text from beginning to middle to end. Most poems, fairy tales, newspaper articles, and even the chapters of this book are written in a linear form. Of course, hyper-novels, hyper-poems, hyper-fairy tales, hyper-newspapers, and hyperbooks are possible, but they would require rethinking of the traditional forms so that they satisfy the Golden Rules of Hypertext.

    Poor design of hypertext is the more common problem. Just because a text has been broken into fragments and linked does not ensure that it will be effective or attractive. Successful hypertext, just as any successful writing project, depends on good design of the contents. The hypertext author who creates a new work or the hypertext editor who takes existing materials and puts them into hypertext form must take great care to produce excellence. The designer who assumes that it is safe to throw everything into the hypertext network and let the reader sort it out will be surprised by the negative reactions.

    Our experience in creating hypertexts and a hypertext system during the past six years has taught us many lessons. Our system, Hyperties (Hypertext based on The Interactive Encyclopedia System), makes a sharp separation in the software used for authoring and the software used for browsing. The embedded menus approach and the simple user interface allow users to tap the substantial power of hypertext for browsing and information search tasks (Figure 1) (Morariu and Shneiderman, 1986; Marchionini and Shneiderman, 1988). Recent additions include capacity for more and larger articles, hot keys for frequent operations (NEXT PAGE, INDEX, HELP), graphic backgrounds, powerful string search, and full path history maintenance. The commercial version of Hyperties (available from Cognetics Corporation, 55 Princeton-Hightstown Rd., Princeton Junction, NJ 08550, (609) 799-5005) runs on an IBM PC while the research version runs on the SUN 3/60 workstation using NeWS.

```
WASHINGTON, DC: THE NATION'S CAPITAL              PAGE 2 OF 3

    Located between Maryland and Virginia, Washington, DC

embraces the White House and the Capitol, a host of

government offices as well as the Smithsonian museums.

Designed by Pierre L'Enfant, Washington, DC is a graceful

city of broad boulevards, national monuments, the rustic

Rock Creek Park, and the National Zoo.


    First-time visitors should begin at the mall by walking

from the Capitol towards the Smithsonian museums and on
-----------------------------------------------------------
SMITHSONIAN MUSEUMS: In addition to the familiar castle and
popular Air & Space Museum there are 14 other major sites.
SEE ARTICLE ON "SMITHSONIAN MUSEUMS"

BACK PAGE NEXT PAGE   RETURN TO "NEW YORK CITY"    EXTRA
```

Figure 1. This Hyperties display on an IBM Personal Computer shows highlighted embedded menu items that can be selected by touchscreen, mouse, or jump-arrow keys. The user can follow a topic of interest, turn pages (BACK or NEXT), RETURN to the previous article, or view the EXTRA features such as the INDEX, TABLE OF CONTENTS, HISTORY, or SEARCH.

Hyperties has been used for museum exhibits, educational course materials, organizational orientation, as a tool for diagnostic problem solving, as an environment for creating checklists for complex procedures, in online help, to browse computer programs, as a public information resource, or to explore cross referenced materials such as scientific journal articles or technical documents:

Hypertext on Hypertext :

Contains the full text of the July 1988 issue of the *Communications of the ACM* which was a special issue containing 8 papers on the topic of hypertext drawn from the November 1987 Hypertext '87 workshop held at the University of North Carolina at Chapel Hill. Additional material was prepared by the hypertext editor, Ben Shneiderman. A review of the workshop by Jakob Nielsen, a bibliography on hypermedia created at Brown University, and biographies of contributors were included. Contains 307 articles and 38 figures. (Available from Association for Computing Machinery, 11 East 42nd Street, New York, NY 10017. $24.95 for members, $34.95 for non-members.)

Guide to Opportunities in Volunteer Archaeology (GOVA):

Provides information on becoming a volunteer at almost 200 sites around the world, as well as information about archaeological methods and historical eras. Contains 11 maps to show geographic locations around the world. Installed in the Smithsonian's National Museum of Natural History during spring 1988, it is travelling to the Los Angeles County Art Museum, Denver, St. Paul, Boston, and Ottawa during the next two years. This special museum version of Hyperties provides touch screen access in two free standing kiosks. The database was created by Dr. Ken Holum (History Professor at the University of Maryland) and his graduate students and is updated regularly to reflect currently available sites.

EDUCOM '88 Guide:

A guide to the October 25-28, 1988 EDUCOM conference, held at the Washington Hilton Hotel. The 120 articles offer information about keynote lectures, luncheons, dinners, sessions, tours, and exhibits. This was distributed to registrants who requested it in advance of the conference.

Hypertext Hands-On!:

Written by Ben Shneiderman and Greg Kearsley for a general interest reader, this introduction covers hypertext ideas, systems, and applications. The 180 articles are prepared in printed book form and on a disk inserted in the back of the book jacket. Readers will be able to explore the relative merits of each version and discover how they diverged as they were created. Figures were superior on paper, but color enhanced some of the on-screen graphics. Longer discussions were more suited to paper, and short articles with links made more sense on the screen. An epilog describing the development process was included on paper, while several example hypertexts were included only on the disk. (Available from Addison-Wesley Publishers, One Jacob Way, Reading, MA 01867, $26.95.)

Training Manual Glossary for Online Bibliographic Searching at the National Agricultural Library:

Novice users of the online bibliographic search system at the National Agricultural Library in Beltsville, MD can take a videodisk-based training course that has an integrated Hyperties database with almost 170 articles. The articles provide definitions of key terms and concepts that are used during the videodisk sessions. This project was produced by the University of Maryland's Center for Instructional Development and Evaluation under the leadership of Dr. Janis Morariu.

Interactive Encyclopedia of Jewish Heritage:

This massive 3-year project will develop 3,000 articles and 10,000 videodisc images into a comprehensive encyclopedia. Sponsored by the New York-based Museum of Jewish Heritage, the project organizers have formed a 12-person board of scholars to oversee the project, develop the list of articles, and write the articles. This project emerged from our first project on Austria and the Holocaust that was written by Marsha Rozenblit, a historian at the University of Maryland.

NASA's Hubble Space Telescope:

On the SUN workstation we have built a small database on the Hubble Space Telescope that supports two large independent windows in which users can traverse the articles and graphics that have been entered from NASA sources. Various multiple window strategies and highlighting strategies have been built and tested. The Hyperties Markup Language on the SUN enables users to specify many more presentation attributes.

NCR College of Management Course Catalog:

This database with more than 200 articles contained course descriptions and maps related to the NCR College of Management in Dayton, Ohio where employees learn managerial skills. It was created on the SUN by semi-automatic loading of information from a database provided by NCR.

Hyperties allows users to explore information resources in an easy and appealing manner. They merely point at topics or picture components that interest them and a brief definition appears at the bottom of the screen (see Figure 1for IBM PC display and Figure 2 for the SUN display). The users may continue reading or ask for details about the selected topic. An article about a topic may be one or more screens long and contain several pictures or videodisc segments. As users traverse articles, Hyperties retains a record of the path and allows easy reversal, building confidence and a sense of control. Users can also select articles and pictures from an index or a Table of Contents. A novel algorithm string search using signature files enables users to type a word (or two words connected by & (and), | (or), or a **blank** (to signify followed by)) and get the list of articles that contain it.

One of the key distinctions of Hyperties compared with the many other hypertext systems is the sophisticated authoring tool on the IBM PC version. Experienced word processor users can learn the features of the author tool within an hour. However, the syntax and semantics of the author tool are only the base from which users construct hypertext applications, just as learning to type is only the base from which authors learn to write novels or scientific journals articles.

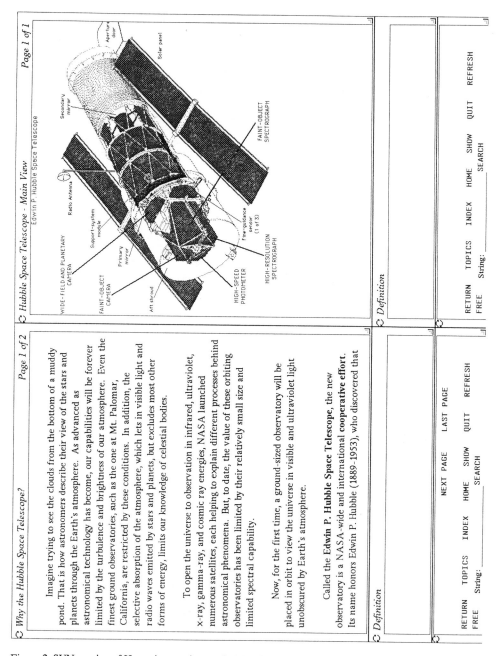

Figure 2. SUN version of Hyperties running on the NeWS Window System. This database provides text and scanned images of NASA's Hubble Space Telescope.

Author system features

Primitive authoring tools from the computer-assisted instruction world were employed to create hypertext documents, but the recent crop of hypertext sytems contain a variety of features to meet the demands of this new environment. To analyse the authoring features we can begin with this tableau of actions and objects:

ACTIONS	OBJECTS
Importation	An article/node
Editing	A link
Exportation	Collections of articles/nodes or webs of links
Printing	Entire database

Hypertext systems should be compared as to their ability to support importation of articles, links, collections of articles or webs of links, or entire databases. There is great variation across systems. Most systems enable each of the actions to be applied to a single node/article from/to an ASCII file, but not much more. For example, most systems enable the author to edit an article at a time, but few systems enable the author to make a global change to all articles with one command. Researchers are developing strategies for exporting entire databases in book formats with links indicated by bold face and a page number. In constructing *Hypertext Hands-On!* (Shneiderman and Kearsley, 1989), we had to build the book version of the hypertext database one step at a time, indicating page numbers by hand. Automation of this process is a natural next step.

Two key issues in the authoring process are the management of nodes and the indication of links. If the hypertext system provides an index of all the nodes/articles that have been referenced and/or created, that will be of great benefit. Figure 3 shows a typical index screen from Hyperties and Figure 4 shows a typical screen for editing an article. The second issue is the indication of links. This process should be simple and easy to manipulate. Marking a phrase or a region can ususally be accomplished easily, but then it should also be easy to indicate the destination of the link. Furthermore, if the same phrase appears many times it should be possible to resolve the link more easily the second time. Automatic facilities for marking and linking every occurrence of a link are attractive, but can lead to an excessive number of links which clutter the screen and distract the reader. One problem that occurs in some hypertext systems is that the link buttons on phrases are marked by regions of the screen, so when the text is edited the link buttons must all be moved. For text articles, the link buttons should move with the words.

Other features to consider in an authoring tool are:

- the range of editing functions available (i.e., copying, moving, insertion, deletion, global change within an article, etc.).

- the availability of lists of link names, index terms, synonyms, etc.

- the range of display formating commands available.

```
┌──────────────────────────────────────────────────────────────────────┐
│ INDEX of ARTICLES                                                      │
│                                                                        │
│    ┌────────────────────────────────────────────────────────────┐     │
│    │ 1. *  ACM USES HYPERTIES                                     │     │
│    │                    ──────── INDEX - 62 entries ────────      │     │
│    │  1. *  ACM USES HYPERTIES                                    │     │
│    │  2. *t ANGELFISH                                             │     │
│    │  3. *t AREAS OF COMPETENCE                                   │     │
│    │  4. *t ARROW KEYS                                            │     │
│    │  5. *t ARTICLE                                               │     │
│    │  6. *t BACKGROUNDS                                           │     │
│    │  7. *t BANKING TERMINALS AND HOME BANKING                    │     │
│    │  8. *t BOOKS ABOUT DAVID SEYMOUR                             │     │
│    │  9. *t BRIEF DESCRIPTION                                     │     │
│    │ 10. *t BROWSER COMMANDS                                      │     │
│    │ 11. *t CBS SOFTWARE                                          │     │
│    │ 12. *t CGA BACKGROUNDS                                       │     │
│    │ 13. *t CGA GRAPHICS                                          │     │
│    │ 14. *t COGNETICS CORPORATION                                 │     │
│    │ 15. *t COMMANDS                                              │     │
│    │ 16. *t COMPLETE ARTICLE                                      │     │
│    └────────────────────────────────────────────────────────────┘     │
│ Press ESC to leave window and access commands.                         │
│ EDIT        ADD          DELETE    RENAME                               │
│ INDEX       SYNONYMS      LINKS     GRAPHICS  PRINT    BROWSE      QUIT  │
└──────────────────────────────────────────────────────────────────────┘
```

Figure 3. A typical INDEX from the IBM PC version of the Hyperties Authoring Tool. The currently selected article is ACM USES HYPERTIES and the available commands are shown on the bottom.

- the availability of search/replace functions for making global changes across multiple nodes.

- control of color (text, background): color can make the text look attractive, but it can also be distracting. Since users are very different in their preferences and tasks, it should be possible for users to reset color usage parameters.

- the capability to easily switch between author and browser modes to test ideas.

- accessing CD-ROM, videodisc, or other devices: new devices are emerging regularly with remarkable storage capabilities. It should be possible to access information on a variety of devices.

- capability to export files to other systems.

- operability on a local area network.

- multi-user, network & distributed databases.

```
Article: "INTRODUCTION"
┌─HEADING────────────────────────────────────────────────────┐
│Introduction to Hyperties                                    │
└─────────────────────────────────────────────────────────────

┌─DESCRIPTION─────────────────────────────────────────────────┐
│This is the General Introduction to the Tour.               │
│                                                             │
└─────────────────────────────────────────────────────────────

┌─CONTENT─────────────────────────────────────────────────────┐
│as1                                                          │
│Hyperties is a "hypertext" product for the IBM PC. You can use it to
│"create databases" of articles, "graphics", "videodisc sequences", all
│linked together.                                             │
│ap                                                           │
│Readers can "browse" through the database, following paths of interest using
│the "arrow keys", a "mouse", or a "touchscreen".             │
│ap                                                           │
│Hyperties can be used in a wide range of applications including:
│al+5                                                         │
│Training and Instruction                                     │
│"Newsletters"                                                │
└─────────────────────────────────────────────────────────────

HEADING    DESCRIPTION    CONTENT    NOTES
RESOLVE    GET            EXPORT              PRINT            INDEX
```

Figure 4. A typical screen from the IBM PC version of Hyperties showing the editing of an article whose title is INTRODUCTION. There are HEADING, DESCRIPTION, and CONTENT windows, plus the set of available commands at the bottom.

- version keeping (can old versions of an article be stored?).

- graphics & video facilities: are there embedded graphics editors and mechanisms for exporing the videodisc.

- collaboration: can more than one person edit the database at one time? Can components of the database written by several people be merged into one hypertext database.

- data compression: compression algorithms can reduce the size of the database and facilitate distibution of disks or dissemination by electronic networks

- security control: is there password control for the database or parts of it.

- encryption: can sensitive nodes be encrypted?

- reliability: does the software perform without bugs, and without loosing data?

- integration with other software/hardware.

- browser distribution: does every user of the hypertext have to acquire a copy of the full system or can the browsing part be included with the database.

There are undoubtedly more items to add, but this list which emerged from our own experience is a start. None of the current systems provides the full set of desirable features.

Authoring or editing hypertext

For at least that last three thousand years authors and editors have explored ways to structure knowledge to suit the linear print medium. When appropriate, authors have developed strategies for linking related fragments of text and graphics even in the linear format. Now, hypertext encourages the non-linear interconnecting links among nodes.

Restructuring knowledge to suit this new medium is a fascinating experience (Koved, 1985; Kreitzberg and Shneiderman, 1988; Weldon, Mills, Koved and Shneiderman, 1985). The first challenge is to structure the knowledge in a way that an overview can be presented to the reader in the root document or introductory article. The overview should identify the key subsidiary ideas and the breadth of coverage. Paper books present a clear vision of their boundaries so readers can know when they have read it all, but in the hypertext world other mechanisms must be created to give the reader a sense of scope and closure. The overall structure of articles must make sense to readers so that they can form a mental image of the topics covered. This facilitates traversal and reduces disorientation. Just as important is the reader's understanding of what is not in the database. It can be terribly frustrating if readers think that something of interest is in the database, but they can neither find it nor convince themselves that it is not there.

In writing articles, the hypertext author is free (and encouraged) to use high-level concepts and terminology. Novices can select the terms to learn about them while knowledgeable readers can move ahead to more complex topics. For example, in a historical database, key events, people, or places can be mentioned without description, and novices can follow the links to read the articles in related nodes if they need background material. The database on Austria and the Holocaust was based on people, places, events, organizations, and social organizations. These could be mentioned freely throughout the text and readers could follow the links to find more. Names of people or places that were not in the database were mentioned only when necessary and with a brief description.

Hypertext is conducive to the inclusion of appendices, glossaries, examples, background information, original sources, and bibliographic references. Interested readers can pursue the details while casual readers can ignore them.

Creating documents for a hypertext database introduces some additional considerations beyond the usual concerns of good writing. No list can be complete, but here again this list, derived from our experience, may be useful to others:

1. Know the users and their tasks: Users are a vital source of ideas and feedback; use them throughout the development process to test your designs. Realize that you are not a good judge of your own design because you know too much. Study the target population of users carefully to make certain you know how the system will really be used. Create demonstrations and prototypes early in the project; don't wait for the full technology to be ready.

2. Meaningful structure comes first: Build the project around the structuring and presentation of information, not around the technology. Develop a high concept for the body of information you are organizing. Avoid fuzzy thinking when creating the information structure.

3. Apply diverse skills: Make certain that the project team includes information specialists (trainers, psychologists), content specialists (users, marketers), and technologists (systems analysts, programmers), and that the team members can communicate.

4. Respect chunking: The information to be presented needs to be organized into small "chunks" that deal with one topic, theme or idea. Chunks may be 100 words or 1000 words but when a chunk reaches 10,000 words the author should consider restructuring into multiple smaller chunks. Screens are still usually small and hard to read, so lengthy linear texts are not as pleasant. Each chunk represents a node or document in the database.

5. Show inter-relationships: Each document should contain links to other documents. The more links contained in the documents, the richer the connectivity of the hypertext. Too few links means that the medium of hypertext may be inappropriate, too many links can overwhelm and distract the reader. Author preferences range from those who like to put in a maximum of one or two links per screen, to the more common range of two to eight links per screen, to the extremes of dozens of selectable links per screen.

6. Be consistent in creating document names: It is important to keep a list of names given to documents as they are created; otherwise, it becomes difficult to identify links properly. Synonyms can be used, but misleading synonyms can be confusing.

7. Work from a master reference list: Create a master reference list as you go to ensure correct citations and prevent redundant or missing citations. Some hypertext system automatically construct this list for you.

8. Ensure simplicity in traversal: Authors should design the link structure so that navigation is simple, intuitive, and consistent throughout the system. Movement through the system should be effortless and require a minimum of conscious thought. Find simple, comprehensible, and global structures that the readers can use as a cognitive map. Be sensitive to the possibility that the user will get "lost in hyperspace" and develop the system so recovery is simple.

9. Design each screen carefully- Screens should be designed so they can be grasped easily. The focus of attention should be clear, headings should guide the reader, links should be useful guides that do not overwhelm the reader. Visual layout is very

important in screen design.

10. Require low cognitive load - Minimize the burden on the user's short-term memory. Do not require the user to remember things from one screen to another. The goal is to enable users to concentrate on their tasks and the contents while the computer vanishes.

Creating the introduction

A key design issue is how to organize the network and how to convey that order to the reader. Some documents begin with an Executive Overview that summarizes and provides pointers to sections. Some reference books have a main table of contents that points to tables of contents for each section or volume. Most books start with a hierarchical table of contents. These models can be a guide to authoring strategies for creating the root document:

1. Make the root document an overview that contains links to all major concepts in the database [glossary strategy].

2. Adopt a hierarchial approach in which the links in the root document are major categories [top-down strategy].

3. Organize the root article as a list or table of contents of the major concepts in the database [menu strategy].

The suitability of the different authoring strategies will depend upon the purposes and anticipated use of the database.

Article size: Small is beautiful (usually)

A major concern to authors of hypertext databases is determining the optimal length for documents. Research suggests that many short documents are preferable to a smaller number of long documents.

An experiment was performed at the University of Maryland using the Hyperties system in which the same database was created as 46 short articles (from 4 to 83 lines) and as 5 long articles (104-150 lines). Participants in the study were given 30 minutes to locate the answers to a series of questions by using the database. The 16 partcipants working with the short articles answered more questions correctly and took less time to answer the questions.

The optimal article length may be affected by such variables as: screen size, nature of task, session duration, and experience of user. One problem with databases consisting of many small articles is that it increases the amount of navigation the reader must perform.

Converting exisitng documents and files

Converting existing documents into hypertext form is a major concern of hypertext developers. Thousands of large online databases already exist and are available via information retrieval systems such as DIALOG, BRS, or Nexis/Lexis. Putting these databases in hypertext format would be a monumental task. Links would need to be placed in each record (document) and browsing capabilities added to these databases. If links were to be established across databases, they would need to have comparable structures.

It seems likely that many existing databases will be converted to hypertext form (for example the Oxford English Dictionary and the AIRS Bible projects). In some cases, only new records added to databases will contain coded links suitable for hypertext.

In the personal computer domain, text conversion is much more feasible since most PC based hypertext systems accept standard ASCII files as input. Most existing documents can be converted to ASCII format. This leaves the task of identifying links using the authoring capabilities of the hypertext program.

Many documents to be converted contain various kinds of graphics. The conversion of graphics to hypertext format is problematic. Graphics file formats differ widely across systems. Modern digitizing technology makes it possible to convert most graphic images from paper to electronic form so they can be incorporated into hypertext databases. However, the degree of manipulation possible with the graphic once in electronic form (e.g., resizing, rotation, cropping, etc.) depends upon the graphic editor available.

There is good reason to hope that processes for automatic conversion will be widely developed. We have already succeeded in converting databases with explicit and consistent structure that contained in document formatting commands. The process involves writing a grammar and parser for the input and a generator to output the articles and the links.

Managing a hypertext project

Each project is different and each manager may have different styles of work, but again our experience may be useful for others. This list can surely be extended:

Identify application that satisfies the Golden Rules of Hypertext

- Large body of knowledge separable into smaller components
- Interrelated components
- User needs only a slice at any time

Design knowledge structure

- Specify goals, market niche & audience
- Decide on scope of coverage
- Identify list of topics and components

     - Choose traversal structures

Prepare material

     - Collect or create material
     - Develop a style sheet for writing articles and creating links
     - Ensure appropriate cross referencing to related concepts
     - Arrange for editing of text and graphics
     - Secure legal permissions
     - Create database in proper formats
     - Work with graphic artists to create images

Run test

     - Insist on multiple reviews of the database
     - Test hardware, software & database
     - Test browsing and fact finding
     - Capture usage data
     - Revise and refine
     - Prepare acknowledgements and credits

Dissemination

     - Develop package design and installation instructions
     - Start with small group and expand
     - Provide consultation for problems
     - Plan improvements

Each of the more than thirty hypertext databses we have built was different. We try to begin by forming a clear concept of the structure of the entire database and its sections. For example, in the database on Austria and the Holocaust, topics were chosen by lead historian Marsha Rozenblit who identified five categories: people, places, events, organizations and social movements. We find it extremely helpful to write an initial list of proposed articles so that authors would have a good idea of which links might be added as they write their articles.

A key step is writing the introductory article which conveys the overall concept and points to the key articles in the database. These key articles point to each other and to secondary articles. The Table of Contents is a second chance to provide orientation for the reader and we generally revert to traditional indented formats found in most books. Adding a Table of Figures to the Table of Contents seems important since most readers of books and hyperbooks like to look at pictures. In many project we use some articles as a sub-index to give a tabular list of articles on a common topic. For example, in the Guide to Opportunities in Volunteer Archaeology, there are lists of dig sites by geographic regions and by historical periods.

Once a few articles, say 10%, have been written it is important to try browsing the database to see if the organization is comprehensible and if the writing style is acceptable. Some projects began with long articles (*CACM* July 1988 Special Issue on Hypertext) which seemed more attractive when separated into smaller articles. Other projects

(EDUCOM Conference Guide) consisted of almost entirely one-page articles. We regularly discuss the number of links per screen and take advice from reviewers and usability testers. A frequent policy is to highlight only on the first occurrence of a term in an article to reduce distracting clutter.

A devoted managing editor is necessary to move the writing along, coordinate with graphic artists, ensure that reviews are done, guarantee that copy editing and final fixes are performed diligently, and to handle the disk production in a timely fashion. Our projects were in the range of 1 to 4 month efforts by 2 to 5 people with additional consultations from reviewers. Sometimes projects stretched over more months if reviews took longer or if later changes were needed. The Hyperties author tool greatly facilitates productivity as we and several others have found: "Overall Hyperties offered the best platform for creating links to references and pictures." (Harris and Cady, 1988).

Acknowledgements and credits should be handled in an explicit and professional manner. The many participants, including the hypertext editors/authors, graphic artists, copy editors, reviewers, and programmers should be recognized. Hypertext, like movie production, can involve dozens of people and it is perfectly acceptable to have a long list with specific roles identified.

Final production details like the packaging design and manufacturing, contents of the disk labels, instructions in paper and disk formats, creation of installation programs, and coordination with distributors must all be handled carefully. An excellent effort on the contents becomes lost if the packaging permits damage to the product or the user can't follow the instructions to load the database.

The Psychology of Hypertext

From the earliest literature on hypertext (e.g., the July 1945 *Atlantic Monthly* article "As We May Think" by Vannevar Bush), much emphasis has been placed on the idea that hypertext structures data in a manner similar to human cognition: in particular, the organization of memory as an semantic network in which concepts are linked together by associations.

If this is valid, it suggests that hypertext should be an efficient way of learning. Learning theory would predict that hypertext should improve meaningful learning because it focuses attention on the relationships between ideas rather than isolated facts. The associations provided by links in a hypertext database should facilitate remembering, concept formation, and understanding.

In addition, the greater sense of control over the reading process may produce increased involvement and desire to read more. In the same way that computer games can be very absorbing because of the high level of interactivity, hypertext databases may be very engaging too.

Getting started

Once you have a feel for hypertext, the next step is to experiment with creating your own hypertext documents. You will need to obtain an authoring system and might start with something familiar such as your Hyper-resume, especially if you already have the contents in machine-readable form. Another modest start would be a personal autobiography or a family newsletter or family tree in hypertext form.

More ambitious projects (a day or two of work) might be to implement part of a personnel policy database where you work, a community Hyper travel guide for your neighborhood (restaurants, stores, emergency services, etc.), or maybe a personal database of your cassette tapes, antiques, or books. These projects would compel you to organize the knowledge in some structured form, recognize relationships within and across groups of nodes, identify the central ideas that would become links from the root document, and decide how to use graphics.

Once you are satisfied with the modest project you can move on to a major project that might occupy you for several weeks or months. There are many attractive candidates and some of them could become viable commercial ventures. Repair manuals, training manuals, advertisements, corporate annual reports, organization trees for large companies, travel guides, sports and entertainment databases, and self-help guides are all possible. And just for fun why not mystery novels, joke books, and adventure games. Let your imagination be your guide!

Acknowledgements

Hyperties has been under development since 1983 and many people have participated in its design and refinement. Dan Ostroff created the initial versions in APL, then converted to C, and has remained an important influence. Janis Morariu and Charles Kreitzberg provided valuable design guidance. Paul Hoffman and James Terry of Cognetics Corporation have worked hard to convert our software to a solid commercial product. Many others participated in developing various versions on the IBM PC and the SUN including major contributions from: Kobi Lifshitz, Richard Potter, Bill Weiland, Don Hopkins, Rodrigo Botafogo, and Catherine Plaisant-Schwenn.

Initial funding came from the US Department of Interior in relation to the US Holocaust Memorial Museum and Education Center, where David Altshuler and Anna Cohn were early supporters of our vision. Later support for our user interface and hypertext work came from Apple, AT&T, IBM, Museum of Jewish Heritage, NASA, and NCR. We are grateful to all the institutions and individuals that recognized the importance of our efforts.

Parts of this paper were drawn from *Hypertext Hands-On!*, written with Greg Kearsley and published by Addison-Wesley, Copyright 1989.

References

Conklin, Jeff, Hypertext: A survey and introduction, *IEEE Computer 20*, 9, (September 1987), 465-472.

Haris, Margaret and Cady, Michael, The dynamic process of creating hypertext literature, *Educational Technology 27*, 11, (November 1988), 33-40.

Koved, Larry and Shneiderman, Ben, Embedded menus: Selecting items in context, *Communications of the ACM 29*, 4, (April 1986), 312-318.

Koved, Larry, Restructuring textual information for online retrieval, Unpublished Masters Thesis, Department of Computer Science, University of Maryland Technical Report 1529 (CAR-TR-133), (July 1985).

Kreitzberg, Charles and Shneiderman, Ben, Restructuring knowledge for an electronic encyclopedia, *Proc 10th Congress of the International Ergonomics Association*, (1988).

Marchionini, Gary and Shneiderman, Ben, Finding facts and browsing knowledge in hypertext systems, *IEEE Computer 21*, 1 (January 1988).

Morariu, Janis and Shneiderman, Ben, Design and Research on The Interactive Encyclopedia System (TIES), *Proc. 29th Conference of the Association for the Development of Computer Based Instructional Systems*, (November 1986), 19-21.

Mumford, Lewis, *Techniques and Civilization*, Harcourt Brace Jovanovich, New York, NY, (1934).

Shneiderman, Ben, User interface design and evaluation for an electronic encyclopedia, *Proc. of the 2nd International Conference on Human-Computer Interaction*, Honolulu, HI, August 1987. In G. Salvendy, Ed., *Cognitive Engineering in the Design of Human-Computer Interaction and Expert Systems*, Elsevier Publishers, Amsterdam, (1987a), 207-223.

Shneiderman, Ben, User interface design for the Hyperties electronic encyclopedia, *Proc. Hypertext '87*, (1987b), 199-205.

Shneiderman, Ben and Kearsley, Greg, *Hypertext Hands-On!*, Addison-Wesley Publ., Reading, MA, 1989.

Weldon, L. J., Mills, C. B., Koved, L., and Shneiderman, B., The structure of information in online and paper technical manuals, *Proc. Human Factors Society - 29th Annual Conference*, Santa Monica, CA, (1985), 1110-1113.

Authoring Tools for Complex Document Sets

Janet H. Walker[1]
Digital Equipment Corporation
Cambridge Research Laboratory

Complexity is the hallmark of large, real-world document sets. This paper describes experience with one such document set, the tools developed for dealing with it, and how using those tools affected both the process of documentation and the eventual result.

Introduction

When any entity increases in size by several orders of magnitude, it changes in nature as well as in size. This observation applies to realms as diverse as organizations and manufactured objects; increasing size leads to qualitative change, not just quantitative change. A number of computer science researchers from diverse corners of software research have also made this observation concerning programming [1, 4, 6].

The same observation holds in the world of writing and documentation -- bigger documents differ in nature from smaller ones. It is significantly more difficult to write a report than to write a memo and more difficult yet to write a large manual than to write a report. The effects of scale on documentation and its writers, however, remain largely unexplored. What are the qualitative effects of increasing size on a documentation effort? Are large documentation projects similar to other complex development efforts? How do designers of document authoring software support this increase in size and complexity? This paper attempts to address some of these questions by example.

An Engineering Metaphor

Building documentation is a form of engineering very similar, from an abstract point of view, to building programs. The similarities in nature of these two activities suggested that there could be similarities in engineering procedure as well. That is, building programs could be used as a metaphor for building documentation; environments for building documentation and software could both provide similar features to their engineers. Since software development had been studied more extensively than document engineering and had more elaborate processes to offer, it was instructive to see what software engineering could offer to document engineering. In this paper, I report on a project that used a software development environment as a model for the general management of complexity in the development process, extending it to apply to document development.

In software engineering, two major concepts are applied to complexity management; they are *modularity* and *abstraction*. Modularity is the result of designing a program as a number of small pieces, the modules, from which the software artifact is constructed. Abstraction is the act of naming something and using it for what it does (in a problem sense) instead of for how it works (in an implementation sense [4]).

In programming, effective modularity is not attained simply by breaking a program into arbitrary pieces. Rather the pieces are designed to serve some specific, clear purpose in the overall system. The essence of modularity lies in designing the pieces so that each does one thing well and can be maintained independently of the others [6]. To achieve that clarity, the pieces must have minimal relationships with other pieces and any remaining relationships must be explicit rather than hidden or implied. Dijkstra [4] points out that clarity has a quantitative aspect as well; something long is not likely to be clear. These considerations suggest that pieces should be small and that their contents should reflect some single, simple purpose. Thus, the goal in software is to define pieces that are small, self-contained, mutually independent, general, and hence easy to maintain.

Completing a large software project, even one with a well-chosen modular design, is a tough job because complexity always remains due to the sheer number of pieces to be managed. Current research in software development environments is directed toward improving the development process through better management of the pieces. A programming environment to manage complexity derives much of its power from knowledge about the modules constituting the software and how they are related to each other. In an environment like Symbolics Genera [14], this base of knowledge is maintained for the most part automatically by the system rather than manually by the programmer.

Modularity in documents

In thinking about complexity and development, one is struck by the thought that the concepts of modularity and powerful development environments could serve writers as well as programmers. After all, writers and programmers work with similar material -- collections of details are composed to constitute an integrated whole. In fact, programs and documents are often closer in structure than such a description might suggest, as a programmer might write a piece of code to implement some element of a modular specification produced by a writer. The correspondences between the products suggest that correspondences between the tools would serve writers well.

Once this premise has been accepted, the first question that arises concerns the nature of modules in a document. Remembering that the essence of modularity is the independent, self-contained nature of the modules, one can rule out arbitrary units such as pages or screens as candidates for the modules in a document system. By analogy with software concepts, a module in a document would be a semantic unit of information. Such a unit would be self-contained, minimally entangled semantically with other parts of the document, and would maintain its facts mostly independently from the rest of the document. Well-designed modules could be developed, tested, and maintained essentially independently of each other.

On one scale, this suggestion is nothing new; modularity in documentation has been espoused by others (for example, Horn [5]). Indeed, modularity such as I have been describing is a fundamental concept of good technical communication. This project took the concept a step further, however, in providing a software environment that made the modularity in documents explicitly visible to the writers and provided support for them to work with it.

An experiment in creating a large modular document set

This part of the paper describes how an existing document set was converted to explicit modular form. The document set in this part of the project was produced by Symbolics, Inc. for Release 4.5 of its software product. The documentation contained approximately 2,500 pages of material, comprising several books and numerous large updates.

The document set was in a state that is all too familiar to computer industry customers. An original set of manuals had been followed quickly by about six sets of release notes to the point where the unintegrated release notes were equal in thickness to the original manuals. The document set was unmaintainable by the then state-of-the-art tools at our disposal. At that point (mid 1983), we made the decision to adopt an experimental modular technology [10] for the manuals in order to solve the immediate problems and to support future expansion and maintenance.

Conversion from machine-readable to modular form

The first step in the process was to convert the existing document set from a conventional, linear, text-file format to the experimental modular format. In this conversion project, we chose to work conservatively, going from a structure that we understood to another one that we understood. As it seemed most reasonable to attempt making one set of changes at a time, we left the organization alone and simply changed the underlying representation for it. That is, we did not undertake to disturb the rhetorical structure of the technical manuals themselves since the conventional organization of technical manuals is familiar to both writers and readers and shows no particular need for redesign.

Our document set used a familiar organizational strategy. It was written as a hierarchical document in which chapters corresponded to major content areas of the system. Within the chapters, introductory conceptual material came first followed by sections with functional groupings of material, each with its own introductory material.

The documents were automatically decomposed into modules along their existing hierarchical organizational lines. The original documents were logically modular but stored phsyically as sequential lines within a file. As shown in Figure 1, a document after the conversion process was explicitly modular, with modules appearing one after another in a file. Logically independent sections were now physically independent as well, with links being used to build up the logical hierarchy in the document.

Each chapter, section, or subsection in the original document became a separate module. Each time that a module was extracted from within another one, it was replaced with a link pointing to the newly created module. As a result, the logical hierarchical information was carried not by physical placement but by explicit links from within one section to another section; sections were thereby only logically contained within chapters instead of physically contained.

For example, one chapter in Figure 1 consists of three sections. After conversion, the piece that represents the chapter contains pointers that identify each of the three contained sections by name. Seeing these pointers makes the structure of each piece clear to the writer and also gives information about the level of abstraction of any particular piece.

At this point in the conversion process, the documents had metamorphosed from simply being "machine-readable" to being physically modular. It is interesting to consider what actually happened to the documents as a result of this process. Most simply, we had created a document that is composed from pieces.

Figure 2 shows a simple, annotated example of part of a document as a

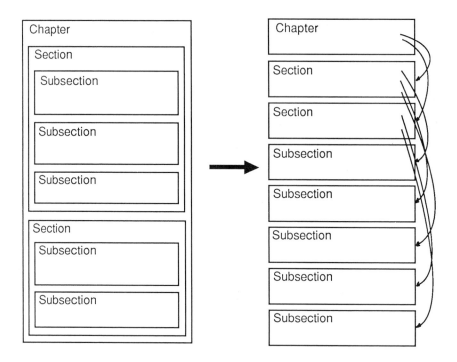

Figure 1. Decomposition of a conventional, hierarchical, linear document to modular form.

writer saw it. The pieces in Figure 2 have visible physical boundaries and all have names reflecting their contents or intent. (The names for the pieces were taken from the original chapter and section names.) The exact internal structure of each piece is visible, consisting of literal content as well as pointers to its various constituent pieces.

The content of a piece tends to vary depending on its level of abstraction in the document. For example, a subsection piece might have no included pieces, just narrative explanation. The further up in the logical hierarchy a piece is located, the more likely it is to consist primarily of pointers to other pieces rather than running text.

In any case, the main difference between the two representations of a book is that, after conversion, the physical structure of the modules mirrors the semantic content of the information. From the writers' point of view, this book is still exactly the same as it was before conversion. Assuming that the material is then formatted appropriately for the readers to see on paper or on a screen [11], it is

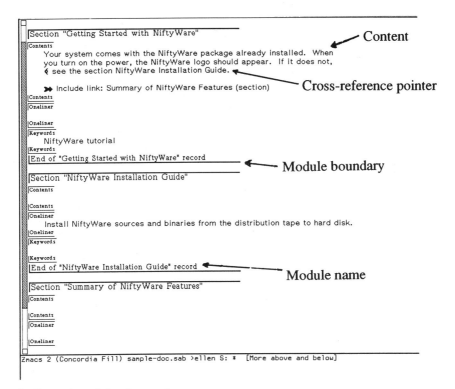

Figure 2. Several modules from a document.

also still the same book to the readers. As a result of the structural conversion, though, the structure of the book is now processable by software. That is, software tools can be written to assist writers in developing and maintaining the books and also to assist readers in using them.

Implementation Detail

The original book sources were in several source languages, including Scribe [8] and a special purpose formatter language from MIT. Translation programs were written to transform the files from these conventional markup languages into the modular form described above. Special cases not handled by the translation software were resolved by hand. At the time of the original conversion, the modular format itself was implemented using a textually embedded language with a syntax like that of Scribe [10]. This textual representation of structure was later replaced by an object-oriented structure whose visible characteristics are described later in this paper.

The whole conversion process took about four months, during which the writers also merged the text of the original documents with the many versions of release notes. The process of converting from one representation to the other was simply a mechanical source translation, taking relatively little time. The process of merging the content was much more daunting; some sections had been updated more than once, others had been deleted altogether or superseded. Identifying and rationalizing all the content changes needed was a challenging project for the writing group.

Further modular refinement

In the course of merging original and revised versions, the writers became aware of major structural problems in the existing documentation. During the next major development phase of the documentation, they undertook to *remodularize* the document set. That is, they made changes that transformed the documentation from being merely physically modular to being functionally modular. For example, the original documentation contained many cases where the material in a section did not match the title, where a jumble of topic areas was treated in a single section, and where certain sections could be understood only in the context of others that were not explicitly cited.

The remodularizing was a necessary precursor to making the documentation really usable online. With online lookup, users can request access directly to any individual section, independent of context. Thus it was essential to put the content where the users were going to look for it, which meant careful modularization.

During this process, the writers worked on making modules exhibit the properties of good modularity. As mentioned earlier, modules should be small, self-contained, and maintainable independently of other modules, with any relationships to other modules made explicit.

The following kinds of changes were made to the document set during the remodularizing project. Having visible module boundaries made it easier to see when material had "slopped over" from an adjoining section; material was then moved into the sections where it belonged. Long, rambling sections were teased apart into their component topics and made into separate modules within a new hierarchy. Locality was improved by putting all material that belonged together into the same module or structure. Titles were modified (usually lengthened) to make them better reflect the intent of the section. Most anaphora was removed, with words like "above" and "below" being banished. Topic sentences were scrutinized to ensure that the first sentence in a module related to its own content rather than being transitional material implicitly dependent on some section that used to precede it. Many explicit cross-references were added to replace the relatedness information that had previously been carried by physical adjacency in the document. Redundant material was identified and moved into independent, re-usable modules.

This process was carried out in parallel with ongoing development activities and took about a year.

Modules and links in a document set

In going through the process described above, we refined our understanding of the nature of modularity in documents and the criteria to use in decomposing some area of knowledge into modular topics in a document.

The primary consideration in creating the modular structure for a document came from viewing its modules as semantic building blocks. Material that con-stituted a self-contained unit of information -- corresponding to a fact -- belonged in a module. The names of the modules formed the set of topics with which users accessed the documentation; hence the naming of the modules was a very impor-tant aspect of the ultimate usability of the document.

In addition to these semantic building-block modules, writers created modules for information, standalone or not, that was needed in multiple places in the document set. For example, a standard phrasing used throughout the docu-ment set to describe a common option would be made into a separate module and simply included throughout. These modules were semantic building blocks of another kind -- ones that were not complete in themselves but were designed to be used only within other modules. They were commonly used only for their con-tents rather than to create a new hierarchical level within the document.

So far in this paper, the process of putting together a document from modules has been described mostly vaguely, using words like "pointers" and "include." In fact, the mechanism for composing modules into a document is called *linking*. The ideas of modules and linking that we used in this project are much the same as those used in hypertext [2, 3].

Links function in two different ways in creating a document. A link can specify that the module it points to is to be included in the document or it can specify that the module is to be referred to, as in a cross-reference. Examples of how these two kinds of links appear to a writer are shown in Figure 3. Each basic kind of link has several variants, which determine exactly what is to be included or how the cross-reference is to appear [7].

The basic *Include* link was used to define the organizational structure of a document. These links were used to put the document set back together after it had been broken up into modules. Other variants of inclusion links simply in-clude parts of other modules transparently, without any effect on the hierarchical

➤ Include link: NiftyWare Installation Guide (section)
➤ Contents link: Summary of NiftyWare Features (section)
❮ Precis link: Summary of NiftyWare Features (section)

❮ See the section Getting Started with NiftyWare.
❮ Getting Started with NiftyWare
❮ Invisible link to "Getting Started with NiftyWare" Section

Figure 3. Examples of how links appear to a writer. The top set shows variants of inclusion links and the bottom set shows variants of cross-reference links.

structure. The cross-reference links serve to define the nonstructural interrelationships and associations between the topics.

Document Engineering Environment

This section briefly describes the engineering environment that was built to assist writers in handling documents composed from distinct modules. The philosophical orientation behind the design was that document engineering is just like software engineering (only harder) and that given tools like those provided by a software engineering environment writers should be able to work more effectively to produce better documents.

The engineering environment, known as Concordia[2], is an extension of the Genera software development environment provided on single-user workstation computers from Symbolics, Inc. [14, 12]. The important aspect of Genera for this discussion is *data-level integration*, that is, the fact that all of the processes running in a machine share the same data objects, so that it is possible to write highly integrated software applications. Concordia offers the same development paradigm to writers as Genera provides for programmers and is implemented as a seamless extension of Genera.

The most important aspect of the document set in its transformed state was its explicit modularity. It was crucial to provide support for modularity so that the modular structure was not just in the minds of the writers. To this end, we built a *structure editor* for the documents. This editor was implemented as an extension of the standard Zmacs editor in the Genera environment [15].

The structure editor was not simply text-based; it had knowledge about the modular structure of the files. The editor maintained an internal representation of the buffers being worked on that was more than simply a stream of characters. Like many editors, the editor maintained its internal representation of the file as a list of lines. The contents of the lines, however, could be data objects rather than simply characters. In addition, the collection of lines was organized as a hierarchical structure in which a top-level editor node corresponded to a module in the document. Essentially, the editor worked with data, not with text. It maintained full knowledge of the modular structure within a particular buffer and provided editing commands appropriate to the kind of data being edited at any given moment.

The editor was implemented so that the writer was working with a mixture of text and data. For material that looked like ordinary running text, the writer used the ordinary text editing commands. For structural material (like module boundaries or links to other modules), the writer used specialized structure commands. Text commands did not apply to structure; conversely, structural commands did not apply to text. In a sense, this distinction was internal to the editor; writers did not have to issue mode-switching commands to move from one kind of editing to another.

The commands themselves knew what they applied to and the editor knew whether any object on the screen represented text or structure. The writer knew which data were which because they looked different. So, if it looked like text to a writer, the editor knew it was text and would permit text-oriented commands to apply to it. Structure commands were similarly specialized in the implementation; link commands were available to operate on links but would not erroneously operate on module boundaries, and so on.

The editor interface supplied specialized commands for dealing with modular structure and linking. Figure 4 shows the editor as it would appear to a writer, with the major module and link support commands appearing in a menu along the right edge.

Writers chose commands from the menu to create or manipulate modules. The main part of the screen in Figure 4 shows two newly created modules. Creating these modules involved choosing the appropriate command from the menu and supplying names and types. The rest of the display was generated by the editor. There is no way to type in or textually modify this structural markup and, as a result, no possibility for syntax errors in markup.

The links between modules were also maintained as structure objects rather than as text. To create links to other modules, writers chose commands from the menu instead of typing in a link. In this way, the links between modules were all *symbolic* and hence the software could keep track of them, providing services beyond what could be offered with text alone. For example, the linking relationships between modules could be examined graphically; all modules making cross-

```
═════════ Concordia ═══════                    📄E    📄P    📄G
Cursor in: Section "NiftyWare Installation Guide" (disconnected)   Editor commands

   ➤ Include link: Summary of NiftyWare Features (section)          Links
|Contents|                                                           Show Links From Record    m-X
|Oneliner|                                                           Show Links To Record      m-X
                                                                     Graph Links From Record   m-X
|Oneliner|                                                           Collect Record Name       m-X
|Keywords|                                                           Create Link               m-X
   NiftyWare tutorial                                                Create Link and Record    m-X
|Keywords|                                                           Find Link                 m-X
End of "Getting Started with NiftyWare" record                       Reverse Find Link         m-X

Section "NiftyWare Installation Guide"                             Records
|Contents|                                                           Beginning                 s-A
|Contents|                                                           End                       s-E
|Oneliner|                                                           Mark                      s-H
                                                                     Create                    m-X
|Oneliner|                                                           Edit                      s-,
|Keywords|                                                           Kill                      m-X
                                                                     Add Record Field          m-X
|Keywords|                                                           Rename                    m-X
End of "NiftyWare Installation Guide" record                         Preview                   s-P
                                                                     Check Spelling            m-X
Section "Summary of NiftyWare Features"                              Show Records in Buffer    m-X
|Contents|                                                           Reorder Records           m-X
|Contents|                                                           Move Records Among Buffers m-
|Oneliner|                                                           Add Patch Changed Records m-X
                                                                     List Changed Records      m-X
|Oneliner|                                                         Markup
|Keywords|                                                           Beginning                 s-(
                                                                     End                       s-)
|Keywords|                                                           Create                    s-M
End of "Summary of NiftyWare Features" record                        Make Language Form        s-L
                                                                     Remove Markup             s-^
Section "NiftyWare Sample Session"                                   Change Environment        m-X
                                                                     Kill                      s-K
                                                                     Find Markup               m-X
                                                                     Reverse Find Markup       m-X
                                                                     Find Markup String        s-S
                                                                     Reverse Find Markup String s-R
                                                                   Topics
                                                                     Show Outline              m-X
Zmacs 2 (Concordia Fill) sample-doc.sab >ellen 5: *  [More above and below]   Collected Record Names
                                                                     Getting Started with NiftyWare
                                                                     NiftyWare Installation Guide
                                                                     Summary of NiftyWare Features
```

Figure 4. Screen display of the structure editor, showing an empty template for a new module.

references to a particular module could be examined one at a time; a module could be renamed without affecting any of the modules linked to it. This base of knowledge about the modules and their relationships, maintained automatically by the software, formed the basis for the services provided by the environment.

Evaluation and Discussion

Has this modular methodology had any effect on the books created by using it? In some ways, no, and in other ways, yes. Although the overall appearance of books to the end user remained almost the same, the process of creating and maintaining the books changed markedly over several years experience.

Effect of modular methodology on books

Rhetorical structure. The rhetorical structure of most books remained the same as before and the same as that conventional for large technical document sets. In some ways, this was a result of a major constraint on the writers, which was the need to produce a set of books that could be printed on paper, serving readers of paper as effectively as books produced with conventional technology. It was also a simple economic constraint, in that no resources were available for completely reorganizing books whose only problem was that they were conventionally organized. Additionally, we knew of no research evidence that the conventional structure fails to serve its readers. Hence, leaving the book structure alone while learning the technology was quite likely the wisest choice.

Several experiments with book organization were possible, however, for new books. In one case, a writer produced a users' guide simply by reusing modules from existing books. The shared modules thus were located in two separate books. Only online readers would have any opportunity to be aware of the two separate contexts for the material. To make it possible to reuse material, writers negotiated compromises about what to cover in a section and how to cover it.

In several new book projects, writers separated reference material and conceptual material into two distinct subvolumes. The first subvolume consisted of explanatory material, functional groupings of concepts, and summaries of capabilities. These sections made heavy use of symbolic references to relevant parts of the second subvolume, which consisted of a "dictionary" of reference material, with the reference modules arranged in alphabetical order. This style of book requires extra attention to making explicit cross-references to related modules, particularly in the reference sections, to replace the relatedness information that is otherwise carried by proximity in a conventionally organized book.

The most interesting change in book organization came in the release notes. In many conventional systems, release notes consist of documentation for each change in the release. Such documents are not integrated with the system documentation. In this experimental release notes structure, changes were put directly into the main document set, and the release notes consisted primarily of links to modules in the main documents. Figure 5 diagrams this experimental approach to release notes.

The amount of effort required to produce release notes was substantially reduced because there was no duplication of effort involved in producing both complete release notes and fully updated main documentation.

Impact of modularity. The books were better organized as a result of the remodularizing project and subsequent attention to modular style. The sections were more self-contained and each unit of information had an appropriate location. More explicit cross-references were used.

Titles became longer and more explicit. Writers found that this helped them during writing to recognize what it was that they were putting into a section. It

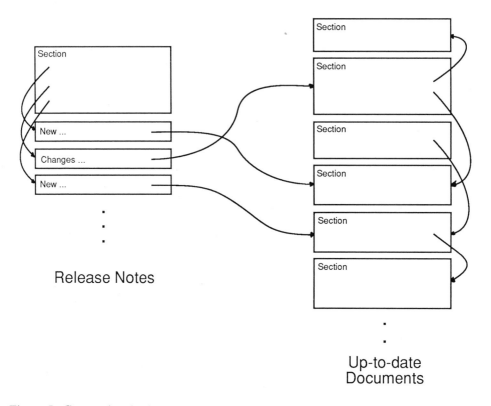

Figure 5. Conventional release notes are independent of the system documentation that they describe. Experimental release notes used links to refer to changed sections without duplication of effort.

also helped readers determine whether a particular section contained what they wanted to find out about. An interesting side effect of the move to more explicit titles was a reduction in the amount of indexing done by hand (since all titles appeared in the index automatically, sorted under each of the major content words).

Effect of modular methodology on projects and process

Distributed responsibility. With the document set organized like a database to which all the writers shared access, writers tended to have topic responsibility rather than the conventional physical volume responsibility. For example, the person responsible for network documentation would write network-related modules to be included in the users' guide and perhaps other books, as well as in the network book itself. Once the writing group had decided on the overall structure of the document set, following through on individual assignments was easier than in conventional projects (where a writer "owns" a physical book).

Moreover, simple errors could be fixed by anyone who discovered them. Some errors were easier to fix than to report; writers and programmers could simply make changes, like fixing typographical errors, unencumbered by ownership constraints on document modules.

A more important manifestation of distributed responsibility appeared in several cases where software developers wrote first draft modules of reference material for the writers. Without having to understand how the writer wanted to organize the book, the programmers could simply provide the basic reference material in a modular form that the writer could then incorporate directly into prototype books simply by creating links to the new material. This turned out to be a more efficient communications medium between programmers and writers than previous methods based on files, interviews, or electronic mail.

Workstyle. The modular development environment supported both major approaches to a writing project: top-down and bottom-up. People who worked top-down could create a fully elaborated set of empty modules, defining the whole structure without supplying any content details. It was easy to work with this structure, modify it, and begin filling in the content without having to change tools (for example, from an outliner to an editor). People who worked bottom-up could start writing modules for facts that they discovered, in advance of making any decisions about how to organize the books. This ensured that material was not lost and avoided the duplication of effort that comes from organizing material twice, once as a collection of rough notes and again as it goes into a book.

The group used both workstyles, with some individuals using both approaches, depending on the project and their needs at the time.

Review process. Because books were being built as a collection of modular pieces, many pieces were complete and ready for use long before the full books were assembled. These completed pieces were available to other writers and to software engineers via the online delivery system for the documentation [11]. As a result, parts of the documentation were in use for months during development. The usability feedback obtained in this way was very useful to writers; the opportunity to give substantive comments early in the cycle allowed programmers to prevent misconceptions from becoming entrenched in documents.

People reported and tracked "bugs" in the documentation using the same tools employed by the software engineering group. Informal reviews were easy to obtain as writers could ask programmers for comments on individual modules. The overall result of these procedural differences was document sets of higher quality for less perceived review effort.

Conclusions

By mid-1988, the Symbolics, Inc. document set maintained with this methodology had grown to around 10,000 pages, roughly quadrupling in size since its original conversion. This dramatic increase, however, had not led to equally dramatic increases in the difficulty of maintenance or production. In fact, most users were unaware of the major changes in the document set. Changes were incorporated easily and manuals reprinted for major software releases with very little production effort. An even larger document set has been created elsewhere with the same technology [9]. These concrete accomplishments, along with interview comments from writers using the system [13], indicate that the approach taken has been effective in the task of managing the complexity inherent in developing large document sets.

Acknowledgments

Many people contributed to the design and refinement of the software described in this paper. Primary thanks are due to Richard L. Bryan for his implementation prowess. Early management commitment was provided by Ilene H. Lang. I am grateful to all the writers and editors in the document engineering group at Symbolics, Inc. for their enthusiasm and support for this project.

Notes

[1] The work reported in this paper was performed while the author was employed by Symbolics, Inc.

[2] Concordia is a trademark of Symbolics, Inc.

References

1. Abelson, H., Sussman, G. J., with Sussman, J.. *Structure and Interpretation of Computer Programs*. MIT Press, Cambridge, Massachusetts, 1985.

2. Akscyn, R. M., McCracken, D. L., & Yoder, E. A. "KMS: A Distributed Hypermedia System for Managing Knowledge in Organizations". *Communications of the ACM 31*, 7 (1988), 820-835.

3. Conklin, J. "Hypertext: An Introduction and Survey". *IEEE Computer 20*, 9 (1987), 17-41.

4. Dijkstra, E. W. Notes on Structured Programming. In *Structured Programming*, Dahl, O.-J., Dijkstra, E. W., & Hoare, C. A. R., Ed., Academic Press, London, 1972.

5. Horn, R. E. Engineering of Documentation - The Information Mapping Approach. Published in 1986. Available from Information Mapping, Inc., Waltham, MA.

6. Kernighan, B. W. & Plauger, P. J.. *The Elements of Programming Style*. McGraw-Hill, New York, 1978.

7. *Concordia Document Set.* 1st edition, Symbolics, Inc., Cambridge, MA, 1988.

8. *Scribe Document Production Software.* 4th edition, UNILOGIC, Ltd., Pittsburgh, PA, 1985.

9. van Sickel, P., Sierzega, K. F., Herring, C. A., Frund, J. J. Document Management for Large Systems of Equipment. RIAO 88: User-oriented content-based text and image handling, Centre de Hautes Etudes Internationales d'Informatique Documentaire, 1988.

10. Walker, J. H. Symbolics Sage: A Documentation Support System. Intellectual Leverage: The Driving Technologies, IEEE Spring Compcon84, San Francisco, 1984, pp. 478-483.

11. Walker, J. H. Document Examiner: Delivery Interface for Hypertext Documents. Proceedings of the Hypertext '87 Workshop, Chapel Hill, N. C., November 1987.

12. Walker, J. H. "Supporting Document Development with Concordia". *IEEE Computer 21*, 1 (1988), 48-59.

13. Walker, J. H. The Role of Modularity in Document Authoring Systems. Proceedings of the ACM Conference on Document Processing Systems, Santa Fe, New Mexico, December 1988.

14. Walker, J. H., Moon, D. A., Weinreb, D. L. & McMahon, M. "Symbolics Genera Programming Environment". *IEEE Software 4*, 6 (1987), 36-45.

15. Walker, J. H. & Bryan, R. L. An Editor for Structured Technical Documents. Protext IV: Proceedings of the 4th International Conference on Text Processing Systems, Boole Press, Dublin, Ireland, 1987.

Limited Freedom:
Linear Reflections on Nonlinear Texts

Joseph T. Jaynes

Apollo Computer Inc.
330 Billerica Road
Chelmsford, MA 01824

The author describes a document retrieval architecture designed to provide electronic access to hardcopy documents generated by multiple publishing systems to readers using a variety of workstations in heterogeneous network environments. He discusses several implications for such a system, focusing especially on the practical and rhetorical limitations of a nonlinear approach to certain classes of instructional texts.

Introduction

Since the earliest days of electronic computing, people have sought to use these machines to help them make sense of the real (and increasingly complex) world around them. Indeed, one might argue that this is the computer's primary function: to order, analyze, and render intelligible the vast sea of information with which we must cope in the daily business of living. It is a considerable irony, then, that the machines themselves have been so difficult to understand and use: so seemingly resistant to "seamless interaction" with those they are intended to serve. The instructional texts associated with their use – often embodied by shelf after shelf of documentation – has itself historically been an imposing barrier to understanding. This vast, impenetrable forest of processed paper has done as much to dampen the spirits of would–be beneficiaries of the power of computers as has the poor quality of the user interfaces which the books struggle valiantly to describe. Even when the books are lucid and well–written, the simple problem of access to the appropriate book in the appropriate revision frequently defeats the reader. It is no wonder then, that people have longed for the day when the machine could serve as an aid to its user, helping to manage and present information about itself as well as about the problems to which it is principally devoted.

Of course, much can and has been done to make user interaction with computers more intuitive and less blatantly obstructive to learning. Yet these improvements have merely reduced the volume of the problem, not removed it. Computer system components (both hardware and software) are intrinsically complex and hence, almost by definition, difficult to describe and more difficult to understand. No matter how "user-friendly" the interfaces become, the sheer number of components and functions mandates explanatory prose in some form or other.

That prose has traditionally taken the form of hardcopy user manuals; it is access to the information in this class of instructional text that concerns us here. As computer power has increased, designers and documenters have envisioned increasingly sophisticated aids for system-related information retrieval and analysis. The fundamental nature of many of the systems being proposed (and in some cases, vigorously marketed) under the banner of "hypertext" or "hypermedia" technologies is increasingly at odds with the more traditional approach to information delivery. This paper discusses a software system which adopts a still more radical approach: namely, it delivers traditional manuals to readers via the agency of the computer screen rather than the printed page. Readers retrieve and interact with hardcopy page images, using retrieval mechanisms which are completely familiar to them from the hardcopy analogs. The "radical" nature of this system lies in the assumption that, at least insofar as instructional texts of this type are concerned, the traditional linear approach to textual presentation of information (albeit enhanced by several extensions made possible by computers) is eminently more practical and theoretically valid than the adoption of more fashionable nonlinear approaches. After we examine the architecture of the system, we move on to a discussion of its practical advantages in real-world publishing environments. Finally, we explore the theoretical foundation for the proposition that the interests of readers engaged in problem-solving are best served by placing limitations on their freedom.

Domain/Delphi:
Putting Apollo's Hardcopy Manuals Online

The Technical Publishing department at Apollo Computer Inc. has long recognized the potential of high-performance workstations to deliver "online documentation" in novel yet effective ways. The advanced technology that characterizes today's technical workstations — bit–mapped displays, high–speed networking, distributed data and computing resources all packaged in units offering mainframe computer performance at personal computer size and cost — makes solutions to document delivery and retrieval that were previously unthinkable now practical and economical.

Domain/Delphi, introduced in February 1988, was Apollo's first serious foray into the electronic document retrieval arena. It provides Apollo customers the option of purchasing manuals in two forms: on paper (hardcopy) or online.

Offering documents electronically as well as in hardcopy provides several benefits to readers. Because the contents of the Domain/Delphi online document databases are identical to those of the corresponding hardcopy books, confusion arising from discrepancies between the information on the screen and in the manuals disappears. Most computer users are familiar with the experience of reading one thing online, only to have that instruction contradicted or confused by a hardcopy rendition of the same information. Which one is to be believed? Since the electronic documents in Domain/Delphi derive from the same source files as the hardcopy documents, such discrepancies are impossible. The documents are guaranteed to be identical. (Unfortunately, consistency does not imply veracity ... but that is a different problem!)

An additional advantage of electronic document delivery is that one electronic document can service hundreds of users in a network, thereby improving the availability and easing the maintenance burden of the document. Documents can be shipped to customers on the same magnetic media as the products themselves, and can be installed in tandem with those products. Users are thus assured of document availability; something which is far from certain when manuals and media take different forms.

For large communities of network users, the cost savings for electronic documents (compared to multiple copies of hardcopy books) can be substantial as well. They can be significantly cheaper for producers to manufacture, warehouse, and ship; those savings are passed on to the users. Our experience shows that electronic documents become cheaper (to say nothing of more useful) for customers with installations of five or more workstations, assuming that such customers would purchase multiple copies of hardcopy manuals to satisfy their user base.

The Domain/Delphi Library Metaphor

Domain/Delphi's state-of-the-art user interface (designed and implemented with Apollo's user interface design tool, Domain/Dialogue™) models the information retrieval tasks that readers already know how to perform. The interface is mouse-driven, with clear, comprehensible functions and universally-available "quick help" prompts to assist the user whenever guidance is necessary. Users are performing productive document searches within minutes. More importantly, Domain/Delphi gives readers of Apollo documentation a single electronic document retrieval interface for a set of manuals produced in a heterogeneous publishing environment. The reader does not know or care whether the document of interest was produced with Interleaf TPS™ or UNIX® troff. The display software makes the differences transparent to the reader and renders the pages of interest in the appropriate fashion.

Since Domain/Delphi is an interactive delivery system for the manuals on a bookshelf, its design reflects their structure. The online document set is represented as a group of libraries, each of which contains several books. Books are composed of chapters and sections, just as they are in hardcopy. When the reader uses Domain/Delphi to locate a piece of information, the program determines the proper portion of a book to be displayed and then presents it for viewing. Displayed pages contain text fonts and graphics identical to their hardcopy counterparts, making the electronic versions attractive and easy to read. Once a document is displayed, the user may scroll from page to page, search for specific text strings in the document, copy and paste text to other Apollo workstation windows, and generally manipulate the pages in the same ways that one manipulates other text on the screen.

Locating Information

When a reader takes a hardcopy manual in hand to search for some piece of information, she has two choices (ignoring, of course, the option of opening the book at random and flipping pages):

- turn to the index to get a pointer to a topic
- traverse the table of contents to locate the information hierarchically

Domain/Delphi gives readers the same two options, extended over multiple books. The reader can perform an indexed search for topics, directing Delphi to search only those books that she thinks are appropriate. And readers can traverse the global "table of contents" to locate their topics hierarchically. Thus readers use Domain/Delphi to retrieve information in ways already familiar to them.

Highlights

Domain/Delphi provides the following capabilities.

- Displayed pages with multiple text fonts and graphics

- User–tailored keyword searches. Readers may constrain topical searches to cover only those books in which they have an interest.

- Hierarchical browsing. Readers may browse through a global "table of contents" to locate pertinent information.

- Personal Reference Lists. Readers may maintain an individualized list of frequently used documents to provide direct access to needed information.

- Dedicated process and window. Domain/Delphi runs in its own process and window; documents are retrieved without interrupting ongoing work in other processes and windows.

- State maintenance between sessions. Domain/Delphi remembers your search constraint preferences and Reference List items from session to session.

- User–friendly interface with universal "quick help." Interacting with Domain/Delphi is as simple as "point and click."

Domain/Delphi and the Domain Environment

Domain/Delphi takes advantage of many of the advanced capabilities of the Domain computing environment. Domain/Dialogue™, Apollo's user interface management system, provides the foundation for Domain/Delphi's graphical user interface. Apollo's CODASYL database management system, D3M™, assures high–speed data access and retrieval. The Public Domain network environment allows hundreds of users to share Domain/Delphi data residing on a single host disk while maintaining "local–disk" performance. Finally, Domain/Delphi is fully integrated with Apollo's Display Manager, making retrieved text available to other windows through the standard "copy and paste" text operations. (For a more thorough discussion of the features of Domain/Delphi, see [Orwick, 1986].)

System–independent Domain/Delphi

But Domain/Delphi does not go far enough. It addresses the heterogeneous publishing system environment to some extent, but only for persons reading Apollo books while seated at Apollo workstations in Apollo networks. Given the headlong rush toward platform independence among computer buyers and software suppliers which typifies the industry today, such limitations are clearly unacceptable. To meet this requirement for openness, Apollo has developed "system–independent" Domain/Delphi: a portable, modular electronic document retrieval system designed to execute on multiple hardware platforms while handling documents produced by multiple publishing systems.

While the intent of system–independent Domain/Delphi is similar to its predecessor — namely, to provide one consistent reader interface into an extended space of electronic documents — the underlying design of the system is radically different. The heart of the architecture (Figure 1) is the "System Core": a set of routines which arbitrate all system functions. The System Core contains three objects:

- the Generic System Manager (GSM), which provides the primary system control functions. It handles program startup, composes database search requests and interprets the results, maintains state information for all system–independent Domain/Delphi functions, and handles orderly program shutdown. The user interface calls the GSM through a standardized, published call interface.

- the Generic Display Manager (GDM), which oversees the rendering of documents on the screen (initializing the display area, opening a document at a specific point, etc.), and interaction with that document (scrolling, copying and pasting, searching for text strings, etc.). When the user initiates a display–related event, the UI calls the GDM to interpret that request and invoke the specific routine(s) in the appropriate Vendor Display Module (VDM) to carry out the request. The user interface calls the GDM through a standardized, published call interface.

● the HyperLink database, which contains data describing cross–reference links between retrievable documents. This database is kept independent of the heterogeneous document database modules (see below) to provide inter–database link capabilities. Both document producers and readers may create links and navigate between documents using this mechanism.

While many of the software modules that make up system–independent Domain/Delphi may be supplied by vendors other than Apollo Computer (indeed, such modularity is a key design feature of this architecture), the GSM and the GDM form the foundation upon which all other functions are built, and remain the prerogative of Apollo. This component will persist in all future implementations of the system.

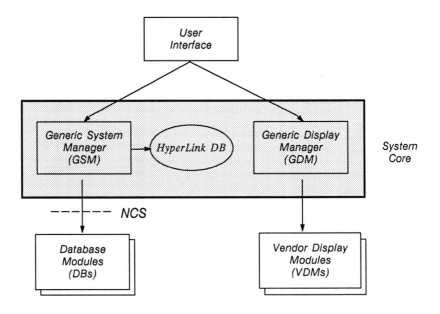

Figure 1. System–Independent Domain/Delphi Document Retrieval Architecture

Other components of system–independent Domain/Delphi include:

- The User Interface (UI), which intercepts user interaction events (keystrokes, mouse movement, etc.) and passes them to the GSM and GDM for interpretation and execution. This may be an Apollo UI implemented with Open Dialogue™, or one provided by some other user interface management system. When implemented in Open Dialogue, the document retrieval user interface is portable to all hardware platforms supporting the X11 windowing system. Thus readers can have a single retrieval interface, regardless of the brand of workstation that they are using.

- Database modules (DBs), which process keyword search and browsing requests and return results to the GSM. Multiple, heterogeneous database modules may execute in multiple processes on multiple computers running in parallel — dramatically improving database performance. Communications and data transfer with the GSM are layered on Network Computing System™ (NCS) protocols, making possible support of foreign databases on foreign hardware platforms. All DBs must conform to the standardized call interface required by the GSM.

- Vendor Display Modules (VDMs), which perform the actual text and graphics display and interaction operations. These modules may be supplied by publishing system vendors to render the documents which they have produced. The VDMs communicate with the GDM via a standardized, published display call interface. The architecture also permits extensions to handle video and audio data, since these may be viewed simply as additional "display types" to be rendered by the appropriate VDM. Users may even add support for their own display types by binding special modules directly to system–independent Domain/Delphi's executable code. All VDMs must conform to the standardized call interface required by the GSM.

Reviewing Our Basic Assumptions

As we have seen, Domain/Delphi provides electronic access to a wide variety of hardcopy document sets. To be sure, the power of networked workstations offers significant extensions to traditional information retrieval paradigms, and Delphi exploits those to the fullest. Hierarchical browsing and indexed topical searching can span multiple volumes; writers and readers can create and maintain dynamic cross–reference links between documents; "documents" themselves can be any textual or graphical object that may be rendered on a computer screen. But the system's fundamental design center — to deliver hardcopy documents electronically — remains intact. This runs somewhat counter to current fashion, which declares that traditional rhetorics and modes of discourse have given way to a brave new world of hyper–everything, where readers are free to indulge their investigative urges in a vast constellation of factual data points. As we will see, this approach to information retrieval — at least as it relates to instructional texts such as computer documentation — fails to fulfill adequately the legitimate needs both of readers and of writers, and so must be reconsidered as the "ultimate answer" for all learning situations (specifically, when problem–solving is the reader's primary motivation).

Practical Considerations

To begin with, let us consider the dilemma facing the writer seeking to illuminate the troubled reader. It is appropriate that we begin by considering the writer, for this individual's needs are almost completely ignored by the hypertext publishing systems being touted today. The writer's primary concerns for the class of texts being considered here are as follows:

1) to provide information that is accurate and complete. To err (either by omission or by commission) is a mortal sin. Instructional texts must be, first and foremost, truthful and sufficient Readers turn to such texts for factual enlightenment, not opinion.

2) to provide information that is on time. Being late is as unacceptable as being wrong, since the documents exist primarily to support other hardware or software products. Those products cannot (or at least, should not) be released without the accompanying documents explaining their use.

> With very rare exceptions, products lacking documentation
> are unfit for use.

3) to provide information that is pertinent to the reader's
    needs. Documents and the knowledge that they contain
    must be relevant and accessible. This is the most intangi-
    ble goal, and hence the most difficult to achieve. Most
    often, writers know only when they have failed on this
    score. At such times, comments such as "I can never un-
    derstand what I'm supposed to do!" or "The instructions
    would be fine if I could just find them in this mountain of
    paper!" signal that relevance or accessibility are lacking.

Any solution or system which hampers a writer's ability to meet any of
these goals will be unacceptable in a real–world publishing environment. For
example, adopting a system that significantly increases the time required to
generate a document (hyper or otherwise) will be ruled out since it violates
principle number 2, even if it enhances principles 1 and 3. Time–to–market
pressures make speed a requirement as well as a virtue. Consequently, any
electronic information delivery system that hopes to succeed in the current
market environment must at a minimum be as time–efficient as current systems.

In similar fashion, any system that requires the writer to maintain one
set of documents for hardcopy production and a separate set for use online
strains principles 1 and 2, since this implies duplication of effort with a resulting increase in maintenance costs and opportunities for discrepancy.
Writers will be the first to say that there is already insufficient time to do a
proper job with one set of books, much less two. And economic realities are
such that few departments can afford the staff needed to duplicate documents required by two production models.

The Domain/Delphi architecture satisfies the writer's fundamental requirements by building on the hardcopy document production process. Instead of requiring that writers duplicate their efforts by creating a separate
production stream for electronic documents, Domain/Delphi delivers electronically the products of the existing hardcopy production stream. Although
this cannot guarantee that documents are truthful, it does guarantee that
hardcopy and online documents are consistent since both systems derive
their content from a single source of information. Coordination and change

tracking problems are thus eliminated. The single source approach also helps the documents achieve the timeliness requirement by streamlining the production process. Finally, Domain/Delphi improves documentation accessibility by eliminating the production, distribution, and maintenance headaches of paper books. The electronic documents are always available, always current, and always easily searched for pertinent answers to pressing problems.

Readers, too, derive practical benefits from this approach. In addition to the benefits which they derive as customers of such a system (discussed previously), they also find Domain/Delphi extremely easy to learn and to use. When we adopt the hardcopy metaphor in the electronic sphere, we hasten reader acceptance and speed learning: everyone already understands how to use books. Training is reduced to an explication of those features which are unique to electronic access, such as index searches spanning multiple volumes and the use of hyperlinks to build and maintain associations between related documents. Even the latter task models the traditional concepts of cross–referencing and footnoting, allowing readers to master the operation quickly.

Theoretical Underpinnings

Yet it is the theoretical foundation upon which this system rests which provides the greatest incentive for acceptance. If there is one fundamental construct upon which the relationship between writers and readers of instructional texts is built, it is this: that the two collaborate in the construction and reconstruction of mutual understandings. Unstructured hypertext environments are by their very nature antithetical to the motivations and requirements of both group of individuals.

Readers *learn* by discerning and internalizing structure. Indeed, "construction and reconstruction" presuppose the existence of structure. But what does "structure" mean in this context? To begin with, structure can be taken to mean "sequence." When we learn (which is our ultimate goal when consulting the types of documents under consideration here), we do so in large part because we perceive — and come to expect — sequence. We scan a painting and absorb its meaning because we have a sense of what has passed and what is to come. When such expectations are violated — for instance, in the paintings of M. C. Escher — we experience a serious sense of disruption and dislocation. While this may be a valid artistic result from Escher's perspective, it is not the result that one appreciates here. In a similar fashion, abstract paintings do not "teach" in the same way that representational paintings often do. This is not to imply that they are without value or somehow less worthy of our appreciation; only that such abstractions create a sense or mood rather than a lesson.

What is it about hypertext that so captures our fancy? I believe that it is the way in which link traversal models the imaginative process. Hypertext systems give readers (often total) control to move through a complex space of data points, exploring those items that tweak their interest, following branches as whim dictates.

The question here, however, can be stated bluntly. Is this what readers of computer books really want — or more importantly — really need? Is this the best way to communicate specific, instructional ideas between the writer (who's job, after all, is to help the reader understand on an intellectual rather than emotional level) and the reader (who has turned to the text specifically for intellectual enlightenment rather than entertainment or pleasure)? I maintain that the unstructured roaming encouraged by conventional hypertext systems is antithetical to the needs of both.

We have no need of hypertext systems to teach us this lesson. The evidence is abundant in reader reactions to traditional "reference" documents. Such documents provide a compendium of information; the reader is usually left to his own devices to figure out how these myriad "chunks" of information interact and pertain to the solution that he is trying to discover. Readers are adamant in their dislike for such forms of documentation, except in those instances when brief, specific memory refreshment is in order. ("Let's see, to print a file I should type 'pr filename ...'") They demand tutorials, and task–oriented handbooks ... anything to provide structure, to synthesize the data into meaningful answers to specific problems. Readers have little time and less interest in exploration; they want to be led.

When we generalize from the small scale bewilderment that characterizes such behavior to the confusion threatened by unstructured access to the vastly expanded information space offered by the networks, databases, and electronic libraries which are becoming commonplace, we cannot help but pity the reader who is told to "enter and explore" to locate the answer to his problem. Now he has an even greater problem; much more than being "lost in hyperspace," he might actually be in danger of the paralyzing vertigo that is said to afflict astronauts engaged in extravehicular activities when they confront the endless depths of space that stretch beyond comprehension in all directions. "Enter and explore" is a condemnation, not a solution.

The reader's need for guidance has much to say about the role of writers. Far more than mere compilers of discrete information "chunks" that are to be assembled at the whim of the reader, writers provide a critical service: they synthesize the available information into forms designed to address the particular needs of particular readers, and thus add important value to the process. They construct meaning out of madness. They take a resume and transform it into a biography.

It is instructive, too, to note the general failure of texts designed from the outset to be free-form and specifically random. The experiment fails in fiction as well as in instruction. As experimental fiction, for instance, William Burroughs' *The Naked Lunch* attempts to demonstrate a formless art.

> [He] sought a self-abolishing structure, and tried to defeat our
> codes of continuity, cultural and temporal, by shuffling his
> prose into random order. "Writers until the cut-up method was
> made explicit," he says, "had no way to produce the accident
> of spontaneity." But it seems that in the logic of the situation
> we shall find such accidents happy only when we see in them
> some allusion, direct or ironical, to our inherited notions of
> linguistic and narrative structure; and I am not surprised that
> Mr. Hassan, a notable exponent of Burroughs, finds the
> method successful only when it is clear that so far from seem-
> ing random the collocations appear to be skillfully contrived."
> [Kermode, 1966]

In a similar manner, "stream of consciousness" novels seek to mimic the unboundedness of the conscious — and often, unconscious — operations of the human mind. These novels are interesting to read, and of great literary value. But they do not teach us useful things except indirectly as we can puzzle them out. Readers of instructional texts come to their books because they already face a puzzle for which they require an answer. For their information retrieval mechanisms to present them with an additional puzzle does them an inexcusable disservice.

Frank Kermode argues persuasively that our "sense of an ending" — in other words, our implicit understanding of the boundedness of our existence (by birth and death, for instance) — is *the* mechanism by which we render reality comprehensible. Without the formalisms that structure provides, the chaos of reality (and the reality of chaos) becomes overwhelming. Of course, an overly strict devotion to structural formalisms can divorce us from reality and result in myth–making: an extreme also to be avoided. Judiciously applied, however, the ordering mechanisms of the human mind protect our sanity and survival.

This ordering mechanism is exactly what a skillful writer provides. Whether the result is a strictly linear text (such as a bound volume) or a more loosely linear text that offers multiple directed pathways through the information web (such as is provided by books made available electronically via Domain/Delphi), the reader is instructed to follow rather than encouraged to wander. Unstructured roaming through the hypertext landscape may be appropriate for a multitude of situations. But when readers need specific answers to specific questions, a more limited freedom is in fact the more efficacious approach.

References

Jaynes, J. T., T. R. Barstow, P. A. Leeds, S. W. Cuti. "Publishing Books Electronically in the Networks of Tomorrow: A Vision of the Present," *Proc. Online Information '88,* (London, 1986).

Kermode, Frank. *The Sense of an Ending: Studies in the Theory of Fiction,* Oxford University Press (New York: 1966), p. 118.

Orwick, P., J. T. Jaynes, T. R. Barstow, L. S. Bohn. "DOMAIN/DELPHI: Retrieving Documents Online," *Proc. CHI'86 Human Factors in Computing Systems,* (Boston, 1986), ACM, New York, pp. 114–121.

Apollo and Domain are registered trademarks of Apollo Computer Inc. D3M, Network Computing System, Domain/Dialogue, and Open Dialogue are trademarks of Apollo Computer Inc. UNIX is a registered trademark of AT&T in the USA and other countries. Interleaf and TPS are trademarks of Interleaf, Inc.

From Database to Hypertext Via Electronic Publishing: An Information Odyssey

R. John Brockmann
Associate Professor, Concentration
    in Business & Technical Writing
204 Memorial Hall
University of Delaware
Newark, DL 19716

William Horton
William Horton Associates
1523 Ward Avenue NE
Huntsville, AL 35801

Kevin Brock
Viar & Company
300 North Lee Street
Alexandria, VA 22314

An information odyssey

This is a story of a journey—of information flowing and changing as it cascades from writer to publisher to reader. It is the story of the writing and publishing of a traditional paper book using electronic publishing tools and of the metamorphosis of that book into hypertext.[1]

We primarily set out on this journey to make use of some bits and pieces of information we had collected over the years and "to make a little beer money." Bill and John had a library of maxims and aphorisms developed during years of teaching students and professionals in technical communication and computer documentation. It seemed that whenever John would encounter former seminar participants, previous undergraduate students, or readers of his textbook[2], he would often find that on quizzing them what stuck in their minds were some key aphorisms or maxims such as:

> The only unchanging rule in technical communication or computer documentation is that the audience is always right
>
> The best type of technical communicator or computer documenter is an ego-less communicator or documenter.

Bill's assorted "Horton's Laws" had appeared in odd corners of pages in a wide number of journals for the apparent purpose of filling the blank space. For example, in the March 1988 issue of *IEEE Transactions on Professional Communication* on a leftover verso half page, the following appeared:

> *Horton's Heuristic #43:*
> Don't start writing on-line documentation until you have good paper documentation.
>
> *Horton's Paradox # 43*
> If you have good paper documentation, you may not need on-line documentation.

Now it's pleasant to know that students remember aphorisms, and that magazines and journals print such heuristics and paradoxes, but it was difficult to collect them all systematically in one place. Thus we wanted to collect all these bits and pieces of information in one place and create a simple, fun paperback book and a hypertext document.[3]

A secondary goal of the journey was to learn first-hand about electronic publishing tools and hypertext; for as Mark Twain said long ago:

> War talk by men who have been in a war is always interesting, whereas moon talk by a poet who has not been in the moon is likely to be dull.

In the tradition of all stories of wandering heroes, we begin our story with a map. Paperback editions of Homer's *Odyssey* often contain a map showing the travels of Odysseus, and Bibles frequently include maps showing the travels of St. Paul. Our map shows the paths traveled by our information on its way to our readers. The path taken is a bit more complex than we originally planned, but then aren't all odysseys? We had anticipated a simple, straight-forward, information assembly line from writers to publisher to reader. But insights, dead ends, discovered opportunities, bugs in the software, and serendipity all combined to turn our assembly line into a rich adventure.

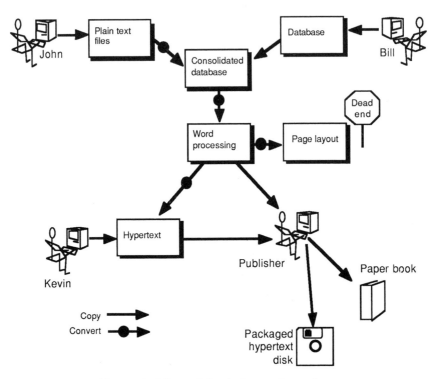

Figure 1 Map of the information odyssey

Throughout this project, our information went through a number of transformations. Each form had its own distinct characteristics and its own inherent advantages and disadvantages. Converting information from one form to the next sometimes required complex procedures to avoid losing organization or formatting added in earlier stages. Often drama and tension accompanied our efforts to convert from one file format to another without losing hard-won information. Sometimes we succeeded, sometimes we did not.

First let us take you with us on our odyssey, and then we'll share with you seven insights we gained during that journey. We think that our odyssey questions Dorothy's claim that "There's no place like home"; for we found much more excitement in electronic publishing than ever we experienced producing books using paper and pen.

In media res: plain text files

As we mentioned earlier, John and Bill had been collecting quotations, aphorisms, witticisms on the business of writing, along with good and bad examples. However, John had collected his in plain text files, while Bill had collected his in a database.

Plain text files are the bedrock of electronic publishing. They are the ultimate in simplicity and the lowest common denominator for all word-processing systems. They make the minimum assumptions about hardware and software; and, except for an ASCII code for representing characters, they have no formatting conventions. Because the ASCII code is used on all but the most ancient mainframe systems, it is the *lingua franca* of computerdom.

Plain text files are open and accommodating. They place no restrictions on what you put in them or how they are represented. This meant that John could enter information quickly without having to meet the requirements of an arbitrary format or structure. It also meant that he could freely intermix different types of information in the same file. This early freedom, however, proved expensive.

Converting plain text files to database

To consolidate our two separate collections, we imported John's plain text files into Bill's database. Consolidating our information this way let us take advantage of the organizing and searching capabilities of the database. Bill's database, *Double Helix II*, could import data from plain text files;[4] but this first required creating a form containing separate fields for each type of information in the plain text files. For quotations this form included fields for the quotation itself, the author's last name, the author's first name, and the source of the quotation. These fields had to be arranged in the order the fields occurred in the plain text file. We also had to flag the corresponding pieces of data in the plain text file by separating them by some special character, a "#", for instance.

We thought we could do this using the search-and-replace feature of a word-processor. We soon discovered a problem: inconsistency For example, the author's name followed the quotation but not always in the same way. Most often it was preceded by <Return> <Tab> <Em-dash> <Tab>. Sometimes the <Em-dash> was a <Hyphen>, an <En-dash>, or two <Hyphen>s. And sometimes the second <Tab> was a <space> or two. Searching and replacing on every combination of characters proved necessary[5], but about 95% of the quotations were imported perfectly. About 3% required minor touch up, and the remaining 2% required retyping. This first surprise on our odyssey made us realize:

> Inconsistency thwarts conversion.

The consolidated database

After importing John's text file of quotations into Bill's quotation database, the consolidated database became the "working draft." In many ways a database is the opposite of plain text files; a database has a very regular, orthogonal structure, while plain text files have no real structure at all.[6]

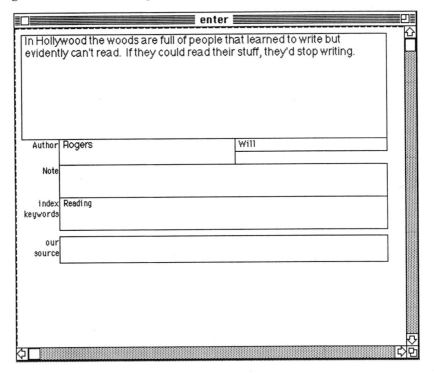

Figure 2: Quotation in the database

The database has certain characteristics that proved valuable, especially when gathering and organizing data. Since information is entered into forms with boxes or slots for each piece of information, the database implicitly prompts the writer to include all the required information. And, by standardizing the entry of information, the database enforces consistency among items; each item has the same components in the same order.

The strongest advantage of the database was its ability to index, sort, and retrieve information based on different criteria. For instance, we could have the database sort quotations by subject or by author's name. We could thus gather all the quotations by Will Rogers as well as all the quotations about the subject of "reading". We could also retrieve quotations on several criteria at once. For instance, we could ask what Will Rogers had to say about reading.

We soon discovered that such retrieval and indexing was valuable in checking and cross-checking information, and with it we quickly identified duplicate quotations. We found, for instance, that the quotation "I would have written less if I had had more time" was attributed to Mark Twain, Benjamin Franklin, and Blaise Pascal, and each attribution had a separate reliable source.

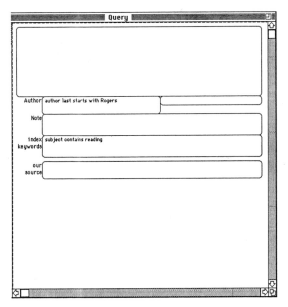

Figure 3: Specifying a query for the database

But a database also has disadvantages; often it is like Procrustes who reshaped and stretched his guests to fit their beds. Since all the information in a database has the same format and the same components, all items are reduced to the same level. While this promotes consistency, it can also distort items that do not fit the mold, and thus tempt the writer either to omit items that do not fit easily or to force fit them into an inappropriate form.

Originally we tried to use just one database, treating everything as if it were a quotation. But examples, Latin aphorisms, historical events, and bad advice simply did not fit this pattern at all. So it was only after much agonizing that we gave in and created separate databases for these items. This second surprise on our odyssey led us to the rule:

Let the data shape the database and not vice versa.

Another disadvantage of some databases is that they reveal only one unit of data at a time. Viewing a single quotation at a time makes comparison and contrast impossible. This narrowing of scope we called the Cyclops syndrome—all the information could be viewed only from one eye rather than the normal two-eye stereoscopic way. (This Cyclops syndrome resurfaced in a different guise in the the *HyperCard* version of the book. See Insight 6 for further exploration of this syndrome.)

The final problem with a database is that it is boring to read: every display looks the same as every other; typography is limited; and all the text in a single field must be the same type face, size, and style. A database is fine for gathering information and for retrieving it, but is boring to browse.

Converting the consolidated database to word-processing files

The next logical step on the odyssey to a published book was to convert the database to word-processing files. The database lacked formatting and page-layout controls necessary to produce camera-ready pages. Converting to word-processing appeared to require no more than dumping our data into a plain text file and reading that file into the word-processing program. But again, we encountered surprises with this approach: a loss of information identity and a loss of indexing.

Within the database, each field had a specific identity, and information in that field was a specific type. The information in the Author's First Name field was always the author's first name and could be accessed as such. In a plain text or word-processing file, text is text.

In the database we had entered indexing keywords to specify the subjects the quotations applied to, and our plan was to use these same terms in the index of the paper book. Our word-processing program, *Microsoft Word 3.01*, could automatically generate an index from index terms embedded in the text, but it required those terms to be in an intricate format, not easily produced directly from the database.

As a result, converting to word-processing required a series of automated and manual procedures to prevent loss of information identity and indexing. (As a side effect of this conversion we were able to consistently and automatically format the text in the word-processing files.) In brief the procedures involved:

1. Writing a simple program for organizing the output from the database. This program was written in the iconic programming language provided by the database. (A segment of the program is shown in Figure 4.)

2. Writing a C language program to rearrange the index terms in the order required by the indexing feature of *Microsoft Word*.

3. Reading the file into *Microsoft Word*.

4. Defining style sheets for each type of paragraph in the file: quotation, author, index entry, horizontal rule, and headings.

5. Use search-and-replace to put the text into the appropriate style and to insert additional characters and codes.

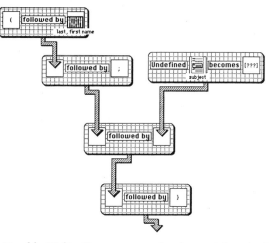

Figure 4: *Double Helix II* program for formatting index entries

With these steps completed, we felt like Odysseus after escaping the cave of the Cyclops; we could now see various pieces of information grouped together on a page allowing, and, in fact, inviting comparison and contrast. We had our normal stereoscopic vision back.

Word-processing files

Word-processing programs are familiar and flexible. The program we used, *Microsoft Word 3.01* for the Macintosh, was a full-featured word-processor with some page-layout features built in; style sheets for defining the formats of similar items and a page-preview window for seeing the layout of the page before printing.

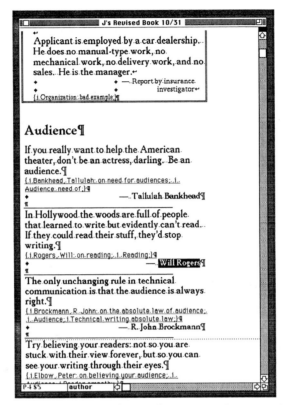

Figure 5: First page of *Almanack* in a word-processing file

But as with other word-processing programs *Word* lacked features for fine typography: its hyphenation and justification routines were rudimentary; it provided no form of kerning; and our choices in lines were limited to thick and thin. But *Word* did have the ability to automatically place page headers and footers, to include graphics, and to compile a table of contents and index from markers embedded in the text—but not without surprises.

Converting word-processing files to page-layout

The conversion to page-layout program was the simplest and least effective of the conversions on this odyssey. We chose a state-of-the-art page layout program, *PageMaker 2.0*, because it claimed to be able to read *Microsoft Word* files and keep *Word's* formatting intact. But in Figure 6 you'll see what the file lost after importing into *PageMaker* (compare this to the Figure 5).

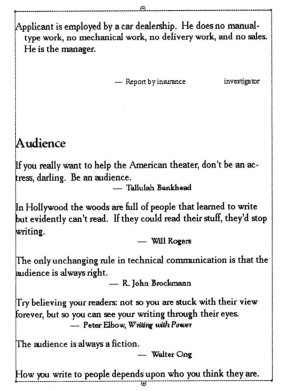

Figure 6: Page format after importing into page-layout program

The claim was half true; character formatting was preserved, but not paragraph formatting. Thus the words that were in bold or italic type in *Word* remained bold or italic, but the spacing of paragraphs and the rules and boxes associated with paragraphs were lost.[7] This third surprise on our odyssey revealed that:

> State-of-the-art software never quite matches writers' state-of-the-art expectations.

Page-layout: A dead-end

Page-layout programs let you apply more sophisticated hyphenation and justification routines than word-processing programs; they give the user precise control over arranging the graphics in a text, and over kerning and other features of fine typography.

But many page-layout programs, such as *PageMaker*, are designed for interactive layout of each individual page, not for automatic batch formatting of a long run of pages.[8] And, the thought of having to manually place 952 rules and to relocate them every time we inserted or deleted text proved to be a daunting blow to our plans.

Another limitation of page-layout programs is that many lack the ability to automatically compile an index, and we certainly did not want to incur Thomas Carlyle's nineteenth century curse:

> Those who write books without indexes ought to be damned ten miles beyond Hell, where the devil could not get for stinging nettles.

In summary, you may have noticed that the page-layout box on our Odyssey map, at the beginning of this article, has an arrow going in but none coming out. This is because for us the page-layout program was a dead-end. Confronted with the loss of formatting and the inability to produce an index, we realized we must compromise our original hopes to achieve our basic objectives with our available resources. This soul-searching forced us to realize that our primary goals were:

- Keeping the price of the final book under $10.
- Designing the book to resemble Benjamin Franklin's *Poor Richard's Almanack*.
- Preserving the "fun" persona.
- Providing an extensive index.
- Delivering the finished product within the seven month contract schedule.

To achieve these goals, we realized we must sacrifice fine control over kerning, rule widths, hyphenation, and justification. This sacrifice reminded us of one of Horton's Laws:

> A good book today beats a perfect one tomorrow.

Converting word-processing files to camera-ready copy

Late in the process we realized how electronic publishing tools had shifted the balance of power, responsibility, and labor from the publisher to the authors.

Traditionally the author submits a typescript and sketches, which the publisher has typeset, illustrated, pasted up, and printed. In our case we had agreed to provide our publisher with electronic camera-ready files. By our use of electronic publishing tools we had taken on nearly all the work but putting ink on paper. (In retrospect, perhaps we should have asked for a larger advance.) The electronic pages we sent the publisher were printed out and collected into signatures, photographed at the printing plant, and turned into printing plates. We don't mean to imply that the publisher was totally passive; he was actively involved in reviewing the various versions, but the control and responsibility for changes remained with the authors. But the shift in publishing balance does imply that we learned rather late in our odyssey that:

> Electronic publishing tools give the author more power, glory, and drudge work.

The first labor is completed: A paper book is born

Two days before Christmas 1988 it arrived—a wrapped package filled with the first fruits of the printing press. Seven months after signing the contract with the publisher, the book was done. Aside from entering the quotations and other items, our total time in designing, formatting, and organizing the book was probably no more than three person-weeks.

How well had we achieved our basic objectives? At $7.95 the price was well under our self-imposed limit. The page layout captured the character of Benjamin Franklin's *Poor Richard's Almanack*. The index was extensive—over 1,000 entries. And, most importantly, our readers felt it was fun and enjoyable to read:

> *The Writer's Pocket Almanack* will help you get your creative juices flowing. (*The Editorial Eye*, September 1988, p. 7)

> Brockmann and Horton's little book of quotations, aphorisms, and trenchant observations on the state of the writing art—and those who practice it—is a pleasant companion for a rainy evening, especially the kind of evening that follows the kind of day that writers and editors have all too often. (*IEEE Transactions on Professional Communication* 31 (3) September 1988, p. 149)

Are you tired of reading technical manuals? Do you long for an escape to fun reading? Well look no further. *The Writer's Pocket Almanack* is for you. (*Los Angeles Technograph* newsletter, May 1988, p. 11)

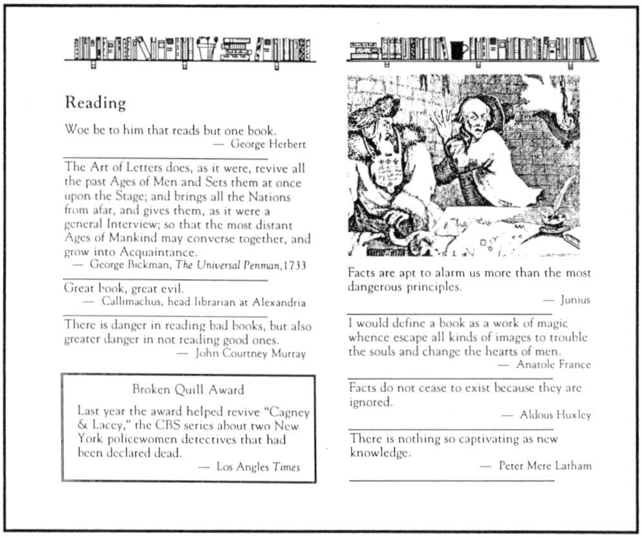

Reading

Woe be to him that reads but one book.
— George Herbert

The Art of Letters does, as it were, revive all the past Ages of Men and Sets them at once upon the Stage; and brings all the Nations from afar, and gives them, as it were a general Interview; so that the most distant Ages of Mankind may converse together, and grow into Acquaintance.
— George Bickman, *The Universal Penman*, 1733

Great book, great evil.
— Callimachus, head librarian at Alexandria

There is danger in reading bad books, but also greater danger in not reading good ones.
— John Courtney Murray

Broken Quill Award

Last year the award helped revive "Cagney & Lacey," the CBS series about two New York policewomen detectives that had been declared dead.
— Los Angles *Times*

Facts are apt to alarm us more than the most dangerous principles.
— Junius

I would define a book as a work of magic whence escape all kinds of images to trouble the souls and change the hearts of men.
— Anatole France

Facts do not cease to exist because they are ignored.
— Aldous Huxley

There is nothing so captivating as new knowledge.
— Peter Mere Latham

Figure 7: Two pages from the *Almanack* paper book

Although the book met its objectives, its very book-ness limited its usefulness:

- Browsing was confined to the book's sequential page order as determined by the authors.
- There was no automatic way to jump to logically associated but spatially distant pieces of information.
- It did not easily merge with our readers' electronic publishing and database tools; reusing material from our book required retyping, reformatting, and re-storing the material.

Publishing an online hypertext edition seemed the next logical step toward overcoming these constraints of the paper medium.

Converting word-processing to hypertext files

Converting the word-processing files from which the paper book was produced into *HyperCard* stacks and cards required all of a Saturday morning's work. (Each unit of information, be it quote or historical fact, was placed by itself on a **card**, a metaphor in *HyperCard* for a single screen. The cards of all the material in a single category, Mal Mots, for example, were then grouped together in a **stack**, a metaphor in *HyperCard* for a file of grouped information.) But crafting the resulting stacks to reuse all of the information imported from the word-processing files required a few more days.

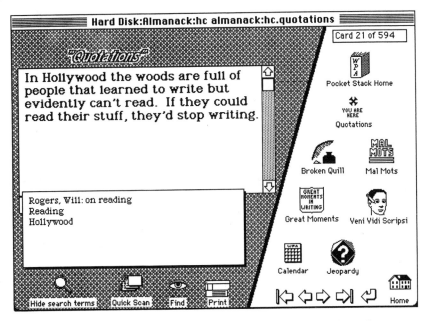

Figure 8: Card from the *Writer's Pocket Almanack*

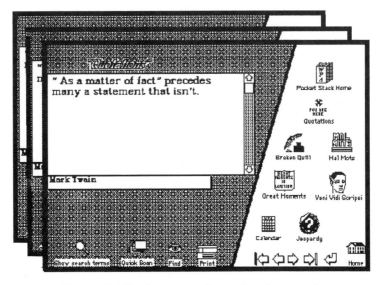

Figure 9: Cards grouped together in a stack

The conversion involved four phases:

1. Again separating Quotations, Mal Mots, Great Moments in Writing, and other items into different files.

2. Using search-and-replace to put <Tab> characters between each component of each entry.

3. Creating a *HyperTalk* script (a program in *HyperCard*'s programming language) to import each word-processing file into a separate stack. (A portion of the script for importing text is shown in Figure 10.)

4. Redesigning the appearance of the resulting stacks.

```
on mouseUp
-- Convert text file to HyperCards
  doMenu New Stack...
  ask "File to import?"
  put it into textFile
  put 0 into numOfFields
  open file textFile
  repeat until it is empty
    read from file textFile until tab
    add 1 to numOfFields
    if it contains return then
      exit repeat
    end if
  end repeat
  close file textFile
  domenu "Background"
  open file textFile
  repeat with x = 1 to numOfFields - 1
    read from file textFile until tab
    ask "Name for field" && x with it
    put it into nameForField
    put the number of background fields into fieldCount
    put fieldCount + 1 into newField
    put "Point and click at place for field"
    wait until the mouseClick
    put the mouseLoc into fieldLocation
    domenu "New field"
    put first item of fieldLocation into right
    add 160 to right
    put second item of fieldLocation into bottom
    add 20 to bottom
    put fieldLocation && ","&& right && "," && bottom into newLocation
    set rect of background field newField to newLocation
    set style of background field newField to rectangle
    set name of background field newField to nameForField
  end repeat
  read from file textFile until return
  ask "Name for field number" && numOfFields with it
  put it into nameForField
  put the number of background fields into fieldCount
  put fieldCount + 1 into newField
  put "Point and click at place for field"
  wait until the mouseClick
  put the mouseLoc into fieldLocation
  domenu "New field"
  put first item of fieldLocation into right
  add 160 to right
  put second item of fieldLocation into bottom
  add 20 to bottom
  put fieldLocation && ","&& right && "," && bottom into newLocation
  set rect of background field newField to newLocation
  set style of background field newField to rectangle
  set name of background field newField to nameForField
```

Figure 10: A portion of the *HyperCard* script used to import word-processing files

The second labor completed: A hypertext is born

In this stage, the data existed on-line and on-screen rather than on the printed page. This gave the data several unique attributes. The material from the book was re-divided into several different categories: Quotations, Broken Quill Awards, Veni Vidi Scripsi, Great Moments in Writing, and Mal Mots (the same categories as in the earlier database stage). And two new ways of using the data were added, a Calendar and a Jeopardy Game.

Because the data existed on-line, it was possible to establish relationships between the individual cards and stacks. In each of the five stacks, Cross-Stack buttons with icons symbolizing the target stack were added to allow the user to jump immediately from one stack to another. These buttons remained in the same place on each card while the icon for the current stack changed to a treasure-map cross mark with the message "You are here."

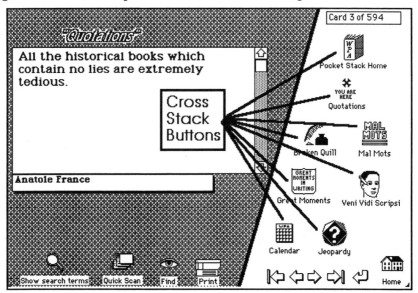

Figure 11: Cross-stack buttons to allow users to navigate between stacks

A Search Terms field was also added to each of the cards to allow the user to skip immediately to related information within the current stack by simply pressing the mouse button while pointing to a word in the field. Each card had several search terms based on the author, context, and content of the quote. The words in this field were transferred directly from the word-processing file's index without the need for additional data entry.

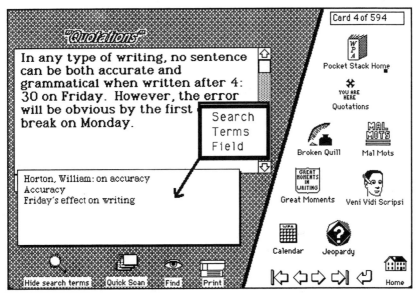

Figure 12: Search terms field with terms the user can select to jump to another stack

The user could also maneuver through the stacks by:

- Choosing the Quick Scan button at the bottom to have the cards in the stack quickly display in numerical sequence—a kind of automated linear browsing.

- Choosing the Find button at the bottom and then typing in a word or phrase to search for; this button allows the user to go anywhere in a stack and not be forced along a stack author's pre-chosen directions—this freedom of movement is one of the essential qualities of a hypertext.

- Choosing the forward or backward arrows at the bottom right to slowly move forward or backward one card at a time in numerical sequence. The arrow with a bar to the left takes the user to the first card in the stacks and the arrow with the bar to the right takes the user to the last card in the stack.

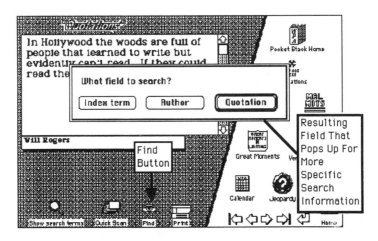

Figure 13: Find button to allow users to navigate within a stack

In addition to the five stacks mirroring the sections of the paper book and the categories of the database stage we added two new ways of displaying and using our information in hypertext, the Calendar and Jeopardy game. One of the advantages of hypertext is that it easily allows information in one hypertext document to be reused in another. This ease of re-utilizing yields not only a practical advantage—retyping, re-editing, and re-storing of information is eliminated—but it also incorporates the notion of inter- or hypertextuality. As John Slatin, an expert on 20th century poetry, points out regarding such texts[9]:

> ... a text (any text) is really a collectivity of texts, so intimately and intricately bound to one another that they have to be described as mutually constituting each other....

The Calendar and the Jeopardy game demonstrate this aspect of hypertextuality because both draw their information from the Quotations stack via search, matching, and randomizing routines, and then display the information in such novel contexts and frameworks that wholly new texts are created.

The Calendar stack is an on-screen page-a-day desk calendar. It demonstrates another way of re-utilizing the data from the Quotations stack. It allows the user to see the current day's quote, look at a different day's quote, and to print out any day's quote.

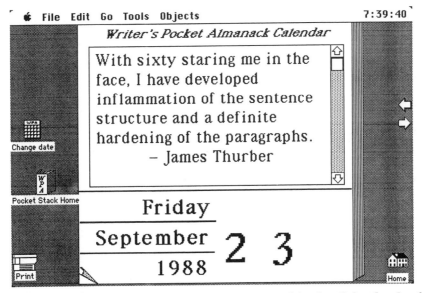

Figure 14: Quotations stack information reused in the Calendar Stack

The Jeopardy Game gives the user a chance to test his or her knowledge of the quotations by organizing some of the quotations into game categories. When the user selects a category and dollar value, the computer assumes the role of Jeopardy's television host, Alex Trebek, and displays a quotation. The user then has to complete the question "Who said ..." with the appropriate source of the quote. If the user is correct, the computer produces the sound of applause and adds points to the score, if the user is incorrect, the computer produces the sound of a honk and subtracts points from the score.

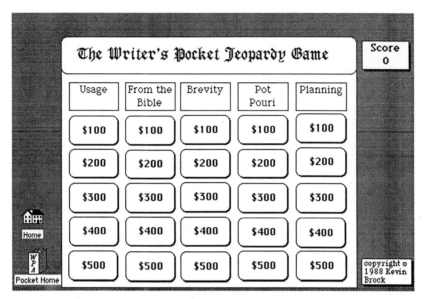

Figure 15: Quotations stack information reused in the Jeopardy stack

At the final step in our odyssey, we sent the completed *HyperCard* stacks to our publisher who then consolidated them onto a single disk, made copies of this master disk, and packaged the copied disks in plastic cases. Again we feel we were successful in creating the *HyperCard* edition of *The Writer's Pocket Almanack*: we kept the price low, $7.95; we delivered it in plenty of time for major 1988 Spring conventions, and again we were able to watch the fun our users had during demonstrations of our stacks.

Insights along the way

Now that you have travelled with us on our information odyssey, and now that our goals have been reached, let us share with you seven of the insights we gained on our journey.

Insight 1. Hypertext is like cayenne pepper.

Hypertext is like cayenne pepper—a little goes a long way. It adds zest to bland fare and sparks the appetite and digestion. But we don't put it on ice cream or add it to iced tea.

The power and risk of hypertext can be seen by looking at the expressive power it adds to the organization of documents. In Figure 16, consider the four different structures for organizing documents: sequence, grid, tree, and web.

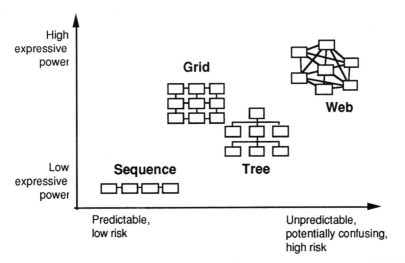

Figure 16. Structures for organizing information—powers and risks

The simplest structure is the sequence. Word follows word, paragraph after paragraph, page by page. In this structure the reader has two choices: forward or backward. It is perfectly reliable but monotonously predictable. It is this safe, sane sequential structure that is the backbone of most paper documents—the paper *Almanack* included.[10] It is also the structure users encounter in our *HyperCard Almanack* as they maneuver through our stacks using only the Quick Scan or arrow buttons.

The grid or orthogonal structure organizes and presents information along two logical dimensions.[11] Imagine a reference manual for a word-processing program or a programming language. Each page contains information on one command. These commands are like the columns of the grid. On each page are the same headings for each command, such as Syntax, Description, Notes, Examples. These headings form the rows of the grids. The reader can read down the columns to learn everything about a particular column or can skim along the row to compare the syntax of various commands. The ubiquitous grid is a permanent and familiar part of our experience; we see it embodied in spreadsheets, tables, game boards, street plans, marching bands, and the rank and file of the workplace. This familiarity makes it a popular way of adding another dimension to the document's structure without great loss of predictability.

The same familiarity is also true for the tree structure. The simple hierarchy is the basis for classification and management. The Vatican, the Kremlin, the

Pentagon, and General Motors all have hierarchical management structures. We see the tree structure in the 3.4.5 style of numbered headings common in technical manuals. Perhaps you can also see a tree structure embodied in the Cross-Stack buttons on the right-hand side of our *HyperCard Almanack* screen.

The web structure, possible with hypertext, is the ultimate in expressive power. Anything can be linked to anything else; associations are not bound to strict rules as for the other structures.[12] Users can see this web structure in our HyperCard *Almanack* as they maneuver through the stacks using either the Find button or the words in the Search Terms Field. Especially in the case of the latter, the users can go any direction they want, and they are unbounded by any of preset passageways. The power of the web structure is that with it the designer can construct the other simpler structures, as well as special ad hoc structures, such as cycles, stars, and diamonds—just as we did in the Jeopardy Game.

The danger, however, with the web structure possible with hypertext is that with multiple structures possible, or with no structure, the user experiences the "classic lost in hyperspace problem."[13]. Users know neither their direction or speed through the information space because nothing is fixed; nothing is necessarily connected or sequenced after anything else.

We protected users of the *HyperCard Almanack* from this classic problem by tempering the web structure of the hypertext (possible through the use of the Find button or Search Terms field) with a sequence structure (embodied in the Quick Scan button, arrow buttons, or numerical card sequence located to the top right), the grid structure (seen in the consistent layout of fields and buttons on each screen), and the tree-structure (embodied in the Cross-Stack buttons). Thus we believe we achieved some of the expressive powers of the hypertext web structure without losing the reader.

Hypertext should not be used as an excuse for the writer to abdicate his responsibility to lead. Writers may be tempted to forego the difficult analysis that linear writing requires and throw the decision of what is important and what to know first onto the reader. But readers expect the writer to lead them through the jungle of information, and although they do not like to be controlled or manipulated, they do expect the writer to blaze a trail for them. They don't want to have to hack their way through hundreds of choices at every juncture.[14]

Thus we believe that hypertext works better as an adjective, not a noun. Hypertext should not be an end in itself but a way of organizing and providing access to information. Hypertext opens new avenues of access, but access is not information. Hypertext must match the information available to the readers' need to access that information. Merely adding links and pointers does not make a document more useful or comprehensible:

> Finally, there is a danger that approaches like ours can lead to sprawling unmanageable systems having little overall coherence.[15]

Insight 2. Inoculate yourself against the disease of information anxiety.

Information is more than words and pictures; it is also organization and format. In information theory, entropy is the loss of useful information. The writing, illustration, and layout activities in our odyssey reduced entropy and allowed us to create information.

As you can see in Figure 17, as content is added, as organization is refined, as formatting is polished, information increases. The climb is not always smooth, as shown in the lower curve. Setbacks occurred in our odyssey when converting from one phase of data representation to another: in converting from database to word-processing, the organization and accessibility of the database was lost, and when the word-processing files were imported into hypertext, formatting was lost. Thus our odyssey's climb from entropy to information was a jagged ascent.

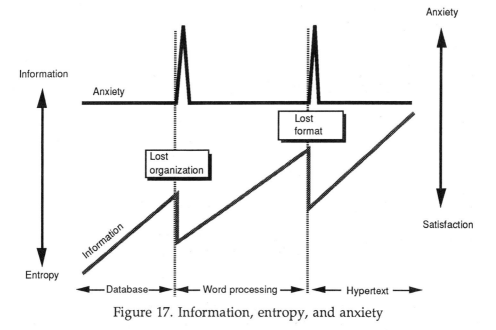

Figure 17. Information, entropy, and anxiety

Along with these setbacks, we noticed a related phenomenon which we called information anxiety. Information anxiety is akin to the feeling a writer gets when after three hours of steady productive work on the computer, the power goes out. Ouch! The writer feels frustration, loss, and anger at not having saved the work in progress. Information anxiety manifested itself to us in our feelings of occasional discouragement and irritability. Usually our morale was high, buoyed by the steady, tangible progress evident in the growing number of quotations or the ever finer format. Anxiety occurred intensely, but only during and immediately after the conversions. This led to our formulation of the law of information anxiety:

> Anxiety rises with the loss of information.

When information is being created, and entropy is being diminished, anxiety is low. When information is suddenly lost and entropy increases, anxiety peaks.

Concern about the difficulty of converting information from one phase to another, and especially in converting existing word-processing documents, with painstakingly crafted layout, to hypertext have been raised by others:

> Those of us who expect the whole world to rewrite its documentation to fit the needs of our new hypertext system are unlikely to have our expectations filled. Instead we must capture existing documents and have some way—even if crude—of automatically imparting structure to it. [16]

Insight 3. 'Tis better to link than re-store.

One of the promises hypertext offers is the easy reuse of information; once something is stored as hypertext, it can be easily linked by later hypertext authors into a new stack or a new document. We wanted to demonstrate this capability by inventing a new way of utilizing our own information in a way that was both educational and entertaining.

We decided to develop a game based on the quotations using the familiar idea of television's Jeopardy game. The structure of the TV game show is such that we could easily use the information in the Quotations stack as the questions and answers given in the Jeopardy game.

We began setting up the Jeopardy game by choosing categories based on the keywords in the Search Terms field of the Quotations stack. After choosing a category name, it scanned through the Quotations stack by clicking on the search term and looking for quotations that fit that category. When we found a quotation that fit, we transferred the quotation and its source into variables within the Quotations stack. After scanning the stack for likely categories and items, we transferred the contents of the variable into a text file outside of the stack and then transferred the contents of the file into a hidden field within the Jeopardy stack. Since the quotations to be used in the game itself would be drawn from the original Quotations stack, we would have achieved our goal of re-utilizing the data. By testing the users knowledge of the quotations and supplying the correct answers when the user is wrong, the game also proved to be educational.

We soon discovered, however, that storing the quotations within the Jeopardy stack took up excessive amounts of memory, and since we had planned on using 15 to 20 categories, this method of storing the quotations would be impractical. This led us to search for a more efficient way to gather and store the game clue data, and we chose to adapt the method used in the Calendar stack. In the Calendar stack, a card number was computed using the number of the day of the year, and then a quotation was read from this card number in the Quotations stack. We set the Jeopardy game up with an array of numbers containing the card numbers of specific cards in the Quotations stack appropriate for each category. Thus when the user chooses to set up the game board at the beginning of a game, the Jeopardy game directly reads these specific cards in the Quotations stack. Thus, only the quotations and sources actually being used in this game are stored in the game at any given time.

By taking advantage of *HyperCard*'s relational database nature and directly linking the Jeopardy game and the Quotations stack, we reused the original data rather than copying and storing it again. The result was that the speed of the game increased, the amount of memory needed to run the game decreased, and we were able to store all our *Almanack* stack on one disk. [17]

Insight 4. Make links between related items visible and audible, not implied.

HyperCard's relational database nature is also expressed to the user in the use of the Cross-Stack buttons, the Search Terms field, and the sound effects of file drawers closing (when the user exits a stack) or pages being turned (when the user moves from one card to another). Rather than have the user guess the relationship between different stacks or cards within a stack, the Cross-Stack buttons and select-able Search Terms provide a visible link between stacks and cards. The two sound effects reinforce these visible links and tend to make the users' connections between controls (selecting a Search Term or pressing a Cross-Stack button) and functions (the actual jumping to the desired card or stack) concrete. These visible and audible links make it easier for the user to make connections. They also fulfill one of Donald Norman's psychological principles of good design—make the control functions visible:

> Why is the automobile, with all its varied functions and numerous controls, so much easier to learn and to use than the telephone system, with its much smaller set of functions and controls? What is good about the design of a car? Things are visible. There are good mappings, natural relationships, between the controls and the things controlled. Simple controls often have single functions. There is good feedback. The system is understandable. In general, the relationships among the user's intentions, the required actions, and the results are sensible, nonarbitrary, and meaningful.[18]

Insight 5   Analogy is the mother of invention and reception. But analogy is only a beginning.

As mentioned in the start of this article, Bill and John began the project with a library of maxims and aphorisms developed over a period of ten years. But, it wasn't until John purchased a facsimile edition of Franklin's *Poor Richard's Almanack* published by Peter Pauper Press[19] that we recognized a means of collecting and publishing the material coherently—it was the analogy of Franklin's *Almanack*, an eighteenth century compendium of poems, aphorisms, and maxims with a slightly tongue-in-cheek tone that gave us the means of packaging our twentieth century material. We also believed that the analogy would also give readers a convenient set of genre expectations that would allow them to make sense out of our *Almanack*—they would have a context or established conceptual niche into which to put our new material. If you compare Franklin's page in Figure 18 to our own in Figure 19, you will see we both have various short bits of information separated by rules rather than integrated in flowing paragraphs. We also tried to maintain the humorous, paradoxical, tongue-in-cheek tone of Franklin.

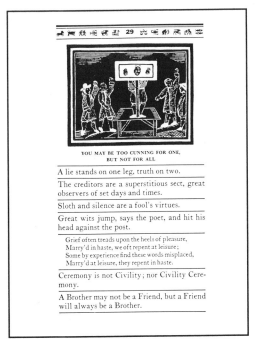

YOU MAY BE TOO CUNNING FOR ONE,
BUT NOT FOR ALL

A lie stands on one leg, truth on two.

The creditors are a superstitious sect, great observers of set days and times.

Sloth and silence are a fool's virtues.

Great wits jump, says the poet, and hit his head against the post.

Grief often treads upon the heels of pleasure,
Marry'd in haste, we oft repent at leisure;
Some by experience find these words misplaced,
Marry'd at leisure, they repent in haste.

Ceremony is not Civility; nor Civility Ceremony.

A Brother may not be a Friend, but a Friend will always be a Brother.

Figure 18. Page from facsimile edition of *Poor Richard's Almanack*

This was the first analogy that was the mother to our invention—it gave us a creative framework on which to hang our new material and it gave our readers a context in which to receiving our material.[20]

But one must go beyond the bounds of the analogy—one doesn't want to remain slavishly imitative. We thought Franklin's *Almanack* would not be visually rich enough or sufficiently varied in content to keep the attention of modern readers. We went beyond the one-dimensional woodcuts to 18th and 19th century line art by such greats as Hogarth and Dürer, and we went beyond Franklin's reliance solely on poems and maxims to include diverse items in our paper text such as:

- Veni Vidi Scripsi—Latin aphorisms in translation,

- Mal Mots—phrases and aphorisms that teach communication truths through their mistaken notions,

- Broken Quill Awards—examples of extremely poor writing, and

- Great Moments in Writing—historical events or inventions that affected the development of the writing profession

Figure 19. Page from *The Writer's Pocket Almanack*

As we began developing the *HyperCard* version of the *Almanack,* the use of analogies again came into play for our invention and for our readers' reception. When we had first converted the word-processing files from *Microsoft Word 3.01* to HyperCard, our draft hypertext had a number of problems. As we have already noted, one of the most common problems in hypertext systems is that readers get lost.[21] Even though hypertext gives readers many different ways of getting at a piece of information, as Steve Weyer pointed out, "Spaghetti looks the same from any perspective."[22]

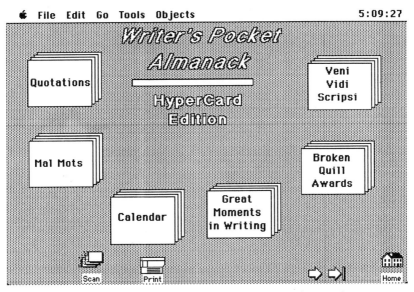

Figure 20. Home card for the draft *Almanack*

As originally designed, our user began at the *Almanack* Home Card, Figure 20, and from there jumped into one of the other stacks, for instance the Quotations stack, seen in Figure 21.

Notice that in this stack users had no easy visible way to return to the starting card of the *Almanack*. The Home button at the lower right would return them to the *HyperCard* Home stack but not to the starting card of the *Almanack*. Hidden were at least three ways of navigating using the built-in *HyperCard* commands. These commands could be selected from pull down menus on the top menu bar, but the top menu bar was hidden.[23] Each of the three methods could be performed from the keyboard, but using keyboard commands assumed an unrealistic level of expertise on the part of users.

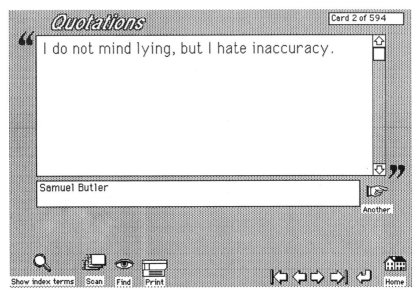

Figure 21. Quotations card from the draft *Almanack*

The sequential structure of the stack was visibly signaled in the Scan button, arrow buttons, and card number box in to the top right. But the stack's web structure was only vaguely implied in the Show index terms button, and the tree-structure of the Cross-Stack buttons and *Almanack* Home Card was totally missing.

In addition, the grid structure of the consistent layout was missing: Figure 21, a Quotations stack card, had a Show index terms button which offered selectable search capability, but Figure 22, a Veni Vidi Scripsi stack card, had a Show Notes button which had no search capability; Figure 21 offered the Another hand button with search capabilities, while Figure 22 did not.

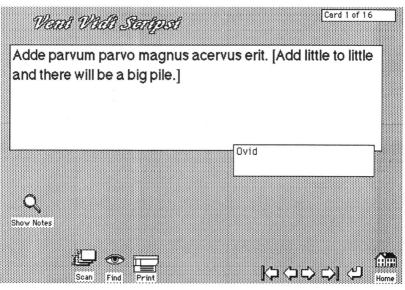

Figure 22. Veni Vidi Scripsi card from draft *Almanack*

In our odyssey, this problem with our design—hypertext spaghetti problems—was our Scylla. Our Charybdis was that in our zeal to more visibly show the reader that our hypertext web structure was tempered by a tree, grid, and sequential structure, we might overload the cards with buttons. We needed an elegant design alternative.

We found our design solution in the layout shown in Figures 23 and 24, the first two cards from McClelland & Danuloff's *HyperCard Typefaces* stack. Figures 23 and 24 are in the order they would be seen by users, and they show how change is tempered by stasis; in a split screen design, the right-hand side changes with the presentation of new information, while the left-hand remains the same to anchor the reader in what is already known.

Figure 23. Title card from *Typefaces* stack

Figure 24. Second card In *Typefaces* stack

In Figures 25 & 26, you can see how we implemented this split-screen format in our stacks. McClelland & Danuloff kept their left side consistent so as to give readers a sense of visual continuity, and we also made the background of our left side consistent again to give the reader a sense of visual continuity.[24]

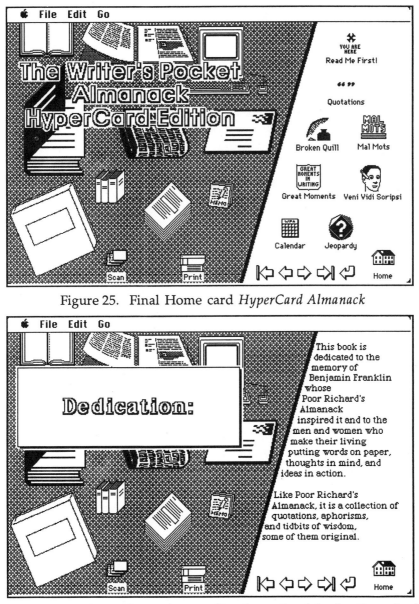

Figure 25. Final Home card *HyperCard Almanack*

Figure 26. A Page of introduction (Read Me First!) in the *HyperCard Almanack*

To avoid button icon overload when the user leaves the Home Card and begins using a stack (Figures 27 and 28), we made the right side static with the Cross-Stack buttons visible. Additionally we leave the top menu bar available for users accustomed to using the *HyperCard* navigating. By comparing Figures 27 and 28, you can see we have visual and interactive consistency in all the cards. Each card has the eight icons to move to other stacks of the *Almanack* or to the *HyperCard* Home card (our tree-structure). Each card also has the searchable index term box—now more appropriately called Search Terms (our web structure). Each card has an author's box in the same location (our grid structure). And each has a treasure-map X indicating which stack the user is in.[25] By these features we escaped the Scylla of hypertext spaghetti and the Charybdis of button overload.

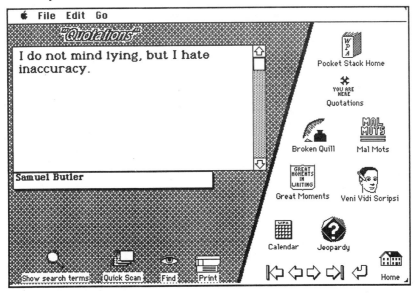

Figure 27. Quotations card from the final *Almanack*

From our design process we learned what creative writing teachers have been saying for a long time. At the University of Delaware, the teachers of creative writing have had a general answer to each of those budding undergraduate novelists, poets, or screenplay writers who want to stop reading the required canon of authors and start writing their own works. What they have said repeatedly is:

> You're not ready yet to write until you've read, read, read, and read some more!

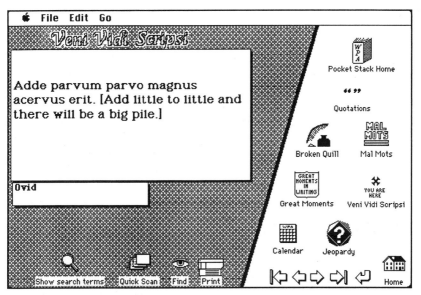

Figure 28. Veni Vidi Scripsi card from the final *Almanack*

These teachers know that creative writers need to understand and appreciate the best writers of the past. Such recommendations should be rephrased for those technical communicators and computer documenters who desire to be desktop publishers and hypertext authors:

> You're not ready yet to perform desktop publishing or develop hypertexts until you've studied examples, studied examples, and studied more examples!

Or as Digital Equipment Corporation wrote in their in-house style guide for documenters:

> Your competition can have useful ideas on content, format, layout, and access methods you might use in your book. Part of your job is to know what competitive products do (and do not) exist so your manual can be "state of the art."[26]

For both the *Almanack* paper book and the *HyperCard* stacks, sifting through example after example led us to discover analogies on which to base our designs. Such analogies allow the reader to understand what we are doing and to navigate through the information.

Insight 6. A way of seeing is also a way of not seeing.
—Kenneth Burke

When we began our two versions of the *Almanack,* we were afraid that readers would find the two versions identical. Instead what we discovered is that the same content had quite different personalities in each medium. We rediscovered what McLuhan meant when he said the "Medium is the message" because what we found is that each medium was communicating as much about itself as a medium as it was communicating our text. In summary, the four major areas that differentiated the personalities of the two media are:

The Paper Book Emphasizes:	The Hypertext Version Emphasizes:
Different relations between viewers and text	
A passive **reader** desires to scan-zoom through the text. This is possible but inconvenient. The reader relies primarily on the author's organization.	An active **user** desires to scan-zoom through the text. This is possible and made very convenient.
Different methods of referencing and integrating	
Referencing is top-down from the table of contents to whole related sections.	Bottom-up referencing is to single cards with a more interactive index search.
Pages simultaneously show a mix of various types of information.	Cards show only one type of information at a time.
Different effects of delivery systems	
Typeface was chosen to communicate a style and tone.	Typeface choice was limited by considerations of portability and cost.
Detailed graphics were used but no sound effects.	Sound effects were used but no detailed graphics.
Closure and progress through the text are physically signified.	Closure and progress are simulated.
Difference between a text as an end in itself and as part of an ongoing process	
The book was an end in itself. Methods by which the reader would reuse our text were not implemented.	The stacks is only part of an ongoing process whereby readers will easily reuse the text. The stack was designed to make reusing easy.
Problems of copyright were not encountered.	Problems of copyright were not addressed.

The different relationships between the viewers and our text in the different media can be summed up in the words we have used to describe the viewers of the two texts, **reader** for the book text and **user** for the hypertext text. Our book reader relies primarily on our linear, numerical page sequence [27] or on the hierarchical sequence of section headings in the table of contents.[28] The user of our hypertext text, on the other hand, is clicking buttons and choosing Search Terms to more actively interact with the text. It is almost an axiom of hypertext that "the author is the reader and the reader is the author."[29]

The reader of our book, of course, can interact with out paper text by annotating it, underlining sections, or putting bookmarks in. On first glance these capabilities seem absent from our own hypertext. But Mark Bernstein suggests that hypertext can offer such annotation facilities; for example, his company's HyperGate™ has screen facilities for margin notes, book marks, note cards, and copy machines.[30] Our own hypertext has similar properties available to the knowledgeable *HyperCard* user: by choosing the Recent command from the Go menu, the user is offered a kind of bookmark in the way Recent shows miniature representations of the 42 most recent screens traversed; and users of our hypertext can add their own links, buttons, and text fields as annotations to suit their own special interests.

Ted Nelson, the coiner of the word "hypertext" in the late 1960's, described the three **different methods of referencing** information. These have been described in the following way:

> In [Ted] Nelson's proposal (as implemented in the Xanadu system), documents are connected by links. The links can be point-to-point, point-to-span, and span-to-span. A point-to-point link goes from one 'point'—a particular location in a document (such as immediately following the asterisk here: *)—to some other point in the same or another document (where the * is repeated).. 'Spans' are regions of text (such as this paragraph). Links connect regions of text (spans) to places in text [points] or spans [regions] to spans [regions].[31]

Readers of our book using the Table of Contents and Index would be primarily performing point-to-span or span-to-span referencing of information. Users of our hypertext using the Search Terms, Find, and Author's name referencing options would all be performing point-to-point referencing. The impact of this change in referencing approaches is that the readers of the book are performing more top-down referencing (e.g., find a Table of Content's high level heading and then go to the specifics in the text), while the users of the hypertext are performing more bottom-up referencing—often after accessing a series of individual cards and observing their common thread, users might recognize a common higher level organizing category (this is exactly how the categories of the Jeopardy game were developed as described in Insight 3). The inability to do top-down referencing beyond the most general level using the Cross-Stack buttons is a problem with the current hypertext design, but it's again not a problem inherent in hypertext—just a very common problem when your design building block in *HyperCard* are separate cards. In the next edition of the *HyperCard Almanack* perhaps we should add a variation on the Find and Search Terms button on the *Almanack* Home Card which would repeat the book's Table of Contents with words as buttons that would jump the user to the first card in that category—doing so would give readers the option of either the current bottom-up referencing as well as a top-down referencing.

But even with replicating the book's point-to-span referencing in the hypertext, the mix of various type of information on a category present in the book is absent in the hypertext. For example, under the heading "Writer's Toil" in the book, the reader finds numerous related quotations, graphics and boxed items such as Veni Vidi Scripsi and Great Moments in Writing. Thus our message in the book to the reader on the topic of "Writer's Toil" is multidimensional—contradictory quotes are juxtaposed and a topic is explored from many different directions. But the user of our hypertext seems to fall into the same Cyclops syndrome we escaped in the "Consolidate Database" episode of our odyssey—the Cyclops syndrome, as you may remember, is a narrowing of scope in which one one quote at a time is presented in the database. Like the database, the hypertext seems to present information for a single eye rather than the normal stereoscopic vision. This is a problem inherent with the hypertext as it is currently designed, and one of the strengths of books that readers have long taken for granted. Unlike the possibility of future replication of the book's Table of Contents in the hypertext, replicating the multidimensional message in the hypertext is not currently possible using our authoring package, Apple's *HyperCard*, because *HyperCard* displays one card at a time—the ideal would be to have multiple cards on one screen and to present information from different stacks simultaneously.

There were also different ways the paper book or the hypertext either enhanced or confounded our communication goals in the **different effects of their delivery systems**. In the book, we spent extra time and effort to purchase a typeface that gave the look and feel of Franklin's eighteenth century typeface, Caslon. Adobe's Goudy Old Style came closest to what we wanted and was available when we needed it. The choice of typeface, therefore, in the book was made on the basis of communication. In the hypertext, however, we needed to realize that users would read our hypertext using Apple's *HyperCard,* and that whatever fonts users had resident in their system would be the fonts *HyperCard* could use to display our hypertext. Since Adobe's Goudy Old Style was new, had to be ordered and specially installed, and cost around $200.00, we could not rely on users having it installed on their systems. We could also have purchased the right from Adobe to include the Goudy font in our package, but that would have more than doubled the cost of our hypertext to users. Therefore, we used the New York font as our design typeface—it is serifed and resident on nearly all Macintoshes, but it does not have the look and feel of Franklin's Caslon. Thus the book allowed us to choose a typeface based on communication considerations, while considerations of portability and cost framed our decision in the hypertext version.

In the book we spent a great deal of time, money, and effort obtaining and integrating quality detailed line art (one of our sources for the line art, for example, was an 1808 English book that was a type of Ripley's *Believe-It-Or-Not)*. But the bit mapped screen of the Macintosh just did not give us the ability to present finely detailed line art. Thus the artwork in the hypertext background and button icons pales next to the line art of the book. On the other hand, *HyperCard* does offer the ability to produce sound effects—a possibility the book cannot, of course, offer. And, the sound effects of file drawers opening and closing or pages turning were not just used to display the gadgetry of *HyperCard*, but to give users audible feedback on actions or controls invoked, and to increase user's understanding of hypertext by providing audible metaphors.

A book, as John has pointed out in his text, *Writing Better Computer User Documentation*, offers a physical analog to its organization—depending on the number of pages in the reader's left or right hands, the readers are physically signalled where they are in the text (beginning, middle, or end). But because of the web structure and lack of integration of the stacks, readers can easily lose that sense of where they are in the hypertext. That's why it took an extra effort on our part to include the "You are Here" treasure mark on the Cross-Stack buttons and the card number in the top-right corner. But again these extra efforts do not provide the degree of context that is inherently signalled by the physical book.[32]

Finally, there are differences between a **text as an end in itself and as part of an ongoing process**. Most of these distinctions were explored in Insight 3, but what remained unresolved by the end of our odyssey were the problems of **copyright** in the hypertext. The problems and solutions to the questions of copyright are well covered in paper books[33], but the same problems and solutions to the problems of copyright in hypertext are only now being defined.[34]

For all their distinctions, there is no clear winner or loser in either medium—both have strengths and weaknesses . By publishing the "same" text in different media we tested the the generality of principles developed for the paper medium.[35]   Only by struggling to convert a document from one medium to another and only after observing how readers interact with the document in each medium do writers realize how media-specific some communication "rules" and "principles" really are.

Insight 7. Three heads are better than one.

Our teamwork during the arduous journey through the odyssey represents the movement throughout technical communication from single heroic figures of classical odysseys to the winning team approach of modern odysseys. In the old days of paper, pen, and typewriter, one heroic technical communicator would attempt to carry out a writing project in single combat. But the complexity of the tools in the post-typewriter age, the shrinking amount of time available to produce ever more and larger texts, and corporate determination to minimize publications costs means that only an effective team can successfully carry out writing projects today.

Integrating the strengths and talents of wordsmith, designer, publicist, programmer, and editor with the tools of word-processing, database management, and hypertext authoring on a team separated by hundreds of miles proved the greatest challenge of our odyssey.

We can say to all those who would follow in our odyssey that the only way to survive the Cyclops, Scylla and Charybdis, the dead ends, technological surprises, and the midnight onslaught of information anxiety is to board your trireme with as strong a crew as you can muster.

Bon voyage.

Notes and references

The authors would like to thank James Martin of Martin Information Services and William F. Meehan of the University of Delaware for their helpful suggestions.

1   The book and hypertext disk discussed in this paper are available by mail for $7.95 each from InfoBooks, PO Box 1018, Santa Monica, CA 90406. The ISBN number of the book is 0-931137-08-X.

2   *Writing Better Computer User Documentation: From Paper to Online* (New York: Wiley Interscience, 1986).

3   Although the publication of this one paper book and hypertext is of no great significance in itself, it does serve as a model for the new electronic publishing process; Honeywell Industrial Automation Systems Division, for example, in their Phoenix facility is using very much the same process and software tools.

4   Throughout this chapter we mention the features, strengths, and weaknesses of several commercial products used in this project. We do not mean to endorse or condemn any products. The observations we make are typical of those of other like products. We mention them because electronic publishing and hypertext tools do shape the end result. In fact, we had little choice in tools, as we had to select tools that both authors and the publisher shared in common.

5   Separating the author's first and last names required a little programming trickery. Using *Tempo*, we were able to identify last names by going to the end of the name and looking backward one word. This worked for most names, but not for compound last names such as *von Braun* and *de Vries*. These we had to handle manually.

6   The database we used was a relational database, *Double Helix* (later upgraded to *Double Helix II*). A flat-file database would have done as well because we used few of the relational features of *Double Helix*.

7   Version 3.0 of *PageMaker*, which was released after our odyssey was completed, promises to alleviate the problems we encountered.

8   R. John Brockmann, "Desktop Publishing--Beyond GEE WHIZ, Part 1: A Critical Overview," *IEEE Transactions on Professional Communication* , 31 (1) (March 1988): 25.

9   John Slatin, "Hypertext and the Teaching of Writing" in *Text, Context, and Hypertext* edited by Edward Barrett (Cambridge, MA: MIT Press, 1988), 115.

10   William Horton, "Toward the Four-Dimensional Page," in *Proceedings of 30th International Technical Communication Conference* (Washington, DC: Society for Technical Communication, 1983), RET 83–86.

11   William Horton, "Minds, Models, and Metaphors," in *Proceedings of 10th Practical Conference on Communication* (Knoxville, TN: East Tennessee Chapter, Society for Technical Communication, 1985), 80–85.

12   William Horton, "Templates of Thought," in *Proceedings of 33rd International Technical Communication Conference* (Washington, DC: Society for Technical Communication, 1986), 302–305.

13   Andries Van Dam, "Hypertext'87 Keynote Address," *Communications of the ACM*, 31 (7) (July 1988): 889.

14   "Along with greater control, of course, comes a greater burden for the readers, who must not only locate the information they need, but relate it to other facts in the network, often without the aid of traditional structural cures." Davida Charney, "Comprehending Non-linear Text: The Role of Discourse Cues and Reading Strategies," in *Hypertext '87 Papers*, November 13-15, 1987, University of North Carolina, Chapel Hill, 111.

15   Randall H. Trigg and Peggy M. Irish, "Hypertext Habitats: Experiences of Writers in NoteCards," in *Hypertext '87 Papers*, November 13-15, 1987, University of North Carolina, Chapel Hill, 1987, 105.

16   P.J. Brown, "Turning Ideas into Products, The Guide System,"in *Hypertext '87 Papers*, November 13-15, 1987, University of North Carolina, Chapel Hill, 39.

17   In choosing the number of categories, we had to balance broadening the categories of the game with minimizing the amount of memory required. Size constraints also led us to realize that where we were performing many similar activities, we needed to try to generalize that activity so that one piece of HyperCard code (HyperTalk) could be used in each of the different instances. This ability of HyperCard allowed us to take a small amount of memory and effectively multiply it by using it more than once.

18   *The Psychology of Everyday Things* (New York: Basic Books Inc., 1988), 22.

19   *Poor Richard's Almanack* (Mount Vernon, NY: Peter Pauper Press, 1987).

20   An interesting fact we have gleaned from published reviews of the books is that many book reviewers do not have this established conceptual niche of almanacks. In many cases the criticisms of our book was not criticisms of our almanack per se, but rather that the almanack was not like their conceptual niche of a normal book—nothing like this had ever been done before in technical communication or computer documentation.

21   "The biggest problem in hypertext systems, which most of us admit in footnotes towards the end of paper extolling the virtues of our systems, is . . . getting lost." P.J. Brown (University of Canterbury, Kent), "Turning Ideas into Products, The Guide System,"in *Hypertext '87 Papers*, November 13-15, 1987, University of North Carolina, Chapel Hill, 39.

22   Steven Weyer, "As We May Learn," in *Multimedia in Education: Interfaces to Knowledge*, (Apple, EAC (in press)).

23   "Most hypertext designers . . . report informal evidence that users may be overwhelmed by the choices." Davida Charney, "Comprehending Non-linear Text: The Role of Discourse Cues and Reading Strategies," in *Hypertext '87 Papers*, November 13-15, 1987, University of North Carolina, Chapel Hill, 111.

24   "The usual approach to this problem [losing location in a text] is to generate a view of the neighborhood around the current position. A straightforward approach is to show a 'zoom out' or 'road map' schematic view of adjoining nodes." Tim Oren, "The Architecture of

Static Hypertexts," in *Hypertext '87 Papers*, November 13-15, 1987, University of North Carolina, Chapel Hill, 296.

25 "Designers of hypertext and hypermedia materials confront two related problems, ... and the second, how to welcome the user on arrival at that destination." George P. Landown, "Relationally Encoded Links and the Rhetoric of Hypertext," in *Hypertext '87 Papers*, November 13-15, 1987, University of North Carolina, Chapel Hill, 296.

26 Digital Equipment Corporation, *The Personal Computer Documenter's Guide* (Maynard, MA, 1983).

27 "Printed text is inherently linear structure." George H. Collier, "Thoth-II: Hypertext with Explicit Semantics, " in *Hypertext '87 Papers*, November 13-15, 1987, University of North Carolina, Chapel Hill, 270.

28 Patricia Ann Carlson, "Hypertext: A Way of Incorporating User Feedback" in *Hypertext '87 Papers*, November 13-15, 1987, University of North Carolina, Chapel Hill, 94.

29 P.J. Brown (University of Canterbury, Kent), "Turning Ideas into Products, The Guide System," in *Hypertext '87 Papers*, November 13-15, 1987, University of North Carolina, Chapel Hill, 37.

30 Mark Bernstein in "Hypertext: New Challengers and Roles for Technical Communicators," in *Proceedings of the 35th International Technical Communications Conference* (Washington, DC: Society for Technical Communication, 1988), 33–36.

31 George H. Collier, "Thoth-II: Hypertext with Explicit Semantics, " in *Hypertext '87 Papers*, November 13-15, 1987, University of North Carolina, Chapel Hill, 271.

32 Tim Oren, "The Architecture of Static Hypertexts," in *Hypertext '87 Papers*, November 13-15, 1987, University of North Carolina, Chapel Hill, 296.

33 Karen Judd, "Copyright," in *Copyediting: A Practical Guide* (New York: William Kaufmann, 1982), 203–205; "Among the Professions: Technical Communication and Law," *Technical Communication*, 32, no. 2 (Second Quarter 1985): 48 (Part I), and no. 3 (Third Quarter): 38 (part II); and the special issue of *IEEE Transactions on Professional Communication* on PC–30, no. 3 (September 1987) on legal issues.

34 Henry W. Jones, "Developing and Distributing Hypertext Tools: Legal Inputs and Parameters, " in *Hypertext '87 Papers*, November 13-15, 1987, University of North Carolina, Chapel Hill, 255.

35 "True online documents can be defined as those documents produced on a computer that are confined to the screen medium. True online documents differ from help screens because they contain much more information (a chapter's worth of information compared to a page's worth) and because they use the computer facilities more fully." R. John Brockmann & Rebecca J. McCauley, "The Computer and the Craft of Writing: Implications for Teachers," *The Technical Writing Teacher* 9 (2) Winter 1984: 132.

Part III
*The Social Perspective: Writers, Management, and the Online
Environment*

Who are we? What are our skills? What will be the role of the writer in light of
changing documentation technology? In Part III John Kirsch analyzes the results of a
survey of practicing technical communicators in the computer industry to focus on
trends in this emerging profession. Muriel Zimmerman discusses technical writing as a
socially constructed reality in order to measure the impact computing technology is
having on the role of the "writer." The matrix of technology, writing, and training in
an organizational context is then addressed by Robert Krull. Lawrence Levine revisions the writer's role as a consultative one based on his analysis of corporate culture
and the computational mediation of work. Jacqueline Stewart presents a first-time
review of *Project Athena* at MIT and the management of educational computing initiatives in a complex social environment. She offers several models for managing
development projects that should be of interest to other academic, as well as industrial,
research communities. Finally, I discuss the *Educational Online System* at MIT in
terms of three models for interaction in any instructional context in order to
demonstrate the suppleness of the online training environment.

Trends in the Emerging Profession of Technical Communication

John Kirsch

TechWriting Affiliates, Inc. *
MIT Sloan School of Management **

I present a model of the technical communication profession and report a questionnaire survey of 85 experienced technical communicators employed by large computer companies in New England. Writing versatility and interpersonal skills discriminated top from average performers. As a group the respondents reported high satisfaction with their careers but low status within the industry; much stronger affiliation with other writers, programmers, and engineers than with customers and marketing or sales staff; and little expertise or interest in writing on-line documentation.

The results suggest the need for more teamwork in the development of new products, and more guidelines or standards in the writing of on-line documentation.

1. Introduction

This paper looks at the emerging profession of technical communication in the computer industry. Because large manufacturers of computers earn increasing portions of net income from software and services, they are hiring more writers to document their products and they are promoting older staff to manage the newcomers. As a result, new jobs and new career tracks are opening up.

My goal in this paper is a better understanding of this fast-evolving occupation, considered both as a profession and, from the individual's point of view, as a career. The main questions on my mind are these:

- How can you tell the best from the rest? What experience or training distinguishes top-performing technical communicators from the merely successful?

- What do technical communicators like and dislike about their work? What are their main non-financial rewards?

---
* 19 Brentwood Avenue, Newton, MA 02159. Telephone (617) 965-5885; fax (617) 965-4669.

** E-mail twa@mitvma.mit.edu .

- Are technical communicators generally satisfied with their career and confident about their future?
- What is the commitment of top management? Does it allocate the resources necessary for technical communicators to perform effectively?

These questions should be of interest to large companies, to educators, and to individual technical communicators. In order to manage groups of writers, large companies will have to translate these concerns into practical tools and techniques for hiring, training, performance-appraisal, and succession-planning. Teachers of technical communication should be interested because these questions may indicate whether their degree programs and courses match the needs and rewards of the workplace. Individual writers and managers should benefit from looking at their own accomplishments and plans in an objective framework.

Edward Barrett asked me to consider these questions in the context of the Fifth Annual Conference on Writing for the Computer Industry, which he directed at MIT in August 1988 (MIT Summer Session 1988). For this purpose, I developed a questionnaire that was mailed to the registrants before the conference (TechWriting Affiliates 1988). This paper analyzes their answers.

The questionnaire was built on a model of the technical writing profession, so I will begin by describing the structure and sources of the model. Then I profile the respondents and identify two subsets for purposes of comparison: "top performers" and "average performers." For the whole sample and each subset, I give basic demographic and employment data.

In the central section of the paper, I tabulate and discuss selected questionnaire results. In reporting on qualifications, I explicitly compare the top performers with the average performers, because I hope to identify correlates of success. But in presenting other variables, I concentrate on the whole sample and mention interesting discrepancies between the two subsets only in passing.

This study is not intended to meet rigorous statistical standards. Instead, it is a stake in the ground, a presentation of ideas and approaches that I hope to amplify and refine in the future. Before drawing my own conclusions from the data, I state the limitations of my methods and compare my sample with a larger survey that has just been published (Society of Technical Communication 1988).

Various parts of the model shed light on the following topics:

- qualifications of top performers
- equal opportunity
- on-line documentation
- teamwork in the development of products

I conclude by synthesizing questionnaire results on these topics. I also suggest approaches and attitudes that may help companies manage technical communicators more effectively and maintain their competitive edge into the next century.

2. A Model of the Technical Communication Profession

The model on which the questionnaire was built had been developed by TechWriting Affiliates, Inc. for consulting and workshops on publication management and professional development. I presented an initial version at the 36th Annual Technical Writers' Institute at RPI in June 1988 (Kirsch 1988b). I expanded and refined the model for the MIT conference the following August. In its current form the model consists of four variables: qualifications, career expectations and self-image, job satisfactions, and management environment (Figure 1).

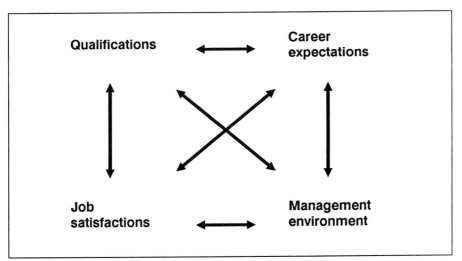

Figure 1. Model of the technical communication profession.

The arrows in the figure represent dynamic relationships between the variables. For example, the management environment of a given company determines to some extent the skills needed to excel there and the satisfactions available to workers. But management is not the only locus of control. Professional staff can affect the environment in many situations — for example, when someone excels at a particular task or when some task is especially unpopular within a group or department.

Similarly, the arrows between qualifications and satisfactions denote the reciprocal relationship between what someone is *good* at doing and what she or he *likes* to do. Finally, the arrows to and from career expectations and self- image suggest that these highly subjective considerations are affected by the other variables and may in turn influence them.

The variables are not monoliths or vague clouds but rather sets of conditions, behaviors, and attitudes that I call factors. The factors in a variable differ in strength from one individual and company to the next. The factors are introduced in the following paragraphs, with a summary in the Appendix.

In the qualifications variable, I seek to identify all credentials that technical communicators in the computer industry acquire through study, training, or work. There are four factors:

- education and training
- technical writing experience
- technical experience
- interpersonal skills

I developed questions for the first three factors by analyzing resumes of 14 top-performing writers in the files of TechWriting Affiliates, Inc.; by comparing help wanted ads for technical writers in the *Boston Sunday Globe*, May-July 1988; and by talking with managers who hire writers at computer companies in the Boston area. I developed the questions on interpersonal skills by applying Schoonover's (1988) behavioral model to my own case studies of technical writing projects (Kirsch 1988a).

In the job-satisfactions variable, I explore psychological and creative factors that contribute to technical communicators' pleasure in work:

- affiliation
- achievement
- power
- verbal
- technical

I adapted the first three factors from the classic literature of organizational psychology. Affiliation denotes the need to interact in a friendly manner with co-workers (Boyatzis 1979). Achievement denotes the need to do something better than it has been done before (McClelland 1966). Power denotes the need to influence co-workers (McClelland 1970).

The last two satisfactions on the list above adapt a creativity motive proposed by Schoonover (1988). The verbal factor tests the pleasure that technical communicators take in writing and editing manuals and on-line texts. The technical factor tests their pleasure in exploring the continuous stream of new technology that their career presents to them.

In the variable on career expectations and self-image, I consider other subjective factors:

- self-image
- job mobility
- career planning

The self-image factor asks about overall satisfaction with job and career, status within and outside the workplace, and creative writing as an avocation. The job-mobility factor explores expectations of change at work and confidence in future employability. The career-planning factor considers goals, plans, and preferred strategies for getting ahead.

In the variable on management environment, the dominant factor is documentation concept: does top management view documentation as an essential part of the company's products or services? Other factors explore how management implements its documentation concept. The other factors are:

- teamwork and specialization
- documentation standards
- quality assurance
- production resources

I abstracted the factors and questions in this variable from my own case studies (Kirsch 1988a).

3. Data Collection and Sample

The Fifth Annual Conference on Writing for the Computer Industry took place at MIT on Saturday, August 13, 1988. Questionnaires (TechWriting Affiliates 1988) based on the model were mailed to all 169 people who had registered by August 2. A cover letter asked them to spend about 45 minutes filling out the questionnaire and to mail it back anonymously. The letter stated that preliminary results would be reported at the conference and that, in general, "the data will facilitate research on... professional identity and competence." The questionnaire was eight pages long and was divided into parts and sub-parts corresponding to variables and factors of the model. There were 112 questions on the four variables; most of them asked the respondents to rate themselves or their companies on a four-point Likert scale:

- "not very descriptive of me" (or "my company")
- "somewhat descriptive"
- "generally descriptive"
- "very descriptive"

There were also 22 questions on demographics and employment status.

One hundred and seven questionnaires were returned by the day of the conference. Three were incomplete; the other 104 came from experienced technical communicators, each of whom answered at least 95% of the questions. From the 104 complete questionnaires, I report here all 85 respondents who stated that they are full-time employees and that their main job function is technical writing or publication management. I exclude 19 editors, consultants, contractors, educators, and part-time employees.

Table 1 profiles the whole sample and two subsets. The whole sample is strongly weighted to people in their mid 30s (median age 34) who have about five years of professional experience, live in New England, and work for large companies. There is a disproportionate number of women (57% in the sample versus 45% in the US

Table 1.
The Sample

	All	54 technical writers	31 managers and senior technical writers
Number of respondents	85	54	31
Live in New England	76%	78%	74%
Median age	34	33	37
Women	57%	63%	45%
Married	62%	61%	65%
With children at home	35%	28%	48%
Spouse employed half-time or more	45%	48%	39%
Employed by large company (1000 or more staff)	73%	70%	77%
1987 median salary			
All	$35,000	$30,500	$45,000
Men	36,000	30,000	45,300
Women	34,000	31,000	45,000
Total years in technical publications (median)	5.5	4	8.5

work force), and 45% of the respondents have a two-career marriage (spouse works half-time or more).

For purposes of comparison I divided the sample into two subsets, average performers and top performers. The average performers are 54 technical writers who reported 1987 earnings under $40,000. I based this criterion on personal communication with employers during the first six months of 1988; they indicated that $40,000 was a threshold reached only by competent "senior" writers.

There are 31 top performers: 11 senior technical writers and 20 managers. The 11 writers are people whose main job function is technical writing, who reported 1987 earnings of at least $40,000, and who do *not* recommend or review anyone else's salary. The 20 managers are people whose main job function is publication management and who do in fact review the salary of others. For all managers, the median number of salaries reviewed is seven. Three managers earned under $40,000; they work for smaller companies (under 500 employees) and review only two salaries.

The top performers are farther along in their careers than the average performers. They are senior in both age and professional experience by about four years. In the average group women have a 63% majority and a slightly higher salary level than men. Among the top performers women are a 45% minority, and the salary levels are about even. As the age difference would lead us to expect, a larger proportion of top performers have children, and a smaller proportion have two-career marriages.

4. Results from the Questionnaire

4.1 How Can You Tell the Best from the Rest?

There were 61 questions on qualifications in the questionnaire. Forty showed either no difference between top and average performers or (in a few cases) higher qualifications on the part of the average. Table 2 establishes a baseline by presenting the most interesting qualifications that do *not* discriminate high performers.

Before proceeding, I should explain how I use "expertise" in this discussion. The questionnaire asked the respondents to state how many times they had written various types of documents, used various classes of software, and performed other technical tasks. In my experience, once a writer has done a task three times, she or he has mastered the generic problems — has climbed the learning curve — and can comfortably repeat the task any number of times. So my working definition of expertise is simply the fact of having written a certain type of document, or performed a certain task, at least three times.

As Table 2 shows, the two subsets are similar in education and training. A bachelor's or master's degree does not discriminate between them, nor does a major in English or technical communication at either level. In fact, the average performers are more likely to have college degrees with honors and more likely to have studied technical writing and computing in college.

Table 2.
Qualifications That Do Not Discriminate High Performers
Percentage of respective subset.

	54 technical writers	31 managers and senior technical writers
EDUCATION AND TRAINING		
Bachelor's degree	83%	87%
Bachelor's in English or technical communication	39	35
Honors in college	50	38
Any master's degree	50	48
Master's in English or technical communication	19	19
Have taken college courses in:		
Computer programming or applications	63	39
Math or statistics	52	48
Technical writing	43	16
Have taken company/other courses in:		
Computer programming or applications	48	58
Technical writing	46	39
TECHNICAL WRITING EXPERIENCE		
Written or re-written three or more documents of this type:		
Training document	21%	29%
System text (menus, commands, messages)	15	16
TECHNICAL EXPERIENCE		
Used three or more operating systems	49%	42%
Performed electronic publishing task three or more times:		
Write typesetting/formatting macros/scripts	22	26
Edit page descriptions (e.g., Postscript)	19	16
Write stylesheets (e.g., Ventura, MS-Word)	19	26

The two groups are also similar in having moderate levels of expertise with operating systems and fairly low levels with advanced electronic publishing tasks. There are also low levels of expertise in writing or re-writing training documents (learning plan, workbook, trainer's guide, programmed text) and in writing or re-writing system text (menus, commands, messages).

Because the average performers have about four years less overall experience than the top performers, uniform expertise in a given skill suggests that the younger group is in some sense "ahead" of the older. This may indicate a trend — for example, growing demand for expertise in advanced electronic publishing.

Table 3 shows qualifications that are more frequently found among the high performers than among the average. The percentage differences between the two subsets fall into two groups, weaker differences (17% or less) and stronger differences (20% or more). I think that the weaker differences may be a function of mere longevity, whereas the stronger ones may indicate skill or experience that is not necessarily acquired by years on the job. By this criterion, the following qualifications are *weak* discriminators of top performers:

- Expertise in writing or re-writing software manuals and on-line documents (help, computer-based training, demo).
- Expertise in using programming languages and in performing other technical tasks (running software diagnostics, removing and replacing printed circuit board, preparing module-level block diagram, installing hard or floppy disk drive, reading circuit schematics).

By the same criterion, the following qualifications are *strong* discriminators of top performers:

- Expertise in writing or re-writing hardware manuals, reference cards or pamphlets, and sales material (data sheet, brochure, newsletter, trade news article).
- Interpersonal skills related to collecting technical information in interviews, handling project problems, and self-presentation.

All the respondents rated themselves more highly on interpersonal skills than on any other set of qualifications. To offset this "halo" effect, the data in Table 3 use only the highest answer on the Likert scale ("very descriptive of me").

In summary, versatility in writing and interpersonal skills are relatively strong distinguishing attributes of top performers in this sample. Software documentation is virtually a baseline capability; top performers must also be able to handle other genres, such as hardware and sales materials.

Table 3.
Qualifications That Discriminate High Performers

Percentage of respective subset. Stronger discriminators are in **boldface** type.

	54 technical writers	31 managers and senior technical writers
TECHNICAL WRITING EXPERIENCE		
Written or re-written three or more documents of this type:		
Software manual	70%	87%
On-line documents (help, CBT, demo)	15	29
Hardware manual	**20**	**42**
Reference card, pamphlet	**20**	**55**
Sales material	**24**	**58**
TECHNICAL EXPERIENCE		
Used three or more programming languages	37%	52%
Performed this task three or more times:		
Run software diagnostics	33	48
Remove, replace circuit board	30	45
Prepare module-level block diagram	28	45
Install hard or floppy disk drive	25	39
Read schematics	26	39
INTERPERSONAL SKILLS (percentage responding "very descriptive of me")		
Interviews		
Establish rapport	**37%**	**65%**
Ask open-ended questions	**41**	**61**
Clarify, summarize important topics	**48**	**77**
Project problems		
See manager about serious problem	**52**	**74**
Suggest how to turn strategies into actions	**44**	**74**
Administrative problems		
See manager when bothered by problem	**13**	**39**
Voice my concerns sensitively, directly	**20**	**45**
Appearance		
Pay attention to grooming, self-presentation	**50**	**71**

It is interesting that expertise in writing on-line information is much less prevalent, among top and average performers alike, than expertise in writing printed material. This comparison is seen more clearly in Table 4, which shows levels of expertise by type of document for the whole sample.

Table 4.
Expertise by Type of Document
Percentage of 85 technical communicators who have written or re-written three or more documents of the given type.

PRINTED

Software manual	77%
Sales material (data sheet, brochure, newsletter, trade news article)	37
Reference pamphlet, card	33
Hardware manual	28
Training document (learning plan, workbook, trainer's guide, programmed text)	24

ON-LINE

System text (menus, commands,messages)	19%
On-line documents (help, computer-based training, demo)	15

4.2 What Are the Main Non-Financial Rewards?

Table 5 presents selected results on job satisfactions. The data in the table refer to the whole sample; interesting differences between the two subsets are mentioned below.

Affiliation appears to me to be the strongest job satisfaction for the respondents. They express very strong camaraderie with other communicators, engineers, and programmers. However, their rapport with customers and marketing or sales staff is notably cooler. The attitude toward marketing or sales staff must be further qualified: there is a wide split between the top performers (74% favorable) and the average (48% favorable).

Table 5.
Job Satisfactions

Percentage of 85 technical communicators responding "generally descriptive of me" or "very descriptive of me."

AFFILIATION

Like spending time working with writers, editors	98%
Like spending time working with programmers, engineers	86
Like spending time working with customers	64
Like spending time working with marketing, sales staff	58

ACHIEVEMENT

More than willing to work overtime on important project	78%
Glad to revise/expand my work for last-minute changes in product	72
Enjoy working under tight deadlines	54

VERBAL

Like working on types of manuals I haven't worked on before	89%
Enjoy polishing my drafts over and over	48
Prefer writing on-line documentation (e.g., help screens) to writing manuals	18
Prefer writing or editing system text (menus, commands, messages) to writing or editing manuals	9

TECHNICAL

Suggest technical changes in my company's products/services	57%
Try out new electronic publishing tools whenever possible	57
Try out new computers/peripherals whenever possible	45
Explore new software releases as soon as possible	40

POWER

Enjoy asking questions, making suggestions at department/team meetings	85%
Like to talk a lot, ask many questions at my own performance-review meetings, regardless of the size of my raise	57

The respondents seem strongly motivated by achievement. They are willing to work overtime if the job is important, and more than half of them even enjoy tight deadlines.

In the questions on verbal satisfaction, the respondents strongly prefer working on new types of manuals to polishing their own drafts. However, on polishing drafts there is a notable gap between the top performers (29%) and the average (59%). There is a uniform and extraordinarily negative attitude toward writing or editing material to be read from the screen, whether it be on-line documents (help, CBT, demos) or system text (menus, commands, messages).

In general, the respondents have a lukewarm attitude toward technical tasks. About half are inclined to suggest improvements in their companies' products and to try out new electronic publishing tools. (However, the top performers are more inclined to suggest improvements than are the average: 74% versus 48%.) There is less overall interest in exploring new hardware and new releases of familiar software.

I could think of only two opportunities for technical communicators to exert power or influence on the job. One is departmental or team meetings; the other, individual performance-review meetings. The respondents like to speak out in the larger meetings, where their confidence is perhaps related to the camaraderie they feel with each other. They are less inclined to talk privately in their own performance-review meetings.

4.3 Is There Overall Professional Satisfaction and Confidence?

Table 6 presents selected results on career expectations and self-image. Again, the data in the table refer to the whole sample; interesting differences between the two subsets are mentioned below.

There are cross-currents in the data on self-image. On the positive side, the respondents express very strong satisfaction with their present employers and careers. On the negative side, when asked how *other* people view their careers, they indicate that they enjoy substantially higher status with people outside the computer field than with those inside it. Thus, many of them do not feel their work is valued by people in the best position to understand it. There is also an interesting spread concerning the attitude of outsiders: 70% of the average performers feel that outsiders are impressed by their occupation, but only 42% of the top performers agree.

The respondents have a positive outlook on the future. They are rather confident of being able to get another job if necessary, but they evaluate changing jobs as a relatively weak strategy for advancing their careers — instead, superior performance is viewed much more favorably. The majority expect to be with their current employers in three years, but this expectation is notably stronger among the

Table 6.
Career Expectations and Self-Image

Percentage of 85 technical communicators responding "generally descriptive of me" or "very descriptive of me."

SELF-IMAGE

Am happy with present employer	89%
Am happy with my present career	88
People outside the computer field are impressed when I say what I do for a living	60
People inside the computer field are impressed when I say what I do for a living	35

MOBILITY

Could easily get another job similar to the one I have now	73%
Will probably be working for same employer in three years	61
Will probably be working in same job role in three years	44

CAREER PLANNING

Superior performance is the best way for me to get ahead	82%
Changing jobs is the best way for me to get ahead	40

top performers (74%) than among the average (54%). Fewer than half the respondents (44%) expect that their job roles will be the same in three years as they are now; in other words, a majority have realistic expectations of change.

4.4 What Is Top Management's Commitment?

Does top management view documentation as an essential part of the company's products or services? This was the first question about management environment, and 67% of the respondents responded positively, suggesting that they think their companies are committed to excellence in documentation. The remaining questions explore the extent to which management implements its commitment with constructive practices. The model groups the latter in four factors:

- teamwork and specialization
- documentation standards
- quality assurance
- production resources

Tables 7 and 8 show results for the entire sample. I will not mention differences between the subsets below because I think the group's overall perceptions are more important.

I start with baseline practices, by which I mean those that at least 75% of the respondents see in their companies (Table 7). Two baseline practices offer important though minimal guarantees of the content of documentation: an editor or supervisor copy-edits new manuals, and at least two drafts are reviewed before camera-ready copy is prepared. The remaining baseline practices have the common denominator of ensuring economical production: page-layout is standardized, text and graphics are integrated by electronic publishing, and layout standards are implemented in software macros or scripts.

Table 7.
Documentation Management: Baseline Practices
Percentage of 85 technical communicators responding "generally descriptive of my company" or "very descriptive of my company."

TEAMWORK AND SPECIALIZATION

Editor or supervisor copy-edits new manuals   75%

STANDARDS

Written guidelines for page-layout   88

QUALITY ASSURANCE

At least two drafts of new manual are reviewed before
*   camera-ready copy*   87

PRODUCTION RESOURCES

Software and hardware integrate text and graphics on
*   on same page*   72
Macros or scripts control page-layout   89

Beyond the baseline are other constructive practices, which 60% or fewer of the respondents see in their companies (Table 8). Teamwork in the development of new products is the most critical factor. I use the term "cross-functional team" to describe teamwork that brings together the various groups that develop, market, and support a new product. Figure 2 shows a cross-functional team for managing a software project. In practice, a management team like this would spin off or create various task-oriented teams with equally diverse membership.

As Table 8 shows, under a third (29%) of the respondents participate in teams like the one shown in Figure 2. So it is not surprising that their verbal skills are not widely used in editing the menus and messages of software products. The problem originates in product plans that do not relate documentation to other development tasks — thereby tacitly denying that documentation is part of the product.

Table 8.
Documentation Management: Beyond the Baseline

Percentage of 85 technical communicators responding "generally descriptive of my company" or "very descriptive of my company."

TEAMWORK AND SPECIALIZATION

New products are developed by teams that include writers or editors	29%
Writer or editor edits menus and messages of new software	33
Written product plan describes how documentation fits in with other development tasks	44

STANDARDS

Written guidelines for on-line documentation	33
Written guidelines for writing and revision process (e.g., number of drafts, who reviews, how tested)	53
Written guidelines for organizing manuals	60
Written guidelines for copy-editing	60

QUALITY ASSURANCE

Documentation is tested, with product, on customers	49
When we're overloaded or have tight deadlines, additional staff is assigned or contractors are hired	51

The respondents report deficits in certain kinds of guidelines or standards — another inconsistency with the asserted importance of documentation. Guidelines or standards provide support for iterated tasks, embody ideas of quality, and ensure consistency in user interface and sales image. As the following list shows, guidelines become less prevalent as companies turn from familiar and concrete features of hard copy, to intangibles of organization and process, and then to the relative novelty of on-line documentation:

- Guidelines for page-layout 88%
- Guidelines for copy-editing 61
- Guidelines for organization of manuals 60
- Guidelines for documentation process 53
- Guidelines for on-line documentation 33

Failure to test documentation on customers is also inconsistent with the assertion that documentation is an essential part of the product. Sometimes the problem is in fact conceptual: why test the manual when we're really selling hardware or software? But in other cases lack of testing stems from lack of time.

Time also underlies the other quality-assurance problem, peak load at the end of project. Underestimates of work and consequent schedule and budget crises are very common in the computer industry. Only half the respondents say that in a crunch management assigns extra staff or hires contractors. Another question

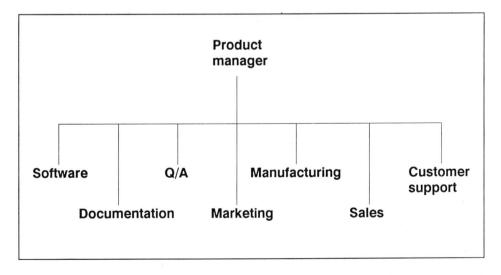

Figure 2. Cross-functional management team for software product.
Source: Kirsch 1988a

(not tabulated in Table 8) confirms the prevalence of two negative solutions: overtime and cutting corners. Sixty-four percent responded that these practices were "generally" or "very descriptive of my company" during peak loads.

The questionnaire results on management environment are clearly inconsistent. While tending to accept top management's assertion of the importance of documentation, the respondents reveal that this concept is not implemented in important ways. At the baseline, management is committed to two drafts, copy-editing, and technology-intensive production methods. Beyond the baseline, there is room for improvement in teamwork, standards, and quality assurance.

5. Limitations of this Study

The questionnaire results that I have presented are preliminary. The sample is small, there was no control group, and the questionnaire was not tested, although it was carefully reviewed. The self-rating data produced could have been refined and analyzed by sophisticated statistical techniques, but such work was beyond the scope of this study. My conclusions are not intended to meet rigorous statistical standards.

Nevertheless, it is interesting to ask whether the MIT conference sample, with its 76% New England component, represents the profession to any extent. Some light is shed on this question by a survey that the STC distributed in October 1987 and published in November 1988 (Society of Technical Communication 1988), while this paper was being written. The STC sent questionnaires to 1,453 people chosen randomly from a national membership of over 12,000, and 610 of the recipients responded. So the STC survey has a good claim to being representative of the profession in the USA.

The STC data of initial interest are median salaries for ten regions. New England is the highest at $37,000, followed by the Carolinas/Georgia at $36,000 and the West Coast at $35,000. Thus the New England population from which 76% of the MIT conference sample was drawn works in the highest-paying market in the USA — and, I infer, the most competitive.

Table 9 compares a few points from the two surveys. Strikingly, the STC's New England median salary of $37,000 is higher than the conference median of $35,000. Similarly, the STC sample shows more professional experience, stated to be "about 7 years," compared with a median of 5.5 years for the conference sample. These comparisons suggest to me that the conference sample represents a relatively young segment within the whole profession and also within New England.

The last point of comparison is the response rate of the two samples. Forty-two percent of the people who received the STC questionnaire actually filled it out, compared with 62% for the conference questionnaire. The difference suggests that the conference respondents are more motivated by achievement than is the national

Table 9.
Comparison of Two Surveys of Technical Communicators

	Median salary in New England	Professional experience— all respondents	Questionnaire response rate (note 1)
STC October 1987 (note 2)	$37,000	"about 7 years"	42%
MIT Conference August 1988	$35,000 (note 3)	5.5 years (note 4)	62%

Note 1.   Completed questionnaires as percentage of all questionnaires distributed.
Note 2.   Source: Society of Technical Communication (1988).
Note 3.   Median both for 62 New England respondents only and for all 85 respondents (Table 1).
Note 4.   Median for all 85 respondents (Table 1). Median for 62 New England respondents only is 6 years.

norm. This inference is supported by the fact that the conference respondents were doubly self-selected: first, by deciding to attend the conference; second, by deciding to fill out the questionnaire. I need hardly add that attendance at a professional meeting on a Saturday in mid-August shows initiative.

Comparison of the two surveys suggests, then, that the MIT conference sample represents a younger, more ambitious portion of the profession than both national and New England norms. This finding is highlighted by the STC regional data showing New England to be the highest-paying market for the skills of technical communicators.

6. Conclusions and Recommendations

The MIT conference questionnaire provides a snapshot of young professionals who are well educated, satisfied with their jobs and career but ready for change, and strongly motivated to do things better than they have been done before. The more recent entrants into the profession seem even better prepared than their older colleagues, as measured by college honors and college courses in technical writing and computing. As a whole, the respondents work for large companies that are committed to excellence in production, where electronic publishing technology provides automated solutions. But the companies are less committed to excellence in the content of documentation, where intangible factors are decisive.

My conclusions fall into four areas: qualifications of top performers, equal opportunity, on-line documentation, and teamwork in the development of products. In each area I will bring together results from different parts of the model.

6.1 Qualifications of Top Performers

The preliminary data presented here suggest that versatility in writing and interpersonal skills discriminate top from average performers in technical communication. If communicators become more active in product teams, interpersonal skills may become an even greater asset for them and their companies alike.

However, because the top and average performers in the sample differ by about four years in age and professional experience, the attributes that seem to discriminate them may simply be a function of time on the job. More research is needed on this question before practical tools and techniques can be developed for hiring, succession-planning, and performance-appraisal in large companies.

The findings may have implications for technical communication curricula. If versatility is defined as the ability to write various types of documents, curricula should expose students to several genres, including software manuals, hardware manuals, sales material, and on-line help. Similarly, it may be possible to teach interpersonal skills in classrooms and workshops, since the main transactions between technical communicators and their co-workers can be modeled. Academic programs that include cooperative or intern arrangements with industry are in a good position to focus attention on interpersonal skills.

6.2 Equal Opportunity

The MIT conference data and the STC survey show a marked trend toward gender-blind salaries. In the conference data (Table 1), women's salaries are slightly higher than men's in the younger subset and barely lower in the older subset. Although the STC's nationwide data still show a large advantage for men, the gap has narrowed from 19% in their 1985 survey ($34,000 versus $27,500) to 13% in the 1988 survey ($37,500 versus $32,500).

There is a bigger obstacle to equal opportunity than salaries: the problem of balancing family and career. The problem is implicit in the following information from Table 1:

- The median age in the sample is 34.
- Almost half the respondents have two-career marriages.
- A growing majority of technical communicators are women.

The 30s are a decade of high career stress and commitment (Levinson 1979) as well as a decade of declining fertility. The data suggest to me that many technical communicators are juggling the most difficult problems of career and personal life — problems that are inherently harder for women than for men. The problems now pervade all professions, but they will become unusually prominent in technical communication because of the growing majority of women.

Crash projects are unacceptable to parents of pre-school children who cannot afford live-in help. Overtime was recognized by a majority of the respondents as one way in which their companies now deal with project emergencies. Management can minimize emergencies by instituting effective teamwork.

Policies of parental leave and flex time, already widespread, should be extended. Large companies should also eliminate career penalties for able people who take extended parental leave. For example, they might provide special management training and accelerated promotion for talented individuals whose career growth has been slowed by family responsibilities.

6.3 On-Line Documentation

It is common practice to distribute documentation of computer products in machine-readable form for viewing on a screen. Therefore, I am surprised by the following results from various parts of the model:

- Few respondents have expertise in writing on-line documents (Qualifications — Table 4).
- Many respondents have a negative attitude toward writing or editing for the screen (Job satisfactions — Table 5).
- Standards for on-line documentation are not widespread (Management environment — Table 8).

I can only offer a range of possible explanations. The most obvious is that the companies represented in the survey are not using on-line documentation! Another is that the companies are converting manuals to on-line format, without authors being involved in the conversion. I know that some large computer companies extract reference sections from printed manuals and convert them with little change to on-line help files.

A variant of this practice will become prevalent, and perhaps dominant, over the next two or three years, as fast optical disk drives come into use. Since an optical disk, roughly the size of a floppy, stores 60,000 to 100,000 pages of text, these disks will become the medium of choice for publishing large sets of manuals. Technical communicators may continue to write manuals as though for printing. The manuals will be transferred to disk, with little involvement on the part of the writers.

Another current practice in product development may contribute to the questionnaire results above. Programmers rather than technical communicators are writing material for the screen (Zimmerman 1989). This is certainly the case for system text (menus, commands, messages); it is likely for help screens too but not for computer-based training (CBT) and demos.

Authoring systems — special software used to write and format some on-line material — are more awkward to use than word processors. This may contribute to writers' negative attitude to preparing on-line text. The most tedious case is CBT, where the writer creates instruction windows and combines them with the product being taught or with a simulation of that product.

Whichever of these explanations may account for the questionnaire results, I have observed a range of problems in on-line information. The most important are unclear wording in menus, commands, and messages; overloaded help screens; and difficult conventions for navigating through text on optical disk and for retrieving items of interest. The first two problems call for more teamwork between technical communicators and co-workers on product-development teams. All three problems call for more attention by large companies to written guidelines or standards.

I commented earlier on the function of guidelines. I should add that they not only help companies improve products and streamline processes; they also help technical communicators confirm the professionalism of their work. In this respect, guidelines, like plans, are documents of power.

Despite the need for written guidelines within companies, on-line documentation cannot be codified at a general level. There are at least four variables:

- storage medium
- genre or type of document
- functional relation between on-line document and printed counterpart
- physical relation between on-line information and the product or task it describes (or is part of)

Technology is changing each variable rapidly. There is only one stable point of reference: all on-line information is ultimately read from a screen. Even this may change if voice-output technology is developed.

TechWriting Affiliates, Inc. has developed on-line documentation standards for several companies. We have found that standards should cover the follow topics to varying degrees:

- selection
- access

- format
- process

By selection I mean what to include in the on-line material and what to reserve for hard copy. By access I mean software conventions for finding needed information and printing it on demand. By format I mean the appearance, and especially the density, of information on the screen. By process I mean who writes the on-line information, who checks it, and how is it tested on customers.

6.4 Teamwork in the Development of Products

Three results from different parts of the model seem to be related:

- Few respondents participate in teams that develop new products (Management environment – Table 8).
- Many respondents feel more affiliation with each other and with programmers, than with customers and marketing or sales staff (Job satisfactions – Table 5).
- Many respondents feel they have higher status outside the industry than inside (Career expectations and self-image – Table 6).

Looking at these three items together, I think the first one determines the other two. Technical communicators lack camaraderie with marketing, sales, and customers simply because they don't work with them. And since they don't belong to product-development teams, their work is implicitly not part of the product and they feel devalued.

These are important challenges for management, whose goal is a work force that feels empowered, not put down. The challenges have practical, and in fact competitive, implications. Large companies risk losing not just the enthusiasm of technical communicators but also their creative input. A great deal of natural language is now built into computer products; it takes the form of both system text (menus, commands, messages) and on-line documentation (help, CBT, demos). It makes sense for technical communicators to be full participants in developing products in which natural language is a major component.

Teamwork has other competitive advantages. Better documentation, both printed and on-line, results when technical communicators understand the business or sales objectives of a new product as well as how it works. By rubbing shoulders with marketing, sales, and customer-support staff, technical communicators learn their language and become more responsive to their needs. In addition, misunderstandings are avoided that might otherwise lead to emergency rewriting toward the end of the project.

The last point suggests that technical communicators can contribute to the process of developing new products as well as to the results of the process. The very term "technical communicator" implies skills of organizing and sharing information that can be valuable to projects and companies as a whole. Lawrence Levine (1988) argues that writers can bridge the gap between the groups that make and the groups that sell, thereby resolving conflict and optimizing the flow of work in the organization. In this role, technical communicators become "process consultants" as well as producers of information.

· · · · ·

At a gathering after the MIT conference, I was talking with someone who manages a writing group at a large company. Concerning the difficulties of her job, she said, "The trouble with tech writing is you're always at the end of the feeding chain!"

The remark stayed with me in part because of the real concern in her voice. The feeding chain clearly referred to time and staff, but there was an implication that she meant energy and morale as well.

Technical communicators need various forms of nourishment for their professional development. Companies should remember that well-nourished professionals are their greatest resource and competitive advantage.

Appendix.
Model of the Technical Writing Profession: Sectors within Variables

Copyright 1989 © TechWriting Affiliates, Inc.

Numbers in parentheses refer to the "Questionnaire on Professional Development" (TechWriting Affiliates 1988).

Qualifications (61 questions)
    Education and training (11)
        Degrees, honors, fields of study
        Total years of graduate study
        Courses in and after college
    Technical writing experience (8)
        Total years in technical publications
        Expertise with seven types of documents
    Technical experience (22)
        Expertise with 11 types of software product
        Expertise in 11 technical tasks
    Interpersonal skills (20)
        Conducting technical interviews
        Obtaining reviews

          Handling project problems
          Handling administrative problems
          Appearance/self-presentation
Job satisfactions (18 questions)
          Affiliation
          Achievement
          Power
          Verbal
          Technical
Career expectations and self-image (14 questions)
          Self-image
          Job mobility
          Career planning
Management environment (19 questions)
          Documentation concept
          Teamwork and specialization
          Documentation standards
          Quality assurance
          Production resources (hardware, software)

Acknowledgments

This paper would not have been possible without the generous input and encouragement of Edward Barrett in his dual capacity as editor of this volume and Director of the Fifth Annual Conference on Writing for the Computer Industry.

For participation in panel discussions that I chaired at the conference, I thank Diane Braff, Ruth Cassidy, Gene Cronin, Lionel Howard, Ilene H. Lang, Lawrence Levine, Leslie Levitt, Philip Rubens, and Muriel Zimmerman.

I also thank Jon Burrowes, Allen King, and Robert R. Rathbone for reading drafts; Stephen Krug and Leonard Muellner of TechWriting Affiliates, Inc., Carol Dietz, and Stephen C. Schoonover for reviewing the questionnaire; John Goldie of TechWriting Affiliates for formatting the questionnaire and setting up the database; Elizabeth Lee-Guckenheimer for consulting on database design and analysis and for supervising data entry; and Nancy Bagot, Winston Braman, Jonathan Mermin, Stanley Silverman, and Nancy Smith for entering the data.

References

Barrett, E. (ed.). 1988a. *Text, Context, and Hypertext: Writing with and for the Computer.* Cambridge, MA: The MIT Press.

Boyatzis, R.E. 1979. "The Need for Close Relationships and the Manager's Job." In Kolb 1979.

Kirsch, J. 1988a "Investment in Computer-Product Documentation." In Barrett 1988a.

_____ 1988b. "Fit To Work: The Relationship between Job Satisfactions and Working Conditions." In *Proceedings of the 36th Annual Technical Writers' Institute.* Troy, NY: Rensselaer Polytechnic Institute.

Kolb, D.A., et al. (eds.). 1979. *Organizational Psychology: A Book of Readings,* third edition. Englewood Cliffs, NJ: Prentice- Hall.

Levine, L. 1988. "Corporate Culture, Technical Documentation, and Organizational Diagnosis." In Barrett 1988a.

Levinson, D. 1979. *Seasons of a Man's Life.* New York: Ballantine Books.

McClelland, D.C. 1966. "That Urge to Achieve." In Kolb 1979.

_____ 1970. "The Two Faces of Power." In Kolb 1979.

MIT Office of the Summer Session. 1988. "Fifth Annual Conference on Writing for the Computer Industry August 13, 1988." Cambridge, MA.

Schoonover, S.C. 1988. *Managing to Relate: Interpersonal Skills at Work.* Reading, MA: Addison-Wesley.

Society of Technical Communication. 1988. "Profile 88." In *Intercom*, Vol. 34, No. 4. Washington, DC.

TechWriting Affiliates, Inc. 1988. "Questionnaire on Professional Development." Newton, MA.

Zimmerman, M. 1989. Paper in this volume.

Reconstruction of a Profession:
New Roles for Writers In the Computer Industry

Muriel Zimmerman

University of California
Santa Barbara, California 93106

The profession of writing is not a cultural absolute, but a socially constructed reality with a history of development and change. At the present time, the profession of writing in the computer industry is changing dramatically because of technological advances like document databases and because the attitudes, expectations, and methodologies of other parties to the computer development process have changed. The work of writers has become more like the work of engineers and programmers. The work of readers has changed as well. Hypercard/hypermedia applications confound our ability to distinguish between reading and writing, as readers read hypercard texts by writing them.

An Endangered Profession

Much of what writers in the computer industry now do is not included in any traditional definition of writing. And much of what we have come to think of as the writer's special contribution to the computer industry — user documentation — has been coopted by engineers and programmers as well as by users themselves.

Early writers in the computer industry worked in product development settings that stressed feasibility and reliability, not user satisfaction. If they were not the central figures in computer advances (no one was shipping the books without the products), they were important parties in the process (very few products could be shipped without the books). As user-satisfaction became the central feature that distinguished one computer product from another, writers were brought earlier and earlier into product development deliberations. Their job titles were often changed; they were now information developers or documentation specialists (21), and they served an increasingly central role in transferring technical information to users who would ultimately need to learn the product.

At the present time, user interfaces are commonly developed with users' needs and capabilities in mind. There are fewer self-referential engineers designing for their own intellectual satisfaction, and fewer occasions on which writers are called in to bail out products by way of written instructions to users. Software engineers have incorporated many of the insights from human factors analysis and educational psychology into product design. Recent articles and books by and for software designers are based on principles indistinguishable from those on which writers have based their materials to help users (12,19). Building products that users are able to use has turned out to be good business. The writer's insight — the writer's methodology — has been incorporated into the technology — an increasingly holistic technology, with less bifurcation of roles between developers and writers. In the best circumstances, usability is now an engineered factor, designed in, not constructed by writing (47,48). Developments like interactive programming and displayable manuals have blurred the lines betwen hardware, software, and information (21). The activities of technical communicators have become, in Roger Grice's words, "more like those of the professionals with whom technical communicators deal" (21, p.137). Dunkle and Pesante, having trouble defining exactly what it is that writers can do, argue that "the key to defining our role lies in the similarities between what the writer does and what the software developer does" (13, p.WE–51). What we are approaching is rhetoric expressed in technology rather than in discourse.

Will there be work for writers if everyone working on computer products functions as a writer? If everyone is a writer, will anyone be a writer? What does it mean for the profession of writing in the computer industry if writing is a function but not a role?

In this chapter, I identify a number of factors that change, and therefore challenge, the profession of writing in the computer industry — a profession, that is, in which the professional writers are a distinct occupational group, in which it is possible to tell who the writers are. This challenge seems to come at a time when writers are getting good at their jobs and when their jobs are getting good. But, I will suggest, writers have continuing important roles to play in the computer revolution that is presently underway. And given what they have learned while doing their jobs, many writers are likely to play important roles in the implementation of the new technology. I will consider the larger problems of professionalism by linking us with all writers who write for money, with all authors whose name is "anonymous," and with all professionals who feel their roles to be ancillary. And I will conclude with some comments about the impact of writing with and for the computer on the socially-created reality we call "writing," an impact which has created new roles for readers as well as for writers.

Playing a Different Role in User Support

A number of technological changes affect the nature of work for writers, including the increased use of the computer itself as the delivery medium for documentation and the increased use of the computer to perform editing and formatting tasks previously performed by writers. Advances in artificial intelligence seem likely to lead to what Mark Haselkorn calls "smart documentation systems" (24), at which time the computer may be the producer as well as the transmitter of documentation. And a blurring of the distinctions between what developers do, what writers do, and what users do has already affected many documentation groups.

Increased use of online documentation. Increased use of the computer as the medium for delivering documentation will of necessity threaten the jobs of writers who cannot program. A cartoon from a 1985 newsletter of the Boston chapter of the Society for Technical Communication, was recently reprinted in the Third Quarter, 1988 issue of *Technical Communication* (p.221). "So I says to my boss, Online? What's online? I have no time for that garbage," explains a former technical writer, now unemployed, to his companion on the proverbial park bench. How realistic is this vision? Will writers who cannot program be obsolete?

Henrietta Shirk predicts that many existing publications departments will become extinct as technical writing shifts from the medium of paper to the medium of online documentation. Shirk notes that most literature about online documentation moves very quickly from using the term "writer" to using the term "designer": "The products of online documentation are, in reality, software products. And this means that these writers are software designers, who happen to specialize in creating (both verbally and visually) information which appears on the computer screens of software products" (43, p.321).

Elsewhere in this volume John Kirsch and Edward Barrett report the results of their 1988 "Issues and Trends" questionnaire on the subject "Is Technical Writing a Profession?" Of the eighty-five respondents who work full-time as writers and managers of writing, 82% prefer writing hard copy to writing or editing on-line material; only 31% have written two or more on-line documents (19% have written three or more on-line documents); and only 28% have edited menus and messages of two or more software products (15% have edited menus and messages of three or more software products). Kirsch cautions that his data are derived from East Coast respondents. However, as the computer industry is generally thought to be moving away from hard-copy documentation and toward on-line documentation, one wonders if it is in fact those personnel who have to date been called "writers" who are doing the bulk of writing and editing for the screen.

Automation of editing functions. In his 1983 paper, "Today's Technical Writers/Editors in Tomorrow's Electronic Mega-Cottage-Industry World of Work: Will They Survive," William Houze predicted that as many as 75% of technical writers will be doing other kinds of jobs by 1990 (26). In his view, technical professionals will no longer need to rely on writers, but instead will have at their disposal software packages which permit them to have immediate access to corrected spelling and grammar, pre-specified document formats, and credible advice about which formats fit which tasks and purposes. In Houze's disturbing vision, a great number of expensive writers and editors will be replaced by "smart software." Some will become document traffic managers; some software writers; some computer language specialists; some computer-generated graphics experts. Most, he thinks, will become typists, inputters of data.

Presently available editing software has not been smart enough to put many writers out of work, but there may be some competition from improving products. Timp Software's advertisement for their new product, "Thelma Thistleblossom," foregrounds the potential threat with the anthropomorphism of both product name and advertising copy, calling the grammar, style, usage, and punctuation checker "Your Personal Copy Editor" (46).

Document Database Methodologies. One of the most interesting challenges to the traditional functions of writers and editors is the idea that the text underlying a document is more valuable than the document; the document is only one of the presentation formats in which captured text can be used (10,27,28,51). The key to unlocking text is declarative structuring expressed in a markup system. Markup systems encode the information necessary to fully develop two products in the document development process: the source file and the printout (10). Files then become more reusable than they have ever been, and if a markup language is standardized, files become more compatible than they have ever been — one reason why Standard Generalized Markup Language is now required to fulfill a substantial amount of writing to federal military specifications.

Technical publications have traditionally been developed by a "batch" methodology. In batch formatting, writers make formatting decisions as they write by entering formatting controls; each decision is a separate one. With declarative structuring, the writer only manipulates the content of the document. The formatter program makes formatting decisions based on that content, according to a standard style definition; the publication style is externally defined (27, pp.8–13).

How does the new document database methodology change the technical publications environment? John Brockmann predicts that the document database methodology will undermine the professional status of documenters and lead to the overcentralization of corporate document design and the "de-skilling" of the documentation profession. Brockmann asks, "By taking away decisions regarding format, layout, design, typeface and size, and even reference aid design, won't this methodology, when married to desktop or workstation publishing technology, lead to a contraction of professional responsibilities and to less of a need to increase documenters' expertise?" (6, p.37). In his prediction, "Fewer people will be needed to produce many more manuals. And the people that remain to churn out the manuals will be divided almost along class lines into those who assemble and develop the generic text and graphic 'screen size' modules and those handful of 'super-documenters' at the home office designing all of the declarative formats" (6, p.38).

Geoffrey James agrees and disagrees: "I agree that the document database methodology will result in readjustments in the publications labor force. This has already happened to some degree – when was the last time you had a conversation with a hot-lead typographer?" (29, p.53). But in James' opinion, the methodology does not pose a threat to the technical communicator because good writing is not tied up with the petty details of document production, and the intellectual effort of synthesizing ideas and expressing them clearly is "a skill that can never be automated" (29, p.54).

Desktop publishing. At some mid-point between realism and paranoia, desktop publishing capabilities can be seen as threats to professional writers as well as to designers. When writing, editing, design, and production functions are decentralized – away from a publications department – and available to individuals and departments, dependence on the specialized skills of writers and designers is reduced. The decline in publications quality associated with desktop publishing is an increasingly urgent subject, and many concerned critics, only half-joking, call for a force of "design police" (20,23). For professional writers who incorporate desktop publishing into their traditional processes of technical communication, the effects of the new technology are not necessarily positive ones. Philip Rubens finds that desktop publishing technology is often poorly developed to support the tasks of writing and does not "adequately mirror the traditional practices in graphics and publication design . . . the technology creates the impression that the design process is trivial, and it subtly discourages the writer from considering the shape of a text before coming to the final stages of document layout" (40, p.298).

AI and Smart Documentation Systems. "The answer is artificial intelligence," write Roger Schank and Colleen Seifert; "What is the question?" (42, p.60). In the publications environment, artificial intelligence is likely to play an important role in conversion of text from one formatting system to another and in the generation of style files (28, p.21). Advances in natural language processing will have an impact on documentation efforts. Mark Haselkorn describes research at the University of Washington to link user issues with system design: "By this approach, a formal representation of the language by which a user specifies a task is mapped to the specification module which defines the functionality of lower level software. This may sound like a far cry from technical writing, but remember that documentation writers are specialists both in the user's perspective and in language" (24, p.6). Advanced expert system development may yield smart, online documentation systems, different from present online documentation because of improved understanding of user's needs (24, p.11) In Schank and Seifert's words, "Those of us who work in artificial intelligence are interested in getting computers to a point at which you don't have to be computer literate. Instead our computers will be 'people literate' " (42, p.60). There is no remaining distinction here between the goals of writers, engineers, programmers, and end-users. Instead of the fragmentation that characterized the early years of computer product development, we have new and overlapping roles for all parties.

New Mindsets for Developers. As usability becomes an engineered factor—designed in, not an add-on provided by writers—the lines between what writers do and what developers do are blurred. Contemporary design teams are user-driven; systems are being built top down, from user's needs, rather than bottom up, from technology availability. When documentation is delivered through the user interface, there is no distinction between interface design and user support—and, as a consequence, there is decreasing distinction between the contribution of the engineer, the programmer, and the writer.

Joseph Dumas' *Designing User Interfaces for Software* is typical of the new thinking of software designers. He defines his audience as professionals who create software, project managers who guide its development, and students who are learning about software development (12, p.xi). His thesis is this: develop the interface first, and emphasize the interface throughout the software development process. What becomes clear is that much of the work of interface building is what has traditionally been thought of as writing. Activities include choosing words that clearly describe options; describing options with parallel grammatical constructions; writing meaningful titles for every menu; and organizing menu hierarchies according to tasks that users will perform rather than according to the structure of the software modules. "The components of this user-software interface that I am concerned with," writes Dumas, "are the words and symbols that people see and read on the computer screen; the content and layout of displays; the procedures used to enter, store, and display information; and the organizational structure of the interface as a whole" (12, p.x). Development groups that accept these goals cannot treat documentation as an add-on, but as part of the product. Of the personnel involved on Dumas' team, which ones are writers—i.e. the information developers and the documentation specialists? I would say they all are. The traditional contribution of the writer has been coopted, and it is part of the job description of all members of the development group.

New Roles for Users. In earlier software development settings, writers functioned as stand-ins for users. With increasing frequency, users are representing themselves as members of development teams. Also with increasing frequency, users are developing their own systems. And user preferences for learning about computer systems are changing both documentation methodology and documentation products.

In their paper "Strategies for Managing User Developed Systems," Behestian and VanWert call attention to the increased frequency in the literature of terms such as "user computing," "user programming," and "user development" (3, p.2). The keywords to their own paper include "End-User Computing" and "User Developed Systems" (3, p.1). The case study "ZOG and the USS Carl Vinson" presents a strong argument for accepting users as equal partners on a development team: "In other words, the relationship should be a peer relationship, like a marriage should be, with neither side trying to dominate the other. Although placing the users in the design loop makes iterative design more difficult, the potential benefit is that both sides accept responsibility for the success of the system" (1, p.904).

Pierson, Forcht, and Moates call the development of non-traditional systems by persons other than information systems development specialists "commonplace" (37, p.142), and they note that the documentation phase in user-developed applications is often skipped. Elsewhere (53) I have described software development settings in which software is developed by protyping, and the task of creating user documentation is deliberately shifted to users, who are encouraged to write whatever they need.

With prototyping methodology, actual users of systems under design sit with developers. Developers ask questions like "is this the type of screen you want? is this the format you want? is this the connection you want between files?" Small versions of systems are built rapidly, followed by a series of revision cycles which involve incremental changes resulting from understandings between developers and users. The process is "intentionally evolutionary" (22, p.136). If documentation is required, it too can be developed in the same way: the developer gets the user to agree that this is what he or she wants.

User preferences for learning in ways other than reading books are increasingly taken into account. Research in technical communication and in related fields like human factors has yielded insights that have changed the ways in which computer products are developed and the ways that writers do the work of supporting users. Our notion of support for computer users is vastly expanded (47), as is our repertoire of strategies for providing support. Most important, I think, we have learned more about the ways that people want to learn about computers. We know that users would rather get something done than learn about a system. "Even the most well-written and comprehensive manual might end up gathering dust on the shelf if users, for one reason or another, prefer to get help elsewhere," writes Barbara Mirel (35, p.349). Word Perfect Corporation reports an average of 10,000 phone calls daily with questions about its new 5.0 software (50, p.1). The marketers of a 5.0 training video advertise it this way, apparently without irony: "Why rack your brain? Learn in the way we were really meant to learn…sitting down, relaxed, in front of a TV set (50, p.3)."

John Carroll's successful minimal manual and training wheels system incorporates this understanding of learning preferences. He developed 20 "guided exploration" cards, representing only a very small part of the 150 page manual, and set users to learn on a "training wheels" word processor program, an abbreviated version of the whole system that makes many error states unreachable (8,9). Stephen Draper has pointed out the naivete of simple notions of expertise, arguing that all of a system's users are in the same general situation of knowing some things and being ignorant of (and therefore sometimes needing help) with others (11, p.468). Users in general typically do not use manuals; they use summaries and they prefer to consult the local expert: "the resident expert is indeed by far the heaviest user of the printed manual, while novices seldom use it, and roughly speaking manual use is proportional to knowledge of the system and not inversely proportional as might have been expected" (11, p.468).

As models of users and of their use of technical manuals are improved (33), we realize that we cannot bully users into learning from books. In work settings in which people traditionally rely on discussions to get information, we have learned that we cannot expect computer users to want to learn in a different way. We know that it may be important to teach people to have conversations about their computer problems, that some sort of social interaction may be important to learning a computer system. We know that users have trouble finding information about systems, but that they can use the information when they do find it (48, p.178), suggesting that we can be better providers of information trails.

From interesting work at the University of Nebraska, Kendall and Losee report on a methodology called FOLKLORE that makes the documentation product flexible and responsive, substituting methods used in gathering traditional folklore for formal documentation methods. FOLKLORE allows documentation to evolve with the incorporation of details from users' customs, tales, sayings, and "art forms" such as blackboards used during meetings to discuss the system (31). In hypertext applications, discussed below, users may well feel themselves to be the authors of the documentation produced by their rich and individualized searches through help trails.

Playing New Roles in a New Game

Computers as Model T's. Rather than seeming the best of all tools, present-day computers increasingly appear to have massive limitations: "This is the auto industry, it's 1902," says Mitchell Kapor; "the state of the art in computing is incredibly primitive" (41, p.60). Classical computer architecture, modelled on an earlier view of the brain, reflects obsolete assumptions (25). The brain is "simply not a logic machine; it is not constructed like a digital computer" (14, p.24). Much software development has been an attempt to imitate what appears to be human activity, reminiscent of the corn-on-the-cob machine in Charlie Chaplin's Modern Times, designed to imitate a human corn-eater. The cob, like a typewriter carriage, zipped past Chaplin's teeth and rotated. Most present-day word processors are imitations of extremely efficient typists and, more recently, of typesetters. In contrast, Geoffrey James' Document Database Methodology is exciting because it is not based on the model of the author as typist or the author as typesetter, and its goal is not to automate a sequence of events that eventually results in a printed piece of paper.

The most radical critiques of computers suggest that their development has been founded on assumptions that limit their potential to serve human undertakings. In his book *The Mechanic Muse*, Hugh Kenner calls his first chapter "In Memoriam ETAOIN SHRDLU." ETAOINSHRDLU are the twelve most frequently-used letters in English, and despite the inconvenience to human operators, they were placed on the two leftmost columns of the linotype machine keyboard, where they obliged the operator's left little finger to make 51% of the keystrokes. They were placed there so that the largest numbers of brass matrixes could make the shortest trip to their places in the line. ETAOIN SHRDLU is now an emblem of obsolescence — recalling years when movements of the left little finger were coerced by technology (32, pp.5–15). The current critique of computers is essentially a critique of the way that certain kinds of presumed rationality are coerced, and other kinds made unavailable, by the computers we have.

Networks and Connections. Terry Winograd and Fernando Flores have written what they call "a new foundation for design" in their important book, *Understanding Computers and Cognition*. They argue that we cannot construct machines that either exhibit or successfully model intelligent behavior when we work from an orientation that equates intelligence with rationalistic problem solving based on heuristic search procedures. Artificial intelligence is founded on assumptions that limit its potential to generate new designs (49, p.143); "current theoretical discourse about computers is based on the misinterpretation of the nature of human cognition and language. Computers designed on this basis . . . are restricted to representing knowledge as the acquisition and manipulation of facts, and communication as the transferring of information" (49, p.78). Is this, they ask, really the only way to be rational?

The title of Heinz Pagels' book *The Dreams of Reason* is both cynical and optimistic. The computer has altered the structure of knowledge. The computer has opened up new windows on reality — or has it? Can we be sure it does not create that reality? When Galileo first used the telescope, he performed many experiments to convince himself that the instrument only magnified objects and did not create new objects or distort existing ones. How can we tell if the reality revealed by the computer is an artifact of the computer (36, p.89)?

Pagels' critique of artificial intelligence theory resembles Winograd's and Flores': the central premise of AI is that a serially organized terminal search is the essence of intelligent behavior. The manipulation of signs — the manipulation of knowledge of an objective world — is treated as the essence of cognition. Pagels calls this view computationalism, and he presents an alternate view, modelled on the image of the network rather than the hierarchy. He calls this alternate connectionism, a view which holds that responding to context-dependent information is more nearly the essence of cognition. Here massive parallelism, distributive information storage, and associative interconnections are the keys to progress in simulating reason. Knowledge is distributed throughout a network, not located in a specific site.

Hypertext and the Future of Writing. In hypertext applications, the metaphor of the network has replaced the hierarchy. A network has no top or bottom, but a plurality of connections that increase possible interactions between components of the network. Hypertext writing is non-sequential: chunks can be linked together in any ways that serve the user's purpose. Hypertext negates all attempts at "progressive-disclosure" writing: the order in which information is presented and received is entirely in the hands of the reader (30, p.ATA–31). Readers can structure their own interface to a document and remedy whatever flaws they find in the generic manual: "the 'bootstrapping' model for automated user response sees revision as a recursive process of incorporating user-generated improvements into the general document" (7, p.104).

Hypertext presents the potential for important changes in the professional activities of writers; the skills required to design such information products are "a giant leap" beyond what we currently use (39). Writers in the computer industry have needed to explain multi-dimensional processes using linear exposition and narrative paired with relatively simple illustrations (52, p.77). Hypertext presents the opportunity for accessing information that incorporates multiple views, n dimensions, so that the reader can move in any direction that seems appropriate. In creation of such systems, says Geri Younggren, writers will be information architects—professionals who build the n-dimensional informational space. People looking for information will perceive themselves to be in the center of an information universe designed specifically for their needs (52, p.78). In this new way of receiving and creating documentation, with deep reader involvement, readers and authors become collaborators (4).

Reconstruction of a Profession

The information we get from a computer is socially constructed: it isn't "out there" or even "in there," waiting for a perfect fit between it and our retrieval methods. We develop retrieval methods that capture certain kinds of data but not other kinds of data. The data that come from a computer—extracted by a programmer's questions and assumptions—can be said to have been created by the computer. The profession of "writer" is also a social construct (15,16,34), and what it means to be a writer has varied over the centuries, before and after Gutenberg, before and after the digital computer. "The author," writes Michel Foucault, "...is undoubtedly only one of the possible specifications of the subject and, considering past historical transformations, it appears that the form, the complexity, and even the existence of this function are far from immutable" (16, p.138).

Technical Communication, Status, and Self-Esteem. In the sense that a profession is a calling requiring specialized knowledge and intensive training and experience, technical communication is of course a profession. But it is a profession many of whose members work in an industrial culture that defines them and their work as ancillary, not central: "the abundance of poor documentation is evidence that its worth is undervalued" (31, p.103). The subject of professional self-esteem is a frequent one in professional journals (17,18,44,45), and though we are convinced that as writers we can see problems to which engineers and programmers are blind, we also know that we are usually not paid or valued as they are. Most writers do far more than repeat or transmit what developers have told them, and often facilitate what no one knew needed to be facilitated. Still, like other support professionals – nurses (17), Hollywood writers (34, pp.73–76), other writers who write for money, and many writers whose signature is "anonymous" – many writers in the computer industry feel themselves to have second-class status. If they need high moral imperatives, few writers will be satisfied. As Edmond Weiss puts it, "We do not document out of moral necessity, but, rather, in pursuit of efficiency, success, and profit" (48, p.176).

The Birth of the Reader. In the next generation of computer documentation, using database methodologies, there may be no unique authors: "each page or module created will go into a data base where it will be maintained and reused by other writers. The systems analysts sometimes call this 'egoless programming' " (48, p.185). Hypertext/hypermedia products are called un-authored, authorless, books without authors – "a book that's sort of written as you read it, by your finger when you touch the screen" (5, p.141). These are books that truly confound our ability to distinguish between reading and writing, because it appears that a reader reads them by writing them. Ithiel deSola Pool considers the copyright implications of computer-authored texts. To read a copyright text is no violation, but to copy it in writing is a violation. The technological basis for this distinction is reversed with a computer text: "to read a text stored in electronic memory, one displays it on the screen; one writes it to read it. To transmit it to others, however, one does not write it; one only gives others a password to one's own computer memory. One must write to read, but not to write" (38, p.214).

Roland Barthes essay "The Death of the Author" provides a formulation that is useful for thinking about these shifting roles: "The reader is the space on which all the quotations that make up a writing are inscribed without any of them being lost; a text's unity lies not in its origin but in its destination" (2, p.148).

Rebirth of the Writer. It seems likely that manual writing will continue for some time; many buyers expect to receive books with their computer products, and some of us will write those books. Many of us will acquire programming skills and write and edit online menus and messages. Some of us will become hypertext information architects. Some of us will have facilitating roles in a technology whose outlines we can only guess at at this time. We may still be called writers – or perhaps "writers" – the inverted commas are used with increasing frequency (24, e.g.). The Massachusetts Institute of Technology may continue to hold a summer conference called "Writing for the Computer Industry" and MIT probably knows something. But it is a mistake to believe that our jobs will continue to be the same. We may continue to be called writers; modern truckdrivers are called teamsters, and firemen ride diesel trains – but I don't think that we will do much of what Thelma Thistleblossom can do, or even much of what we presently do.

For predictive purposes, the surest bets are that paper will be obsolete as a primary means of teaching users about computer systems and that the present computer will be obsolete as a primary means of communication. The question comes down to what kinds of machines we are likely to need to teach people to use: our knowledge of the ways that users want to learn from machines will give us continuing important roles in enabling users in the next computer revolution.

Acknowledgments. Thanks to Edward Barrett of MIT and to Caron Caligor, Eric Dahlin, and Everett Zimmerman of University of California, Santa Barbara, for comments on early drafts and other assistance and support.

References

[1] R.M. Akscyn and D.L. McCracken, "ZOG and the USS Carl Vinson: Lessons in System Development," *Human-Computer Interaction*, ed. B. Shackel, Elsevier Science Publishers, 1985, pp. 901–906.

[2] R. Barthes, "The Death of the Author," translated S. Heath, *Image, Music, Text*, Hill and Wang, 1977, pp. 142–148.

[3] M. Beheshtian and P.D. VanWert, "Strategies for Managing User Developed Systems," *Information and Management*, Vol.12, 1987, pp. 1–7.

[4] M. Bernstein, "Hypertext: New Challenges and Roles for Technical Communicators," *Proceedings of the 35th ITCC, Society for Technical Communication*, 1988, pp. ATA33–ATA36.

[5] S. Brand, *The Media Lab: Inventing the Future at MIT*, Penguin Books, 1988.

[6] R.J. Brockmann, "Exploring the Connections Between Improved Technology – Workstation and Desktop Publishing and Improved Methodology – Document Databases," *Text, Context, and Hypertext*, ed. E. Barrett, MIT Press, 1988, pp. 25–49.

[7] P.A. Carlson, "Hypertext: A Way of Incorporating User Feedback into Online Documentation," *Text, Context, and Hypertext*, ed. E. Barrett, MIT Press, 1988, pp. 93–110.

[8] J.M. Carroll, "Minimalist Training," *Datamation*, November 1, 1984, pp. 125–136.

[9] J.M. Carroll, "Minimalist Design for Active Users," *Human Computer Interaction*, ed. B. Shackel, Elsevier Science Publishers, 1985, pp. 39–44.

[10]   J.H. Coombs, A.H. Renear, and S.J.DeRose, "Markup Systems and the Future of Scholarly Text Processing," *Communications of the ACM*, Vol. 30, 1987, pp. 933–947.

[11]   S.W. Draper, "The Nature of Expertise in UNIX," *Human Computer Interaction*, ed. B. Shackel, Elsevier Science Publishers, 1985, pp. 465–471.

[12]   J.S. Dumas, *Designing User Interfaces for Software*, Prentice-Hall, 1988.

[13]   S.B. Dunkle and L.H. Pesante, "Role of the Writer on the Software Team," *Proceedings of the 35th ITCC, Society for Technical Communication*, 1988, pp. WE51–WE53.

[14]   G.M. Edelman, "Neural Darwinism: Population Thinking and Higher Brain Function," *How We Know*, ed. M. Shafto, Harper and Row, 1985, pp. 1–29.

[15]   E.L. Eisenstein, *The Printing Press as an Agent of Change: Communications and Cultural Transformations in Early-Modern Europe*, Vols. 1 and 2, Cambridge University Press, 1979.

[16]   M. Foucault, "What is an Author?" translated D.F. Bouchard and S. Simon, *Language, Counter-Memory, Practice*, Cornell University Press, pp. 113–138.

[17]   T.R. Girill, "Technical Communication and Nursing," *Technical Communication*, Vol. 31, 1984, pp. 62–63.

[18]   T.R. Girill, "Technical Communication and Planning," *Technical Communication*, Vol. 35, 1988, pp. 65–66.

[19]   J.D. Gould and C. Lewis, "Designing for Usability: Key Principles and What Designers Think," *Communications of the ACM*, Vol. 18, 1985, pp. 300–311.

[20]   J. Greitzer, "Design Police: Corporations Lay Down the Law for Design Standards," *Publish!*, Vol. 1, November/December, 1986, pp. 48–52.

[21]   R.A. Grice, "Information Development is Part of Product Development – Not an Afterthought," *Text, Context, and Hypertext*, ed. E. Barrett, MIT Press, 1988, pp. 133–148.

[22]   R.A. Guillemette, "Prototyping: An Alternate Method for Developing Documentation," *Technical Communication*, Vol. 34, 1987, pp. 135–141.

[23]   J.T. Hackos, "Redefining Corporate Design Standards for Desktop Publishing," *Technical Communication*, Vol. 35, 1988, pp. 288–291.

[24] M.P. Haselkorn, "The Future of 'Writing' for the Computer Industry," *Text, Context, and Hypertext*, ed. E. Barrett, MIT Press, 1988, pp. 3–13.

[25] W.D. Hillis, *The Connection Machine*, MIT Press, 1985.

[26] W.C. Houze, "Today's Technical Writers/Editors in Tomorrow's 'Electronic Mega-Cottage-Industry' World of Work: Will They Survive?" *Proteus*, Vol. 1, 1983, pp. 23–28.

[27] G. James, *Document Databases*, Van Nostrand Reinhold, 1985.

[28] G. James, "Artificial Intelligence and Automated Publishing Systems," *Text, Context, and Hypertext*, ed. E. Barrett, MIT Press, 1988, pp. 15–24.

[29] G. James, "The Ethics of Automated Publishing Systems (A Reply to Dr. Brockmann)," *Text, Context, and Hypertext*, ed. E. Barrett, MIT Press, 1988, pp. 50–54.

[30] S. Jong, "The Challenge of Hypertext," *Proceedings of the 35th ITCC, Society for Technical Communication*, 1988, pp. ATA30–ATA32.

[31] K.E. Kendall, "Information System Folklore: A New Technique for System Documentation," *Information and Management*, Vol. 10, 1986, pp. 103–111.

[32] H. Kenner, *The Mechanic Muse*, Oxford University Press, 1987.

[33] R.P. Kern, "Modeling Users and Their Use of Technical Manuals," *Designing Usable Texts*, ed. T.M. Duffy and R. Waller, Academic Press, 1985, 315–375.

[34] A. Kernan, *Printing Technology, Letters, and Samuel Johnson*, Princeton University Press, 1987.

[35] B. Mirel, "Designing Field Research in Technical Communication: Usability Testing for In-House User Documentation," *J.Technical Writing and Communication*, Vol. 17, 1987, pp. 347–354.

[36] H. Pagels, *The Dreams of Reason: The Computer and the Rise of the Sciences of Complexity*, Simon and Schuster, 1988.

[37] J.K. Pierson, K.A. Forcht, and W. Moates, "Factors Affecting Level of Documentation Required for User-Developed Applications," IEEE *Transactions on Professional Communication*, Vol. 31, 1988, pp. 142–148.

[38] Pool, I.deS., *Technologies of Freedom*, Harvard University Press, 1983.

[39] A. Rockley and G. Graham, "Hypermedia — A Web of Thought," *Proceedings of the 35th ITCC, Society for Technical Communication*, 1988, pp. ATA10–ATA12.

[40] P. Rubens, "Desktop Publishing: Technology and the Technical Communicator," *Technical Communication*, Vol. 35, 1988, pp. 296–299.

[41] D.E. Sanger, "High-Tech Rebel," *The New York Times Magazine*, September 11, 1988, pp. 60, 64–68, 90–92.

[42] R.C. Schank and C.M. Seifert, "Modeling Memory and Learning," *How We Know*, ed. M. Shafto, Harper and Row, 1985, pp. 60–88.

[43] H.N. Shirk, "Technical Writers as Computer Scientists: The Challenges of On-line Documentation," *Text, Context, and Hypertext*, ed. E. Barrett, MIT Press, pp. 311–327.

[44] C.H. Sides, "Commentary: Land of Milk and Honey? Technical Writing in Israel," *J. Technical Writing and Communication*, Vol. 17, 1987, pp. 367–372.

[45] E.W. Smith, "Professionalism," *Technical Communication*, Vol. 35, 1988, pp. 164–166.

[46] "Thelma Thistleblossom," Timp Software, Orem, Utah 84057.

[47] E. H. Weiss, "The Next Wave of User Documentation," *Computerworld*, September 9, 1985, pp. 15–23.

[48] E.H. Weiss, "Usability: Stereotypes and Traps," *Text, Context, and Hypertext*, ed. E. Barrett, MIT Press, 1988, pp. 175–185.

[49] T. Winograd and F. Flores, *Understanding Computers and Cognition: A New Foundation for Design*, Ablex, 1986.

[50] "WordPerfect 5.0 — A Smash Hit!" *WP Corp Report*, Vol. 2, 1988.

[51] H. Wright, E. Severson, and M. Szcyzygiel, "Taking Full Advantage of Text," *Graphic Communications Association*, Vol. 1, 1988, pp. 7–10.

[52] G. Younggren, "Using an Object-Oriented Programming Language to Create Audience-Driven Hypermedia Environments," *Text, Context, and Hypertext*, ed. E. Barrett, MIT Press, 1988, pp. 77–92.

[53] M. Zimmerman, Are Writers Obsolete in the Computer Industry? *Text, Context, and Hypertext*, ed. E. Barrett, MIT Press, 1988, pp. 278–287.

Online Writing from an Organizational Perspective

Robert Krull

Department of Language, Literature, and Communication
Rensselaer Polytechnic Institute
Troy, New York

This chapter argues that, although many computer products promise to improve the productivity of technical writers, not every writer in a company should use every product. Many products require writers to have both subject-matter skills and product-specific training. Writers should learn products they will use frequently and for which they have or easily can obtain subject-matter skills. Specialists should be left to work with other software.

Introduction

The technical writing process may be improved through careful application of electronic writing and printing tools. Unquestionably this would involve drafting and editing documents, word processors being the most helpful electronic tools. Desktop publishing could be useful in document production.

However, closer examination of professional technical writing shows that writers do much more than just write and that, from an organizational perspective, document management requires information search, document standards, document archiving, personnel training, and resource allocation. Taking this broader perspective, I have divided technical writing into two areas:

* the writing environment -- how technical writers work in organizations;
* the organizational writing process -- options for managing electronic resources and the people who use them.

To give an integrated picture of organizational writing, I will draw on research about how writers work, about their learning to use electronic tools, and about the organization's perspective on the tools costs and benefits.

The Writing Environment

Writers write. Well, yes, they do that. For example, Kalmbach, Jobst, and Meese (1986) found that one group of technical writers spend 30 percent of their time writing and 14 percent editing. But technical writers also collect and organize information. Kalmbach, **et al.**, found writers spend 23 percent of their time in research, 7 percent field testing, 13 percent in meetings and 11 percent in document design. Writers' tasks change during their careers, experienced writers doing more project management and less writing (see also Green and Nolan, 1984).

Writers also don't work alone. Several studies have shown that most technical writers work in teams (Ede and Lunsford, 1985; Kalmbach, Jobst, and Meese, 1986). Working with others means sharing information and documents, and coordinating effort.

This task mix suggests that several kinds of computer software could help technical writers. Table 1 matches tasks to software. The table also lists the subject-matter skills writers need to use these tools.

The chart suggests that many computer products could help technical communicators. It also implies that writers will need considerable skills in two areas: being able to use the computer products themselves; and knowing about the tasks the products are intended to support. Many trained writers are familiar with word processors; a few are familiar with outliners, database managers, and spelling and grammar checkers. Fewer know remote online databases, drawing programs, statistics programs and project managers. Learning to use these additional electronic tools may provide dividends in increased performance; but they also require time to learn how to use them and, for companies, the costs of purchase, maintenance, and updating software. These demands are substantial, as we shall see (see also Reitman, 1987).

Productivity Gains from Word Processing

One illustration of the time required to learn computer programs is how long it takes writers to become proficient with word processors. Gilfoil (1982) found that typists needed nearly 20 hours to move from a novice's to an expert's way of operating. Technical communicators, whose writing tasks are more complex than those of typists, would need at least that long. Twenty hours may be a small price to pay for the increased writing speed word processors seem to provide (Beck and Stibravy, 1986).

However, word processors used in industry are updated, if not completely replaced, about every two to three years. Writers' keeping up with these changes might mean 10 additional hours' learning during this period. Still, the total amount of learning time, compared to the amount of time writers use word processors is small. If writers spend 40 percent of their time writing and editing (Kalmbach, **et al.**, 1986), they might use a word processor about 15 hours a week. This would mean that, for a maximal usage case (50 weeks at 15 hours per week), a writer might spend 750 hours a year with a word processor. The true number is likely to be smaller because few people work 50 weeks at the same kinds of tasks; but it will do as a rough estimate.

Computing a percentage for learning-time versus usage shows that people would initially spend 20 of 750 hours learning word processing -- or about three percent. Keeping up with the updates to the word processor might require an additional percent or two a year.

Table 1: Computer Software for Technical Writers

Task	Software	Skills
Research	Remote database	Know the online system.
		General knowledge of the technical topic.
Information Organization	Database manager	Know the DBMS.
	Hypertext	Ability to organize information in a computerizable way.
Planning Documents	Outliner	Know the outliner.
		Know outlining methods.
Drafting Documents	Word Processor	Know the processor.
		Know how to write.
Editing Documents	Word Processor	Know the tools.
	Spell and grammar checker	Know how to apply their advice and when to ignore it.
Generating Illustrations	Drawing Program	Know the tools.
	Scanner System	Know how to illustrate ideas.
Field Testing	Statistics Programs	Know the stat program.
		Know statistics.
Document Design	Desktop Publishing	Know the publishing system.
		Know layout and design.
Project Management	Project Manager	Know the manager.
	Electronic Mail	Know work organization and people's skills.

For this learning cost, writers might be able to produce text more rapidly. Precise figures for the acceleration of writing are difficult to come by. Most writers perceive themselves to work more rapidly with a word processor than by hand or with a typewriter (Beck and Stibravy, 1986). Unfortunately, several studies have shown that, at least initially, writers take longer working with word processors (Daiute, 1986; Haas and Hayes, 1986). After the learning period, though, writers perform more rapidly. However, even here the gains are not clear-cut. Beck and Stibravy have shown that writers use the time saved by word processors to continue tinkering with texts. Colette and Oatley (1987) showed that in spite of several other benefits, online editing takes longer than traditional editing of paper manuscripts. Using several studies of computer-supported typing, Johnson and Rice (1984) demonstrated that speed changes varied from a loss of one percent to a gain of 20 percent. The variation in productivity gains depended on how the work process was organized.

If technical writing teams are optimally organized, speed gains could be 20 percent or larger. Twenty percent would give nearly an eight-to-one gain for the first year when a write learned a word processor. The gain would be nearly ten to one for later years. One could produce similar computations for gains in writing quality, if studies of writing quality were available. I will explore this issue further in the section on editing procedures.

Productivity Gains from Other Electronic Tools

Desktop Publishing. Among the computer products listed in Table 1, five probably would take about the same amount of time to learn as a word processor: the remote database, database manager, drawing program, desktop publishing system, and project manager. However, since writers would spend a smaller proportion of the workday using them, the resulting productivity gains would be smaller. For example, Kalmbach, **et al.**, found that writers spend about 11 percent of their time on document design. A desktop publishing system could support this task. Writers might use such a system 220 hours a year. If it took a writer 20 hours to learn to use the system, this would mean that about nine percent of contact the first year would be instructional. Since publishing systems are still changing rapidly, writers would have to spend more time in learning updated publishing systems than updated word processing systems. Therefore, writers might allot about five percent of their time annually to re-learning publishing systems.

How much productivity increase would using desktop publishing produce? That depends on how one looks at the role of the process in a company. Doebler (1987) shows that an internal composition department may save 10-15 percent in costs over external suppliers. If layout and design can be folded into the editing function, he contends, a company may be able to save 75-85 percent of the cost of outside composition. However, Doebler does not include the cost of training technical writers to use a desktop publishing system. Webb (1987) found that in one case, while desktop publishing reduced the document production cycle from 90 days per 100 pages to 45 days, the amount of time spent by editors actually increased. The reason is that editors gained additional responsibilities. So an apparent gain for the firm in printing cost and a shortened production cycle had a hidden cost of increased work for writers and editors.

The overall productivity of a company still may increase because a company it can complete more quickly. Measures of productivity of individual writers, however, would show **decreased** performance when measured by pages produced per day. Writers and editors would seem to have written fewer pages because they would have spent more time electronically laying out finished pages.

Another variable limiting writers' use of publishing systems is their skill at layout and design. Training them in these skills would also take away from productive work and would yet again reduce the cost advantages of desktop systems. Let me explore this problem further by describing writers' using electronic illustration tools.

Drawing Programs. For most writers, drawing programs are a less promising product than either word processors or desktop publishing. Benzon (1988) argues that writers can learn to draw adequate illustrations for technical reports. While this may be true, professional-quality graphics for widely distributed manuals and other documents are beyond the skills of many writers. Writers will at least take more time to produce the same quality work as graphic artists can.

Computer-supported drawing programs themselves may demand about the same learning period as the other programs I have discussed. However, most writers were trained to write, they were not trained to present ideas visually. Some writers have learned to write well by spending four years of undergraduate school plus one to two years to earn a master's degree. Adding illustration skills may not take another five to six years, but some time is necessary. So, while drawing programs may allow writers to generate illustrations, many writers may be less efficient than graphic artists if they try to do illustrations. From a company's perspective, it probably is more efficient to let artists continue to do illustrations and to have only a few writers work with layout and design.

Database Managers and Hypertext. When used for information retrieval, database managers and hypertext, a special kind of database manager, are as easy to use as word processors or drawing programs. They probably also draw on fewer subject-matter skills. Learning to set up a database is easier than learning to write or to draw. However, database managers exact another cost -- someone has to go to the effort of entering the information. Depending on the size of the database and how specialized its information is, data entry can be trivial or a major undertaking, requiring years of effort.

If information is entered in the normal course of other tasks, it can be more easily searched in a database than in a word processor file. When some of the information is graphic, it can best be handled by a hypermedia system (Shneiderman, 1987). For example, Apple's Hypercard allows parts of pictures (say, eyes in photographs) to be linked to each other. A user can point at a segment of a picture and then follow a sequence of pictures, each containing an example of that picture segment (other examples of eyes).

Use of electronic data management programs is described further in the section on collecting information during document production.

Outliners, Spelling Checkers, and Grammar Checkers. Some software products are comparatively simple to learn and require skills writers already possess -- outliners, spelling and grammar checkers. These programs augment, rather than tax, existing writing skills.

The outliner is most effective when a writer already knows the properties of a good outline (Krull and Hurford, 1987). Professional writers customarily do. It is possible that outliners may also help new writers, such as some technical area specialists, become more capable writers. The time spent learning outliners probably would have at worst a small, short-term negative effect on writer productivity. Two to three hours' learning could turn into 20 hours' use annually.

Some spelling checkers can be mastered in a few minutes. Most professional-level word processors in fact now include spelling checkers. Using them may save writers some time proofreading documents. Because spelling checkers are not infallible (for example, missing correctly-spelled erroneous words), writers must still proof documents (Peterson, 1980). So the total effect of spelling checkers on writer productivity is not straightforward. I have not found research documenting how much time spelling checkers actually save. However, this is the most-used feature of the Writer's Workbench, signifying its comparative value among other writing aids (Cherry, Frase, Gingrich, Keenan, and MacDonald, 1983). There is, to be sure, some effect; and since the learning time is so small, using spelling checkers would help writers to some degree.

Grammar checkers are an even more complex case. Swerdlow and Gooding (1986) have analyzed errors in business writing. The types of errors they find -- grammar, abbreviations, subject-verb agreement, word usage and so on -- are ones that grammar checkers can identify. However, since grammar checkers have a limited capability to interpret language, they may suggest changes that make a document worse. So the quality of a grammar checkers' suggestions limits its value for writers (Krull and Hurford, 1987).

The checkers' greatest potential advantages may be in helping technical specialists produce better source material for technical writers and in helping skilled writers get a first evaluation of their texts. Both would save professional writers' time.

If one were to compute the gains due to a grammar checker, one could begin with Kalmbach, et al.'s, estimate of their respondents' spending 14 percent of their time editing. That would amount to about 280 hours per year. Perhaps 5 percent, or 14 hours, of that editing time could be saved by a grammar checker. It probably takes three to four hours thoroughly to learn a checker. The productivity gain during the first-year's use, then, would be about three to one, lower than for word processing, but higher than for most writers' using drawing programs.

Similar computations could be generated for the other products in Table 1. Remote information databases, statistics programs, and project managers probably are products whose subject-matter skill requisites make them unsuitable for most writers. They would be more useful for specialists, of whom a company might have a small number.

Taken together, then, there are several tools likely to enhance writer productivity with comparatively little cost:

* outliners
* word processors
* hypertext and database management (for retrieval only)
* spelling checkers
* grammar checkers.

Several other tools may be valuable to companies or to a group of writers, but might better be left to specialists:

* remote database programs
* database management (for database generation)
* drawing programs
* statistics programs
* desktop publishing
* project management programs.

In the next section I suggest how a company can use these programs to optimize the document production process.

The Organizational Writing Process

From an organizational perspective, technical writing involves interaction among several people who may have different views of the topic and of the proper writing approach. Electronic tools can help coordinate writing groups while they collect information, organize it, produce a draft, exchange the draft for comments, and produce the final copy. Group members will play different roles in the process, using different tools.

Project Planning

Planning, the first stage in a documentation project, can be quite extended and complex. Duffy, Post, and Smith (1984) argue that most documentation projects have problems because writers plan them poorly. Important steps of project planning include the following: recognizing requirements, defining the need, defining the audience, determining the development time frame, considering resources, and incorporating others' ideas.

Many companies may provide standards for how documents are to be developed and how they are to look. Some of this information may be provided electronically. For example, document style may be incorporated into the word processors made available to writers. The other planning steps may involve collecting and organizing information. In a purely paper process, writers might do this using notecards and file folders. In an electronic system, writers could do the same tasks using their electronic counterparts.

For example, once a product specification is produced, it could be put onto a word processor disk. The disk could be duplicated so that different departments have records on an electronic mail system to be accessed from a computer terminal. Wheeler (1988) argues that this kind of record keeping is very important to a writing shop and that a librarian should keep this document up-to-date.

The advantage of using computers for this purpose is that specifications of critical project parts are quickly available to everyone in a company. Disadvantages are that access to planning documents requires a computer; users need to know how to navigate the document retrieval system; and disks may be misleading about which documents are current. After projects reach a certain size, however, the computer's advantages outweigh its disadvantages. Team members can no longer remember all the documents they have generated or which document contains specific information. The solution can be a database that allows writers access by specifying document type, content, authors, keywords, and other index features (Whalen, 1986).

Planning documents can be a fruitful application of hypertext. Once a specialist designs a hypertext-based specification, writers can access information easily. If the specification includes graphics, hypertext could include them in the specification database, something not possible with most database managers.

Another aspect of project planning is determining resource and personnel scheduling. Electronic project managers can aid this stage of projects but, as I have argued, they are sufficiently complex that many technical writers will not want to use them. Duffy, **et al.**, also do not see this as a role for most writers. One individual in a documentation group, perhaps the lead writer, could handle the scheduling system. This person would distribute task schedules to other writers.

Collecting Information

Writers need to collect at least two kinds of information:

* information produced outside the writing group or the company;
* information produced by company technical area specialists about the products they have designed.

The sources, character and methods of collection differ. External information could be acquired through a remote electronic database, such as Dialog, or through testing. Internal technical information could be obtained through interviews or internal documents. These kinds of information probably should be managed in different ways.

Collecting Outside Information. External databases, being complex to use, should be manipulated by a specialist. Technical writers would make search requests of the online specialist and would later receive the information retrieved. The company would have to determine the procedures for making requests for information. Johnson and Rice's (1984) description of word processor groups is germain here.

Johnson and Rice maintain that different access arrangements affect the productivity gains from electronic tools. A system of technical writers' directly dealing with the remote database specialist might work well if a company is small. For larger companies, the database specialist could become overwhelmed by requests, not having the power to control work load. In such cases a supervisor might control workflow. If a data processing or library system manager were to play this role, control would be outside the writing group. The supervisor may not be able to judge the relative merit of requests. Optimal supervision may include both writing group and technical group managers.

A different genre of external information, usability testing, has already been mentioned. Duffy, **et al.**, (1987) and Vreeland and Grice (1986), among others, argue that usability testing produces better documents than does skillful editing alone. Testing can take advantage of statistics programs and electronic data collection systems. However, elaborate statistical analyses and formal laboratory testing require more training than many technical writers can afford. They should be left to a human factors group. Informal testing, using procedures that look very much like writers' other interviews, does not require computer support and can be handled by most writers.

Collecting Technical Information. Collecting internal information from technical area specialists can be assisted by several kinds of software. Some companies maintain complete records of production processes. These include engineers' notes about products and correspondence among team members.

Several authors have described the value of this information (Brooks, 1982; Wheeler, 1988; Weiss, 1985). It can be used to coordinate development teams, thereby increasing their productivity.

Many of these documents could be handled electronically as word processor files. They can be stored on computer disks or on a central computer connected to a network. In either case, electronically accessing the documents would require knowledge of a company's document inventory system and knowledge of a word processor or text editor. Writers should already know how to use a word processor to write. If a company is small and the documents are few, using the electronic catalog can be simple. Conversely, large companies with many documents may have a complex catalog, requiring the services of a company librarian (Wheeler, 1988; Whalen, 1986).

Outlinining the Document

Once writers have collected and organized their information they can flesh out their outline. A writing group could work from a general outline specifying chapter titles and major headings. Individual writers then could develop detailed outlines for modules of a document (Weiss, 1985; Walker, 1988).

The advantage of doing this electronically is that outlining programs allow writers to share outlines, helping coordinate their work. If writers work with a word processor that supports windowing, they can draft in one window while looking other writers' sections in another window. Being guided by outlines may keep writers consistent with each other.

Walker (1988) argues that writers produce text more easily when they treat documents as dynamic entities. Using hypertext, writers can generate independent electronic text modules that they later link into a complete document. Outlining and linking are both included in several hypertext authoring systems.

The First Draft

Writing and revising drafts are the two tasks computers, and particularly word processing programs, are best known for. From a company's viewpoint, word-processed drafts may be superior to paper ones. The reason is that, since writers work on documents in groups (Kalmbach, et al., 1986; Ede and Lunsford, 1985), they can more easily assemble text sections from electronic than printed copy. Print needs to be glued physically; electronic copy can be collated more quickly and neatly. However, electronic assembly is not the only task needed to produce a complete, polished, usable document. Writers must identify revisions before they can be made.

Editing

Methods of editing documents vary among writers and among companies. As editing style varies, so will the electronic tools appropriate to the process. Bandes (1986a, 1986b) points out that 91% of managers value editing for format, style and language. Only 18%, she found, edit for technical accuracy. To please managers, writers might concentrate on producing pretty, wordsmithed texts. The most helpful electronic tools are spelling and grammar checkers to identify changes and word processors to make them. Grammar checkers also may help maintain consistency among documents produced by different writers. Checkers could save companies money if writers would check their own documents electronically and only then pass them onto editors.

All this suggests that spelling and grammar checkers are beneficial to a company; but careful analysis reveals that editing cannot simply be handed over to computer programs. I have already mentioned Bandes' finding that most document revision enhances language rather than content. Bandes (1986a, b), Vreeland and Grice (1986), and Duffy, et al., (1987) all stress that effective technical editing involves more than wordsmithing. Human editors still need to read that texts to assure their accuracy and to ask for testing to assure their ease of use.

Another kind of problem with online editing is a company's sharing online documents among several writers and editors. Whether writers are working on modules or an entire document, they must access the most up-to-date version and make clear to others what they would like to change (Colette and Oatley, 1987;

Fenno, 1987). How these problems are controlled depends on two issues -- how a company operates and on the editing medium.

Some companies allow editors to make changes in documents without their having to consult writers. That means no record of changes, or rationales for them, are kept. Companies asking closer cooperation among personnel may require editors to mark changes they think are needed and then to collaborate with writers in making changes. The other issue, the editing medium, involves whether editors and writers trade printed documents or work entirely on computer screens. Paper copy allows easier annotation, comparisons among text sections, and is more legible. The CRT's limited screen size and poor legibility makes editing considerably more difficult (Farkas, 1987; Haas and Hayes, 1986; Kruk and Muter, 1984; Krull and Hurford, 1987). There are ways around these difficulties, but describing them goes beyond the scope of this paper.

Layout and Transmission

Depending on the technology used, layout, transmission and production of documents are separate steps carried out by separate people, or are combined into one step. Modern technology makes it possible for one person to go from a raw idea to camera-ready copy; but, as I argued earlier, people's limited skills make this unlikely. Many writers may be able to design simple layouts and transmit files to other workers for printing. The result can be a decrease in printing cost, but at an increase in document editing cost (Webb, 1987).

Layout. An optimal system for layout and production may be to have a company produce standard layouts for typical documents. The layouts are encoded through the style-sheet features of word processors. Writers indicate that they want to produce a certain type of content (for example, a top-level heading or a paragraph) by calling for its style. The computer program takes care of layout. A company can pre-specify the typeface, typesize and placement of headings, and the margins and line-spacing of a paragraph. The advantages of this system are that it reduces the amount of time writers need to spend on layout and increases consistency among documents produced by different writers.

An efficient arrangement for in-house production of camera-ready copy has graphic artists produce illustrations. Writers generate manuscripts with style-sheet markings for text sections they have generated. Then a specialist integrates text and graphics in finished pages. The writers' only role after editing drafts is to review camera-ready copy for errors.

Transmission. Traditionally, documents are sent to printers as paper manuscripts. Producing a finished document requires setting text in type and turning art into screened masters. Both processes take time and provide an opportunity for error. Two alternatives exist. First, writers could create the finished product in-house, using laser printers and desktop publishing software. Second, writers could transmit text electronically, either carrying a computer disk to the print shop or transmitting files over telephone lines. Either system reduces errors; both require close coordination between the writing group and the printer's staff (Orr, 1988).

From an organizational standpoint, text transmission requires that at least one person be skilled in solving technical problems. That person must be familiar with company document formats. He or she also must know the printer's coding system for generating these formats. If possible, the company's word processor could be used to generate printer code automatically. Otherwise a computer program is needed to translate word processing codes to printer codes. This could mean that the company's text transmission specialist would have to be a programmer as well.

Altogether, the specialist would have to check documents for conformance to printer standards, run documents through a translation process, transmit documents over phone lines, and check printer proofs. Since this is an involved process, it is not be efficient if every writer did it for his or her own documents.

Summary

The popular press, anecdotal reports, and detailed research all suggest that computers can increase the efficiency and work quality of individual writers. How much computers help writers working in organizations is less certain. Strassmann (1987) asserts that time and money invested in writers' producing high-quality documents repays itself by reducing costs of supporting customers who read them. Computerized writing tools should be one kind of investment in the documentation process.

I have suggested a strategy for allocating resources to computing -- besides the cost of hardware and software, consider the costs of training personnel to use software and hardware, training in the subject-matter skills, and take into account the period for which software and hardware are up-to-date. Based on this strategy, managers should only expect writers to master a handful of computer tools. Tools requiring complex subject-matter skills or computer skills should be used by only one or two specialists in a writing group. Having all writers learn every computer program is a waste of their time and of company resources. I have described ways of implementing computer software that draw on skills writing group members already have.

References

Bandes, H. "Defining and Controlling Documentation Quality." **Technical Communication**, 33(1), First Quarter 1986a, 6-9.

Bandes, H. "Defining and Controlling Documentation Quality -- Part II." **Technical Communication**, 33(2), Second Quarter 1986b, 69-71.

Beck, C.E. and Stibravy, J.A. "The Effect of Word Processors on Writing Quality." **Technical Communication**, 33(2), Second Quarter 1986, 84-87.

Benzon, W.L. "Computer Graphics for the Technical Communicator." In Robert Krull (Ed.) **Word Processing for Technical Writers**. Amityville, NY: Baywood Publishing, 1988, 115-137..

Brooks, F. P. **The Mythical Man-month: Essays on Software Engineering**. Reading, Mass.: Addison-Wesley, 1982.

Cherry, L.L., Frase, L.T., Gingrich, P.S., Keenan, S.A., and MacDonald, N.H. "Computer Aids for Text Analysis." **Bell Laboratories Record**, 61(5), May/June, 1983, 10-16.

Colette, B. and Oatley, L. "Online Editing: Is It Worth the Trouble?" **Proceedings of the 34th International Technical Communication Conference**, Denver, May 10-13, 1987, WE59-62.

Daiute, C. "Physical and Cognitive Factors in Revising: Insights from Studies with Computers." **Research in the Teaching of English**, 20(2), May, 1986, 141-159.

Doebler, P.D. "Productivity Improvement Through Electronic Publishing." **Technical Communication**, 34(4), Fourth Quarter 1987, 250-256.

Duffy, T.M., Post, T., and Smith, G. "An Analysis of the Process of Developing Military Technical Manuals." **Technical Communication**, 34(2), Second Quarter, May, 1987, 70-78.

Ede, L. and Lunsford, A. "Research into Collaborative Writing." **Technical Communication**, 32(4), Fourth Quarter 1985, 69-70.

Farkas, D.K. "Online Editing and Document Review." **Technical Communication**, 34(3), Third Quarter, August, 1987, 180-183.

Fenno, C.R. "Interactive Online Editing: A Review of Current Techniques." **Proceedings of the 34th International Technical Communication Conference**, Denver, May 10-13, 1987, WE55-58.

Fenno, C.R. "But What if the Shoe Doesn't Fit?: User Comfort in the Electronic Office." **Technical Communication**, 34(3), Third Quarter, August, 1987, 146-149.

Gilfoil, D.M. "Warming Up to Computers: A Study of Cognitive and Affective Interaction Over Time." **Human Factors in Computer Systems**, Gaithersburg, Maryland, 1982, 242-250.

Green M. and Nolan, T.D. "A Systematic Analysis of the Technical Communicator's Job: A Guide for Educators." **Technical Communication**, 31(4), Fourth Quarter 1984, 9-12.

Haas, C. and Hayes, J.R. "What Did I Just Say? Reading Problems in Writing with the Machine." **Research in the Teaching of English**, 20(1), February, 1986, 22-35.

Johnson, B.M. and Rice, R. "Reinvention in the Innovation Process: The Case of Word Processing." In Ronald Rice and Associates (Eds.) **The New Media: Communication, Research, and Technology**. Beverly Hills: Sage, 1984, 157-184.

Kalmbach, J.R., Jobst, J.W., and Meese, G.P.E. "Education and Practice: A Survey of Graduates of a Technical Communication Program." **Technical Communication**, 33(21), First Quarter 1986, 21-26.

Kruk, R.S. and Muter, P. "Reading of Continuous Text on Video Screens." **Human Factors**, 26(3), 1984, 339-345.

Krull, R. and Hurford, J.M. "Can Computers Increase Writing Productivity?" **Technical Communication**, Fourth Quarter, 1987, 243-249.

Orr, D.T. "Text Preparation and Transmission for Word Processing." In Robert Krull (Ed.) **Word Processing for Technical Writers**. Amityville, NY: Baywood Publishing, 1988, 138-145.

Peterson, J.L. "A Note on Undetected Typing Errors." **Communications of the ACM**, 23(2), December, 1980, 676-687.

Reitman, P. "The Trouble with Larry: A Look at the Problems Facing a New Writer." **Technical Communication**, 34(2), Second Quarter, May, 1987, 103-104.

Shneiderman, B. "User Interface Design and Evaluation for an Electronic Encyclopedia." In G. Salvendy (Ed.) **Cognitive Engineering in the Design of Human-Computer Interaction and Expert Systems**. Amsterdam, Holland: Elsevier Science Publishers, 1987, 207-223.

Strassmann, P.A. "Improving the Productivity of Technical Documentation." **Technical Communication**, 34(4), Fourth Quarter 1987, 236-242.

Swerdlow, S. and Gooding, E.H. "The Essential Skills for Effective Writing: Do Writers of Technical Correspondence Meet the Standards of Business Communication? **Linking Technology and Users**. New York: IEEE Professional Communication Society, 1986, 167-175.

Vreeland, J. and Grice, R. "How We Used Data from Our Quality Program to Revise Our Process." **Linking Technology and Users**. New York: IEEE Professional Communication Society, 1986, 163-166.

Walker, J.H. "The Role of Modularity in Document Authoring Systems." **Proceedings of the Conference on Document Processing Systems**, ACM, Santa Fe, New Mexico, December, 1988, 117-124.

Webb, R.E. "Synergistic Publishing." **Proceedings of the 34th International Technical Communication Conference**, Denver, May 10-13, 1987, ATA146-148.

Weiss, E.H. **How to Write a Usable User Manual**. Philadelphia: ISI Press, 1985.

Whalen, E. "A Computerized Document-Tracking System on UNIX." **Technical Communication**, 33(2), Second Quarter 1986, 62-68.

Wheeler, W. "Word Processing for the Technical Writer: A Case Study." In Robert Krull (Ed.) **Word Processing for Technical Writers**. Amityville, NY: Baywood Publishing, 1988, 31-44.

Consulting Skills for Technical Writers

Lawrence B. Levine

Digital Equipment Corporation
Bedford, MA 01730

This article addresses the increasing attention by practitioners and researchers to the roles of technical writers. Building on previous research about how technical writers can benefit from understanding corporate culture, it argues for approaching the work of technical documentation as a form of consultation. There are three primary elements of consulting: roles, skills, and process. The article presents a range of consulting roles from directive to nondirective and how they apply to technical writers. It distinguishes the skills of consultation from other related skill sets. It provides a theoretical framework underlying consulting process and applies it to examples drawn from everyday life and the work of technical writing. The conclusion considers further evolution of the technical writer role in response to the changes in work design and work environment being introduced by increased computer mediation of work.

What I propose in this article is no more true for technical documentation professionals than it is for trainers, MIS staff, and other "coordinating" and "intermediary" corporate functions which serve the more traditional functions which "make product" and "sell product." In fact, the notion of conceiving of one's work role as consultant and one's product as a form of consultation may be useful to anyone who has encountered the barriers and frustration of what Peter Block calls "getting your expertise used" (Block, 1981). The focus of this volume, however, is technical writing and the technical writer, and this article will consider how reconceiving writers' roles to more consultative ones can help writers and their departments address some of Documentation's traditionally thorny problems.

Traditional Problems and the Failure of Traditional Solutions

Documentation Departments share some common problems. A few of these are:

- second-class status
- not feeling appreciated
- product developers not invested in documentation
- product developers do not use the documentation
- product developers and marketers overdefine documentation tasks
- unrealistic time requests for publication turnaround
- last-minute product changes
- limited access to information sources, usually product developers.

Solutions such as improved graphic design, expensive production tools, and increased attention to the verbal presentation of technical information (what Weiss aptly calls the "wordsmith fallacy") have had minimal impact on these fundamental problems. They can be better addressed in terms of "expanding the role of the technical communicator" and enlarging the context in which writers view these problems. The former concept has been documented by a number of researchers since the early 1980s, including (Thedens, 1983), (Knapp, 1984, 1985), (Grice, 1988), (Weiss, 1988), and (Levine and Bosch, 1985). I introduced the latter in "Corporate Culture, Documentation, and Organization Diagnosis" (Levine, 1988) in which I argue for enlarging the view of these classic documentation problems to managing resistance to change, understanding organization culture, intergroup conflicts, and new roles for "intermediary" or "coordinating" functions. I suggested that these "problems" are "opportunities" for Documentation to reconceive its role from at best a "necessary evil" to one of "strategic value" much as the Information System departments have done over the last ten years (Levine, 1988, p. 163). "Armed with a greater understanding of corporate culture," I concluded (Levine, 1988, p. 167), "the Documentation function may be able to discover its true value to a corporation and thereby raise its own self image, enhance its organizational effectiveness, and make a contribution far beyond what anyone ever expected."

What emerges from these two lines of theory and practice as the primary barrier to "expanding the role of the technical writer" and to "enlarging the Documentation view of its world to place it squarely in the corporate action" is something more than, but deeply connected to, our limited view of ourselves. In the "Culture" article cited above I addressed these issues directly, but in retrospect feel that article was slightly off the mark by offering less than a clear target and adequate aiming tools for making the proposed changes.

I propose here to address that shortcoming and to offer a clearer, more direct way technical writers can address the most common and aggravating problems they face. First, the precise role to which I recommend writers expand is the role of consultant. This is the clearer target. Second, the aiming tools are the skills of consultation. This article addresses how writers can reconceptualize many of their most common problems, refashion their roles in ways that improve their self image, and more effectively influence the culture (beliefs, behaviors, and assumptions) of their information sources. The proposed target is the adoption of a consulting role via the aiming tools of mastering the basic skills of consultation and approaching documentation work (design, planning, research, writing, editing, review, and publication) as the phases of a consultative process.

Technical Documentation Work as a Form of Consultation

How does a technical writing project typically get started? An organizational player usually commissions or hires a writer to do some task that will fill a perceived need. In other words, there is a problem to be solved, and someone or more than one person perceive(s) benefit from having it solved. Too often writers (and their managers) are willing to be just "problem solvers." They are too trusting that the requestor must know what s/he really wants and what the document audience really needs, and they are too eager to burrow into the research and writing. The automatic tendency is to problem-solving action rather than reflection and research on the context of the request. We work hard, but not smart, preferring the "footwork" of doing to the "headwork" of understanding.

Technical writers' primary expertise is need clarification and problem-solving in the lear-ning and communication of technical information. The problem in any writing project — not unlike any training, programming, construction, or consulting project — is that the requestor is often not empowered to or informed enough to decide a solution; however, this same person often dictates the correct solution without ever clearly articulating the perceived problem. In Documentation that translates to: the requestor wants a piece of writing that serves some purpose, but does not explicitly charge the writer with *first* clarifying the intended purpose and *second*, inventing an optimal solution. In short, you are being used, but your primary expertise is not.

"Getting Your Expertise Used" is the primary goal of Peter Block's famous book, *Flawless Consulting* (Block, 1981), and six-day workshop on consulting skills. I believe that "getting your expertise used" is precisely what technical writers need to do better in responding to and executing requests for their services. I am not arguing, as Muriel Zimmerman does that technical writing is quickly disappearing as a profession (Zimmerman, 1988), nor do I feel a great need to rename the activity or the job title of the technical writer. What I am arguing is that the process of developing a document in a product development environment obeys many of the rules and requires many of the skills of consultation. With this clarification of how consulting roles, skills, and process can help technical writers do the job they already do, this article explains and illustrates the roles, skills, and process of consulting and how they can be applied to the work of technical documentation.

Consulting Roles

What do consultants do? Consultants are most commonly described as "helpers" of some kind. Some provide more general help, perhaps assistance in figuring out "what is my problem?" Others help address or solve clearly defined problems by virtue of their expertise in a specific discipline or knowledge area.

Although the variety of help offered by consultants to clients is great, the roles consultants play in providing that help tend to have more limited patterns. Most consultants have to play multiple roles, and the internal consultant (which most clearly applies to documentation people, or any "staff" service person) often has to play a richer set of roles and has greater difficulty shifting between them.

Two common models of consulting roles are the Tannenbaum-Schmidt and Lippitt and Lippitt (Lippitt and Lippitt, 1975) models. Both have slightly different names for the 8-10 roles across the spectrum of possible consulting roles, but both name the opposite poles the same — directive and nondirective. Exhibit A shows a combination of the models with the role names positioned along the continuum.

Applying the model to the work of technical writers, you may play a number of the roles outlined on the continuum. For example, most commonly you "find facts." However, what you do with them often shifts the work to another role. The writing serves to educate or train, or explain something to the user. The growing role of writer as repre-sentative of the user places you in an advocate role. As QA evaluator of the product — applying the notion that if I cannot write about it, how will anybody use it — you play the role of judge.

Different people, on different projects, in different departments and companies, with different personal styles, for different audiences may play these roles more or less often, but the range provides a checklist of possible ways you work in the process of developing and producing technical documentation.

Edgar Schein (Schein, 1969 and 1987) has a similar and simpler way of conceiving of consultant roles. He distinguishes between *expert* consultation, and *process* consultation. The connection with the above model is clear — the experts provide advice, leadership, and judgement based on a specific content expertise; they give the client answers. In this sense, the client's autonomy goes down while the consultant's responsibility goes up. This also means that the client becomes more dependent on the consultant. Clients are more likely to give up their autonomy for expertise they do not have, like brain surgery. However, the client is no better able to apply the learning or solve the problem next time. This kind of consultation is most effective for clearly defined, tangible problems, that will likely not recur.

Schein's specialty is Process Consulting. Here the consultant forms a partnership with the client, does not provide answers, but is firmly in the facilitative role of observing, reflecting, and questioning. This form of help is often perceived as no help, especially by technical experts and in an American society that is hungry for quick answers and formulas. Based on the nondirective therapeutic style of Carl Rodgers (Rodgers, 1961), it emphasizes active listening and objective feedback to the client about how s/he is thinking, feeling, and behaving. It is most effective when the client knows there is a problem but is unclear about what the problem is.

Schein and Block's approach on this matter are very similar. Schein emphasizes that this kind of "help" is not equivalent to psychotherapy. He also stresses that he is not advocating that all consultants make their primary expertise process consultation. What both clearly offer to consultants who have expertise in any field from law to medicine to technical description is the following. When problems are clearly defined and the requestor is clearly the one in control of the solution, expert consultation works extremely well. However, when problems are less defined and the client is less clearly able to act on possible solutions, any expertise may not get fully utilized unless the consultant first plays a less directive, process role with the client to help the client

Exhibit A. Continuum of Consultant Roles

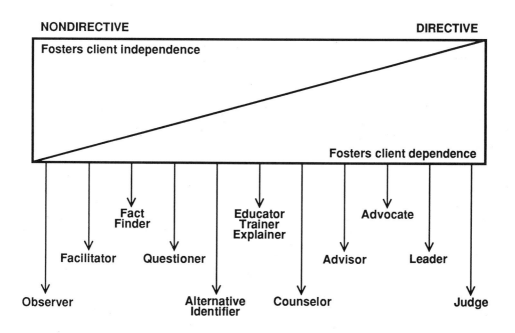

Adapted from Lippitt and Lippitt, 1975, and Tannenbaum-Schmidt.

define the problem and clarify his/her influence in implementing a solution. Thereafter, the client and consultant can agree on roles and responsibilities which can take any number of forms along the directive-facilitative continuum.

In this sense, documentation people would benefit tremendously from understanding the need to play this <u>process</u> role as an integral part of ensuring that your documents meet the real client needs and will have the impact on users and on product success that they potentially can have.

In summary, writers play a consultative role as internal consultants. A variety of roles from directive to nondirective may be appropriate and necessary under different circumstances. The distinction between *process* and *expert* consulting can help a writer know when to work in which mode.

Is There a Consulting Skill Set?

Peter Block asserts that there is a consulting skill set distinct from a host of other connected but separate skill sets. In the consulting skills program I run at Digital Equipment Corporation, we are often asked by participants about such skill sets as negotiation, influence, assertiveness, and interviewing. We explain that these are separate skills that will be used and in some cases partially assumed in the work of the Consulting Skills course; however, they are not included in the work of consulting skills.

What then are consulting skills? Block is quite emphatic that consulting requires three distinct skill sets: (1) technical skills — the expert knowledge specific to your discipline, such as engineering, planning, marketing, writing, system analysis, or auto repair; (2) interpersonal skills — including assertiveness, listening, interviewing, influence and group process; and (3) consulting skills.

Block defines consulting skills as a specific set of behaviors a consultant practices in framing and completing the tasks of each phase of the consulting process. These behaviors read like training objectives or resume bullets, beginning with active verbs and targeting very specific actions. For example, during the "Contracting" phase he lists:

- Dealing with concerns about exposure and the loss of control by the client.
- Asking at the end of a contracting meeting, "How are you feeling about this meeting, and what are your reservations about doing this work together?"

On dealing with resistance, he says:

- Identifying and working with different forms of resistance.

In the later stages of consulting, Block points out:

- Running group meetings.
- Not taking it personally when a client does not follow your recommendation.

These are the set of effective behaviors a consultant will practice in completing the tasks of each phase of the consulting process. A critical feature of approaching consultation in terms of *behaviors* and *skills* is the implication that they are *learnable* and *teachable*, not just attributes of personality that one does or does not possess.

These behaviors fit into a larger consulting process, and for Block identifying the needs of, recognizing the gaps, and completing each phase of the process provides the framework in which the skills of consulting have purpose.

Consulting Process

By consulting process I refer to two separate but linked ideas. First, I mean the phases of a consulting project. Second, I mean a theoretical model central to most applied behavioral science theory — the action research model. The phrase "action research" denotes a process of gathering data about a "human system," taking some helping action based upon that data, and gathering further data to determine the effect of the action upon the system behavior (Lewin, 1946 and French, 1969). Kurt Lewin, a social psychologist in the 1940s and 1950s and often deemed founding father of Organization Development (a philisophy and set of tools for applying social science to organizational improvement), has two famous quotes that help explain the action research model:

1. "No action without research, and no research without action."

2. "If you want to understand something, try to change it."

Exhibit B illustrates the action research model at the center of the stages of a consulting project. An action research approach can be taken by anyone within a system; the additional steps of Entry, Contracting, and Follow-Up are critical (even for internal consultants) to position them within the system to gather data and take action.

For example, you probably use the action research process (without the additional consulting phases) each morning in your kitchen or at the local donut shop. If you drink coffee or tea with milk or cream, you may experience something resembling the Morning Routine description in Exhibit C.

The most striking thing about this example is its simplicity. The action research model, like the scientific method, is not meant to be obscure, esoteric, or mysterious, but rather is a natural outgrowth of human intuition, analytical skills, and observation. My goal is not to mystify a simple process or cloud what you already know and do in jargon. In fact, the familiarity of this basic process and the fact that you already do it most of the time is a real plus for seeing the importance of consulting skills and consulting process in doing technical writing. Another example illustrates this for the start of a new writing project, Exhibit D.

This is an idealized version of a documentation project, but one that captures in many respects the primary events and activities of technical writing work. The key issues and advantages to thinking in terms of these phases are briefly explained in the following guidelines.

1. In the ENTRY and CONTRACTING phase ask yourself, and possibly the requestor and your manager: "Who is the real client?"

2. In CONTRACTING, ask yourself and work out with the requestor: "What is the problem?"

Exhibit B. Action Research Model with Added Phases of Consultation

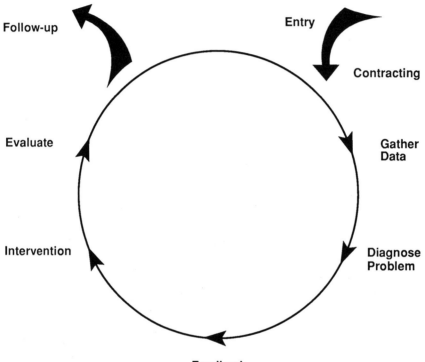

Exhibit C. Consulting Process Example One — Morning Coffee

My Morning Routine

Lifting a freshly brewed cup of coffee, you...

1. **DATA GATHERING**   Gather data on its temperature.

   Question: Is the coffee the right temperature for you?
   Method: Touch the cup.
                                  Put your finger in the coffee.
                                  Taste.

2. **DIAGNOSIS**   Formulate and state the problem, the gap between the
                                  current "state of the system" and the desired state.

   Problem
   Statement: The coffee is too hot. OR
                                  The coffee is too cold. OR
                                  The coffee is just right.

   Question: Does the data confirm my diagnosis?

3. **ACTION (INTERVENTION)**   Take action, or intervene, in the system to address the
                                  problem.

                                  Add milk.   OR
                                  Wait.   OR
                                  Throw out and remake.

   Question: Does the intervention address the problem (diagnostic)
                                  statement?

4. **FEEDBACK AND EVALUATION**

   Question: Is the temperature of the coffee just right for me now?
   YES: Drink it, and get on with your life.

   NO: Repeat the action research process beginning with
                                  gathering data on the temperature.

Exhibit D. Consulting Process Example Two — New Writing Assignment

<u>NEW WRITING ASSIGNMENT</u>

You have just been given a new writing assignment by your manager.

ENTRY	You arrange to meet with the person making the work request to get a sense of how you can work together, what the need is, scheduling constraints, scope of the work, and who the key players are.
CONTRACTING	You meet with the requestor, hopefully not the first meeting, to discuss the problem to be solved in some detail. You voice concerns you have about the project, limitations you see, barriers to possible success, and you state what you need to do a successful job. You negotiate over time, money, resources, and problem definition. The result is some form of "contract," such as an initial Document Plan.
COLLECT DATA	You determine what data to collect from whom and by what means. For example, reading old documents, going to design meetings, one–on–one interviews, and testing the software.
DIAGNOSIS	You meet with the requestor and perhaps others to test the initial contract against your initial data gathering to develop a joint problem statement or diagnosis. This should yield a revised and complete "contract" or Document Plan if appropriate. This is a step that rarely happens.
INTERVENTION	You write the document; that is, take the prescribed action to address the problem as agreed upon in the DIAGNOSIS.
EVALUATION	This is the document review process, and is often where the "failure to complete" the steps of the previous stages may be first articulated or felt.
FOLLOW-UP	Occurring rarely, this would entail a variety of methods for gathering data from users and requestors about the usefulness of the document and whether it succeeded at addressing the problem agreed upon in the DIAGNOSIS.

3. Meet the client where s/he is in stating a "presenting problem" without asserting that the problem statement is wrong. The challenge becomes how to accept the work based on the <u>presenting problem</u> while stating your own needs and moving toward a truer picture of the problem.

    The way to do that is gather data that moves the requestor toward a truer version of the problem statement so that the DIAGNOSIS is a joint decision based upon gathered data.

4. In CONTRACTING, make a contract <u>to collect data</u> and then feed it back to the requestor for a joint DIAGNOSIS. Try to avoid the trap of committing to defining and designing the <u>answer to the problem</u> or the INTERVENTION at this point.

Addressing these critical questions in this way during the early consulting phases will help you manage conflicts over the fundamental issues:

*   Who wants it?
*   What is IT?

As presented thus far, the phases of the action research model may appear to be deceptively linear and sequential. In reality, they blend, intermix, and loop back on each other. However, it is helpful, from an educational standpoint, to clarify the purpose and dilemmas of each phase. Another reason is especially important to Peter Block. He argues that consulting "flawlessly" has absolutely everything to do with "completing the business of each phase before moving on to the next phase." When I first read *Flawless Consulting* in 1983, I was so put off by that idea that I dismissed much of the what Block had to offer.

In the context of some more recent learning from adult development, particularly Daniel Levinson's *Seasons of a Man's Life* (Levinson, 1978), I now understand how to accommodate Block's insistence on completing the business of each phase with my caveat that clearly bounded "stages" of the process do not match reality.

Levinson studied adult development in males, extrapolating the common developmental model of child and adolescent development through clearly marked stages of physical and psychosocial development. (Levinson's work is the research base for Gail Sheehey's famous *Passages*.) He posed that for each stage of adult growth, there are specific "tasks" that need to be addressed and completed. These tasks and stages appear comparable to Block's business of each phase, with "Stating your own wants" as an example of a task which must be addressed before a consultant can complete the phase of CONTRACTING.

The analogy is even more useful when applied to the obstacles that prevent us from completing each consulting or developmental phase smoothly. Levinson implies that perfectly completing the tasks of any given phase is not possible; I apply this to Block's flawless completion of the tasks of any consulting phase. However, the real learning comes from thinking in terms of unfinished tasks which create incomplete phases. I would argue that these leftover, unfinished tasks of previous consulting phases often become the primary causes of the problems in subsequent phases. In conclusion, what the tasks (and skills) are to complete each phase helps us *try* to complete them as Block suggests; however, even when that proves impossible, we can at least diagnose problems backwards to unfinished tasks in previously uncompleted phases.

Another way that overly clear boundaries between consulting phases may misrepresent real consulting work concerns how the name of each phase refers to activities that actually occur throughout every phase. Activities like building rapport, establishing and checking expectations, gathering data, and diagnosing the problem occur throughout the entire consulting process; that is, the primary tasks of the early phases do not stop while the consultant designs an intervention and performs feedback and evaluation tasks.

The opposite is true as well — intervention is not just the main event. A consultant is intervening in a human system and in individuals' thoughts and behavior by his/her very presence. "Everything a consultant does to a client," according to Schein (Schein, 1987, p. 38), "from the moment the client makes contact with the consultant is an intervention of some sort." This is also true for documenters' involvement in product development activities to an extent only beginning to receive attention in Documentation literature (Levine, 1988). Data gathering and diagnosis are both interventions. Sometimes they are so powerful in themselves that no main event as such needs to take place. For example, it is possible that during ENTRY and CONTRACTING your helping a document requestor more fully understand the basis for the request, or consider possible conflicts among audiences, or recognize product design problems that might argue against writing a certain kind of document or perhaps not writing any document could lead to your not writing the originally requested document. In this case there would have been no INTERVENTION *phase*, or main act, but your behaviors with the client would have provides strong components of both DIAGNOSIS and INTERVENTION.

The final consideration in representing consulting process as a series of discrete, bounded phases to be completed in sequence concerns the larger purpose of any consultation. Block emphasizes that independent of consulting phase and consulting task, every consultant–client interaction is an opportunity to:

- Diagnose and handle resistance
- Build client commitment.

The implication of this approach is subtle but critical — all tasks within all phases of the consulting process are oriented toward maximizing the likelihood that the consultant's recommendations will be implemented and have beneficial impact.

Consulting Role Again — Role Conflicts of the Internal Consultant

To some extent, consulting skills and the consulting process may be approached independent of the consultant's role. Role, however, can have a tremendous influence on what skills are needed and appropriate at which phase in the project. The notion of role conflict is critical to walking the tightrope of consulting, and is even more aggravated for internal consultants (Steele, 1983).

For example, in seeking partnership between client and consultant, it sometimes becomes difficult to find a balance between inclusion and responsibility. Becoming included in product meetings or remembered for published lists of product changes, or even invited to team celebrations can be a major issue for technical writers serving product teams. On the other hand, Development has a responsibility for providing access to people with information, system resources, and ensuring the technical accuracy of documentation. Finding a balance of inclusion but without becoming entirely responsible is a key role conflict for an internal consultant.

Another role conflict is multiple loyalties. For example, writers can often find themselves understanding differing opinions of developers and marketers in competing groups more objectively than any other party. The same applies to team members and team leaders. The writer needs to maintain objectivity in these cases, and sometimes the best way to do that is not passive withdrawal, but active facilitation. In short, the writer can actively play the nondirective role of observer, reflector, and questioner.

Finally, internal consultants often find themselves assigned to projects without clearly contracting about what the work is and how the parties will work together. The writer begins working under an implicit contract prior to any negotiation about role or result. Implicit contracts are extremely hard to change; they are even harder to become aware of. Although making a formal contract for time and money in the pure business sense is an anxiety internal consultants may be spared, the flip side is that formal contracting provides an opportunity to state needs and wants of both sides at the outset, before implicit contracts lock either party into assumptions about each other and the work.

Identifying these specific dilemmas of consulting as an internal person can help writers anticipate problems about expectations and outcomes and understand these problems more clearly when they do occur.

Summary of Consulting Roles, Skills, and Process

In the previous sections I have addressed the possible roles of consultants from directive to nondirective and how they apply to writers. I explained Peter Block's definition of consulting skills, distinguishing them from interpersonal and technical skills. Finally, the section on Consulting Process provided a theoretical framework and two examples for applying consulting process to everyday life and to technical writing. Exhibit E summarizes the main points about consulting roles, skills, and process.

Exhibit E. Summary of Main Points about Consulting Roles, Skills, and Process

Consulting Roles

Two Poles:

DIRECTIVE ↔ FACILATIVE

As client autonomy goes
down, consultant
responsibility goes up.

Clients are more likely to
give up autonomy for an
expertise they do not
have.

Internal consultants have
particular problems with:

a. partnership: inclusion
   vs responsibility

b. multiple client
   loyalties

c. difficulty of becoming
   aware of and changing
   implicit contracts

Consulting Skills

Behaviors at each stage
of Consulting Process,
such as: (1) state your
concerns about client
partnership and (2) do
not take resistance
personally.

What consulting skills
are not:

- Technical Skills
- Interpersonal Skills
  – Influence
  – Assertiveness
  – Negotiation

Consulting Process

Entry — Build rapport.

Contracting — Agree on
how to work together.
What is the problem?

Data Gathering — What
data, from whom, and by
what means?

Diagnosis — Agree on
the problem based on
initial data gathering
presented for feedback
and development of
collaborative diagnosis.

Intervention — Take
action to address the
problem considering
level and magnitude of
intervention.

Evaluation & Feedback —
Gather data on whether the
intervention had an effect
on the stated problem.

Follow-Up — Inquire
about the impact of the
work, offer more help,
and diagnose possible
resistance to change.

The Evolving Role of the Technical Writer — Next Steps

If Information Systems researchers are on the right track, and many think Shoshana Zuboff's major work *In the Age of the Smart Machine* (Zuboff, 1988) is at the forefront, new and more influential roles for technical writers may be an integral part of major shifts in the ways developers, top management, and users conceptualize and plan for job and work change caused by and enabled by computerization.

Zuboff distinguishes between the automating and informating effects of technology. Whereas the automating capacity of computerization tends to "displace the human body and its know–how (a process that has come to be known as *deskilling*), the informating power of the technology simultaneously creates pressure for a profound *reskilling*" (Zuboff, 1988, p. 57). The later increases what she calls "intellective skills" required by users and are characterized by increased abstraction, critical judgement, and inferential reasoning. "Taken together," she writers, "these elements make possible a new set of competencies that I call *intellective skills*.... Mastery in a computer–mediated environment depends on developing intellective skills" (Zuboff, 1988, p. 75–76). This approach reconceptualizes the impact of computers on work, communication, coordination and competition on the level of replacing vacuum tubes with transistors.

Like the clerks in Zuboff's studies whose jobs were most affected by computerization, documentation jobs can move in the direction of informating (enhancing the value, skill level, and impact of the work) or in the direction of automating (making the added value of documenters more narrow and limited).

One of the most exciting trends in Information System development and selling is the reconception of the business. If the 1970s were a technology–driven era of "moving iron," the 1980s will be thought of as the era of solution selling. That means that hardware–software integration in the form of understanding the customer problem and designing a solution will be the watchword. Based on what major computer manufacturers are currently doing, the 1990s will again reconceptualize the business and its approach. Digital Equipment Corporation (DEC) is combining not only technical knowledge with business knowledge, but also fully recognizing that it is selling large–scale human systems change. Jobs, work space, worker–supervisor relationships, management skill sets, and basis of competitive advantage are precisely the objective of long–term investments in the next generation of computers. If computer companies like DEC and Hewlett–Packard are actively reconceiving of their business (much the way railroads did not change their business to more general transportation) from "movers of iron" past software solutions to "architects of change," then suggesting that technical writers rethink their products and roles to include the notion of "consultation" seems a pretty small reconceptualization relative to their business environments.

Given these changes in the computer business, what would be the next step in the evolution of technical writing work? Zuboff's research provides some clues. She is articulate about how organizations are becoming "textualized." "The electronic text is the result of a ... radical centralization: a wide range of information can be gathered and codified in a single computer system. However, this radical centralization enables an equally radical decentralization: in principle, the text can be constituted at any time from any place. The contents of the electronic text can infuse an entire organization, instead of being bundled in discrete objects, like books or pieces of paper" (Zuboff, 1988, p. 180). In this way, "information technology becomes the receptacle for larger and larger portions of the organization's operating intelligence" (Zuboff, 1988, p. 69).

However, the skills and know–how that characterized pre–computerized work remain substantially encased in the social network and contextual factors of a culture that is more oral than written. She quotes from scholars on oral culture such as Walter Ong to show how some corporate segments have resisted the codification of their work competencies in writing. The price of revering codification over the messy, uncontrollable, intuitive social processes for getting work done is buying the small–scale increases in volume, cost reduction, and accuracy possible through an automating process, but selling out the much longer–term benefits of informating.

Zuboff presents these two alternatives as a choice, depending on management's support for new behaviors and organization structures that will challenge its own traditional source of power and control. The possibility of tapping the informating benefits of technology would appear to depend in part on quality instruction in how people can interact with the equipment and with each other in using the equipment in totally new ways. It also appears to depend on capturing the expertise of pre–computerized ways of doing the work that exist only in the oral culture of the work environment. In assisting this transformation, technical writers may have a profoundly challenging and exciting new role to play.

Combining Zuboff's notion of "capturing the social context" of work with the bardic notion of one very articulate software developer (and former technical writer) that "writers are the scribes of the lore of software development groups," I propose that technical writers consider thinking of themselves as anthropologists of software development cultures. If the software are artifacts of software groups' various intelligent, tool–using activities by collections of individuals according to unique physical and social arrangements, then perhaps what users need is less the conclusion and objective product of all that work and more the flavor of the context in which commands are named, screen layouts are rejected, data structures are planned, and user needs are allowed to drive development or "dropped on the floor" as unimportant.

Writers like Robert Pirsig and Tracy Kidder come to mind. Pirsig's book, *Zen and the Art of Motorcycle Maintenance* (Pirsig, 1974), argued vehemently that the product and its document should not be conceived of as separate from the spirit of their creation. His conception of that creation, however, was not that of a social or cultural arrangement. Kidder, *The Soul of the New Machine*, (Kidder, 1981), on the other hand, approaches computer product development precisely from this social vantage point. His book to remains the pillar of description about computer product development.

I am not proposing that every manual be an ethnography, but I cannot help but wonder how (particularly large) documentation sets would be enhanced if perhaps one book per set were an ethnographic account of the development group and its software task. Although only speculation at this point, I submit that the skill set and desire to serve users and development groups this way may be very similar to an activity that Zuboff's informating approach requires to prepare work environments to take advantage of the kinds of positive change offered by computer manufacturers acting often more as information system and human system consultants.

With these kinds of changes in our educational, product development, and customer environments, documentation professionals cannot be satisfied with the skills we currently value or the roles we currently play. The notion of software development or human systems ethnographer is certainly an idiosyncrasy in any environment or profession. In any case, it would be a long way off. However, positioning ourselves for such an impact begins with the more immediate next step which I have argued throughout this article — the revamping of our roles and skills via an approach to our work that emphasizes the ways technical writers already are and can be better consultants.

Works Cited

Block, Peter. *Flawless Consulting*. Austin, Texas: Learning Concepts. Distributed by University Associates, Inc., San Diego CA, 1981.

French, Wendell L. "Organization Development: Objectives, Assumptions, and Strategies," *California Management Review* 12:23–34, 1969.

Grice, Roger A. "Information Development Is Part of Product Development — Not an Afterthought," *Text, ConText, and Hypertext — Writing with and for the Computer*, edited by Edward Barrett. Cambridge MA: MIT Press, 1988.

Kidder, Tracy. *The Soul of the New Machine*. Boston MA: Little, Brown, 1981.

Knapp, Joan T. "A New Role for the Technical Communicator," *Proceedings of the 32nd ITCC*, Seattle WA, 1984.

Knapp, Joan T. "Getting Cinderella to the Ball: How We Can Improve the Status and Quality of In–House Documents." *Proceedings of the 33rd ITCC*, Houston TX, 1985.

Levine, Larry, and Tim Bosch. "Technical Communicators and the Technical Design Process," *Proceedings of the 33rd ITCC*, Houston TX, 1985.

Levine, Lawrence. B. "Corporate Culture, Technical Documentation, and Organization Diagnosis," *Text, ConText, and Hypertext — Writing with and for the Computer*, edited by Edward Barrett. Cambridge MA: MIT Press, 1988.

Levinson, Daniel J. *The Seasons of a Man's Life*. New York: Ballantine Books, 1978.

Lewin, Kurt. "Action Research and Minority Problems," *Journal of Applied Behavioral Science* 9(4):423–68, 1946.

Lippitt, Ron, and Gordon Lippitt. "Consulting Process in Action," *Training and Development Journal*, 29(5): 48–54; 29(6): 38–44.

Pirsig, Robert M. *Zen and the Art of Motorcycle Maintenance*. New York: William Morrow and Company, Inc., 1974.

Schein, Edgar H. *Process Consultation: Its Role in Organization Development*. Reading MA: Addison–Wesley Publishing Company, 1969.

Schein, Edgar H. *Process Consultation Volume II: Lessons for Managers and Consultants*. Reading MA: Addison–Wesley Publishing Company, 1987.

Steele, Fritz. The Role of the Internal Consultant. New York: Van Nostrand Reinhold, 1983.

Thedens, Melinda. "Earning the Respect and Confidence of the Technical Staff," *Proceedings of the 31st ITCC*, St. Louis MO, 1983.

Weiss, Edmond H. "Usability: Stereotypes and Traps," *Text, ConText, and Hypertext — Writing with and for the Computer*, edited by Edward Barrett. Cambridge MA: MIT Press, 1988.

Zimmerman, Muriel. "Are Writers Obsolete in the Computer Industry?" *Text, ConText, and Hypertext — Writing with and for the Computer*, edited by Edward Barrett. Cambridge MA: MIT Press, 1988.

Zuboff, Shoshana. *In the Age of the Smart Machine — The Future of Work and Power*. New York: Basic Books, Inc., 1988.

How to Manage Educational Computing Initiatives - Lessons from the first five years of Project Athena at MIT

Jacqueline A. Stewart
Manager of Applications Development, Visual Computing Group,
and User Services

Project Athena
Massachusetts Institute of Technology

This chapter briefly summarizes the evolution of the Athena computing environment during the first five years of the Project. The goals are identified and conflicts described. Some measurements of progress towards these goals are specified. As the Project heavily involves people as well as machines a brief commentary on some of the subcultures which comprise the overall MIT culture gives the sense of the constraints and incentives we have experienced. The process of software development is abstracted and explored within the context of Athena. Characteristics of models for development are described including cost as compared to effectiveness against the backdrop of a moving computational platform. Some observations and reflections on our experiences in this Project to date are offered. Finally, our objectives for the extension of Project Athena are expressed.

Introduction

Numerous projects have been initiated by faculty at MIT to acquire or develop software to be used in the academic curriculum under the auspices of Project Athena which was prophetically named after Athena, the mythological Greek warrior-goddess, goddess of prudent intelligence, and goddess of the arts of peace. The conflicting goals of the Project - implementing leading edge technology versus curriculum software development often presented significant challenges to the MIT community. Compounded by a "make" versus "buy" tension, and a range of computational sophistication which varies widely across departments as well as the culture of the various MIT organizations, no one way of implementing educational computing initiatives clearly emerges. Instead, a number of models for development have been identified. The analysis of problems we have encountered and lessons we have learned should prove helpful not only for other educational institutions which we believe will follow in the tracks of the MIT experience in one way or the other but also should prove valuable for applications in industry.

Project Athena - a chronology of the first five years

In the Fall of 1982 an *ad hoc* MIT faculty committee assembled to define the types of applications various faculty wanted to create and to establish the requirements for an instructionally-oriented computational environment that would serve instructional needs in the 1990's. At first it was envisioned as a Project within the School of Engineering but it became obvious that maximum benefits would be achieved if it were MIT-wide. From then through the Spring of 1983 industrial sponsorships were solicited, and in May 1983 Project Athena was announced with Digital Equipment Corporation and IBM as the major sponsors. It was originally budgeted at 70 million dollars over a five year period, with 50 million dollars coming from the industrial sponsors in the form of equipment grants and maintenance, and 20 million dollars to be raised by MIT. Of the MIT portion, about 10 million dollars was targeted towards the support of the development of educational software.

Equipment was to be allocated roughly as follows - Digital Equipment Corporation (DEC) workstations would go to the School of Engineering while IBM equipment would serve the needs of the Schools of Science, Humanities and Social Science, Management, Architecture and Urban Planning, and various Programs. The monies for curriculum development were to be allocated in parallel to equipment grants by two Resource Allocation Committees which focussed on proposals from faculty and funded awards based on committee recommendations.

The chosen computing environment was based on the *BSD4.x UNIX* operating system. The Project was divided into two phases. Phase I would provide interim development and prototype facilities using DEC equipment in a time-sharing mode with access to the campus network on one hand, and IBM PC's locally networked to a shared printer on the other. In Phase II, both of these types of facilities would be replaced by fully networked advanced function workstations.

Year one, Phase I. In January, 1984 the first time-sharing system based on DEC equipment was opened for public use by faculty. In February the first round of solicitations, proposals, and grants for Athena curriculum development projects was completed. Seventy-six proposals were submitted requesting funding totaling 2.5 million dollars; 440 thousand dollars were awarded. In March two more DEC time-sharing clusters opened for public use. The first IBM XT's (*DOS*-based) for use as standalone real-time laboratory workstations were drawn against the grant. By the end of this first year of the Project a total of 10 million dollars had been drawn against the equipment grants.

The second year. A major system release of *BSD4.2 UNIX* occurred in September, 1984. By the end of this second year of the Project, 1.4 million dollars had been granted to date to faculty for curriculum development projects; additionally, the first

IBM AT workstations using *DOS* as an operating system had been deployed to staff and advanced faculty development projects. The equipment grant draws for the year totalled 5.5 million with a total to date of 15.5 million dollars.

The third year. The first public release of the *X Window System version 9* to the time-sharing machines occurred in September, 1985. In the Fall of 1985 the first three IBM AT public clusters opened using a combined *DOS/UNIX*-like system. In the Spring of 1986 the sixth round of funding by the DEC and IBM Resource Allocation Committees was completed with 26 projects receiving funding. 92 separate projects had been funded to date through the Resource Allocation Committees. Total amounts drawn against the equipment grants for the year totalled 5.2 million dollars for the year with a total of 20.7 million dollars at the end of the first three years of the Project.

Year four - the beginning of Phase II. The first of the DEC time-sharing clusters was taken out of service in the Summer of 1986 and in September, the first DEC workstations were deployed outside of the staff area in two public clusters. By October, there were 200 of these workstations up and running. In November another major system release of *BSD4.3 UNIX* with the *X Window System version 10* occurred. By the end of this fourth year of the Project some IBM RT PC workstations had been deployed with a smaller complement of software than their DEC counterparts. Total amounts drawn against the grants for the year were 9.6 million dollars with a total to date of 30.3 million dollars.

The fifth year: a fully networked system. In the summer of 1987 the change-over from time-sharing to fully networked workstations in the field was completed. September saw another major system release with the implementation of the *X Window System version 11*. Major breakage in educational applications occurred as a result of incompatibility with the earlier version of *X*. The Visual Workstation public cluster was opened in January, 1988 for experimental use by subjects and developers. A number of departmental and public clusters with DEC and IBM workstations were opened. All the IBM AT's had been pulled from public service and reallocated to individual departments. The networking infrastructure consisting of DEC VAX/750's was completed, and in many cases in need of replacement after five years of service. Approximately eight million dollars had been awarded to curriculum development projects over the life of the Project. A total to date of 33.3 million dollars had been expended against the equipment grants.

Goals and conflict

The main objectives of the Project were to improve education at MIT over five years by creating a new educational computing environment built around high performance graphics workstations, high speed networking and servers of various types. There were three main subgoals - the *educational goal* of fostering innovative projects by MIT faculty, the *physical goal* of putting in place and operating a system of approximately 2000 workstations for use by the MIT academic community, and the *technical goal* of designing and implementing a new computing environment. This goal had five aspects: first, the accommodation of heterogeneous hardware since MIT would never be a single computer-vendor campus; second, the provision of machine-independent interfaces for programmers and users, permitting importability and exportability of software; third, encouragement of the sharing of information; fourth, provision of an environment scalable to 10,000 workstations; and fifth, the support of workstations that could be purchased after the end of the five year Project by an MIT student for a total system cost of about 10% of MIT tuition.

Although each of the goals by itself was laudable, trying to realize them in parallel resulted in chaos. Since this was an effort to support educational needs immediate development of software for curriculum use was encouraged. Applications software development at the very least requires a stable hardware and operating systems software environment. It also needs to have a known delivery environment for users to run the applications software on. And for this software to have any lasting value, the base on which it is developed cannot change unexpectedly or rapidly. The physical goal of deploying several thousand *advanced function workstations* required replacing the temporary *time-sharing* and *personal computer* workstations as rapidly as possible. The technical goal of providing a uniform network of *UNIX*-based mixed-vendor advanced-function workstations with machine-independent interfaces required constant pushing of the next generation (often incompatible with the earlier generation) improved hardware, software tools, and operating system versions into the computing environment. These physical and technical victories, outstanding achievements in their own right, were diametrically opposed to the requirements for developing and delivering curriculum software. The initial decision to split hardware (and inherently software) by Schools resulted in two different tracks, the *DEC - time-sharing - VAXstations track*, and the *IBM - AT's - RT's track*. It has been very difficult to bring these tracks to convergence.

The *DEC track* allowed for a straight-forward process of migration of faculty-developed software from the Phase I time-sharing systems to the Phase II workstations. A small number of third-party packages did not make the transition since either the vendor did not port to the *X Window System* at all or ported to *X, Version 10* but not yet to *X, Version 11*, the current Athena supported version. Other requirements for a vestigial time-sharing machine resulted from the problems of using a relational database management system in a distributed computing environment.

The *IBM track* was somewhat discontinuous. Software that strictly adhered to *FORTRAN* and *C* migrated successfully from the AT's to the RT PC's. Faculty who used or developed software in *BASIC* and *Pascal* and other languages or who relied on specific display or device characteristics of the AT were stone-walled. In Phase II AT's were no longer supported by Athena either in faculty offices or in Athena public clusters. Users of such popular packages as *Lotus 1-2-3* or *Personal Consultant Plus* were left without public facilities for student use. Also, color was no longer available - the new workstations were all monochrome.

Software developed in either *track* that survived the Phase I - Phase II migration has a good chance of being delivered on both DEC and IBM workstations, the concept of source-level code coherence being realized.

Progress towards goals at the end of the first five years

In spite of this conflict significant progress was made towards achieving each of the three main goals. In the *educational* arena, Athena has fostered 125 curriculum development projects. Major Athena projects have had far reaching effects within departments, and in several cases have cut across traditional departmental boundaries. All Schools were involved with a surprising number of projects in the School of Humanities. Athena-provided programming resources demonstrated the value of providing faculty with technical help. The use of Athena curriculum software in the classroom has been well-received by faculty and students alike. This has been done via the use of projection of live demonstrations on a workstation and in an electronic class-room equipped with a number of workstations. A series of evaluation studies suggest significant educational benefits and directions for further enhancing Athena's educational effects.

The *physical* goal of widespread deployment of workstations has resulted in the provision of approximately 800 ports. There are 14,000 accounts with 5,000 active Athena users. About 100 subjects per semester use Athena with a combined enrollment of 3,500 students. 82% of undergraduates reported using Athena during the 1987-1988 academic year. In the first week of May, 1988, approximately half of the MIT undergraduates had at least one Athena session.

Progress in the *technical* area points to development of a wide array of network-based services that are operational at MIT. There has been a complete export of the *X Window System*, now an industry standard, with beta test exportation of the authentication and name servers. A high degree of source code compatibility exists across supported platforms. There has been an implementation of a color Visual workstation, including initial specifications of video extensions to the *X Window System*, and ongoing development and prototyping use of an authoring language, supporting a set of curriculum applications. *UNIX* has been re-engineered to meet the requirements of public workstations rather than time-sharing systems. There is a working *Service Management System* for operating this distributed environment.

MIT Culture

So far we have been focusing on the computer-related characteristics of the Project. Let's now take a look at the people-side and briefly view some of the subcultures which comprise the overall MIT culture. MIT is primarily a single campus covering 135 acres along the Charles River in Cambridge; MIT's Lincoln Lab is 15 miles away in Lexington. A view of the overall pecking order (top-down) of the Administration, faculty, students, and staff from the standpoint of Athena looks roughly something like this:

- President, Provost, Vice-Presidents, Deans

- Tenured Faculty and Junior Faculty (numbering 1000) and Research Staff; total teaching staff numbers 1,800 including teaching assistants)

- Administrative Staff

- Support staff and other employees (total employment of the Institute numbers 9,900)

- Students (9,600 of which 4,700 are graduate students, 4,500 undergraduates, and 400 special students; international students comprise 20% of the student population)

Some generalized observations follow. MIT is the model on which matrix organizations are based. Tenured faculty members are the preferred heads of everything. Key sources of educational innovation are the Junior faculty who run into conflict/risk with research requirements to gain tenure. Management is by committees. Planning is generally confined to a one year span.

There are some observations related specifically to Athena. From MIT at large two key items are visible: first, computer professionals are thought to be commercially over-valued, therefore budgeted salaries are substantially lower than counterparts in industry; and second, the need and value of professional management is not recognized. From within Athena the pecking order (top-down) appears as follows:

- Telecommunications (part of Information Systems)

- Physical plant (MIT-wide organization)

- The MIT Administration

- Athena Technical Architect-Director

- Athena Director

- Athena Systems Development

- Athena Operations/Deployment (contract service from Information Systems)

- Athena Applications Development & Visual Courseware Group

- Athena User Services

- MIT Students

- MIT Faculty/Developers

- Athena Support staff

There are several ordering differences in the internal Athena pecking-order as compared with that of MIT overall; this is local to Athena. Included among the Athena culture are the following norms. Technical might makes right, i.e. technical expertise is the most highly valued skill which overrides everything else. Staff must use the experimental system to deliver products to the field. The Project is technically driven. "Flaming" (refers to inflammatory messages) is broadcast through electronic mail. Internal Athena organizations operate independently -- planning is bottom-up -- group goals are often in conflict. There is no central integrated plan. Communications occur after the fact. Visiting Engineers and Scientists from other universities and industry are encouraged to participate. Professional staff work at Athena because they love the work, its challenges, the encounters with bright colleagues and students and faculty, the opportunities to do exciting things that are new, and because they really believe in the educational mission of Athena. And because they believe in the overall idea that permeates MIT -- we are a world-class institute comprised of world-class people.

Social customs vary widely by department and organizational unit at MIT. A number of departments are very conservative in their approach to the use of computers in the educational process while others have enthusiastically employed computer technology. There is a tension between centralization of computer resources and decentralized or departmental or individual control. There is also a fundamental tension between whether it is better to buy software off-the-shelf or to make it yourself.

MIT students are often thought of as having technical blood flowing through their veins. It is a common misconception to interchange technology and computers. A surprising number of our students are chary of using a computer and try to avoid doing so. This is true of the faculty as well.

All of the above combine to form the milieu of MIT culture which forms the backdrop of constraints and incentives for the process of implementing educational computing initiatives.

Process of development

The development of software to be used in the curriculum involves:

- *Conceptualization* of the mapping of a problem in learning (see Figure 1) to a solution using the computer in a particular role (see Figure 2). This includes a definition of what it is you want the software to do and how you envision the student using it.

- *Finding* something that already exists that could satisfy these requirements, such as a commercial package or software developed by a colleague or student, or *designing and implementing* the software yourself or with the aid of others.

- *Delivering* the software in a subject to students.

There are a number of factors which constrain the process. Constraints against curriculum software development may be classified into three main types -- *empowering, environmental,* and *value.*

Empowering agents are those which affect the ability to create curriculum software. These include the following:

- *Computer expertise* either on the part of the faculty member or through access to programming resources.

- *Programming environment* including languages and tools.

- *Productivity aids* such as worksheet programs, presentation graphics, electronic mail, and word processing.

- *Authoring languages* which permit knowledge experts such as faculty to interact directly with the system instead of through a technical intermediary.

- *Ease of use* - friendly user interfaces which tame complex systems.

- *Documentation* and *training* aids.

Figure 3 shows a classification of the empowering elements available to curriculum software developers at Project Athena. Appreciable applications development support has been provided through the funding of individual projects by the Athena Resource Allocation Committees. In addition, there has been a central group of about twelve professional application development programmers to support curriculum development projects. The selection of languages has been limited; the debugging tools are also restricted. Most of the *productivity aids* available today on Athena are still oriented to a line terminal mode of interaction and do not take advantage of the full screen display and graphics capabilities. There are no fully supported authoring languages on Athena although one is in the process of being developed. Athena has been a very difficult arena in which to construct applications software. The *UNIX* operating system does

- Visualization
- Translating mathematical formulation into intuition
- Creating realistic design experiences
- Dealing with large amounts of data
- Individualization
- Abstraction of complexity (model construction)

Figure 1: Key Problems in Learning

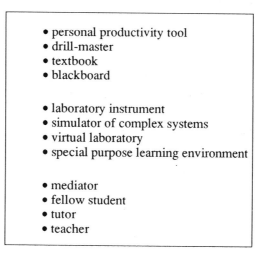

- personal productivity tool
- drill-master
- textbook
- blackboard

- laboratory instrument
- simulator of complex systems
- virtual laboratory
- special purpose learning environment

- mediator
- fellow student
- tutor
- teacher

Figure 2: Role of the Computer

not provide a friendly user interface; it is arcane and difficult to learn. *UNIX* is most appreciated by programmers who are used to low-level languages. The reason it was initially chosen as an operating environment for Athena is its ability to support networking. Partially as a compensation for these deficiencies Athena has a good support system in the area of basic documentation for end-user applications, and in the area of live training for students and faculty. This past year all basic documentation has been put online for user access. A main benefit of this is that a user can get the most recent version of documentation everytime while the Athena documentation team can manage centralized updates for distributed environment. Training is provided for both programmers and end-users, much of it regularly scheduled as well as on-request.

Class	Item	Availability
Computer expertise	Programmers (UROP students and Graduate students)	yes - funded Athena projects
	Professional programmers for contract programming	yes - limited to a few funded Athena projects
	Professional consultants	yes - central Athena resources
Programming environment	*FORTRAN*	yes
	C	yes
	Saber C - debugger	yes
	LISP	yes
	Pascal	no
	BASIC	no
	X Window System	yes
	X Toolkit	yes
	Andrew Toolkit	yes
	Prolog	yes but unsupported
	BLOX graphics interface	yes
	GKS graphics	yes
Productivity aids	*2020* spreadsheet	yes but poor quality
	ProChart presentation graphics	yes
	Xmath graphics	yes
	RS/1 laboratory worksheet	yes for VAX only
	Xmh - X Window System mail handler	yes
	Emacs text editor	yes
	Scribe text formatter	yes
	PostScript viewer	yes - prototype
Authoring languages	*Athena Muse* - visual courseware development	yes - prototype
	CMU Tutor - CT	no - not ported to *X*
	HyperCard	no - not ported to *X*

Figure 3: Classification of Project Athena Empowering Elements

Environmental constraints are those which affect the ability to use or gain access to computing resources. These include:

- *Equipment accessibility* either in faculty offices or/and programmer development facilities.

Class	Item	Availability
Ease of use	Friendly *UNIX* interface Online help Online consulting	no no yes
Documentation	Online *UNIX* man pages Online Athena documentation Hardcopy Athena documentation	yes yes yes
Training	Online tutorials Live Minicourses Personalized faculty instruction Application developers courses - *C, X*	sparse yes - readily available yes - on request yes - live and videotape

Figure 3: Classification of Project Athena Empowering Elements, continued

- *Network accessibility* to get to printing services, file services, and communications services.

- *Delivery resources availability* to provide an appropriate platform for students to use the software.

Figure 4 shows a summary of workstation facilities and servers available from Project Athena. Today, significant numbers of workstations are available for student use. A number of faculty offices have not yet had requested workstations installed. The physical impediment of old architecture has delayed the process of bringing the network into a number of MIT's facilities. The Athena workstation model does not support standalone workstations - they must be connected to the network. Although good delivery facilities for software developed for the Athena workstation environment are ubiquitous, lack of facilities containing platforms that are dissimilar but popular constitute a major impediment to delivery inside and outside of MIT. Thus some excellent software developed in Phase I of Project Athena may not be generally deployable at MIT unless the department in which it was developed has its own equipment in sufficient numbers for student use in a subject.

Values which are attitudinal or cultural in nature also constrain educational computational initiatives. Some examples of these are:

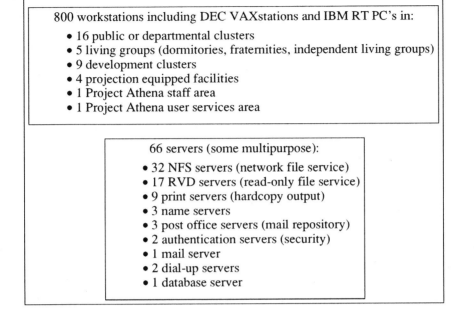

800 workstations including DEC VAXstations and IBM RT PC's in:

- 16 public or departmental clusters
- 5 living groups (dormitories, fraternities, independent living groups)
- 9 development clusters
- 4 projection equipped facilities
- 1 Project Athena staff area
- 1 Project Athena user services area

66 servers (some multipurpose):

- 32 NFS servers (network file service)
- 17 RVD servers (read-only file service)
- 9 print servers (hardcopy output)
- 3 name servers
- 3 post office servers (mail repository)
- 2 authentication servers (security)
- 1 mail server
- 2 dial-up servers
- 1 database server

Figure 4: Facilities

- *Departmental support* - degree to which only a few mavericks are tolerated or time and resources are made available for development.

- *Tenure process* - degree to which research requirements dominate educational contributions.

- *NIH* - degree to which the "Not Invented Here" syndrome prevails over the "snarfing" principle, i.e. importation from other educational institutions is encouraged.

- *Personal incentives* such as exportation for use by colleagues and the world outside of MIT, and opportunities to incorporate software into a textbook.

The amount of development and amount of use are dependent on the *environmental* constraints. The amount of development and the complexity of development are dependent on *empowering* constraints. Everything is influenced by the *value* factors. The Athena experience of the type and complexity of educational computing initiatives may be viewed as a function of value constraints. When the value constraints are low the value impediments are minimal and are not barriers. When highly constrained by values the likelihood of strong initiatives is lessened. Figure 5 shows the curriculum software development environment as a function of environmental and empowering factors for low value constraints, while Figure 6 shows the outcome of development under highly constrained value conditions.

These Figures also highlight the software profile for each cell in the curriculum software development matrix. "Import" means bringing in an application from another institution and "buy" refers to third party vendor purchases, "make" indicates local development while "export" indicates developed software is being used outside of MIT.

The most favorable conditions for educational computing initiatives are when all constraints are low resulting in a "make/export" software profile. Here we see the development of complex modules with widespread use. The software is exported to other institutions and commercial enterprises. An example of this at Project Athena is the package developed by the department of Aeronautics and Astronautics for fluid mechanics and thermodynamics. Consisting of twenty-two modules coded primarily in *FORTRAN* with some *C* routines, it uses *BLOX* as a user and graphics interface layered on the *X Window System*. In addition to running on the Athena VAX workstations and RT PC's, it is in the process of being ported to the Sun and Apollo workstations for use outside of MIT. At the other end of the development matrix the least favorable conditions for educational computing initiatives are when everything is highly constrained resulting in an "import/buy" software profile. This is characterized by the buying of packages for limited use. An example of this at Project Athena is the use of a purchased software package such as *Lotus 123*. The cost per copy limits use to a small number of users as does the necessity for the particular department to provide the computers for student use since the package does not run on the Athena supported *UNIX* workstations.

Models for development

Several models for development have been identified in our experience at Project Athena. These have been dubbed by the Athena applications developers as the *Jump Start, SIG, Group Therapy, Contract Programming, Triangle, College*, and *Service Rep* models.

Jump start. A faculty member and/or department programmer meets with an Athena consultant to learn what Athena has to offer in software, hardware, and services. Athena provides initial direction setting. The faculty member and/or depart-

	Low Environmental Constraints	High Environmental Constraints
High Empowering Constraints	**Import/Buy/Make** • Buy packages • Develop small modules • Widespread use	**Import/Buy/Make** • Buy packages • Develop small modules • Limited use
Low Empowering Constraints	**Make/Export** • Develop complex modules • Widespread use • Export	**Import/Buy/Make/Export** • Buy packages • Develop modules of moderate size & complexity • Limited use • Export

Figure 5: Curriculum software development under low value constraints

	Low Environmental Constraints	High Environmental Constraints
High Empowering Constraints	**Import/Buy** • Buy packages • Wide-spread use	**Import/Buy** • Buy packages • Limited use
Low Empowering Constraints	**Import/Buy/Make/Export** • Buy packages • Develop small modules • Widespread use • Export	**Import/Buy/Make** • Buy packages • Develop small modules • Limited use

Figure 6: Curriculum software development under high value constraints

ment programmer usually goes off and proceeds on their own. Often, Athena does not
see them again until they are ready to use Athena facilities for subject delivery. If the
time lapse between initial contact with Athena and actual delivery is short, the
developer usually does not run into any problems. If a significant period of time
elapses before delivery, there is a good chance that the environment will have slipped
out from underneath the developer and the software will break.

SIG. The Special Interest Group consists of a number of Athena consultants with
various specialized knowledge and a number of departments' faculty and programmers
who have similar interests. For instance, several Athena consultants have knowledge
of *GKS, BLOX, Xmath*, various statistics packages, etc. Several departments may be
interested in applying *BLOX* or in using statistics libraries or packages. The SIG is a
matching of these interests. The consultants often provide implementation assistance.
For a long time at Athena, there was a committee which met regularly on the problems
with finding and using appropriate statistics packages. The SIG concept could also be
extended across subject areas, such as common interests in "Optimization" and
"Thermodynamics" which could span a number of departments. For instance, the
project on "CAT: A New Methodology of Computer-Aided Thermodynamics" from
the department of Mechanical Engineering has developed software which is used by
several departments.

Group therapy. A faculty member and/or department programmer comes to
Athena with a project they wish to implement. Athena consultants are brought
together, representing an array of expertise needed to tackle the problem. The Athena
consultants work with the faculty and/or department programmer to provide implementation assistance -- cradle to grave support. No dollars are provided by Athena, just
limited consulting support and use of Athena facilities. During Spring of 1988 and
throughout the Summer Athena has supported the "MIT/Kennedy Space Center Teles-
cience Testbed" pilot project from the department of Aeronautics and Astronautics.
This project was developed by staff and programmers from the Aero Department in
conjunction with some outside knowledge-based consultants versed in payload systems. The pilot project pushed the envelope of technology at Athena, using satellite
communications, direct data links with the Kennedy Space Center, the color Athena
Visual Workstation for collecting and processing live moving video, and audio data.
Athena provided space, workstations, and help ranging from creative wiring to consulting on use of the Parallax graphics display processor and the *X Window System, Version 10*. Students were able to participate in the experiments and observe the live links
which were prominently displayed in an Athena cluster in the center of campus. This
application provides students with the opportunity to observe, gather data, and learn
from experiments conducted on board the space shuttle from the comfort of an Athena
cluster. This project represents a "proof of concept" which will form the basis for
follow-on proposals.

Contract programming. This type of support may be provided by professional programmers or/and by student programmers. A department project may be funded to have an Athena consultant assigned to do programming of courseware. The Athena consultant usually works for only one or two projects at any given time. Examples of these are in the projects for developing "Computer-aided Teaching of Crystal Structure, Crystallography and Crystal Defects" in the department of Material Science and Engineering and in porting "Common Ground, a Conferencing System" originally developed for PC's, to the *UNIX* workstation environment for the department of Biology. The department may also have a non-Athena staff member support such efforts. Examples of this are the projects for "Computer-based Educational Tools for Probability and Statistics" and "Computer Aided Electromagnetic Field Instruction" in the department of Electrical Engineering and Computer Science. In the latter case, there is a risk of short-term longevity for the developed software if the department programming staff does not remain well-connected to Athena development staff.

There are some excellent examples of applications that have been developed for nonstandard Athena workstations by Athena funded projects. They represent limited use, specialized applications that do not fundamentally require use of the Athena networked services. Several of them require real-time processing that can only be achieved in a standalone mode. They deserve special mention as follows:

- In the department of Music, IBM AT PC's outfitted with MIDI keyboards and synthesizers are used with applications software written in the *LogoMusic-Writer* language. It is designed to explore melody, rhythm, pitch relations, and procedural composition. This department has a laboratory outfitted with ten of these workstations for faculty and student use.

- A recent top prize award winner for educational software, the "Graphing Utility Programs in the Teaching of Special Relativity" were developed in the department of Physics on IBM XT and AT PC's in *Pascal* and *C*.

- Another award winning software application originated out of the department of Economics. "CASCON -- Computer-Aided System for Information on Local Conflicts" was designed for use in political science courses on foreign policy and international relations. Written in *C* it runs on the IBM AT PC computer.

- The Athena "Real-time Laboratory Workstation" project evolved out of the department of Ocean Engineering. The software and the hardware were designed to collect and analyze experimental data in the laboratory. IBM AT PC's and PS2/30's have been configured with Metrabyte data acquisition boards. There are *FORTRAN* and *C* versions available. About 100 of these workstations are being used by students in laboratories at MIT. Some of the software is also distributed commercially.

Triangle (department). This is a team approach model consisting of a faculty member(s) in a single department, a department software coach or programmer (resident in the department), and an Athena consultant. Often, this team represents a partnership that is long-lasting with potential for deep penetration into the department. The combination of talents should not be confused with the "classical" approach of a three member team where the department software coach is replaced by a design expert who is experienced in individualized instruction and the computer medium. The *triangle* has been a particularly successful model for providing a good chance of long-term survival for software that is developed for the curriculum. A strong sense of commitment and ownership has been generated by the departments involved. Several examples include projects in the School of Humanities and Social Science, the School of Science, and in the department of Aeronautics and Astronautics.

In the School of Humanities and Social Science the "Athena Writing Project" consists of two faculty members, an Athena consultant who has expert knowledge in the field of text and document systems, and a department programmer (augmented by student programmers). This *triangle* relationship at times was over-dominated by the technical staff. The writing staff were unfamiliar with *UNIX* and the Athena software and hardware environment before embarking on this project. About half-way through the project, the faculty were able to take control and concentrate on developing the environment for writing which they envisioned. This is an evolving project.

In the department of Chemistry in the School of Science, the project "Computer Applications in Chemistry Education" has expanded from a finite development project into an ongoing process of incorporating new applications into the department. This *triangle* consists of several faculty members, a departmental software coach, and an Athena consultant who provides part-time assistance in programming, finding, importing and buying external software. The department has implemented several modules which they developed, incorporated a commercial package, and acquired a videodisc-based module from another university.

The department of Aeronautics and Astronautics is particularly unusual in that development has occurred on a department-wide basis. This *triangle* consists of virtually all department faculty, a department-resident software coach/programmer, and an Athena-based consultant who is also a knowledge expert. Examples of several of their projects are "Computer Pedagogy in Structural Mechanics" and "Computer Enhanced Curriculum for Fluid Mechanics". A significant portion of software has been developed and is in the process of exportation to a number of universities. New modules continue to be added.

College. In this model which is a very broad version of the *SIG* model, a number of Athena consultants with various skills are assembled into a team to tackle a large problem which is shared in common by many departments; for example, the Visual

Computing Group at Athena. This group is involved in designing, creating, and delivering a hardware and software environment to support easy authoring of visual courseware and delivery to students. Faculty in Languages, Neuroanatomy, Aeronautics and Astronautics, Mechanical Engineering, Architecture, etc. share these same interests. This collegial model is a long-term effort with a lot of synergy. A good example of this model that is department-based rather than relying heavily on Athena resources occurs in the School of Architecture and Planning. Here faculty and students are involved in the creation of a graphics environment for educating architects, planners and developers. Their efforts are aimed at developing an integrated graphics environment and design support system that would otherwise exist piecewise across the School.

Service rep. The idea of having a one-stop service has been proposed a number of times. For example, a faculty member calls someone in Athena to find out what has happened to the workstation he was expecting from Athena six months ago. Currently, he usually gets the equivalent of the Athena staff telephone list and told "Good Luck". The service representative in Athena would walk the problem through the Athena (and broader MIT) labyrinth, hopefully obtaining positive resolution, but at least providing reliable information. This service does not exist today. This model is included as a model of development because of the tight coupling of *environmental* factors with the requirements for the development process mentioned earlier.

Cost and effectiveness

The relative dollar cost and duration of the various types of models are indicated in Figure 7.

Each of the models is effective for what it is trying to accomplish. There is a more fundamental problem about getting a project connected initially to the correct model. All of these models depend on the faculty member initiating the contact with Athena.

Observations and reflections

Writing innovative educational software is *hard work*, not a task to be undertaken as a side activity. Assuring the results will have a *future* is even more difficult, requiring programming practices that permit the generation of maintainable code, a constant eye to products in the pipeline and those that are slated for replacement.

Model	Cost	Duration
Jump start	Low	Short
SIG	Medium	Sporadic
Group therapy	Medium	3 - 6 months
Contract programming	Medium - High	6 months - 2 years
Triangle (department)	High	1 - 2 years
College	High	2 - 3 years
Service rep	Low - Medium	Sporadic

Figure 7: Cost and duration of curriculum development models

Users should be involved in decisions affecting them. The pervading idea of faculty and students was that Athena was doing something *to* them not *for* them. An informed user is in a better position of anticipating potential problems and weighing risks versus rewards in a conscious manner. "Buy in" is important!

Understanding the business we are in is essential. The faculty are in the business of research and education, not programming per se. Students are in the business of getting an education through formal instruction and exposure to research, not programming per se. Software professionals are in the business of creating programs to accomplish a desired set of functions which are maintainable. Linking the right skills together results in a usable product. Less than that is amateurism.

The interest of the faculty is in the *initial development* of the educational software, *not in its ongoing maintenance*. The expectation is that once the software is written it should continue to run, indefinitely. The computational model of networked workstations with its tendency to change has far different implications than a personal computer where the operating system can be frozen forever.

Objectives for the extension of Project Athena

After the first five years of the Project, a three year extension has been granted in order to gather more information about its educational impact so that the MIT Administration can make an informed decision about future directions of the MIT computational environment. In keeping with the spirit of this article the following goals and functions for the next three years of Project Athena are given from the prospective of the curriculum applications development group's planning process.

Goals. The following goals have been proposed for educational and technical support of faculty's educational computing over Athena's next three year phase:

- Focus on departments as the basic institutional units for development and use of educational computing in the curriculum with provision for school-wide or Institute-wide initiatives.

- Implement new forms of partnership between Project Athena and the departments, making use of a range of models for the provision of technical and educational support for faculty initiatives.

- Make the boundary between educational and research computing more permeable.

- Under the umbrella of Athena, integrate less technically sophisticated computing systems.

- Increase the visibility of applications software developed and used within MIT.

- Improve the match between faculty members' needs for educational computing and Athena's technical directions, including specification of software development tools and user interfaces.

- Sustain attention to the diffusion of promising innovations and development of new uses of the computer in MIT's curriculum.

- Provide an intellectual home for faculty interested in educational computing as broadly defined, encompassing all such efforts, whether or not they use Athena hardware and software.

In connection with this last goal, critical to Athena's success as an educational experiment, we believe Athena should evolve as an informal collegial forum in which faculty can learn from what they do and explore together the exciting intellectual questions raised by their educational initiatives -- for example, How do engineers think? How do students learn to think like engineers? Like composers or chemists? How might computers help them do so? What are the specific educational benefits of educational computing? What are the best classroom environments for educational computing? What impact will a campus-wide communications network have across the curriculum? How can it best be used to foster educational innovation, and to support conventional classroom practices?

Functions. In support of the goals outlined above, in addition to the provision of hardware, maintenance and user support services, Project Athena should fulfill the following functions through the *Educational Computing Initiatives* Group (formerly known as Applications Development):

- Assist faculty in formulating curriculum development proposals and locating external funding for them.

- Continually assess software tools and create specifications for tools that faculty need; upgrade and augment when appropriate.

- Training for faculty who wish to develop new educational uses of the computer, including introduction to Athena's computing environment.

- Assist faculty in importing and exporting educational software, across institutional boundaries, including demonstration and evaluation of existing software.

- Provide support to interested faculty in conducting "self studies" for the planning, monitoring and evaluation of educational computing initiatives.

- Organize "cluster" seminars on educational computing issues that cut across departments, for example, computer environments for design and computer processing of laboratory data.

- Maintenance of a repository for software in use at MIT, to reduce burden on faculty.

Significant progress has already been made on these redefined goals and functions. Athena, the tripartite mythological Greek warrior-goddess, goddess of prudent intelligence, and goddess of the arts of peace may now lay to rest her first scepter of war, and take up, one in each hand, the scepters of prudent intelligence and peace.

Acknowledgements

The material in this article reflects many of the experiences of a number of us at MIT. Some of the Figures and information in the discussion of the goals and progress towards goals comes from materials prepared for various presentations by Professor Steven R. Lerman who was the Director of Project Athena for the first five years and is a member of the department of Civil Engineering. The information relating to the objectives for the extension of Project Athena comes from a planning instrument developed by a number of faculty who participated in a curriculum applications development planning committee chaired by the author of this article prior to the end of the first five years of the Project.

Textual Intervention, Collaboration, and the Online Environment

Edward Barrett

Writing Program
Massachusetts Institute of Technology

By modeling the social processes of meaning-making, the Educational Online System at MIT integrates textual intervention, collaboration, and developmental writing. This design approach suggests a new role for writers in the computer industry.

Introduction

This chapter completes a trilogy of articles defining a conceptual framework for the design and implementation of a networked instructional and conferencing system, the Educational Online System (EOS) (Barrett and Paradis, 1988; and 1988 in Barrett, 1988). After a brief background discussion of EOS, I will present three models for interacting in an instructional or conferencing environment. Then I will analyze the changing dynamic of interaction effected by this system in terms of those three models.

Background

The Educational Online System (EOS) was developed at MIT as part of the Athena Writing Project. Continued development of this system is currently funded by the MIT Writing Program, with technical assistance provided by Project Athena. EOS uses a fully-distributed computer network in conjunction with specially designed programs to support conventional classroom activities: text creation, text exchange, text display, and textual annotation. These activities can be viewed as paradigmatic and constitutive of all subjects if "text" is defined broadly as "work;" thus, a problem-set in math is a "text," or a discussion in a history class, as well as a written report in a literature class. EOS is used in real class-time as part of an *ad hoc* electronic classroom outfitted with twenty DEC VS2000 workstations and a Hughes light valve for large screen projection of text files.

The design of EOS, therefore, was essentially subject neutral although it was fully expected that, at least initially, its main use would be within the province of its principal investigators: writing subjects in the School of Humanities and Social Science. However, EOS has migrated to twenty different subjects within the School of Science and the School of Engineering. This fact certainly justifies the "subject neutral" aim of its designers and supports the notion that EOS is highly tailorable to a range of constituencies (Barrett and Paradis, 1988) although it does problematize the question of computer support for humanities subjects. Of course, science and engineering faculty may be in general less resistant to computer technology and, therefore, more supportive of it in instructional domains, especially since its use may correlate so strongly with advancement in their fields of study (both within and outside the academy). EOS was recently extended to support activities in the MIT Writing Cooperative (Barrett, 1988), in which faculty from the Writing Program and faculty in Science and Engineering collaborate in training students to write technical and scientific reports. No objective data exist as yet to support the notion that EOS either improves, impedes, or leaves unchanged progress in these courses at MIT. Nevertheless, anecdotal material in the form of instructor journals, student questionnaires, and student memoranda strongly suggests that this particular application of computer technology to writing classes changes the dynamic of classroom interaction and enriches in-class work. In an attempt to gather more objective data, MIT is participating in a year-long, nationwide study, supported by the Fund for the Improvement of Post Secondary Education (FIPSE), which will investigate the effects of computing technology on writing subjects (Kirsch, 1988).

Three Models for Interaction

1. Interventionism and 2. the Developmental Perspective

Of course, it is difficult to assess "progress" in writing. Instructors grapple with this question in varying degrees each semester. Industry, too, wrestles with this issue in various forms: in-house standards are formulated, outside consultants (frequently those same academics grappling with these issues within their own domain) are called in to offer short-courses, or computer systems of varying sorts are implemented to make "writing" somehow easier or more procedurally intelligible. Companies will also pay for their employees to take academic courses to improve writing skills. But no really adequate standard exists for the training of individuals since individual competencies vary so much--both between any two individuals, as well as within the individual who switches from one task to the next. As a result, the management of documentation cycles in industry and the academy frequently falls back on set formulae to articulate hypothetical processes that are supposed to be "happening" when one is writing; or the more profound questions are put aside and substituted in their place is an emphasis on skill-training--that is, the effort to train a writer in the outside performance aspects of texts that have already been judged successful or at least adequate.

It is always easy to establish "baseline" standards for each writer and to rate individual deviations from that standard through a series of highly structured tests. Indeed, computer-based training (CBT) is an ideal engine for such transactions, at least from the point of view of simplistic stimulus-response theories of learning (Skinner, 1961). But it is difficult to correlate deviations from that initial baseline with improved performance in writing since "writing" itself, at least within the academy, is used to facilitate (and then test) content acquisition in a subject, as well as to further more "developmental" perspectives. Of course, these two aims of writing in the academy apply equally well to writing within the computer industry: writing facilitates the exchange of information about something, and increasingly, as in the development of hypertext delivery systems, writing with and for the computer is viewed through the perspective of various cognitive process models of performance and analysis.

Thus, two strong and sometimes opposing strategies for teaching, assessing, and producing writing exist: *interventionism*, which is usually perceived as a rear-guard movement stressing normative behavior in text creation (standard usage, sentence and paragraph development, style, etc.) and the *developmental* perspective which stresses the maturational potential in all writing (Kroll, 1980): writing that is explorational, hence contingent, disjunctive, demotic.

Both the interventionalist school of writing instruction and the developmental approach share a certain fascination with process-driven, performance aspects of writing. For interventionists, like Skinner, all learning can be reduced to basic skills, and the best method for teaching and acquiring these skills is through programmed learning models. Thus, a pedagogical approach which some see as rear-guard allies itself quite naturally with avant-garde educational technologists who support the introduction of advanced computing techniques into the classroom. The computer, they say, is a most effective learning machine because of its rigid hierarchical ordering of material and its "genetic" reliance on a programmed sequence of steps which the student can manipulate and internalize. The developmental approach also relies upon a process model for instruction although here the sequence of steps is perhaps less rigid because the goal, self-actualization, is more nebulous. The developmental approach uses the "protean power" (Papert, 1980) of the computer for simulation: the computer is programmed to simulate the cognitive processes that presumably attend various performance levels; by following the prompting of the machine the user can map these programmed simulations to an internal intellectual and affective organization.

3. The Collaborative Model

The dialectic between interventionism and the developmental approach is complicated by a third perspective which in a sense displaces attention away from the individual to the community of which she is part. Perhaps the most well-known advocate of this approach is Kenneth Bruffee. Bruffee's revisionism of the work of Lev Vygotsky (Bruffee, 1972, 1982; Vygotsky, 1962, 1978) on the social construction of knowledge was undoubtedly influenced by his experiences as a member of the English Department at Brooklyn College during a decade of massive demographic, economic, and political change at CUNY. Faced with a new, stunningly ill-prepared student constituency that nevertheless was desirous of learning, the community of scholars at his institution had to assess traditional methods of instruction, as well as deeper questions of historicity and value in their presentation of curricular material. Bruffee's work on peer tutoring lead him to assert a new model for the analysis, composition, and review of texts, a model that stresses collaborative groups and the definition of socially justified belief systems in the construction of meaning and knowledge.

Bruffee's radicalization of the learning model also easily allies itself with educational technology. In this model user-machine interaction is viewed as an element of a larger social process of learning, and less as a one-to-one interaction between user and screen divorced from the communal peer group. Thus, process-driven programs for learning are subordinate to electronic messaging of various forms within and among peer-groups. The individual machine is an enabling device by virtue of its connection to other machines on a network (Schwartz, 1984).

Following the collaborative model, it is easy to see how various electronic activities can be used in the construction, exchange, and review of writing, or "text" in general: electronic mail for messaging, text editors for composition, and hypertext systems for remapping topologies of information sequences as the social constructs of meaning-making change. However, each one of these electronic forms is by itself too limited to sustain the social constructionist's model. Electronic mail supports text exchange and peer response, but not text editing; text editors are in general a solipsistic tool; and hypertext permits annotation and review but largely preserves authorial imperative because the conceptual ordering of information in hypertext is so ingrained by the initial programming.

"Writing" in the Computer Industry

Each of these three models is a necessary although not sufficient element in the design of an electronic instructional and conferencing system for "writing." I set off "writing" in quotation marks for two reasons. First, as stated above, activities that fall under this term are varied; usually in any particular environment only a subset of these activities is being invoked. Second, with specific reference to the computer industry, "writing" and "writer" may be shibboleths as well as functional job descriptions

(Zimmerman, 1988). As documentation moves online, the "writing" skills necessary for producing such text will probably coalesce with programming skills (Shirk, 1988)-- especially as delivery systems move closer to modified hypertext environments. "Writers" will be more integral members of product development teams (Grice, 1988).

This new job function will also complete the evolution of one current role of a writer, the writer as user-surrogate. However, the term "surrogate" seems to possess two meanings for practicing technical writers in the computer industry. The first meaning is more fruitful: the "writer" as surrogate represents the end-user in product development, a sort of pre-test subject and Socratic gadfly to engineering departments--obviously a valuable role to be played.

The second implied meaning is a less fulfilling one. For the past two years, in addition to directing the annual conference on *Writing for the Computer Industry*, I have served on the faculty of the MIT summer seminar *Communicating Technical Information*, directed by my colleague, James Paradis. As part of my work for this seminar, I have collected anecdotes from technical writers both within and outside the computer industry regarding their perceptions of self in relation to job function. For both groups, the use of the word "surrogate" is opprobrious: it represents a perceived lack of status for writers and writing within their industry. In fact, the term carries with it another marking, this time a specifically *feminine* one--as reported by both male and female respondents although most strongly noted by female writers, especially females who have been in the field for five years or less. For these writers, to be called "surrogates" connotes the economic and political disparity between men and women in the larger culture of the United States; the term seems to stand for perceptions of an exploitative relationship in their jobs, a second-class citizenship within engineering or-ganizations.

The Collaborative Model and the Role of the Writer

As computer systems evolve out of the single-screen single-user dynamic, and if hypertext systems develop into more than navigational devices in structured databases, writers, as product developers, will need to study the social content of the interface. In this view, interface is more than a means for controlling submerged machine functions. The social content of the interface is the mapping of social operations on to the machine. When interface is construed to mean simply control of machine function, it is also usually linked to presumed cognitive processes going on in the mind of the user, a result most likely of the severely personal use of some computing technology. Herbert Simon points out that "interface" is always between inner and outer environments--between organization and functioning (Simon, 1985). Yet, a major use of computers in knowledge-making and writing involves no "outer" environment, only inner environments, the inner organization of the machine and the mind.

With emphasis upon the social content of the interface, however, focus is changed to the social constructs (as opposed to purely interior, intellectual ones) that engender meaning-making, information, knowledge, and communication. In this view, the writer's role as developer is determinant (Barrett and Paradis, 1988). The social construction of information switches emphasis away from cognitive process models of meaning-making in the development of information architecture and delivery systems. A writer (ideally, a writer with experience in a range of writing activities) helps to define these social constructs; design follows suit. The society of mind, personified in the machine, is replaced by the society of text--a paradigm shift. In this new paradigm, it is not enough to say that the computer has textualized work (Zuboff, 1988); we must also textualize the computer.

The Ascent of Forms: Online Environments and the Integration of Intervention, Collaboration, and Developmental Writing

EOS uses the online environment of the Athena-supported distributed network at MIT to integrate textual intervention, collaboration, and developmental writing. This integration fundamentally changes the dynamic each of these models possesses in the conventional classroom. Thus, traditional textual intervention (a one-to-one, student-instructor dynamic) is permitted and enlarged to include a many-to-one, many-to-many text exchange in-class and out-of-class by means of specially designed text-exchange programs. This new dynamic of intervention, therefore, integrates the social processes that are part of writing: in other words, it invokes collaboration. And finally, EOS enhances developmental writing not by forcing the student to internalize a pre-programmed "process" of development. Instead, EOS uses the linearity of the computer to integrate n different processes in parallel. Students perform various actions on texts (the text of the paper and the developing text of discussion and revisioning) and emerge with a different perspective on how they, and others, write.

Virtual Environments

Of course, the online environment is the ideal space to study, as well as implement, these changing dynamics of intervention, collaboration, and development. By its very nature as a *virtual environment* an online system can merge public and private domains of interaction. On the most basic level, space itself is more malleable. The inherited forms we all bring to any instructional/conferencing space still adhere in the electronic classroom, but they are deconstructed and reassembled in ways that change the psychology of interaction. Since all files and all annotation and text display software are available to anyone at anytime anywhere on campus (or through a modem, at home) the stark discontinuity between going to class and being in class is submerged into an environment that expands notions of class-time and class-room. Furthermore, the in-class environment provides a more "plastic" space for the exchange, display, and review of texts. Since all texts are online, they may easily be viewed on the light valve (a large screen projection device) as well as individual workstations. Thus, the light valve is simultaneously an electronic chalkboard (Stefik, 1987), overhead projector, and collaborative arena. The workstation screen itself is more than an electronic stylus (Daiute, 1983); it assembles or invokes the forms of "notebook" (through scratch text editing windows), "textbook" (through online curricular files accessible in other windows), "notepassing" (through "hidden" student-to-student talk facilities), while remaining a theater for the analysis, composition, and review of student texts (see Figure 1).

Text As Object

EOS translates forms of thought (texts) into representational objects upon which the class and instructor may perform various operations. The most typical operation, classical textual intervention--making notes on a paper, correcting usage, etc.--is of course supported by EOS (see Figure 2). Yet this fairly mundane activity is transformed in the electronic classroom. In the conventional classroom, the instructor uses a set of traditional and idiosyncratic marginal symbols to refer to a larger set of ideas, conventions, and models for writing. The instructor may also question the validity of certain rhetorical devices or the logic of certain arguments through marginal commentaries. But these handwritten notes are bound by certain physical limitations (available margin space, legibility), and by the feeling that the bold symbology of "marking up" papers tilts the transaction towards the grader--after all the grader's comment are *written over* the author's text.

In the electronic classroom there is a basic shift in the political dynamic of annotation. As we see in Figure 2, the grader's online comments are as intrusive as ordinary hardcopy annotation. Yet the instructor's comments now ride within the original author's. The bold symbology of red ink and squiggly lines or underscoring (indeed, crossing out in various stages of vigor) is missing. Instead, text is inserted that exists upon the *same plane* as the original. Grader and author now reside within this plane of text, equally responsible for its status as text. Furthermore, the grader's comment in this new form cannot rely upon the usual telegraphy of annotation (lines, question marks, circles, etc.) that gesture toward a meaning but rarely articulate it fully. Now the grader is forced into making comments that must assume a status of text equal to the original. In other words, the grader has now become less authoritarian (although her authoritative status is unchanged), more equal on the plane of text. Essentially, the "grader" has become an collaborator on the revision.

At first, there was some question as to what we were losing by sacrificing the usual machinery of textual commentary in EOS (Barrett and Paradis, 1988). It is clear, however, that the benefits of online critiquing far outweigh the loss of the gestural vigor of hardcopy annotation. Comments may now be expanded within the original without the physical limitations noted above. Furthermore, observations of students

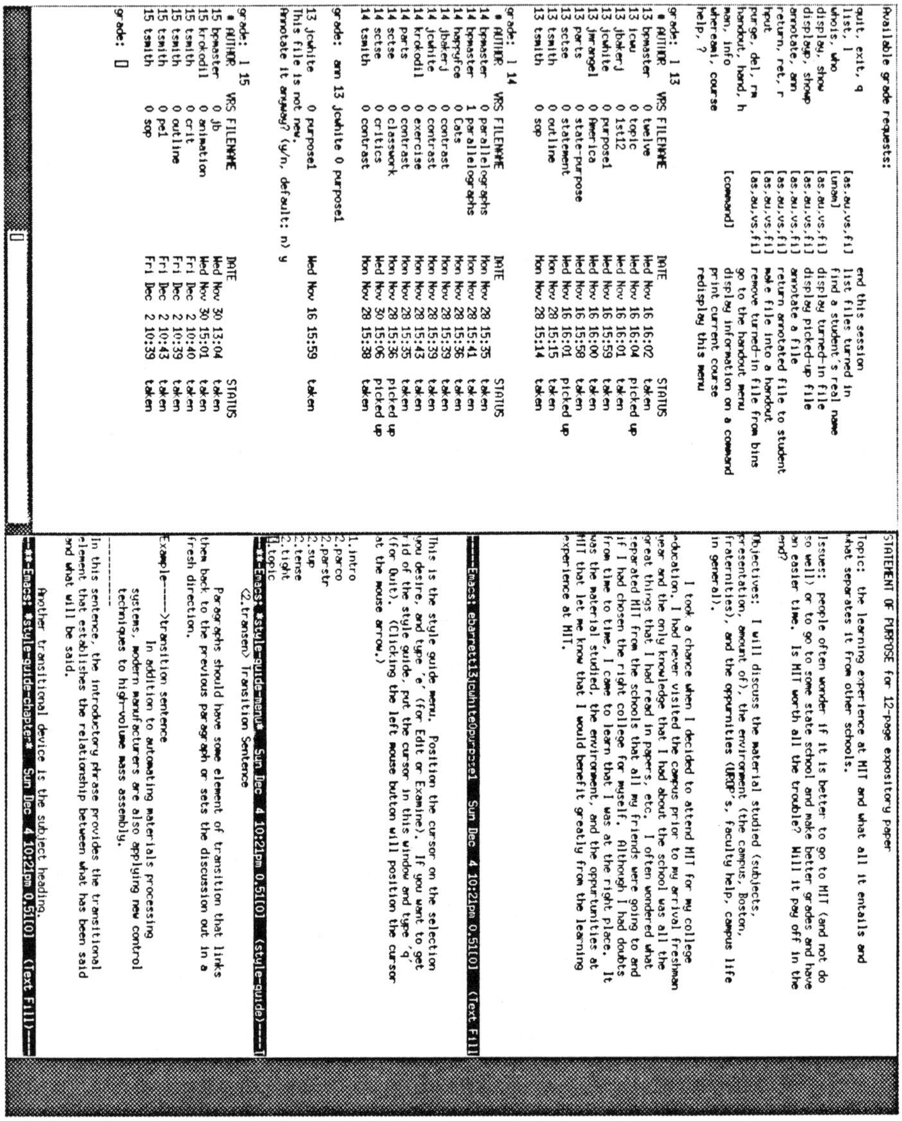

Figure 1. Instructor's annotation screen.

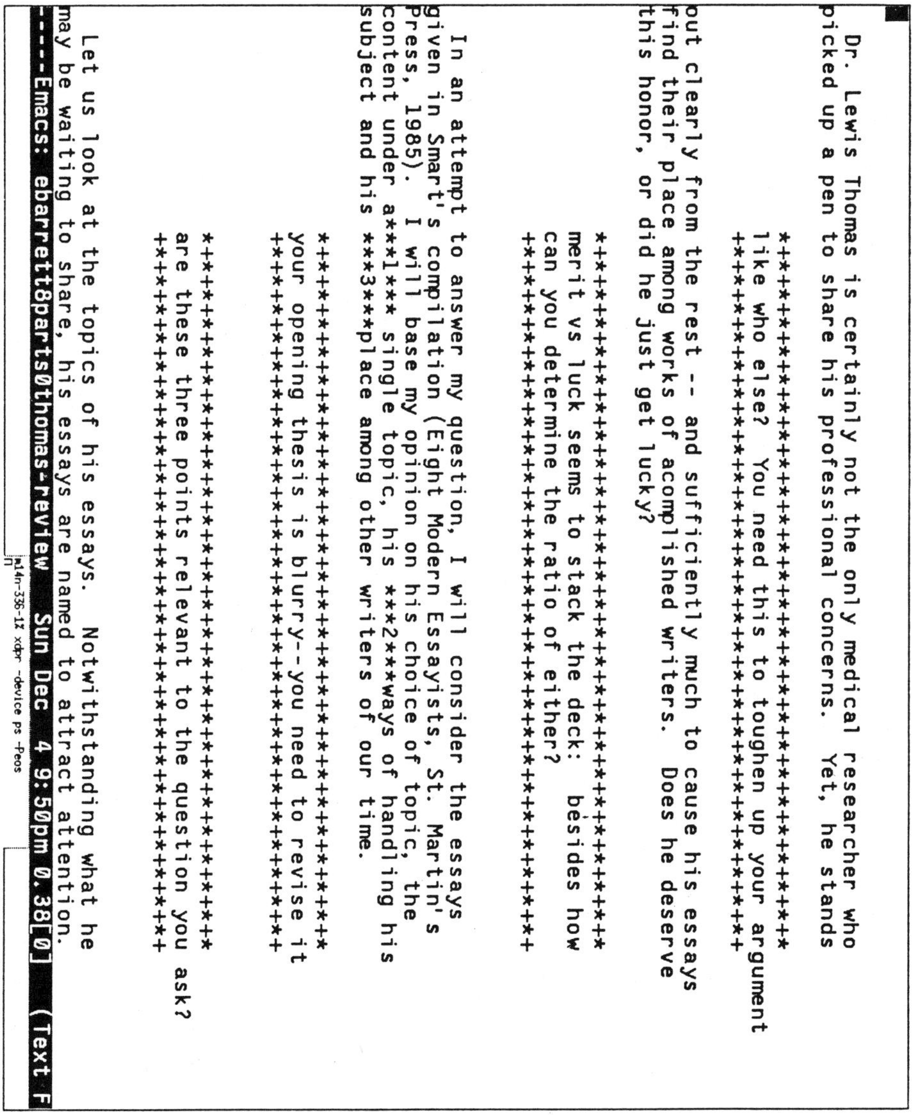

```
 Dr. Lewis Thomas is certainly not the only medical researcher who
picked up a pen to share his professional concerns.  Yet, he stands

      *+*+*+*+*+*+*+*+*+*+*+*+*+*+*+*+*+*+*+*+*+*+*+*+*+*
      like who else?  You need this to toughen up your argument
      +*+*+*+*+*+*+*+*+*+*+*+*+*+*+*+*+*+*+*+*+*+*+*+*+*+

out clearly from the rest -- and sufficiently much to cause his essays
find their place among works of acomplished writers.  Does he deserve
this honor, or did he just get lucky?
      *+*+*+*+*+*+*+*+*+*+*+*+*+*+*+*+*+*+*+*+*+*+*+*+*+*
      merit vs luck seems to stack the deck:  besides how
      can you determine the ratio of either?
      +*+*+*+*+*+*+*+*+*+*+*+*+*+*+*+*+*+*+*+*+*+*+*+*+*+

 In an attempt to answer my question, I will consider the essays
given in Smart's compilation (Eight Modern Essayists, St. Martin's
Press, 1985).  I will base my opinion on his choice of topic, the
content under a***1*** single topic, his ***2***ways of handling his
subject and his ***3***place among other writers of our time.
      *+*+*+*+*+*+*+*+*+*+*+*+*+*+*+*+*+*+*+*+*+*+*
      your opening thesis is blurry--you need to revise it
      +*+*+*+*+*+*+*+*+*+*+*+*+*+*+*+*+*+*+*+*+*+*+

      *+*+*+*+*+*+*+*+*+*+*+*+*+*+*+*+*+*+*+*+*+*+*
      are these three points relevant to the question you ask?
      +*+*+*+*+*+*+*+*+*+*+*+*+*+*+*+*+*+*+*+*+*+*+

 Let us look at the topics of his essays.  Notwithstanding what he
may be waiting to share, his essays are named to attract attention.
----Emacs: ebarrett8parts0thomas-review    Sun Dec  4 9:50pm 0.38[0]    (Text F
```

m14n-336-1% xdpr -device ps -Peos

Figure 2. A student's text with instructor's comments.

reading online commentary in their reports seem to suggest another gain. Just as instructors are now forced to make more intelligible comments on a text, students are forced to read these comments interspersed throughout their original drafts. Students in EOS find it difficult to gauge an instructor's reaction as quickly as they once did simply by glancing at the amount of red ink spilled over the paper. The equality of status afforded commentary within the plane of the original apparently invites more considered review by students. Of course, to speak of a student "reviewing" an instructor's comments points to the changing power structure in the electronic classroom. If an adequate *Theory of Marginalia* were ever to be articulated, it would have to speak to this important dynamic of writer/reviewer status. Finally, the surface contiguity of the author's original text and a reviewer's commentary reifies the fact that in the electronic classroom, writing is being used to comment upon writing. The instructor may lose the gestural efficacy of a red arrow; what is gained is the more important dialogue in language, written language, that supports the larger concept of the value of writing to communicate ideas. The instructor must, then, reside on the same plane as the student as a test almost of the usefulness of writing to communicate ideas. The instructor now connives in the production of a next draft as collaborator, as well as mediator of traditions and conventions. Needless to say, these same functions are available to every other student in the electronic classroom--everyone potentially collaborates in the production of a text.

Another aspect of textual intervention that we are studying as part of EOS is the *record/replay* program developed by David Custer (Custer, 1988). Essentially, this program opens a "dribble file" which creates a keystroke-by-keystroke record of a text editing session. This record can then be replayed in- or out-of-class by student or instructor. The replay provides a video-like recreation of textual composition, keystroke-by-keystroke, with all deletions, insertions and cursor movements included. *Replay* allows the class to see vividly into the actual moment of composition in order to identify and comment upon composition strategies. Thought protocols are obviated since we have a "moving picture" of the thought-as-object being played out right in front of us. This program provides a dynamic illustration of typical compositional signatures (a writer who always begins with certain subordinate clauses, for example, only to delete them for a simpler, more direct syntax). *Record/replay* also allows authors to speak about compositional strategies after the fact with the actual composing event unfolding before them.

Figure 3 is a screen-dump showing the kind of textual intervention now possible in EOS with *record/replay*. This screen-dump is taken from a typical instructor's review of a student's text editing session. The top of the screen is the "video-like" keystroke-by-keystroke replay in action (here of course the action is frozen). In the lower left-hand corner of the screen are two windows that depict the final stage of the editing session. The bottom lower left-hand screen is the final paragraph written by the student. The window directly above it symbolically represents the kinds of editing the

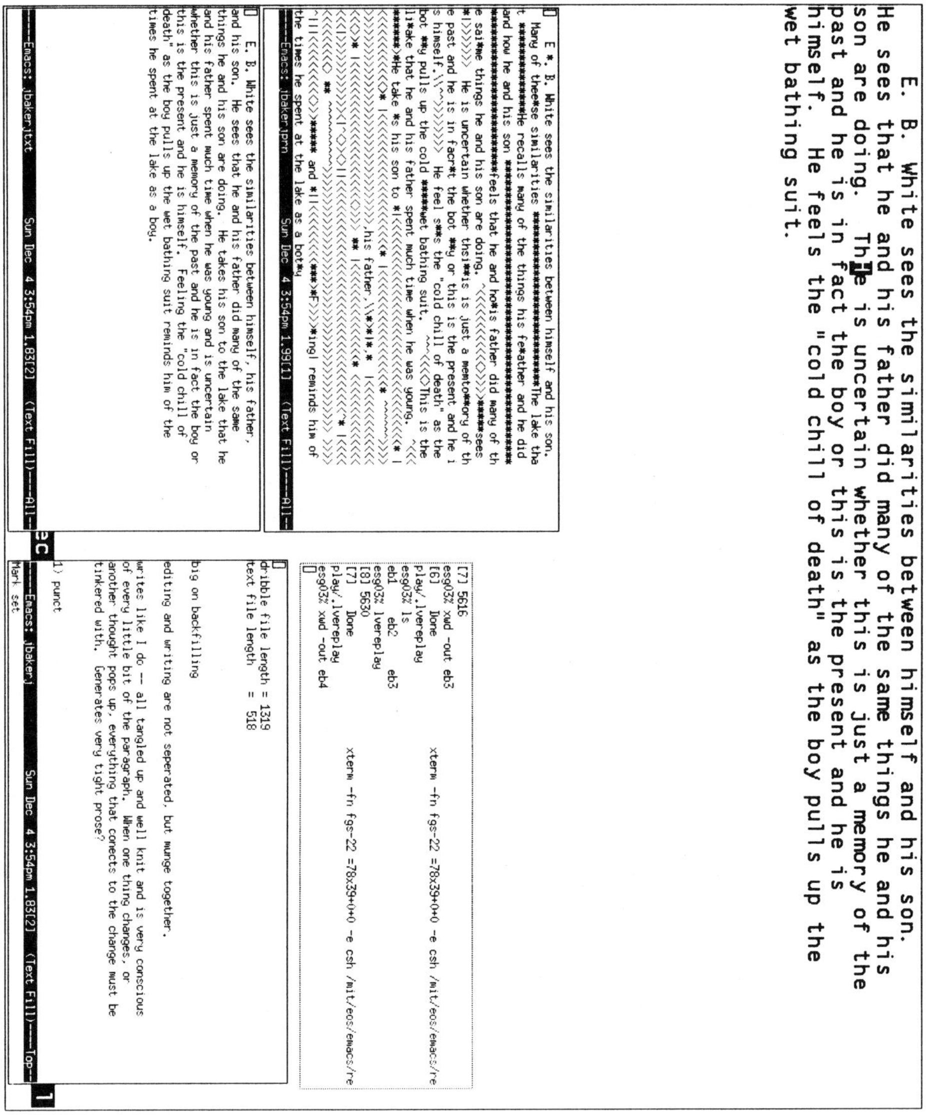

E. B. White sees the similarities between himself and his son.
He sees that he and his father did many of the same things he and his
son are doing. The is uncertain whether this is just a memory of the
past and he is in fact the boy or this is the present and he is
himself. He feels the "cold chill of death" as the boy pulls up the
wet bathing suit.

E. B. White sees the similarities between himself and his son.
Many of these similarities ============The lake tha
============He recalls many of the things his father and he did
and how he and his son ==========
e sa==me things he and ho=is father did many of th
e feels things he and his son are doing. \^\<<<<<<\<<>>>======sees
t >>>>> He is uncertain whether th=is=is is just a mem=o=mory of th
e past and he is in fac=t the bot =my or this is the present and he i
s himself.\^\>>>>>>> He feel s=ees the "cold chill of death" as the
bot =my pulls up the cold =====bwet bathing suit. ^~\<<\<>This is the
litake that he and his father spent much time when he was young. \<<
=======He take *s his son to *I\<<<<<
\<\<\<\<\<\<\<\<O\>* I\<<<<<<<<<<<<(<\<* ~^~~~~/,his father.\/*#I*.* \>
\^I\<<<<<<<<<\<<O\>* I\<<<<<< ## I\<<<<<
^~I\<<<<<<<<<<<<<O\>*****#* I\<<<<<<<\<<* I\<<<<<
^/I\<<\<<<<<O\>*****#>F\>>*#Ing1 reminds him of
the times he spent at the lake as a bot#y

---Emacs: jbaker.tpm   Sun Dec 4 3:54pm 1.99(1) (Text Fill)---All-

E. B. White sees the similarities between himself, his father,
and his son.   He sees that he and his father did many of the same
things he and his son are doing. He takes his son to the lake that he
and his father spent much time when he was young and is uncertain
whether this is just a memory of the past and he is in fact the boy or
this is the present and he is himself. Feeling the "cold chill of
death" as the boy pulls up the wet bathing suit reminds him of the
times he spent at the lake as a boy.

---Emacs: jbaker.txt   Sun Dec 4 3:54pm 1.83(2) (Text Fill)---All-

[7] 5616
esg03z xwd -out eb3   xterm -fn fgs-22 =78x39+0+0 -e csh /mit/eos/emacs/re
[6]   Done
play./iverepay   xterm -fn fgs-22 =78x39+0+0 -e csh /mit/eos/emacs/re
esg03z is
eb1   eb2   eb3
esg03z iverepay
[8] 5630
[7] 5630
play./iverepay   xterm -fn fgs-22 =78x39+0+0 -e csh /mit/eos/emacs/re
esg03z xwd -out eb4

dribble file length = 1319
text file length   = 518

big on backfilling

editing and writing are not seperated, but merge together.

writes like I do -- all tangled up and well knit and is very conscious
of every little bit of the paragraph. When one thing changes, or
another thought pops up, everything that conects to the change must be
tinkered with. Generates very tight prose?

1) punct
Mark set:
---Emacs: jbaker.j   Sun Dec 4 3:54pm 1.83(2) (Text Fill)---Top-

Figure 3. A screen running the *record/replay* program.

student was doing: deletions, insertions, cutting-and-pasting and so forth. Finally, in the bottom lower right-hand window is the instructor's log of this editing session, identifying the operations the student was performing on this text, and offering suggestions about the rhetorical strategies the student was using, as well as more typical statements about effect (excellent, poor, etc.).

We have also employed *record/replay* with all editing functions disabled. The student writer, therefore, could not correct mistakes on any level of composition. Instead, students were literally pushed forward to complete the syntactical/logical trajectory of any particular sentence or group of sentences. This exercise forced students to "write through" problem areas in a particular passage. Results of this in-class exercise demonstrate that a student writer will usually write fluently after a few minutes of uncertainty, apparently riding the crest of a developing idea, now that responsibility for correcting "mistakes" has been removed.

The *record/replay* program promises to be a fertile ground for the study of compositional strategies since it permits a fairly objective review of an editing session without ever having to resort to highly subjective protocol analysis.

Social Processes as Objects in EOS

Perhaps the most important design element of EOS is the use of the computer to model the social constructs behind the creation of texts. In this view, the social content of the interface is predominant--the computer is used to facilitate the social processes that go into the creation, analysis, and review of texts. Interface, therefore, mediates the social construction of knowledge in this environment.

One corollary to this design principle is that networked, online instructional and conferencing systems are best developed *in situ* by the end-user. Our experience with the development of EOS supports this idea (Barrett and Paradis, 1988). Discussions about developing a system that would employ the Athena-supported network to teach writing classes went on for several years before design and implementation. And it was only after the end-users of this system (that is, writing instructors) asserted control of the design process and wrote out specifications based upon their needs that a workable system was produced.

Using the computer to model the social constructs behind the creation and assessment of texts resulted in several design choices. First, it was essential that a central repository of all files (both student and curricular) be formed (see Figure 4). Without this core storage facility it would be difficult to trace development over a period of time. In this sense, EOS does not address problems involved with updating databases. As writing instructors we needed a stable "geology" of record keeping to order the daily stratum of drafts that any writing environment produces. EOS, therefore, stores

```
grade:  l 9
 # AUTHOR     VRS FILENAME          DATE               STATUS
 9 bpmaster    0 exercise9          Wed Oct 26 15:37   picked up
 9 cheryl      0 exercise9          Wed Oct 26 15:36   picked up
 9 cheryl      0 thomas             Wed Oct 26 14:33   picked up
 9 happyfce    0 ex9                Wed Oct 26 15:38   picked up
 9 icwu        0 critique           Wed Oct 26 17:27   picked up
 9 icwu        1 critique           Sun Oct 30 23:18   picked up
 9 icwu        0 ex.9               Wed Oct 26 15:40   picked up
 9 icwu        1 ex.9               Wed Oct 26 15:58   picked up
 9 icwu        0 exercise9          Wed Oct 26 16:21   picked up
 9 jbakerj     0 critique~          Wed Oct 26 15:37   picked up
 9 jbakerj     0 exercise9          Wed Oct 26 15:47   picked up
 9 jbakerj     1 exercise9          Wed Oct 26 16:17   picked up
 9 jbakerj     0 exercise9~         Wed Oct 26 15:38   picked up
 9 jcwhite     0 exercise9          Wed Oct 26 15:36   picked up
 9 jmrangel    0 exercise9          Wed Oct 26 15:38   picked up
 9 jmrangel    1 exercise9          Wed Oct 26 15:43   picked up
 9 parts       0 exercise9          Wed Oct 26 15:38   picked up
 9 sctse       0 exercise9          Wed Oct 26 15:37   picked up

grade:  ann 9 cheryl 0 exercise9

 9 cheryl      0 exercise9          Wed Oct 26 15:36   picked up
This file is not new.
Annotate it anyway? (y/n, default: n) y


grade:  l 10
 # AUTHOR     VRS FILENAME          DATE               STATUS
10 bpmaster    0 bonehead           Mon Nov  7 11:30   picked up
10 bpmaster    0 d3                 Wed Nov  9 16:23   picked up
10 bpmaster    0 opp                Wed Nov  2 15:48   picked up
10 icwu        0 critique.unk       Wed Nov  2 15:49   picked up
10 jbakerj     0 Thomas             Wed Nov  2 15:49   picked up
10 jbakerj     0 peress             Sun Nov  6 23:38   picked up
10 jcwhite     0 personal           Wed Nov  9 14:29   picked up .
10 jcwhite     0 thomasopposite     Wed Nov  2 15:49   picked up
10 jmrangel    0 AutoLewis          Wed Nov  2 15:50   picked up
10 krokodil    0 Personal_Essay     Mon Nov  7 13:00   picked up
10 krokodil    0 intro              Wed Nov  2 15:49   picked up
10 parts       0 Thomas-again       Wed Nov  2 15:48   picked up
10 parts       0 personal-essay     Mon Nov  7 13:12   picked up
10 tsmith      0 pe2                Mon Nov  7 15:41   picked up

grade:  l 11
 # AUTHOR     VRS FILENAME          DATE               STATUS
11 cheryl      0 personal           Thu Nov 10 02:10   picked up
11 cheryl      0 revise             Wed Nov  9 16:22   picked up
11 jcwhite     0 revision           Wed Nov  9 16:14   taken
11 jmrangel    0 Autonomy1.mss      Sat Nov  5 16:34   picked up
11 jmrangel    0 Death              Wed Nov  9 16:15   taken
11 parts       0 purpose-outline    Tue Nov 22 17:35   taken
11 parts       0 revision           Wed Nov  9 16:14   taken
11 sctse       0 personal_essay_review Wed Nov  9 16:19   picked up

grade:  l 12
 # AUTHOR     VRS FILENAME          DATE               STATUS
12 dldeb       0 ads.mss            Tue Nov  8 23:01   picked up
12 jmrangel    0 Memories.mss       Mon Nov  7 14:56   picked up
12 tsmith      0 crit               Wed Nov 23 11:21   taken
12 tsmith      0 pe1                Tue Nov 22 10:42   taken

grade:  █
```

Figure 4. Central class list in EOS.

all drafts in weekly directories, classified according to author, version number, and filename; in addition, it records what actions have been taken on a particular draft.

With this core established, EOS translates social processes of intervention and collaboration into objects that can be manipulated in real class-time. Thus, files can be created in class, turned in to the instructor and sent to the rest of the class for review (all annotation software is shared by instructor and students to make peer review possible). These shared files can then be reviewed, annotated, and rewritten for another cycle of exchange. The student must identify the problems (or the successes of a text) and improve upon it, or use it (if the text is successful) as a model for another text. Throughout this process, discussion of various forms of textual intervention is encouraged by the large screen projection of drafts and by the sharing and manipulation of texts at individual workstations. Thus, the machine itself is not analyzing a text, or leading a student through a programmed sequence of steps in composition; it is supporting the social dynamic of analysis and review. Interior, cognitive processes are not mapped to the computer in this dynamic; instead, the computer supports the social construction of knowledge through its modeling of the collaborative processes of analysis, composition, and review.

For example, one typical class in expository writing from midsemester began with the instructor sending to students at their workstations sentences for revision: a sort of warm-up exercise. Students then revised these sentences and turned in their revised files to the central repository (they retained copies in their permanent home directories also). Several students, however, were asked to broadcast the contents of their screen to everyone else for review and discussion. With this warm-up concluded, the class was then asked to call up a file from their online curricular files stored in the "handout" bin (a modified version of an online electronic textbook). This handout contained a model text showing the development of a statement of purpose for a longer, critical essay. Students discussed the formal and stylistic qualities of this model. The class was then asked to take twenty minutes to write a statement of purpose for a critical essay due the following week. These statements of purpose were then shown for class discussion. After suggestions were given for improvement, or difficulties in understanding the statements were addressed, students were asked to write introductory paragraphs for this essay. These drafts were recorded in the *record/replay* mode, and displayed in class for review and analysis. Of course, all files during this ninety-minute class were permanently stored online for the instructor to annotate outside class. The *record/replay* mode was analyzed by the instructor and returned to students before the next class.

Ideally, students leave a class in this environment with a deeper understanding of different approaches to writing and an awareness of their place within this spectrum of compositional strategies and performances. Typically, a consensus is formed identifying effective texts, with abundant reasons for that effectiveness discussed in class. The student writer sees a repertory of writing skills and rhetorical strategies displayed in class, some more successful than others given a particular context for writing. Furthermore, the student may be able to apply these alternative writing strategies to future writing sessions. Most importantly, in this scenario the student is learning to incorporate critical skills with intervention strategies through the medium of textual exchange and peer review.

Summary

EOS represents a new paradigm for the design and implementation of online systems for educational purposes in industry and the academy. Instead of modeling interior cognitive processes, EOS models the social constructs by which analysis, composition, and review cohere in knowledge-making. This decision to map the social constructs of knowledge-making to the machine (what is called here the social content of the interface) puts writers at the center of the design process, rather than at the periphery.

Acknowledgments

Work on EOS during the past year was funded by the MIT Writing Program. I wish to thank Kenneth R. Manning, Head of the Writing Program, for his support of this project.

I am especially grateful to my colleague in the Writing Program, James Paradis, for our many discussions of the main points in this chapter. I also wish to thank David Custer for our discussions of the *record/replay* program.

References

Barrett, E. *Text, ConText, and HyperText: Writing with and for the Computer*. Cambridge, Ma.: MIT Press, 1988.

Barrett, E. *Proposal for an Online Writing Cooperative at MIT*. 1988.

Barrett, E. and J. Paradis. "Teaching Writing in an On-line Classroom." *Harvard Educational Review* 58 (1988): 154-171.

Barrett, E. and J. Paradis. "The Online Environment and In-House Training." In Barrett, 1988.

Bruffee, Kenneth A. "A New Emphasis in College Teaching: The Context of Learning." *Peabody Journal of Education* 50 (1972).

_____. "Liberal Education and the Social Justification of Belief." *Liberal Education* 68 (1982): 90-114.

Custer, D. "Text Editors as Tools for Writing Instruction" (forthcoming).

Daiute, C. "The Computer as Stylus and Audience." *College Composition and Communication* 34 (1983):134-145.

Grice, Roger. "Information Development is Part of Product Development--Not an Afterthought." In Barrett, 1988.

Kirsch, M. *National Project on Computers and College Writing*. Fund for the Improvement of Post Secondary Education. City University of New York. 1988.

Kroll, B.M. "Developmental Perspectives and the Teaching of Composition." *College English* 41 (1980): 741-752.

Papert, Seymour. *Mindstorms: Children, Computers, and Powerful Ideas.* New York: Basic Books, 1980.

Shirk, H. N. "Technical Writers as Computer Scientists: the Challenges of Online Documentation." In Barrett, 1988.

Simon, H. A. *The Sciences of the Artificial.* Cambridge, Ma.: MIT Press, 1985.

Skinner, B.F. "Why We Need Teaching Machines." *Harvard Educational Review* 3 (1961):377-398.

Stefik, M., Foster, G., Bobrow, D.G., Kahn, K., Lanning, S., and Suchman, L. "Beyond the chalkboard: computer support for collaboration and problem-solving in meetings." *Communications of the ACM* 30 (1987):32-47.

Schwartz, H. J. "SEEN: A Tutorial and User Network for Hypothesis Testing." In Wresch, 1984.

Vygotsky, L. *Thought and Language.* Cambridge, Ma.: MIT Press, 1962. Rev. ed. 1986.

_____. *Mind in Society: the Development of Higher Psychological Processes.* Michael Cole, Vera John-Steiner, Sylvia Scribner, Ellen Souberman, ed. Cambridge, Ma.: Harvard University Press, 1978.

Wresch, W. *The Computer in Composition: A Writer's Tool.* Urbana: NCTE, 1984.

Zimmerman, M. "Are Writers Obsolete in the Computer Industry?" In Barrett, 1988.

Zuboff, S. *In the Age of the Smart Machine: the Future of Work and Power.* New York: Basic Books, 1988.

Part IV
Sensemaking, Learning, and the Online Environment

Part IV addresses a range of issues relevant to working in an online environment. Christine Neuwirth describes the *User Message System* at CMU designed to support collaborative online work. Liora Alschuler reviews an experiment in hypertext documentation and assesses its effectiveness for information retrieval. Thomas Duffy, Brad Mehlenbacher, and Jim Palmer derive a conceptual model for evaluating online help systems from their analysis of the cognitive tasks required of users. Judith Ramey provides a tonic assessment of stylistic ambiguities in online text and shows how computer systems may be viewed as "rhetorical entities." Jill Gaulding and Boris Katz present a model for certain types of "word knowledge" reasoning in a natural language processing system. And finally, John Carroll and Amy Aaronson study the usability of a simulated intelligent help facility and discuss the implications of their findings for further research into the design of intelligent help systems.

Techniques of User Message Design:
Developing a User Message System to Support Cooperative Work

Christine M. Neuwirth

English Department
Carnegie Mellon University
Pittsburgh, PA 15213

1 Introduction

User messages (including prompts, requests for confirmation, and error messages)
are now acknowledged to be a crucial factor in the success or failure of a software
product: user messages can significantly affect user performance and satisfaction
(Shneiderman, 1986). The successful development and testing of user messages
requires cooperation among people with substantially different substantive knowledge
and methodological skills: software engineers, writers, graphic designers, human
factors psychologists, and domain specialists. No one of these individuals typically
knows enough to create successful messages. For example, a software engineer, often
the person who creates the original message, typically knows the conditions under
which a message appears; however, the software engineer, who is necessarily highly
knowledgeable about the system, may fail to anticipate the needs of less
knowledgeable users (Hayes & Flower, 1986). A writer knows how to create or revise
a message to maximize its comprehensibility and usefulness according to such criteria
as specificity, positive tone, user-control, consistency and so forth; however, the writer
is often at a loss to know how to revise a particular message, for example, how to
make a message more specific, because of lack of easy access to information about
what conditions cause a message to appear. A human factors psychologist knows how
to develop test procedures, test scenarios, and associated materials; however, the
human factors psychologist is often hampered by the difficulties involved in creating
or managing a system that uses both the original and revised messages, and in creating
scenarios that cause the messages to appear.

This paper has two goals. First, it describes a User Message System (UMS),
designed to provide the support these people need in order to work together
effectively. The paper details the application of the UMS to message creation,
revision and testing for a software program that received extensive use by novice
computer users. The second goal of the paper is to describe a study in which UMS
was used to investigate whether writers are able to predict the effectiveness of user
messages.

2 The development context

The User Message System was developed to facilitate work on computer tools for writing that are under development at Carnegie Mellon's Center for Educational Computing in English (CECE). This report discusses our experience with the UMS in the context of the Comments program, a computer tool that supports response to writing (Neuwirth, Kaufer, Keim, Gillespie, 1988). To provide a context for the support needed in the development of user messages, this section will describe the Comments application, its intended users, our method for testing user messages, and the problems associated with achieving the test plan goals that the User Message System addresses.

2.1 The target application

The Comments program allows writers and readers to "talk" about a piece of writing over a campus-wide network of advanced-function workstations.[1] The program is intended to make it easier for student writers to perform the following tasks:

- Share their work-in-progress with other members of a class, friends, and their teachers. To facilitate sharing, the Comments program is integrated with Carnegie Mellon's campus-wide local area network. Its user interface simplifies the task of copying files across the distributed, shared file system and setting appropriate access permissions.

- Discuss the written comments themselves. Students can ask for clarification of written comments, share plans for revision based on written comments, and communicate about whether a draft has addressed previous comments. To facilitate the communication required, the Comments program is a hypertext application (Conklin, 1987). When users make a comment, a link is created between the original text and the comment and an active icon allows users to access the text at the end of the link. The system supports "comments on comments," so users can carry on a written hypertext "dialog."

Two aspects of the Comments project necessitated intensive, cooperative development and testing of user messages. First, the Comments program is intended for use in freshman English classes at Carnegie Mellon.[2] Thus, the challenge that the user message group faced was to construct a set of messages that allowed users to understand what actions they need to take without needing to understand the complexities of a distributed, shared file system or a shared, hypertext database. Second, the Comments program was developed through a process of evolutionary system design (Sandewall, 1978). In evolutionary system design, the final version is not determined before implementation takes place. Rather, a small version of a large system is implemented, used, evaluated formatively through interviews with users and tests, then expanded based on the formative evaluation. Thus, in evolutionary system design, there is a special need for a system that allows the user message group to work together efficiently.

2.2 Description of users

In the design of the Comments program, our immediate audiences were students in our Freshman writing courses at Carnegie Mellon and their teachers, many of whom have some computer anxiety. We anticipated that users of the Comments program would range from approximately 16 to 70 years in age and would include the following types:

- novice computer user--has little or no previous computer experience (< 1 year, no programming course).

- infrequent user--has some or extensive computer experience, but uses the Unix operating system, the Andrew system or the Comments program infrequently (less than once a week).

- frequent user--may or may not have extensive computer experience, but uses the Comments program frequently.

- expert user--has extensive computer experience (> 1 year frequent use; 1 programming course).

We wanted user messages to accommodate the novice or infrequent user group, but not be tedious for frequent or expert users. We logged cases in which these two goals conflicted as problem reports. Most problem cases were resolved by having an additional online help button available for the message so that novices could choose to get more help while experts were not burdened with reading information unnecessary to them (O'Malley, 1986). We set a goal that the messages be usable under conditions of minimal outside support, with online help sufficient to lead a novice user through a session.

Another goal for user messages concerned terminology and complexity. The system design document for the Comments program specified that the users should not be assumed to have knowledge of computer terminology beyond what is introduced in (1) *The Andrew System User's Guide*, a document that contains system information all Freshman learn in a required *Computing Skills Workshop* and (2) *The Comments Program User's Guide*. The messages were to minimize all computer terminology and Comments program terminology. The system design document further specified that the reading level of messages should be appropriate to a wide undergraduate audience.

2.3 Iterative design plan for user messages

The plan for the testing of user messages was an iterative design, with steps 4-7 to repeat until a criterion for usability was met:

1. Specify criteria for user messages.

2. Develop user messages.

3. Construct tests for messages.

4. Test messages.

5. Analyze and diagnose any message problems uncovered through testing.

6. Revise user messages.

7. If needed, revise tests or criteria.

The messages were to be developed and tested by creating scenarios of the Comments program in operation. Scenarios help in addressing functional procedures and problems (Spencer, 1985).

2.4 Criteria for user messages

General criteria for user messages included how appropriate each message was for the types of users we anticipated and their computer environment. The specific criteria included the following research-based guidelines developed in Schneiderman (1982):

- specificity and constructive guidance--the user knows exactly what has happened or gone wrong and what to do about it.

- positive tone--the message avoids words like kill, abort, execute, and so forth.

- user-control--the message allows the user maximum control rather than enforces program control.

- physical format--the message format is attractive and readable.

The following criteria, although not specifically based on empirical research concerning effective messages, were also included:

- style--the message avoids redundancy, unnecessary technical jargon, and so forth (Dean, 1982).

- consistency--the message is consistent, both in content and format, with other messages (Dean, 1982) and with other sources of program information (e.g., the program's menus, documentation).

- necessity--the message is necessary; the message is the only source of feedback; the user needs to see the message (i.e., there is not a better, alternative design that would eliminate the need for the message) (Lewis & Norman, 1986).

- completeness--all program actions which need messages in fact have messages (Dean, 1982).

3 The User Message System

3.1 Requirements and problems

As noted in the introduction, the development and testing of user messages requires cooperation among people with substantially different substantive knowledge and methodological skills: software engineers, writers, graphic designers, human factors psychologists, and domain specialists.

When these people are able to work together successfully, the quality of the product can be substantially improved because of a synthesis of perspectives and criticisms they can provide each other. Such collaborations, however, require making implicit knowledge explicit and "can be particularly difficult when people are involved in complex technical tasks such as programming ... where knowledge of what has been done, what has been learned, and what remains to be done exists at a pre-verbal level ..." (Kraut, Gelegher & Egido, 1988). Moreover, the research literature suggests that people with different functional backgrounds will bring different knowledge and attitudes to the task and that these differences will be a source of conflict (Gabarro, 1987), resulting in even more difficulties than collaborations in which members share disciplinary assumptions, knowledge, and attitudes.

Besides the difficulties of communicating in technical tasks and high potential for unproductive conflicts, interdisciplinary collaboration in developing user messages involves other costs. There are delays because individuals are no longer able to make decisions autonomously and indeed, may be completely dependent on another person. For example, because the human factors psychologist must depend on the software engineer to implement new user messages, they must coordinate their activities, often leading to delays. Of course, further costs occur during the course of a large project when the people occupying these functional roles change. The impact of role changes is exacerbated when there has been a great deal of effort devoted to establishing working assumptions and common knowledge.

In our previous systems development, we had experienced these difficulties. We designed the User Message System to attempt to overcome the difficulties inherent in cooperative work by providing the following support:

- A shared problem representation--The system makes the type of information needed by other participants explicit. For example, when software engineers using UMS create a user message, they record the conditions under which it appears with the message, rather than with the source code.

- Tools and resources--The system provides a set of tools that are designed for working with user messages. For example, the system provides easy to use search mechanisms to help writers maintain message consistency; the system provides automatic collection of user message statistics to help writers and human factors people assign priorities for revising and testing messages. Olson (1982) notes that a technology that changes the quality and availability of information can change the distribution of authority and control.

3.2 Shared problem representation

3.2.1 Structured knowledge

The User Message System organizes user messages in a database, with each message constituting one record.[3] A database record structures information and constitutes an hypothesis about the information that the group needs to represent or to share in order to create useful user messages (Mears, 1981):

Number	A unique message id number, generated by the system. Required by the database program.
Name	The symbolic name given to a message that the Comments program uses to identify which message is to be displayed (e. g., CMT_SUCCESSFUL_SAVE). Although the "Number" field could be used, a symbolic name is less error-prone and constitutes good programming practice.
Type	The type of message (see below).
Module	The source code module or modules (e.g., cmt_internal.c) in which the user message appears. This field is useful to programmers for locating the occurrences of messages in the program's source code.
Message Text	The actual text of message to the user. It can include formatting information such as bold, italic, centering, and so forth.
Buttons	Message response "buttons" that will be displayed to the user and which the user will select to indicate his or her response to the message.
Conditions	The conditions under which the message appears. This field is maintained by the software engineer, but is used by writers as a basis for revising messages and by human factors psychologists to create the conditions for messages to appear.

Revised Text	A proposed revision, if any.
Revised Buttons	A proposed revision to the buttons, if any.
Modified	The last date that any of the complete record information was modified, in the format <yy/mm/dd>. This field is useful for members of the group to locate those messages that might have been added or altered since the last time they examined the message database file.
Remarks	Any remarks about a particular message (e.g., questions about program logic, revisions, conditions, etc.) This field is useful for members to communicate about the messages.

Maintaining two fields for messages and buttons, the original and the revised, is intended to facilitate testing messages. If revisions do not require changes in program logic, the revised messages can be run by invoking the program with a switch in the command line. If the revisions require changes in program logic, the changes must be coded and the program must be conditionally recompiled. Of course, the number of revisions that require logic changes depends on many factors, including the quality of the conception of the user interface and the stage in the program's development.[4]

The following illustrates the information found in typical user message record:

Number	003
Name	CMT_NO_ROOM_FOR_COMMENT_ARRAY
Type	um_acknowledge
Module	cmt_internal.c
Message Text	The program required more memory than is available on the workstation. Please exit from other programs, then try this action again.
Buttons	Acknowledge
Conditions	malloc() returned NULL
Revised Text	In order to complete your request, the program requires more memory than is currently available. To make more memory available, you can quit from other programs you are running, then click on Continue.
Revised Buttons	Continue
Modified	4/23/88
Remarks	And if this does not work?

3.2.2 A typology of user messages

We created a typology of user message types that allowed programmers and writers to create messages according to standard format:

Message line	A single line message in a "message line" area at the bottom of an Andrew window (see Figure 1). Informal user testing indicated that users often failed to see messages displayed at the bottom of a window, possibly because of the large screen size of advanced function workstations. Thus, we limited the use of these messages to status messages, such as "Saved at Sun Oct 23 17:33:59 1988."
Console	A single line message gets printed to the Console window, an Andrew application that monitors the operation of the Andrew system and its applications (see Figure 1).
Acknowledge	A multi-line message displayed in an overlay at the center of the window. One button, displayed below the text of the message, allows the user to acknowledge the message.
Multiple choice	Just like Acknowledge, except that there can be any number of buttons that allow the user to answer a question or express a choice.
Type in	A multi-line message displayed in an overlay with a type-in box that allows the user to type in information (see Figure 1).[5] There can be any number of buttons.
Scrollable	A multi-line message displayed in an overlay with a scrollable document displayed below the message. A scrollable document allows the program to display information that might not fit within the available screen space. There are three types. *Type 1* simply allows the user to look at the document; it is used primarily to display online help. *Type 2* allows the user to click in the document and select one of the lines of text for action; it is used primarily to display items such as lists of files. *Type 3* allows the user the select any number of lines of text; it is used to allow the user to select more than one item. There can be any number of buttons.
Fill in the form	A multi-line message displayed in an overlay, with a scrollable document containing a fill-in form displayed below the message. The user can fill in the form with values. There can be any number of buttons.
Custom layout	Whereas the other message types have standard graphic design layouts, this message type allows programmers and graphic designers to create custom-built layouts for those messages that need it (e.g., the display of printing options uses a custom-built layout).

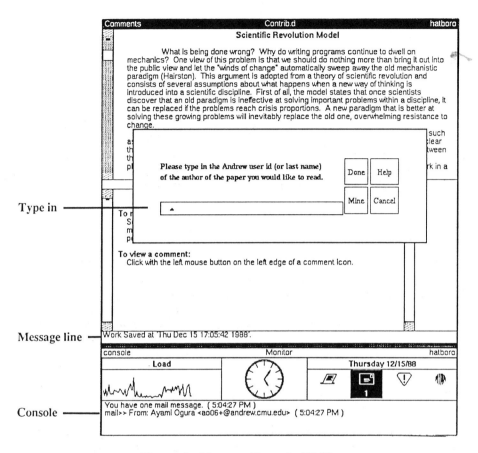

Figure 1: Message Types in UMS

3.3 Tools and resources

3.3.1 Visualization

In order for group members to use the UMS effectively, they must be able to locate the relevant messages. They could search the UMS database by using keywords and boolean combinations of keywords. But as Williams, Tou, Fikes, Henderson and Malone (1982) note, there are two major sources of difficulty for database interfaces based upon boolean keyword searches: (1) the user does not know what descriptive terms are needed to create a query. For example, if a writer wanted to locate all the messages with negative wording, there are innumerable words (abort, fatal, catastrophic, kill, twit, etc.) that would need to be included as descriptive terms in a query. (2) The user does not know or has difficulty with the boolean expression language itself.

In response to these difficulties, Williams et al. created an interface that allowed retrieval based upon partial descriptions and examples. The creation of such a system was beyond the scope of the UMS project. As Shneiderman (1986) notes, however, a large part of the success and appeal of the query-by-example approach (Zloof, 1975) to data retrieval is due to the direct representation of the data relations on the screen. Thus, we speculated that we could alleviate these two problems, especially the first, by providing a simple direct representation interface to the database of user messages. The interface allows writers to scroll through a list of words used in the database. Database visualization helps writers detect inconsistent wording and negative language.[6]

3.3.2 Statistics collection

When trying to assess the effectiveness of a message, a writer has recourse to guidelines about user messages and intuitions about an imagined reader. But guidelines and an imagined readers are not always effective (Wright, 1985; Hayes & Flower, 1986). Response time data (such as time for a user to read a message, time for a user to react to a message, errors, etc.) can provide the writer with information on whether the user message is meeting goals. The User Message System supports the collection of response time statistics on both the original and any revised messages.

4 The effectiveness of the User Message System

The CECE staff has been using the User Message System for the development of its software for two years. The User Message System appears to serve as an effective focus for communication on the project. Our experience has shown that the time between developing a message and evaluating it should be as short as possible. When too much time elapses, the software designers and writers forget too much about the purpose of the message and why it was written as it was.

The UMS has not replaced face-to-face interactions among the various group members, but supplements it. For example, even though software engineers record the conditions under which messages appear, writers and human factors testers still meet to discuss this information with the engineers. The written information requires much more thought to provide than briefing face-to-face in which response from the other person can guide how much detail is needed (Krauss & Weinheimer, 1966; Kraut, Lewis, & Swezey, 1982). A good deal of the face-to-face interaction concerns further clarification and revisions to such written communication in order to provide more detail.[7] Nonetheless, written information seems to serve as a record for review and reevaluation, and minimizes the effects of group turnover. It seems to help new group members develop shared expectations about what the task of developing user messages involves and, since there is a written record of important information, it seems to speed the acquisition of the knowledge need to operate effectively.

These informal observations raise many questions about effectiveness of the system that deserve systematic study (e.g., Are staff members able to work more efficiently using the User Message System?). At the present time, we have undertaken a systematic evaluation of only one aspect of the User Message System: its data gathering facilities for testing user messages. In his article, "How and When to Collect Behavioural Data," Andrew Monk (1987) argues that behavioral data should be collected at three points in the software engineering cycle: during system specification, implementation, and evaluation. Despite the value of behavioral data collection, collecting and analyzing behavioral data is relatively expensive. Moreover, some messages, especially those whose conditions (e.g., campus-wide network down, user's disk quota full) are difficult to create upon demand, do not lend themselves easily to the testing paradigm of the User Message System. We reasoned that if writers can do a good job of predicting the performance of users, then it would be best not to collect data at all points of the development process. In particular, we would not need to collect behavioral data during the implementation stage, but only during the evaluation stage.

Thus, we had two objectives in testing the user messages: (1) to determine whether the Comments program user messages could be used effectively and easily by novice users. The result of the testing should be that the messages are comprehensible and useful; (2) to determine whether experienced writers could rate user messages accurately according to how difficult users would find them.

4.1 Experimental evaluation of experienced writers' predictions

To determine how well experienced writers' rankings of user messages predict users' actual performance times, we did an exploratory study. In the first part of the study, we asked experienced writers to rank the Comments program user messages from best to worst. Then we collected actual users' response times and, in a *post hoc* regression analysis, determined how well the length of the message and the experienced writers' rankings predicted those response times.

4.1.1 Writers' rankings of messages

Rankers. Four graduate students in English served as rankers. It was important for the rankers both to be good writers and to have some understanding of human-computer interaction issues. Three of the students were enrolled in the Carnegie Mellon English department's Masters in Professional Writing Program and had completed, with a grade of B or better, a required course, Computers and Writing. The course introduced students to theory and research on the human-computer interface, including the design of successful user messages, and required them to practice applying theory and research to actual design problems. The fourth subject, a student in the Carnegie Mellon English department's Ph.D. in Rhetoric program, was actively pursuing document design research and had extensive knowledge of the theory and research on user messages as well as experience in writing user messages. All were experienced with the Andrew system (all had used the system for at least several months and all had used it recently). None of the subjects had prior experience with the Comments program.

Training of the rankers. Rankers were told that they were to familiarize themselves with the Comments program in preparation for revising its user messages. They were provided with *User's Guide to the Comments Program*, a document that has been used successfully to teach novice computer users how to operate the program. After reading the user's guide, each subject was asked to run the program and to send a paper to one of the investigators for comments, read the comments, and delete them. This procedure was designed to give subjects a working knowledge of those messages that they would be asked to judge.

Ranking task. After reading the documentation and running the program, subjects were given screen dumps of ten user messages and were asked to rank the messages from best to worst, basing their judgments on which messages they thought would confuse and hinder a user and which messages a user would be able to understand easily and act upon correctly. Subjects were told to "imagine that you have a limited amount of time to revise the set of user messages and that you want to rank the messages so you can revise the worst ones first, so that, in the event you are not able to revise all of them, at least the worst ones will be corrected." Figure 1 depicts one of the user messages in the study.

4.1.2 Users' responses to messages

Users. There were 40 student users. All were experienced with using the Andrew system (all had used the system for at least several months and had used it recently), but none had experience using the Comments program.

Task. The task performed by the users was designed to be representative of the normal uses student writers would make of the Comments program. Users were asked to send a paper to another user for comments, to read a paper that had comments, to view the comments, to delete the comments, and to restore the paper to its original location in the file system.

Procedure. Users performed the task in individually scheduled sessions of approximately 15 minutes each. To establish that users knew the basics of responding to a user message in the Andrew system, the investigator asked each user about his or her computer experience. Then the investigator showed each subject a practice user message of the type used in the Comments program and asked the subject to use the mouse control device to make an appropriate response. All subjects were able to respond to the practice message.

For each of the five tasks (send a paper, read a paper, view comments, delete comments, restore the paper to its original location in the file system), the investigator gave each user a description of the task to perform and asked the user to perform each task. As the user worked, the response time for each user message was recorded automatically. Response time was measured from the time the message appeared on the screen to the time the user made a response.

4.1.3 Results

Rankings. The Spearman rank correlation (Glass & Hopkins, 1984) was computed between subjects for all pairs. Two of the rankers were in significant agreement about the messages. Their rankings were significantly, positively correlated ($r = .67$, $p < .01$). The other two rankers disagreed with this pair as well as with each other.

Users' responses. All users eventually completed all user message interactions. Except for the first message in which half the subjects needed online help or made an error, the number of errors users made was very low and suggests that the messages were, overall, fairly comprehensible.

In addition to errors, however, it is important to consider how easily users can respond to a message. To examine ease-of-use, we analyzed response times for those messages that users responded to correctly. Table 1 shows the mean correct response times in seconds, the standard deviations, and the number of subjects with correct responses for the ten messages, as well as their length in words. Obviously, the longer messages had the longest response times, but length does not appear to be the only source of variance.

4.1.4 Discussion

One major finding is that writers were not able to agree about the effectiveness of user messages. This result is somewhat surprising considering that these writers were selected because of their previous training in human-computer interaction. Their lack of agreement may be due to the lack of variation in the messages. This explanation has support from the other major finding that users were fairly successful at responding to the messages. Therefore, writers may have been unable to distinguish between messages that users found to be relatively comprehensible. However, there is reason to believe that this might not be the whole story. Even though all of the users were ultimately successful, they took much longer to respond to some of the messages than others. Therefore, it is interesting to consider whether some of the writers' rankings were sensitive to these differences. In order to explore these possibilities, we conducted a *post hoc* analysis to see whether any of the writers were able to predict users' response times.

For each of the rankers, a stepwise multiple regression analysis was performed to determine any relationship of message length and rank score to response time. The

Message	Response Time			Length
	M	SD	N	
1	17.5	7.8	20	15
2	6.5	2.4	40	11
3	12.4	7.3	39	25
4	13.9	7.1	38	15
5	5.6	2.4	40	13
6	6.6	2.0	40	18
7	6.7	1.7	40	15
8	4.6	2.5	40	11
9	27.6	14.1	39	123
10	5.2	2.7	39	10

Table 1: Mean Correct Response Times and Message Lengths

variable with the largest correlation with the remaining variance in response time was entered into the regression equation at each step. As is typical with response times, the distribution of response times was skewed. Since regressions can be substantially affected by skewness, a log transformation was applied to convert to a metric in which the distribution was more nearly normal.

Of the four rankers, only the two whose rankings were significantly positively correlated were able to predict response time. For Ranker 1 (see Table 2), ranking accounted for 66% of the variance in response time; length accounted for an additional 29%. Together these variables accounted for 95% (93% adjusted) of the variance, $F (2, 7) = 64.3$, $p < .01$. For Ranker 2, length entered the regression first, accounting for 51% of the variance; however, ranking accounted for an additional 29%. Together these variables accounted for 80% (74% adjusted) of the variance, $F (2, 7) = 14.0$, $p < .01$.

One explanation for why these two writers were able to predict users' response times and other two were not is difference in background knowledge. The two writers who were able to predict response times were relatively novice computer users (no programming experience and less than three years computer use) whereas those writers who were unable to predict were more expert (programming experience and more than five years computer use). This explanation is consistent with the finding that revisers with prior content knowledge are less able to predict where readers will have trouble with a text than those less knowledgeable about the content (Hayes,

	Step	Variable	R^2
Ranker 1	1	Ranking	.66
	2	Length	.95
Ranker 2	1	Length	.51
	2	Ranking	.80

$p < .01.$

Table 2: Stepwise Multiple Regression on Response Time

Schriver, Spilka, & Blaustein, 1986). If this explanation is correct, it should not be taken to mean that writers should avoid learning programming. Writers who know programming seem to have some advantages over those who do not (e.g., writers who know programming seem better able to judge whether a message is necessary or not).

5 Conclusions

Our experiences with using the User Message System suggest that it provides valuable support for the cooperative work required to create successful user messages. It is also clear that one primary component in a User Message System should be a facility to collect users' response times. The results of the exploratory study suggest that as a whole, writers were unable to agree about the effectiveness of user messages. However, the *post hoc* analyses indicate that the writers' background knowledge may be an important factor and would allow us to distinguish those writers who are able to predict the effectiveness of user messages. Further research needs to be done to determine what distinguishes those writers who were able to predict users' responses from those who were not.

6 Acknowledgments

The work reported in this document was supported in part by grants from the Fund for Improvement of Post-Secondary Education (FIPSE), the Alfred P. Sloan Foundation, the Pew Memorial Trust, and the A.W. Mellon Foundation as part of the Warrant Project, Preston Covey, Cheryl Geisler, David S. Kaufer and Christine M. Neuwirth, Co-Principal Investigators.

Thanks to Rick Chimera, Keith Evans, Steve Hoffman, Aaron Oppenheimer, and Thom Peters for their work on the User Message System. Thanks to Davida Charney for her comments on earlier drafts, Dick Hayes for his advice on the exploratory study, and Terilyn Gillespie for her help throughout the project.

7 Notes

[1]The Comments program runs on advanced function workstations--IBM RTs, SUN2s and 3s, and VAX-stations. It runs under Andrew, a window-management and user interface toolkit environment for UNIX 4.2 BSD (Morris et al., 1986; Palay et al., 1988) and a distributed, shared file system (Howard et al., 1987).

[2]We have operated Comments in about five sections of Freshmen English courses for four semesters where it has been used to gather research data about computer-based response to writing.

[3]We used Grits, an Andrew-based database management system with both a command language and subroutine library interface (see T. C. Peters, *Grits Programmer's Guide*, Information Technology Center, Carnegie Mellon University, Pittsburgh, PA 15213). Greif and Sarin (1987) note that a central concern in any computer-supported cooperative work activity is coordinating access to shared data. To coordinate sharing of the database, we used an existing Unix-based work tool, RCS, Revision Control System (Tichy, 1982), a system that helps manage multiple revisions of text files by automating the storage, retrieval, logging, identification and merging of revisions.

[4]In the first iteration of Comments message revisions, 13 (12.5%) of the proposed revisions required logic changes. These included messages which writers judged to lack specificity and constructive guidance (e.g., the program reports a problem--a help file could not be found, but the problem could be due to one of two very different causes--an environment variable not properly set or a virtual memory error--so the user does not know what to do) and user-control (e.g., the program forces the user to perform an action that should be optional or has a flow of control that is not as helpful as it might be).

[5]An optional parameter allows the program to prompt the user with a string.

[6]To provide a direct manipulation interface to the user messages database, we used an Andrew-based tool called GRIN (see T. C. Peters, *GRIN User's Guide*, Information Technology Center, Carnegie Mellon University, Pittsburgh, PA 15213).

[7]In the first iteration of the Comments message revisions, writers asked programmers to elaborate or clarify what caused messages to appear for 20 (18%) messages.

8 References

Conklin, J. (1987). Hypertext: An introduction and survey. *Computer*, *20*(9), 17-41.

Dean, M. (1982). How a computer should talk to people. *IBM Systems Journal*, *21*(4), 424-453.

Gabarro, J. J. (1987). The development of working relationships. In J. W. Lorsch (Ed.), *Handbook of Organizational Behavior*. Englewood Cliffs, NJ: Prentice-Hall.

Glass, G. V., & Hopkins, K. D. (1984). *Statistical methods in education and psychology*. Englewood Cliffs, NJ: Prentice-Hall, Inc.

Greif, I., & Sarin, S. (April 1987). Data sharing in group work. *ACM Transactions on Office Information Systems*, *5*(2), 187-211.

Hayes, J. R., & Flower, L. (Oct. 1986). Writing research and the writer. *American Psychologist*, *41*(10), 1106-1113.

Hayes, J. R., Schriver, K. A., Spilka, R., & Blaustein, A. (1986). If its clear to me it must be clear to them. Paper presented at the Conference on College Composition and Communication, New Orleans, LA.

Howard, J., Kazar, M. L., Menees, S. G., Nichols, D. A., Satyanarayanan, M., Sidebotham, R. N., & West, M. J. (1988). Scale and performance in a distributed file system. *ACM Transactions on Computer Systems* , *6*(1), 51-82.

Krauss, R., & Weinheimer, S. (1966). Concurrent feedback, confirmation, and the encoding of referents in verbal interaction. *Journal of Personality and Social Psychology*, *4*, 342-346.

Kraut, R., Lewis, S., & Swezey, L. (1982). Listener responsiveness and the corrdination of converstaion. *Journal of Personality and Social Psychology*, *43*, 718-731.

Kraut, R., Galegher, J., & Egido, C. (1988). Relationships and tasks in scientific research collaborations. *Human Computer Interaction*, *3*(1), 31-58.

Lewis, C., & Norman, D. A. (1986). Designing for error. In D. A. Norman & S. W. Draper (Eds.), *User centered system design*. Hillsdale, NJ: Lawrence Erlbaum Associates.

Mears, P. (1981). Structuring communication in a working group. In R. S. Cathcart & L. A. Samovar (Eds.), *Small Group Communication*. Dubuque, Iowa: Wm. C. Brown Co.

Monk, A. (1987). How and when to collect behavioral data. In R. M. Baecker & W. A. S. Buxton (Eds.), *Readings in Human-Computer Interaction*. 95 First Street, Los Altos, CA 94022: Morgan Kaufmann Publishers, Inc.

Morris, J. H., Satyanarayanan, M., Conner, M. H., Howard, J. H., Rosenthal, D. S. H., & Smith, F. D. (March 1986). Andrew: A distributed personal computing environment. *Communications of the ACM, 29*(3), 184-201.

Neuwirth, C. M., Kaufer, D. S., Keim, G., & Gillespie, T. (Jan. 1988). *The Comments program: Computer support for response to writing* (CECE-TR 3). Center for Educational Computing in English, English Department, Carnegie Mellon University.

O'Malley, C. E. (1986). Helping users help themselves. In D. A. Norman & S. W. Draper (Eds.), *User-centered system design.* Hillsdale, NJ: Lawrence Erlbaum Associates.

Olson, M. H. (Dec. 1982). New information technology and organizational culture. *Management Information System Quarterly, Special Issue,* 71-92.

Palay, A. J., Hansen, W. J., Kazar, M. L., Sherman, M., Wadlow, M. G., Neuendorffer, T. P., Stern, Z., Bader, M., & Peters, T. (Feb. 1988). The Andrew toolkit: An overview. *USENIX Conference Proceedings.* Dallas, TX: USENIX.

Sandewall, E. (March 1978). Programming in an interactive environment: The LISP experience. *ACM Computing Surveys, 10*(1), 35-72.

Shneiderman, B. (1982). System message design: Guidelines and experimental results. In A. Badre & B. Shneiderman (Eds.), *Directions in human computer interaction.* Norwood, NJ: Ablex Publishing.

Shneiderman, B. (1986). *Designing the user interface.* Reading, MA: Addison-Wesley.

Spencer, R. H. (1985). *Computer usability testing and evaluation.* Englewood Cliffs, NJ: Prentice-Hall.

Tichy, W. F. (Sep. 1982). Design, implementation, and evaluation of a revision control system. *Proceedings of the 6th International Conference on Software Engineering.* Tokyo: IEEE.

Williams, M. D., Tou, F. N., Fikes, R. E., Henderson, A., & Malone, T. W. (August 1982). RABBIT: Cognitive Science in Interface Design. *Proceedings of the Cognitive Science Society.* Ann Arbor, MI: Cognitive Science Society.

Wright, P. (1985). Editing: Policies and processes. In T. M. Duffy, & R. Waller (Eds.), *Designing Usable Texts.* Orlando, FL: Academic Press, Inc.

Zloof, M. M. (1975). Query-by-example. *Proceedings of the National Computer Conferences.* AFIPS Press, Montvale, NJ: AFIPS.

Hand-crafted Hypertext—Lessons from the ACM Experiment

Liora Alschuler

Miles-Samuelson, Inc.
New York, New York

This chapter asserts that certain types of hypertext are characterized by "hand-crafted," non-systematic linking and that in hand-crafted hypertext the program and composer have a strong impact on the information presented. The chapter also shows that hand-crafted linking is problematic and in many cases is not as suitable for the presentation of technical material as a simple search on a keyword or phrase.

Hypertext on Hypertext

In July of 1988, the Association for Computing Machines (ACM) devoted an entire issue of their journal Communications to reprinting six of the papers presented at *Hypertext '87,* a conference which was held in November of that year at the University of North Carolina.[1] Following the special issue, ACM re-published the same material, this time as *Hypertext on Hypertext,* in various hypertext formats providing first-hand exposure to the issues discussed in the six papers. The first hypertext products were published using HyperCard™ on the Apple Macintosh® by the Institute for Research in Information and Scholarship (IRIS) at Brown University and Hyperties™ for IBM PCs® and compatibles by the University of Maryland. A third version of *Hypertext on Hypertext,* using KMS™ on a SUN-3™ workstation was prepared by Knowledge Systems Inc. and published in November, just as this chapter goes to press. A fourth version, written with Owl's Guide™ is anticipated for 1989.

Why Study Thrice-published material?

The publication by ACM of a single collection of articles both in print and in various hypertext formats presents a unique opportunity to make direct comparisons between hypertext systems. Existing hypertexts either are "toy" databases[2] or operate on specialized texts which prohibits direct comparison between hypertext systems.

™ HyperCard is a trademark of Apple Computer, Inc.
® Macintosh is a registered trademark of Apple Computer, Inc.
™ Hyperties is a trademark of Cognetics Corporation.
® IBM PC is a registered trademark of International Business Machines.
™ KMS is a trademark of Knowledge Systems Incorporated.
™ SUN-3 Workstation is a trademark of Sun Microsystems, Inc.
™ Guide is a trademark of Owl International, Inc.

Comparing presentations reveals the latitude that a hypertext composer has with this type of algorithm and the impact of an individual program on the material.[3] The experience sheds light on the idea of "intertwingledness" which was given such emphasis by Ted Nelson when he first coined the term "hypertext " (Nelson,1974).

Now that we can compare print with various versions of hypertext, we are in a position to ask whether this type of electronic presentation is mind-expanding or mind-constricting. Is the original material clearly and objectively presented or is it colored by its hypertext presentation? What determines the effectiveness of the linking?

This chapter explores how individual programs and authors affect the way information is interconnected by tracing links and webs in three hypertext versions of the ACM *Hypertext on Hypertext*. The goal of the study is not to imply that there is a single correct way to do hypertext, but to dispense with the illusion that converting text to hypertext is a neutral process.

Hand-crafted Links and Subjective Hypertext

While there are considerable differences between the three platforms used for *Hypertext on Hypertext*,[4] all three share the same type of hypertext linking—what I call "hand-crafted" as opposed to random, intelligent, or automated linking. Hand-crafted links are created individually by the hypertext composer. The exact method for creating links varies between composers and programs, but in all the programs that use this type of linking, the decision to link is in the hands of the composer.

Automated linking, in contrast, can use a simple keyword search or techniques adapted from artificial intelligence and expert systems. Hand-crafted linking also contrasts with structured linking in which connections between nodes are explicit in the structure of the hypertext document.

Examples of hypertext with automated linking are askSam™, which many do not even consider as hypertext, and ViaInsight™, a program that is not considered hypertext, but which is called "live documentation" because of its ability to generate a report directly from source code (Alschuler and Schneider, 1988). The premier example of structured-link hypertext is Concordia® (Walker, 1988).

The categorization of hypertext in terms of a typology of linking allows us to ask if hand-crafted linking is subjective, and if it is not subjective, on what is it based? How does the fact that it is hand-crafted affect the presentation of material? Does the print hierarchy relate well to the hypertext structure? Is hand-crafted linking suitable for technical or non-technical material?

™ askSam is a trademark of Seaside Software, Inc.
™ ViaInsight is a trademark of Viasoft, Inc.
® Concordia is a registered trademark of Symbolics, Inc.

Method

This chapter gives an overview of the *Hypertext on Hypertext* programs, compares their node structure, then traces various topics through their web of interconnections. The questions asked are as follows:

- How different are the nodes?
- How are they related to print structure?
- What type of nodes are linked together?
- Is the linking thorough and consistent?
- What subjects are indexed?
- Is it like a conventional index?
- How does the index relate to the direct links?
- How effective is the keyword search?

Limits of the Study

While the ACM material allows us to avoid comparing apples and oranges, we are still comparing mandarins with navels; the tart with the sweet. Of the three elements—hardware, software, and data—the applications share only the data. It is not useful to compare these packages in terms of speed and overall performance because they run on different platforms. Hyperties might be a different animal on a System 30 instead of an old XT. Although it may be appropriate at certain points to comment on speed, presentation, and ease of use, it should be emphasized that this is not a product review and was not done under laboratory test conditions. The premise of this chapter is that even if faster, prettier, or friendlier, the individual programs would still lack systematic linking, a distinction which is not directly related to their hardware platform.

The second limitation in terms of evaluating this type of hypertext program for the presentation of technical material, is that the material presented is generally descriptive and academic in nature, as opposed to purely technical. For this reason, I avoided, for the most part, tracing links among the more abstract subjects.

When comparing links, the number of connected nodes, or the number of references, is deceptive because a single node in one system may contain several of another system's nodes, so that the numbers themselves do not reflect the amount of information collected.

Finally, this is not an evaluation of original composition with hypertext, although some of the same objections on subjectivity might apply to that process as well.

General Description and Node Structure

HyperCard

The HyperCard version of *Hypertext on Hypertext* uses the familiar rolodex card analogy. A card is the basic unit or node of information. The cards are organized into 11 stacks, which correspond to the six original articles, plus stacks for "HELP," "INDEX," "HOME," other shared functions, and editors' notes. The cards have sequential numbers within their stack that are unique identifiers.

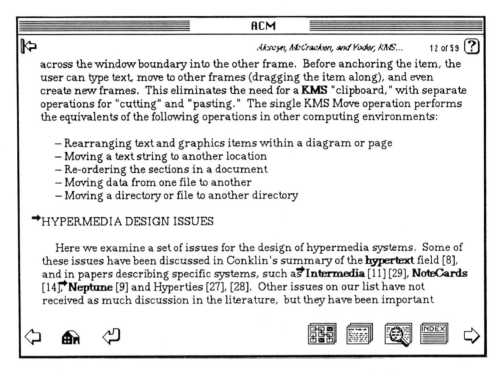

Figure 1.   HyperCard display and node structure

Each card within an article stack uses screen display conventions similar, but not identical, to the original print publication. For example, a card uses large, bold letters for article titles, italics for authors and so on. The type face conventions are not, however, part of the hypertext structure. There is no way to search and display authors' names or primary headings based on screen display coding.

While the stacks follow the division of printed material into articles, the cards, for the most part, do not follow the logical divisions within the print-ed material. This seems to be only partially because of spatial constraints on the screen. Nodes often ignored author's structure; they have no title and can be found only by the sequence of the card in the stack.

Figure 1, which is the twelfth card in the Akscyn, McCracken, and Yoder stack, combines text from two major headings and a bulleted list. In other instances, cards break text in the middle of bulleted lists, but give no indica-tion whether the list continues on the next card. Without the logical docu-ment structure the user must navigate in a "linear" fashion (i.e., flip through cards sequentially) because there is no other way to know if a thought con-tinues or not.

The primary way to navigate this HyperCard application, apart from paging through it sequentially, is to follow trails of connections through the index, the map, the embedded links, and the search function.

KMS

KMS divides the articles into nodes called "frames." Each frame has a title, an alphanumeric identifier (not shown on figures) and may have both linked and unlinked text (see figure 2). KMS nodes are logical units, each one having a title and a logical relationship to those around it. While HyperCard and Hyperties tend to use the same amount of text per screen, the amount of text varies substantially in KMS nodes because the editors were more concerned with logical structure than with screen-fit.

KMS connects frames in a hierarchy using frame titles to create an outline. The outlines show the structure of the article and act like a menu of links. On figure 2, the items marked with a small open circle are subheadings subordinate to the frame title and linked to other frames. The KMS composers used the existing document titles, headings, and subheadings for their frame titles, adding subheadings where necessary to complete the hierarchical structure.

The "PARENT" button in the lower right-hand corner always takes the user to the next higher level of document hierarchy. While the relationship of a KMS node to subordinate nodes is always clear, there is no indication of how many levels of hierarchy are above the node being viewed. Printed articles usually do not list subheadings at the beginning of each section, although this technique is used in technical and instructional material. A case might be made that KMS uses structured linking because it adheres to hierarchical print conventions. However, while it preserves print conventions and document hierarchy, the connections between nodes are initiated only when the composer chooses to install a link. There is no requirement to link any set of nodes, regardless of their hierarchical relationship. Theoretically, it is possible to adhere to hierarchical print conventions without the appropriate linking because the hierarchy is not organic to the hypertext structure. The frame title is position sensitive, whatever text is in the designated part of the frame becomes the title. There are three primary ways to thread together information with the KMS *Hypertext on Hypertext*. The first is to follow the embedded hierarchical links from heading to subheading; the second is to use the indexes to connect nodes of related information; the third is to get a "linear" presentation of the text corresponding exactly to the printed material. (This is equivalent to using the HyperCard "NEXT CARD" button to read through all the stacks in order or following all the hierarchical links in order.) "SEE ALSO" references appear on certain frames linking to a related index frame. In addition, KMS has a search capacity that builds a temporary index for a keyword or phase. These temporary nodes can be accessed in the same way as the other indexed nodes.

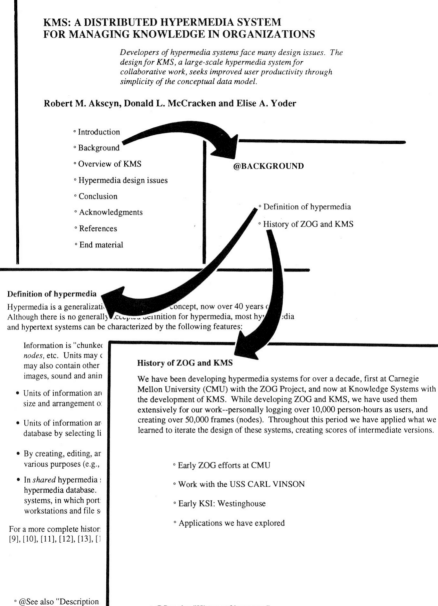

Figure 2. KMS hierarchy and node structure

Hyperties

The Hyperties version of *Hypertext on Hypertext* divides material into 307 "articles." (I will continue to refer to Hyperties "articles" in quotation marks to avoid confusion with the original six articles and with the usual sense of the word.)

Unlike the other two programs, Hyperties nodes are not single screens of information. The Hyperties "articles" are smaller than the original article and contain from one line to a dozen screens of information. The division between "articles" corresponds to document structure and agrees fairly closely with the KMS division into major topic headings, but the division between screens within an "article" is a function of how much text can be displayed. The first hypertext "article" often lists the headings of the "article" that follows, but often, as in figure 3, this list is not the first screen of the "article." The topic names that correspond to "articles" are highlighted and the user can click on them to jump to the first screen of that "article."

Unlike KMS, this convention is not consistent at all levels. For example, the Akscyn, McCracken, and Yoder article contains "articles" numbered 4.0, 4.1, 4.2.1, 4.2.2, 4.3, and 4.4. The 4.0 article incorporates a list of the subjects of 4.1-4.4, but not in the same format as the other top frames. There is no list showing the subtopics under 4.2. Whether or not this was an oversight is less important than the fact that, as with KMS, the hierarchy itself is not integral to the hypertext structure. The primary method of navigation is the table of contents which lists the original articles plus some related material such as first hand reports from the *Hypertext '87* conference. There are also the hierarchical links, an index, some direct links, and a search function.

Links

While all links in each version are installed at the discretion of the hypertext composer, from the user's perspective, links are either sequential, that is, they connect nodes in the order that they would appear in print, or they are cross reference links that connect related, non-sequential nodes.

In this chapter, the term "indirect link" refers to cross-referenced nodes connected through an index or map. "Direct link" refers to links that jump directly from node to node.

The type of cross-reference linking varies in the three applications. KMS and Hyperties link primarily to hierarchical or sequential nodes of information. Their cross-reference linking is done indirectly through an index. The HyperCard application has direct cross-reference links as well as an index and a map for indirect linking.

HyperCard Direct Links

The direct links from card to card are designated by small black arrows placed next to the text in question. See figure 1.

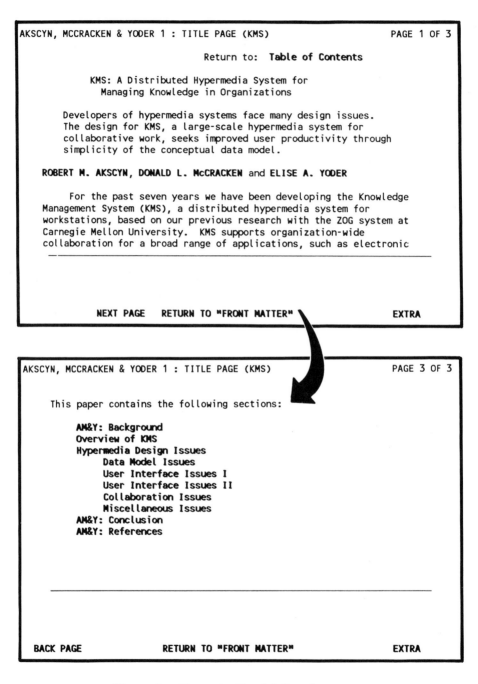

Figure 3. Hyperties "article" and screen

Following the "Definition of Hypermedia" from the first card in the editor's introduction (Smith and Weiss), the direct links are as follows:

ARTICLE	CARD #
Smith and Weiss	1
Akscyn,..	2
Smith and Weiss	5
Garg	9 (also goes to Garg 33 and back)
Smith and Weiss	1

The links work in a circular pattern, returning to the original when the loop is completed. One loop links cards 1,2,5 and 9 and a smaller loop connects Garg 9 and 33. Regardless of which link is followed first, eventually the whole circle can be traced, as long as the user follows the links.

The decision to connect the Smith and Weiss definition (card 1) with the definition in the Akscyn, McCracken and Yoder article, rather than the Smith and Weiss elaboration on card five may have been based on the fact that they are the two most explicit definitions. If, on the other hand, it is true that the more general definitions should be presented together, then it will not make sense for the user who starts with the Akscyn, McCracken and Yoder article definition. This user will go to the Smith and Weiss elaboration, then to Garg's abstract, mathematical definition and only then, back to the basic definition given by Smith and Weiss.

While the loop structure of the links guarantees that if a user is not distracted by another topic, they will eventually cover all linked nodes, the user is then in the position of "linearly" leafing through related nodes in no particular order.

There are several other quirks in the direct HyperCard links. Sometimes direct links connect to other articles, then, following the same topic, return to the original article. Links may take you to other topics before finding all references to the original topic.

The hidden buttons used with HyperCard can be confusing. Clicking as little as 1/8″ apart can produce entirely different results. Figure 4 shows a

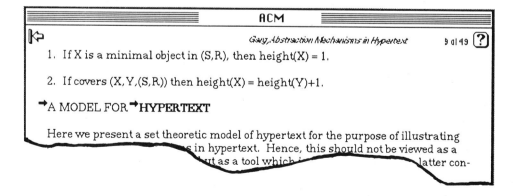

Figure 4. Direct links in HyperCard heading

heading from the Garg stack. The first arrow goes to the 33rd card in the stack which is an abstract definition of hypertext. The second arrow goes to the first card in the Smith and Weiss stack, which is a general definition of hypertext. Clicking on the boldface term "HYPERTEXT" connects to the hypertext card of the index.

Most direct links were repeated, even covered more extensively, through the index which is described below.

KMS Direct Links

Direct links within KMS use the original document hierarchy to guide the user to different parts of the document.

KMS links cut across document hierarchy with "SEE ALSO" references. These references connect to index frames that list places where similar subjects are covered. They are discussed below under index links.

Hyperties Direct Links

The Hyperties application had few direct links that were not hierarchical, and those that were included were of a specific nature, i.e., to bibliographic and biographical references.

The introduction lists the "hypertext opportunities" where links were embedded:

1. Cross links to the Smith and Weiss Overview
2. Links to the hypertext editor's overview
3. Links to Nielsen's trip report
4. Links to authors' names and biographies
5. Bibliographic references

With the exception of the two overviews, the composer did not try to link between articles. We were not able to find direct links between the Nielsen trip report and the other report on the conference in the Special Section on Hypertext.

Link Indexes and Indirect Links

Each of the three *Hypertext on Hypertext* applications has a topic index. Both KMS and HyperCard have 26 first-level topics. The common number seems to be a coincidence because only three of the 26 subjects match, while five others are similar. The Hyperties index has only five topics.

In each case, the "Index" is more a list of links than a traditional index. Each subject is broken down until there is only one entry under each topic. This may be done to avoid referring to the nodes by title or a numerical identifier, which would be required if there were two or more citations per index entry. Most of the embedded, direct links are included in and summarized through this index of links. Each of the hypertext indexes, at some point, stops using alphabetical order and other standard index conventions.

HyperCard Index

The user searches for references in the HyperCard index by clicking the mouse when the cursor is over the name of the desired topic. The index topic then expands showing all the second-level references under that topic. The user can view a node by clicking on its reference. Items that appear in the index are shown in boldface on the cards (see "KMS", "hypertext", "Intermedia", "Notecards", and "Neptune" on figure 1). Clicking on a bold-faced item in the text takes the user to the appropriate index card.

The HyperCard index topics have a second, and in some cases, a third level. The first level is organized topically, rather than according to printed sequence, although second level topics are not arranged alphabetically or in any other easily identifiable sequence. Under "History of Hypertext," the headings are, in this order, Vannevar Bush, Memex, Neptune, History of KMS and ZOG, Hypertext Editing System, FRESS, Doug Engelbart, Ted Nelson, and References.

While the HyperCard index seems to be structured around the links embedded into the text, the index also adds nodes that are not directly linked within the text. For example, the "Definition of Hypermedia" loop of nodes is listed on an index card with an additional reference to the fourth card in the Smith and Weiss Overview. There is no readily apparent reason why this node should be indexed together with the others under "Definitions of Hypermedia," and yet not be part of the direct-link loop.

HyperCard Map

Each of the rectangles on the map card links to a list of subordinate topics. Selecting a topic brings up the map of that topic. The map icons represent nodes containing related information. Lines between the icons represent the links between those nodes (figure 5.) The user can view the nodes by clicking the mouse on the corresponding icon.

The exact relationship of the HyperCard map to the index and to the embedded links is not entirely clear. The map does not include all indexed or embedded links and appears to add another level of subjectivity because it is not organically connected to either of the other navigation methods. For example, in figure 5, a map called "Definition of Hypermedia" shows the *Overview* article connected to the Garg article on abstraction mechanisms and to the Akscyn, McCracken and Yoder article on KMS. The map shows no connection between the definition in the *KMS* article and the Garg article, although embedded links connect the two definitions.

In addition, the map, because it has only one icon per article, cannot direct the user to more than one node in an article.

The same is true of the "Navigation" map which is a subtopic of the same Hypermedia card mentioned above. The map connects the *Keynote* address to the *Reflections* article and the *KMS* article to the *Keynote,* but shows no connections between the *KMS* and *Reflections* articles. The embedded links connect all three nodes in a circular fashion.

The map of hypermedia definitions leads to the same loop of five nodes described above, no matter which of the three icons is chosen. Excluding these connections from the map seems confusing, but is understandable. Since the map is not organically linked to the hypertext structure, it is another arbitrary web of connections.

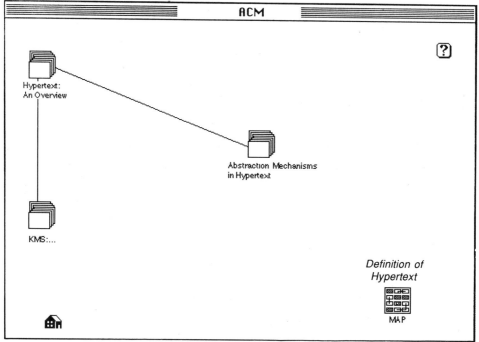

Figure 5.   HyperCard "Definition of Hypermedia" map

KMS Link Index

Links between KMS frames that are not sequentially or hierarchically connected can be direct or indirect. By choosing where to position the cursor,
KMS users can go directly to the next reference in the index or back to the
index and then to any of the indexed nodes. This convenience, being able to
go to the next- referenced node without returning to the index itself, in effect creates direct links through the index.

Although the mechanics of using the KMS index are particularly graceful
in comparison with other schemes, the index made no pretense at being
comprehensive in its subject coverage. The KMS composers introduced the
frames holding the second-level listings with statements like: "Here are a few
sections that provide overview descriptions of actual hypertext and
hypermedia systems (see also ..." The significant phrase here is "a few sections..." indicating that the index is not comprehensive. The other index
frames start with similar disclaimers.

The index was not organized so that the connection between scattered
nodes was easy to see. Subtopics on index lists are organized according to
the article in which they appear—a curious concession to the sequential
structure of the original material. For example, the "Systems" index card
listed the relevant nodes according to article titles, not subject categories. To
find references in different articles, the user must read the full list. A traditional subject index would list the system names in alphabetical order, then
give the entries with or without further explanation.

Index items link to a single frame, which may cross reference another index list. Cross links are always indirect, through the index.

Hyperties Index

The Hyperties "index" lists all 307 "articles" alphabetically using author's last name, then the sequence number, then the title of the "article."

Example: "FRISSE 1: TITLE PAGE (MEDICAL SEARCH)"
"FRISSE 4: PRINCIPLES OF HYPERTEXT QUERY
PROCESSING"

This system is not practical for navigation because information is not arranged by subject. For example, the Frisse article, "Searching for Information in a Hypertext Medical Handbook," would not be found under "m" for "medical," or "s" for search, but under "f" for "Frisse."

The 307 "articles" include the authors' biographies and a list of all 132 bibliographic references in the form [WEGN87] plus an alphabetic bibliography. However, the bibliographic references are not linked to the source of their citations. For example, the user can click on [GUID86B] to get the full reference to the Guide user's manual, but there is no way to know where it was cited.

The references duplicate what the author provided in the original text, and no more. For example, in Hyperties, the Halasz article contains a reference to an earlier article by Garg, but doesn't reference material by Garg in this publication. An automated search function would bring the additional reference to the user's attention.

The only items within the 307 "articles" listed in a traditional fashion are the authors biographies which are scattered alphabetically among the other listings.

The "Table of Topics" index is similar to the indexes in the other programs and can be used for navigation. It includes only the five topics listed below with a combined total of 16 citations, approximately one citation for every 20 of the 307 "articles," so it is not a primary method of navigation.

Topics:	Number of references:
Database structure/model	5
Search and Query	6
Input	2
Collaboration	2
Versioning	1

The order of listing is curious. Conspicuously missing are the history, future and definition of hypermedia, navigation, mapping, and hypertext systems.

Entries list the referenced "article," but since the "articles" cover so much material, up to several pages of text, there is no apparent scheme for indexing topics within "articles."

Tracing the links on "Collaboration", the first reference is to the Akscyn, McCracken and Yoder article. There are no links to other material on collaboration. Interestingly, this same "article" includes material on annotating which is related to versioning, another of the indexed topics, but this node is not referenced under "versioning" in the index.

Keyword Search

The user has the ability, in all three applications, to create a list of connections based on a keyword or string search. In each application, more nodes were found through search than through embedded links or the index or the map.

HyperCard Search

The HyperCard search uses the HyperCard "FINDER" utility, which, unfortunately, only searches the current stack. To search all cards, the user must re-initiate the search in each stack.

I used the topic "KMS" to compare information supplied by the various forms of HyperCard navigation. The HyperCard map gives one reference to "KMS" in the Smith and Weiss *Overview* and one reference to the index. The index lists seven nodes in the Akscyn, McCracken and Yoder article plus the ZOG index.

A search on "KMS" yields all the references within the Akscyn, McCracken and Yoder article plus three hits from *Reflections*, an abstract of the article by Akscyn, McCracken and Yoder and a second hit from the Smith and Weiss *Overview*, (KMS as predecessor to ZOG), which did not show up on the map or the index. The first reference in *Reflections,* on p.840 of the text, places KMS in the hypertext lineage; the second reference, p. 848 of the text, evaluates the programs's support for collaborative work. The third is a bibliographic reference to another article.

The index leads indirectly to the ZOG reference through the ZOG index frame. However, there is no readily apparent reason why the abstract of the article is omitted or why the passage on support for collaborative work is not included in the index or the map.

The hypermedia/hypertext index lists six topics. Four of the citations lead into the same loop described above under direct links and the hypertext map. A fifth citation led to another reference in the Smith and Weiss *Overview* explaining increased interest in hypertext. This node has a link to a node in the van Dam keynote speech on the same subject. The sixth index reference led to the "History of Hypertext" index card.

A search on "hypermedia" yielded 21 nodes. Most of these, except some within bibliographic citations, lead back to the index. One that did not connect to the index was the heading "Hypermedia Design Issues" (figure 1) which was linked to two other nodes in Halasz and Frisse on design questions, but not to the hypermedia index. Because the links to the index are hand-made and not automatic, not all indexed words are connected to the index.

KMS Search

KMS search is nicely implemented. The search creates a frame listing the title of all frames that contain the search string. The user can go directly through the list using the "NEXT" button without returning to the index frame. The implementation would be better, however, if the hierarchy were integral to the document. When a keyword is part of a frame title which is subordinate to another frame, the search finds two "hits" which actually lead to the same node of information, but the program has no way to interpret the embedded links and understand the relationship between the two hits.

It is hard to compare the KMS index and search capacities, because the index groups entries by article, not by subject. There are two index references to "Doug Engelbart" in the history index, one to the *Overview* and one to the *Keynote* address. These two references do not include a description of Engelbart's demonstration of hypertext in 1968. The keyword search uncovers this and other references and gives a classic example of a "bad hit," the most common reason for not relying on keyword search. The keyword search on Engelbart includes the node titled "Ted Nelson" that starts out, "So much for my paean of praise to Doug Engelbart."

Hyperties Search

Hyperties also allows for key word and string search and builds a temporary index card, in the same manner as KMS, although, as with all Hyperties connections, the user must first return to the temporary index card before going on to the next reference.

Searching on "KMS" yields links to the entire the Akscyn, McCracken and Yoder article as well as information on KMS in the *Hypertext '87* reports and the other feature articles.

Searching on "Doug Engelbart" yields a biography and various references to articles that mention Engelbart and also the Nielsen report on what van Dam said at *Hypertext '87*. The same remarks are, of course, in the *Keynote* article itself, but there are no direct links between them. Nielson gives a short biography of Engelbart which has no direct reference to the other biography.

A hindrance in using the Hyperties index is the size of the Hyperties "article." One search reference leads to a discussion of Engelbart's views on augmenting intellect. All three pages of this "article" contain information on Engelbart, in fact, he is subject of the whole "article," but no way to know this except to keep reading. The other screens are not referenced.

Of course, this search yields the same "paean" bad hit as in KMS.

A direct comparison between the Hyperties index and its search capacity is possible with the topic "versioning." This topic is more abstract than "KMS" or "Engelbart" and should show the work of the indexer over the blind capabilities of the search.

"Versioning" has one index reference. A search on "versioning" gives several other useful sources. The index lists Halasz "article" 5.5 where he states that versioning is one of his "Seven Issues for the Next Generation of Hypermedia Systems," but omits his comments on versioning in his classification scheme for hypertext and in his conclusions and, more significantly, in the other articles—Akscyn, McCracken and Yoder, Nielsen and van Dam.

Conclusions

This chapter concludes by comparing the *Hypertext on Hypertext* applications with each other, with text search programs and with print, and finally examines future directions for hypertext experiments, for this type of hypertext platform and for technical documentation.

Comparisons Between the Hypertext on Hypertext Programs

Even in so limited a task as connecting six related magazine articles, there are vast differences in the way information can be structured. The difference between the programs is not merely one of speed, efficiency, elegance or the care with which they are presented (I have held my tongue on the subject of the user interface)—but a qualitative difference due, at least in part, to inconsistent adherence to document structure and to the subjective nature of their linking systems.

The way the hypertext composer relates to the printed document structure determines the node structure. On one extreme, the HyperCard composer paid no attention to document structure, and on the other, the KMS composer divided frames strictly by document hierarchy. Hyperties fell somewhere in the middle, using logical subdivisions for "articles", but not for screens.

The different link structure does not appear to be the result of design decisions, but of the subjective nature of this type of hypertext. The lack of relationship between different linking schemes, even within the same program, the random order of embedded links and their erratic coverage of the subject matter are hallmarks of hand-crafted hypertext links.

The difficulties with the linking process did not escape the notice of the hypertext composers themselves. When I spoke with Elise Yoder, President of KSI, about the process of composing *Hypertext on Hypertext*, she said that at the beginning, they wanted to connect everything, but that this was not feasible. By the end of the project, in her words, they were "practically fabricating" meaningful connections in order to install more links.

In the Hyperties "Special Section on Hypertext," there is a passage that describes the hypertext composition process. After a month of work and after doing about 30 hypertext "articles", the editors became "painfully aware (of) how hard it is to convey to the hypertext reader what the contents are and how to navigate successfully. The Hyperties alphabetical INDEX of article names provides some help, but we have become more aware of the need for a meaningfully structured Table of Contents." That the words "Table of Contents" form a button connected to the actual Table of Contents rather than to one of the many passages on hypertext structure seems to underscore the composers plight. Ben Shneiderman told me that his work on *Hypertext on Hypertext* confirmed his suspicion that this type of "linear" text could not be translated into hypertext.

This type of linking fosters the illusion of connectivity, but falls short of the all-connectedness or "intertwingledness" envisioned by Ted Nelson.

Was this poor showing due to sloppy, hurried construction rather than the fundamental limitations of the programs? Each group had a team of two or three people and reported spending approximately two months preparing for hypertext publication. While much time was spent by each group cleaning up the original source code, the hypertext development time was not insubstantial. Other composers would have handled these issues differently, but it would be impossible to find three more qualified individuals than those responsible for the applications—Nicole Yankelovitch at IRIS, Elise Yoder at KSI and Ben Shneiderman at the University of Maryland. It does not seem likely that lack of development time or talent was an issue.

Future Hypertext Experiments

The ACM publishing venture points to interesting directions for future hypertext experiments. Two or more authors could create a hypertext script from the same material using the same hypertext system. Even more valuable would be to compare hand-crafted hypertext directly with a structured hypertext like Concordia or an inverted index like askSam using the same data. While "bad hits" are more common with automatic linking, speed and thoroughness of connection can make compensation for the inconvenience.

While this analysis has focused on linking, the same material could be used to analyze the ability of hypertext to deal with complex material.

Linear Hypertext

Opinion is divided over whether hypertext is intended to overcome the deficiencies of "linear" print or of sequential on-line text. With only one entry per topic listing and only one destination for every direct link, this type of hypertext may be more "linear" than printed text. Even in hyperspace, without multiple windows, the user goes to only one place at a time.

It may be that the "linearity" of print derided in the hypertext literature is less constricting for the reader than the blind loops and directional links of subjective hypertext. Unless mitigated by a number of clear choices, hypertext linking is not only "linear", but blind. (Let's hope that it is not "blind and therefore insane" as in the old joke about the computer translation of "out of sight, out of mind.")

Future Hypertext

The techniques of hand-crafted hypertext are applicable to certain types of information where broad interconnectivity is not an issue. Instructional or training material where connections are well-defined by the subject matter, like foreign languages and anatomy, are well-served by the requirement to insert each link by hand.

In each case where a direct comparison was made, keyword search was more thorough than hypertext linking. More abstract topics would not do as well in keyword search, however, hypertext programs built on an inverted index, like askSam, should be considered as alternatives to subjective hypertext linking, especially when the time and cost of development is considered. While it took months of effort to convert these articles and link them by hand, the entire Commerce Business Daily is converted to hypertext everyday with minimal intervention by a hypertext composer.[5]

With hand-crafted hypertext, at the very least, the node structure should retain the logic of print hierarchy, the index should be traditional and links should be as systematic as possible. Composers would be better off, if they cannot connect things in a structured and meaningful way, to use boolean search with traditional indexing techniques. It appears curious that structure and hierarchy or key-word-search may foster more intertwingledness than random, subjective linking, but real-world implementations often complement and refine original visions.

Those looking for solutions for technical documentation should look at automatic linking, linking by machine intelligence and structured linking, while keeping in mind that without the intervention of the composer, even systematic bibliographic references are less useful.

Acknowledgements

Miles-Samuelson, Inc., made this work possible because of its corporate commitment to hypermedia documentation conversion.

I am grateful to Matt Vignieri and Reynold Jabbour at Sun Microsystems in Broadhollow, N.Y., and to David Bantz of the Center for Computing in the Humanities, Dartmouth College for generous use of their facilities.

Many thanks are due to Elise Yoder at KSI, Ben Shneiderman at the University of Maryland and Nicole Yankelovitch at IRIS for their help and cooperation. Mark Mandelbaum and Bernard Rous at ACM headquarters in New York initiated *Hypertext on Hypertext*, introduced me to the project and shared their enthusiasm with me at every step of the way. Debra Schneider of Computer Documentation read an early manuscript and is not to blame.

Finally, I want to express my appreciation to the typesetters, editors, proofreaders and illustrators at Miles-Samuelson for their work on this project.

NOTES:

1. The six conference articles are Akscyn, McCracken and Yoder, 1988; Halasz, 1988; Campbell and Goodman, 1988; Garg, 1988; Raymond and Tompa, 1988; and Frisse, 1988. In addition, *Communications* contained the "Hypertext '87 Keynote Address" by Andries van Dam and "An Overview of Hypertext" by editors Smith and Weiss.

2. "Toy" databases is a phrase used by Robert Glushko, et.al., to distinguish between their experience translating the Engineering Data Compendium into hypertext and the type of fanciful material used in most hypermedia demonstrations. See Glushko, 1988.

3. I use the phrase hypertext "composer" to designate the individual who creates the hypertext or hypermedia document. This phrase avoids the awkward and improper use of "author" as a verb.

4. For descriptions of the three platforms see Goodman, 1987 on HyperCard; Shneiderman, 1987, on Hyperties and Akscyn, McCracken and Yoder, 1988, on KMS.

5. The CBD Electronic Edition is published by Mercury Computer Services, Inc.

BIBLIOGRAPHIC REFERENCES:

Akscyn, R.M., McCracken, D.L., and Yoder, E.A. "KMS: A Distributed Hypermedia System for Managing Knowledge in Organizations." *Communications of the ACM,* 1988.

Alschuler, L. and Schneider, D. "Ban the Book? Interactive Documentation and the Writer's Responsibility for the Human/Machine Interface" *Proceedings of the ACM SIGDOC,* 1988.

Campbell, B. and Goodman, J.M. "HAM: A General Purpose Hypertext Abstract Machine." *Communications of the ACM,* 1988.

Frisse, M.E. "Searching for Information in a Hypertext Medical Handbook." *Communications of the ACM,* 1988.

Garg, P.K. "Abstraction Mechanisms in Hypertext." *Communications of the ACM,* 1988.

Glushko, R.J., Weaver, M.D., Coonan, T.A., and Lincoln, J.E. "'Hypertext Engineering': Practical Methods for Creating A Compact Disc Encyclopedia." *ACM Conference on Document Processing Systems,* Santa Fe, NM, 1988.

Goodman, D. *The Complete HyperCard Handbook.* Bantam Books, 1987.

Halasz, F.G. "Reflections on Notecards: Seven Issues for the Next Generation of Hypermedia Systems." *Communications of the ACM,* 1988.

Nelson, T. *Computer Lib/Dream Machines.* (first edition, fifth printing), 1974.

Raymond, D.R. and Tompa, F.W. "Hypertext and the New Oxford Dictionary." *Communications of the ACM,* 1988.

Shneiderman, B. "User Interface Design for the Hyperties Electronic Encyclopedia." *Hypertext '87 Papers,* Chapel Hill, NC, 1987.

Smith, J.B. and Weiss, S.F. "An Overview of Hypertext." *Communications of the ACM,* 1988.

Van Dam, A. "Hypertext '87: Keynote Address." *Communications of the ACM,* 1988.

Walker, J.H. "Supporting Document Development with Concordia." *Computer,* 1988

The Evaluation of Online Help Systems: A conceptual model[1]

Thomas M. Duffy
Indiana University
Learning Resources
004 Franklin Hall
Bloomington, In 47405

Brad Mehlenbacher
Carnegie Mellon
Baker Hall 160
Pittsburgh, PA 15232

Jim Palmer
Carnegie Mellon
and Apple Computer
10500 De Anza Blvd. MS: 27AR
Cupertino, CA 94051

There are an increasing number of software applications providing users with assistance online. We might even anticipate that online assistance will be the standard means of aiding a user in the near future. This chapter examines one online strategy for aiding a user: online help. Help systems are distinguished from other types of assistance and a conceptual model for analyzing online help systems is presented. Finally efforts to use that model in designing an online help evaluation system are described.

1. Introduction

> *Technology, properly interiorized, does not degrade human life but on the contrary enhances it.*
>
> Walter Ong

New technology, as Walter Ong notes in *Orality and Literacy*, has the power to *restructure* human consciousness: to transform the ways we interact with and think about the world. Writing itself is a technology: it requires a whole array of tools and "equipment." Moreover, the technology of writing has transformed our way of viewing the world. It allows us to form grapholects such as standard English (with nearly 2 million words) and to develop fully analytic and abstract modes of thinking. We fail to regard writing as technology because we have interiorized it (Ong, 1982).

The computer extends the technology of writing to a new medium. For example, accountants who once balanced books using ledgers and adding machines can now interact with electronic spreadsheets. As a new tool, the spreadsheet requires the accountants to perform their original tasks in new ways; ultimately, it transforms the way in which they understand those tasks.

To use the computer effectively, users must "properly interiorize" its technology, much as a concert pianist must interiorize the technology of the piano and a musical score. We claim that **helping computer users to interiorize technology** is the ultimate goal of training and assistance (such as tutorials and documentation). Training and assistance should help users to

1. establish a context for using an application,

2. learn how to achieve their goals using that application, and

3. acquire the skills necessary for performance.

We also believe that users will always require some training and assistance, no matter how simple or obvious a computer design aims to be (cf. Carroll & Mazur, 1985).

Delivering training and assistance online seems to be a natural way to use the flexibility provided by the computer. In theory, at least, presenting documentation and tutorials online has several advantages over the print medium (Brockmann, 1986; Shneiderman, 1987; Walker, 1987; Duffy, Gomoll, Gomoll, Palmer, & Aaron, 1988). Online delivery allows

Greater availability   With networks and portable computers becoming more prevalent, online information can provide a reliable source of information as hardcopy documentation becomes less available or less convenient to access.

Easier access   Online, the system can provide mechanisms for efficient access to the relevant information, especially in cases where that information might span many volumes of hardcopy documentation.

More interaction   Online, both the user and the system can interact with the information. For example, the system can use the state of the application (its current context) to determine what information to provide to the user, or a monitor capable of plan recognition could help debug users' faulty or inefficient procedures.

Low cost/High accuracy   In general, online information is less expensive to store, produce, and update. Hardcopy documents require much longer production cycles. As computer companies adopt shorter and more efficient software development cycles, the pressure to adequately document a product increases. The time it takes to produce a book after it is written—layout, formatting, and printing—becomes a bottleneck. Either manuals go into production well before products are stable (resulting in manuals that are inaccurate or incomplete) or a company incurs costs in order to make the necessary changes and to begin the production cycle again.

Multimedia and AI   Online information can exploit multiple media, such as video, sound, and animation, and can apply techniques from Artificial Intelligence (AI).

Of course, there are disadvantages to the online medium as well. First, with most computer systems users cannot work in the primary application while using the online information. In contrast, users can work comfortably with an application while using a hardcopy tutorial or manual. Second, it is well documented that most computer displays diminish the readability of text and the legibility of characters, two factors which make reading from screens more difficult than reading from a book or manual (Muter, Latremouille, Treurniet, & Beam, 1982; Kruk & Muter, 1984; Haas & Hayes, 1987). In general, these types of problems are *technological*: advances in computer hardware and software may reduce or eliminate the difficulties. There also remain *conceptual* problems. For example, the familiar strategies for navigating through books do not apply to online information (cf. Robertson & Akscyn, 1982; Elm & Woods, 1985). Users, therefore, must learn how to interact with the new medium.

Our goal is to address some of the problems posed by online training and assistance. In particular, we want to provide a conceptual model for understanding online help systems. We derive our model from an analysis of the cognitive tasks required of the **user** of the online help system. From this model we develop several methods for evaluating existing online help systems. The same model can also be used to guide the design of help systems, although we do not focus on design issues in this paper. To present our conceptual model for evaluating online help, we will

- more formally define online help;

- discuss the goals and methods of evaluation; and

- present our method of evaluation based on a cognitive task analysis.

2. What is online help?

Unfortunately, the term online help carries a number of competing connotations. One way to define online help is to classify various implementations of online information along some scale. For example, Shirk (1988) creates a taxonomy of online information based on two scales: increased writing complexity and progressive self-containment. At the low end of the scale she places system messages, at the high end, computer-based training. In contrast, we follow an approach based on Kinneavy's *Theory of Discourse* (1972) and reframe the question from one of classifying products (various implementations of online information) to one of classifying the aims of users in specific situations or contexts: what do they want or expect from online information? What questions should online systems be able to answer? Note that we view the function of information with respect to the context of its use, not the writer's intentions or the static description of its form (cf. Bethke, Dean, Kaiser, Ort, & Pessin, 1981).

The core idea behind our effort is to match the information provided to users with the different kinds of knowledge that they require. This focus allows us to establish general distinctions that do not rely on the specifics of an implementation (for example, does the system have a mouse?). Actual help systems, then, are a cross between content and the constraints imposed by online presentation. These constraints obviously include different hardware and software platforms, as well as available resources and creative differences among designers. But whether one is designing help for an IBM-PC or a Unix-based workstation, our goal is to match content to the user's goals and to present that content effectively.

Two basic types of user-accessed online information[2]

1. *Primary sources (Browsing)*. The exemplars for this category include an online encyclopedia or a bibliographic system for retrieving articles about various subjects. The **reference** of this discourse is primary in that the information supports the solution of a real-world problem, such as writing an article on electricity or finding the current stock prices in the Wallstreet Journal. Its **audience** is all users, and their **goal** is to browse or look up information relevant to their primary task.

2. *Secondary sources (Understanding).* The exemplars for this category include a wide variety of forms considered "electronic documentation," which we discuss in more detail below. The **reference** of this discourse is secondary, in that the information supports the use of a tool which itself is used to accomplish a primary task. In general, its **audience** is all users and their **goal** is to understand the tool itself.

In focussing upon secondary sources, we first note that the user's goal—understanding the primary application—takes different forms depending on his or her situation. Thus we can further classify secondary sources as follows:

Three types of secondary sources (electronic documentation)

1. I want to *buy* it. The exemplar for information that meets this goal is the sales demonstration. The **audience** is usually prospective buyers. Their **goal** is to (perhaps) buy the product or to understand how they can use its services; ultimately, the information reflects a persuasive aim.

2. I want to *learn* it. The exemplars for this category include tutorials and guided tours (which may emphasize a successful first experience—the affective response of the user—as an adjunct to the goal of learning). The users' **goals** are to learn what they can do with an application and how they perform some set of important or fundamental tasks. Constraints on attention generally limit this set of tasks to a group of basic skills, although more elaborate forms of instruction, much like a course or curriculum, also exist. From the user's point of view, however, the distinguishing feature is the goal of learning rather than performing. The **audience** includes both the prospective buyer and the novice or transfer user. Typically, the **context** is a set of artificial situations constructed so that the user can practice using the application; the user is not actually performing his or her own work.

3.   I want to *use* it. The exemplars for this category include online help or online documentation, although neither of these labels identifies the necessary functionality required of the information. Critically, the **context** is the actual work situation where the user is trying to perform a task with the application. The users' **goals** are to overcome impasses that prevent them from proceeding on their task. The **audience** is all users, depending on the type of knowledge they require. For example, the novice typically needs task-oriented information, while the expert wants access to reference material.

For our purposes, the difference between a learning-oriented aim and a performance-oriented aim is critical. We restrict our use of the term online help to systems that support performance; online tutorials and training support the goal of learning. It is important to understand that implementations can certainly mix the two functions in one system—designers might allow access to a tutorial from help, or deliver both via some other framework. Ours is a functional definition, since we believe that the reasons users come to help should determine the way in which help is delivered.

Characteristics of performance-oriented support systems

In studying performance-oriented systems (like online help), we really want to understand

1. how the user accomplishes tasks with the application,

2. how the user deals with breakdowns in task performance, and

3. how the help system can get the user back on task.

Note that the user will not try to access performance-oriented information as long as the task is going smoothly. All users, however, encounter breakdowns (Winograd & Flores, 1986); that is, they reach points in tasks where they lack the procedural or semantic knowledge to continue. An analogous situation is our use of a car. Under normal operation, we do not interact with the car as a tool, but use it to take us places. But when the car breaks down, we must interact with it as a tool: Is the battery dead? Must I change a tire? For some breakdowns, the only recourse is to take the car to a specialist who can both diagnose the problem and then repair it.

A similar series of events occurs when the goal-directed activity of the user breaks down. After Brown & VanLehn (1987), we call such a breakdown an *impasse*. On encountering an impasse, users can no longer interact with the application as a tool for accomplishing a task; rather, the impasse itself becomes the focus of attention. To continue, users must *diagnose* their problem and then access knowledge that will allow them to *repair* the impasse. That is, the users must engage in secondary problem solving. If they lack the requisite knowledge directly (that is, in long term memory or via inferencing), users may turn to secondary sources for the information (they can also, for example, ask other people or experiment with the system).

Performance-oriented information, then, has two primary functions:

- to aid diagnosis by allowing access to information based on the *types* of impasse a user will encounter; and

- to aid performance by providing specific information that gives the user one (or more) repair strategies.

Traditionally, online help systems provide little support for the diagnosis stage[3]. For example, a user may represent his impasse as a procedural question (How can I get a listing of my documents?), but only access an alphabetical list of topics, a list that, in the worst case, contains just the commands from the application program. He must then decide which of the various commands will best answer his question.

As designers, we need to change our strategy: first, we must determine the information that users need to know; then we must present that knowledge in ways that meet their expectations. But how does one characterize the kinds of information needed by the user? Of the many ways to view human-computer interaction—internal-external task mapping (Moran, 1983), Cognitive Complexity Theory (Kieras & Polson, 1985), Task-Action Grammars (Payne & Greene, 1986), and GOMS (Card, Moran, & Newell, 1983)—we have found Ben Shneiderman's model of user knowledge a useful way to represent the information needs of the user (see Figure 1).

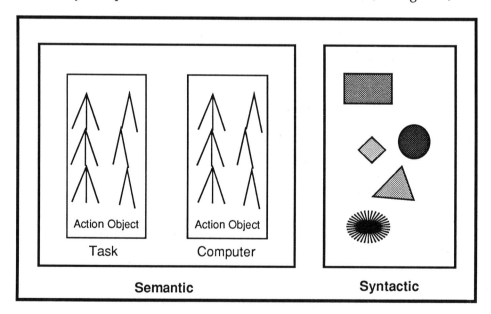

Figure 1: A representation of user knowledge in long-term memory (based on Shneiderman, 1987, p. 43).

Shneiderman's model allows for a syntactic and semantic component to a user's knowledge. The syntactic component includes all the device-specific knowledge necessary to perform actions. The semantic component involves

- real-world tasks and actions;

- computer tasks and actions (for example, using two windows to display different parts of a document) and

- a mapping between the two.

For example, a real-world writing task might be to *compare* (action) two parts of the same *document* (object), perhaps in order to check the citations against the reference list. Similarly, there might exist a computer task that allows users to *split* (action) a *window* (object) into two parts or *subwindows* (object). Related to this action is the appropriate syntax for performing it (in the current environment)—perhaps by typing the name of a command called "split window," by pressing 2 while holding the control key (^2), or, with a direct manipulation interface, by dragging an icon to the middle of the window. Finally, users must learn to map the real-world task into the corresponding computer task or tasks: to compare two parts of the same document, one can split the current window, and so on.

But how do we relate information to these types of knowledge? The user's knowledge of specific actions, objects, and syntax matches descriptive information, for example, a command reference that details all the commands in a system. The Unix **man** system, for example, provides online information for all the possible Unix commands. Each **man** unit includes a description of the command name, its function, a synopsis of its syntax, and related commands. The focus is on documenting the commands, not on how to use them to achieve real-world tasks. The basic **man** system even fails to help users relate computer objects and actions to their syntax. If users know that they want to list the contents of their directory, but they do not know some syntax—the specific name of the command for doing this, ls—they cannot get help.

The user's knowledge of the tasks they want to accomplish matches task-oriented, or procedural, information. Again, most help systems provide procedural information that supports computer tasks, such as how to split a window or how to open a new file. Few systems, however, relate real-world tasks to the computer tasks. That is, a user may know that she wants to move various pieces of text to another document (a task represented using real-world actions and objects). But the help system may only support computer tasks such as splitting windows, opening files, and cutting and pasting text. Once the user discovers the correct computer semantics—for example, that splitting the window is part of the task—she still must correctly order the various subtasks to achieve the overall task.

Obviously the help system cannot anticipate every real-world task that users will want to accomplish. It is important, therefore, to determine a range of prototypical real-world tasks using task analysis. From these tasks (and concrete examples), users will be able to apply their knowledge to novel situations. A task-orientation, therefore, will help users to learn the necessary computer semantics and syntax.

Medium constraints on help information

We have defined online help based on the needs of users in specific situations. In this sense, our description is implementation-independent; certain aspects of it apply to either online or hardcopy information. We chose this approach to emphasize the functional role of information—what does the user need to know? We do not want to suggest, however, that putting information online does not present special problems over and above the specification of content. We recognize that the constraints of presentation online have great impact on the design and evaluation of content as implemented in any one form (cf. James, 1985; Brockmann, 1986).

Based on interviews we conducted with nine professional writers who had at least five years of experience in the computer industry and who had primary responsibility for developing at least one online help system, we can begin to make several assertions about the difference between the online and hardcopy mediums (Duffy et al., 1988). Constraints imposed by the new medium include

Screen size

Writers disagree on whether online help should be formatted in the same way as hardcopy documentation. Certainly, limited screen size forces writers to chunk information in new ways. In this respect, writers suggest that a computer screen demands physical structuring as well as conceptual structuring even more than the page does because of the disorientation that many users experience when working with an online document.

Access mechanisms

The traditional hardcopy Table of Contents and Index do not transfer easily to computer. Writers

	are often responsible, not only for the content of the help system, but for the organization of and access to that help information.
Memory limitations	Although technological advances in this area are diminishing the importance of this constraint, memory still figures into the design of online information. The constraints of the software and hardware influence the amount of information designers can provide online.
Lack of context	There is no parallel navigation problem in a hardcopy document because the physical manual provides a "compass" with which users can orient themselves to other sections of the documentation (for example, "Now I am in the front of the book; now I am in the index"). Unlike the users of hardcopy, users of online information tend to "get lost in space."

Summary

We have defined online help based on the type of information the user needs, taking into account the various constraints presented by the new medium. Now we want to consider methods for evaluating existing online help systems . Then we will present our method of evaluation based on an analysis of user's tasks.

3. Goal and methods for evaluating online help systems

In this section we discuss the goals and methods for evaluating online help systems. In particular, we consider how the choice of goals determines which data are relevant for the evaluation. We then examine some of the constraints on the evaluation process and discuss alternative evaluation methods in light of these constraints.

The goals of evaluation

As defined in section 2, an online help system should support the secondary problem solving behavior of its users. Users come to a help system after reaching an impasse with the primary application. A *usable* help system, then, is one that aids the user in diagnosing and repairing their problem (impasse) with a minimum expenditure of time or effort.

When we evaluate help systems, our primary goal is to provide an operational definition of usability. That is, we want to provide a set of specific criteria which, taken together, indicate usability. Our secondary goal is to develop an instrument that is robust—one, in short, that meets the needs of both the researcher and the practitioner. We recognize that practitioners typically do not have the resources to engage in large-scale experiments or studies.

But what factors make a help system usable? For example, it is not sufficient to determine whether users can find the necessary information; the evaluation must determine how *efficiently* users can find this information. Moreover, as Borenstein (1985) stresses, one must certainly consider the quality of the information itself. Is it well written? Is it accurate? We argue that questions regarding usability fall into four basic categories:

1. the accuracy of the information presented;

2. the completeness of the information presented;

3. the ease of accessing the information; and,

4. the ease of understanding of the information.

A significant deficit in one category tends to make the system unusable. Providing a complete database of information matters very little if that information is inaccurate, and neither completeness nor accuracy matter much if the text is so poorly written that the user cannot understand it. Even if the information is easy to understand, it will not help if the user cannot find it, as when tasks are not represented explicitly or when relevant information is scattered throughout the system.

Our goal for evaluation, then, is to rate help systems based on the criteria of accuracy, completeness, access, and comprehensibility. Given this goal, we must now develop a methodology for achieving it. The appropriate methodology, however, partly depends upon the audience for the evaluation, that is, who will use the data.

The audience constraint

We can define two specific audiences for our evaluation data. The first audience includes the developers or designers of the help system. They may use many types of evaluation to provide feedback about their design. In general, this type of evaluation is called *formative evaluation*. Formative evaluation aims to guide the iterative process of design and revision: it may unearth problems with a design and, potentially, identify strategies for solving those problems.

The second audience for evaluation includes users and their representatives (those who review the product in order to advise customers on its advantages or disadvantages). The customer who wants to buy an application program should have data about the usability of its help system. Similarly, software reviewers for magazines should not only review the application program, but also the strengths and weaknesses of its help system. In general, evaluation of an existing product is called *summative evaluation*. Summative evaluation happens independently of the developers. Since the primary goal of summative evaluation is to rate the usefulness of an existing product, it should allow the reviewer to compare help systems against one another or against some reference standard.

Methods of evaluation

We can now examine evaluation methods in light of the above goals and audience constraints. Schriver (1988) identifies three groups of methods used to evaluate documentation:

1. expert review

2. document analysis, and

3. performance assessment.

Expert review includes all the ways in which both subject matter experts and design experts review a document. Document analysis includes such strategies as the use of readability formulas, syntactic analysis, and discourse analysis. Finally, performance assessment involves examining the performance of intended users of the system as they work with it. Most of these evaluation strategies are methods for formative evaluation.

Protocol-Aided Revision. Schriver (1988) argues that one variety of performance evaluation, protocol-aided revision (or PAR), is more effective than either expert review or document analysis for formative evaluation. In the PAR approach to the evaluation of online help, one first identifies tasks for users to perform with the application. The end users are then asked to complete those tasks using the help system as their only resource. Importantly, the end users are instructed to think aloud as they work on the task. That is, they are asked to verbalize their thoughts. From a transcript of the session, the evaluator tracks how users formulate their need for help (when they reach an impasse in the application program), how they search for information, and how they apply that information to overcome their impasse.

While we agree with the value of PAR for formative evaluation, the approach does not easily provide comparative data for summative evaluation. Think-aloud protocols yield data about the usability of a particular system; because of the verbalization, protocol analysis cannot be reliably used to compare either versions of the same system or different systems without greatly complicating the design of the test. For example, the evaluator must establish a valid and reliable system for categorizing comments into categories relevant to the comparative evaluation. Then he or she must develop a scoring system for each category, one that is not influenced by the "talkativeness" of a user. Finally, the evaluator must identify tasks that generalize from one system to another.

Our interest is in summative, rather than formative, evaluation. That is, our goal is to develop a strategy that will provide comparative data on the effectiveness of help systems. We want a tool for reviewers and potential users of a system that allows them to (1) make detailed ratings of a help system; and (2) reference their ratings to a database of ratings of other help systems.

Benchmarking. Benchmarking is a form of summative evaluation that does aim to provide comparative data (Lewis & Crews, 1985). Like PAR, the evaluators first define a set of problems that can be solved on all the systems being tested. Then, they establish a specific experimental methodology to examine users performing those tasks. Finally, they collect speed and accuracy data for novice users. These dependent measures become the basic data for comparing different systems.

Roberts & Moran (1983) describe a benchmark for comparing word processors. They define a matrix of word processing *actions* (for example, delete, move, and copy) and *objects* (for example, characters, words, sentences, and paragraphs). From this matrix, they derive a set of basic word processing tasks and, using standard material and testing procedures, compare the accuracy and speed with which novice users do those tasks on different word processors. While the approach has received some criticism (Borenstein, 1985), others have used the database established in Roberts & Moran's (1983) original study to evaluate new word processors.

Unfortunately, developing a benchmark to evaluate online help is problematic. A benchmark uses a set of common tasks and compares the time and accuracy of performance. Initially, one can question whether it is possible to define tasks common to even a representative subset of help systems. After all, help systems document different application programs and therefore support different types of tasks. (As discussed later, however, we think that a cognitive task analysis of the user's encounter with a help system can form the basis for comparative evaluation.)

The main difficulty with benchmarking arises not with defining common tasks, but with its emphasis on speed and accuracy of performance. We do not believe that comparing the speed and accuracy of users on a task in the application will necessarily reflect on the usability of the help system. For example, a complex application program, that is, one with a large command set, will require a more complicated help system In this case we would expect slower and potentially less accurate performance, not because the help system is poorly designed, but because it is large and complex. Moreover, the nature of the application program (for example, a word processor versus an operating system) and the quality of the applications interface may also impact the help system negatively if the only measure of usability is speed and accuracy on a task.

4. A conceptual model for the evaluation of online help systems

In contrast to PAR and benchmarking, our approach to evaluation has two distinguishing features. First, our evaluation focuses on the tasks a user should be able to perform within the help system itself. Second, we distinguish between the evaluation of accuracy and completeness and the evaluation of access and comprehensibility. The accuracy and completeness of the help information are intimately related to the application software; one can only determine whether help accurately supports a complete range of tasks by fully testing its information against a list of those tasks.

One can determine, however, the ease of accessing and comprehending information in the help system independently of the application program. The basic concept is that the user of the help system always engages in certain tasks specific to using the help system, such as scanning a menu for topics. Even though the content of the help system should support the tasks of the primary application (word processing, database management, and so on), the actual use of the help system itself has many regularities.

A task analysis of the use of online help

What is the situation of the user when he or she turns to online help? As established in section 2, users are trying to complete some primary task using an application. When they reach an impasse, they turn to help in order to obtain information that will let them overcome the impasse. Task analysis identifies those tasks the user must perform to solve this secondary problem. Eight major tasks, as shown in Figure 2, are identified in the task analysis.

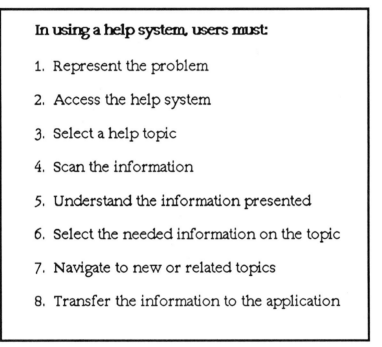

In using a help system, users must:

1. Represent the problem

2. Access the help system

3. Select a help topic

4. Scan the information

5. Understand the information presented

6. Select the needed information on the topic

7. Navigate to new or related topics

8. Transfer the information to the application

Figure 2: Primary tasks that users must perform while using a help system.

1. *Represent the problem.* Users will somehow label their impasse or information need. Although the required information is unknown, users usually won't stop with a statement of "I don't know what to do next." Rather they develop two hypotheses. First, they guess a likely name for the needed information. This naming process may be at a very general level, such as the class of activities involved, or it may be very specific, such as a likely command name. Second, users must guess how the help system will represent the needed information. That is, they will attempt to reformulate

their representation of the impasse into terms that they expect to work in an information search task.

2. *Access the help system.* Given a representation of the problem, users must access the help system. Here we simply mean actually getting into the help system—a task that is a significant problem for some systems.

3. *Select a help topic.* Once in the help system, users must select a help topic that they feel will probably provide the information they need. In essence, they need to find a topic that explicitly matches their original representation of the problem or one that seems to provide the best fit given the impasse.

4. *Scan the information.* Once users get to a help topic that they selected, it must be scanned to determine if it contains the needed information. If the help information is just a text file with little discourse structure, scanning may be difficult if not impossible.

5. *Understand the information presented.* Once they locate a relevant section of information to read, users must be able to understand the text and graphics.

6. *Select the needed information on the topic.* If the information is on the correct topic and is understood, users must extract the particular information needed to complete their task in the application. This includes being able to translate the general help information provided into the specific actions needed for the application.

7. *Navigate to new and related topics.* If they did not find all the needed information, users must go to another topic. In general, users must be able to navigate through the help system. Of course, as they come to new topics, users will step through tasks four, five, and six again. If they ultimately fail to find the necessary information, users may start over by reformulating their problem (or give up in exasperation).

8. *Transfer the information to the application.* Finally, users must take the information from the help system and apply it in the application program in order to remove the impasse.

When we speak of the usability of a help system we mean how well the help system supports each of these tasks. While our method for evaluating access and comprehensibility may differ from our method for evaluating access and completeness, both forms of evaluation must be framed in terms of this task analysis.

Evaluating usability: access and comprehensibility

The goal of summative evaluation is to provide comparative data on the usability of help systems. If we are to use the task analysis described above, we must be able to score any help system in terms of each of the eight user tasks. But what are we to score and how do we obtain reliable and comparable scores?

First, let us consider what we are to score. If we focus on the access and comprehensibility components of usability, then we must score each user task in terms of how easy it is to access and understand the information that is relevant to performing that task. For example, in terms of the first task, Problem Formulation, we may assess how well the system tries to match the user's formulation of the problem.

We could assess the system through user testing. However, as we have argued earlier, the user's speed and accuracy of performance in the help system is significantly affected by the complexity, generality, and design of the application program. Instead, our evaluation system employs expert judgement to provide the basis for the evaluation of access and comprehensibility. Of course, if we are to have comparable ratings, then the expert judgement must be tightly constrained. In essence, the expert must have very specific criteria on which to rate the system.

We are using specific guidelines for effective design as the mechanism for constraining or guiding the expert judgment. We have taken the guidelines for effective design from the literature on help systems, interface design, and document design (for example, Smith & Mosier , 1986; Kearsley, 1988; Meyhew, in press; Duffy, Palmer, & Mehlenbacher, in preparation) and recast them as statements to be used in rating a help system. While there is some question of the guideline approach as a means of directing the activities of a writer or designer (Duffy & Kabance, 1982; Duffy, 1985b; Mosier & Smith, 1986), guidelines have been used to evaluate products successfully (Duffy, 1985a). That is, well designed material will exhibit characteristics recommended by guidelines.

We use two criteria for selecting guidelines. The first criterion is that the guideline should indicate reduced information processing demands on the user. A usable help system is one in which the user can obtain information with a minimum of time and effort, that is, with minimal information processing. Therefore, the guidelines used to judge a help system should clearly reflect a reduction in information processing requirements. This may happen by reducing the demands on any one of the three human information processing subsystems: perceptual, motor, or cognitive.

The second criterion is that the guideline should address one (or more) of the eight tasks identified in our task analysis. For example, guidelines having to do with the organization of items on a menu would be grouped under user Task Three, *"Select a Topic,"* while guidelines addressing the nature of the items on the menu (or in a keyword system) would be classified under Task One, *"Represent the problem."*

The final evaluation system consists of 49 items arranged into categories based on their relevance to the eight user tasks. The items guide the expert to review the help system thoroughly and to rate it based on the presence or absence of particular features (for example, help on help) or on the judged quality of a particular feature (for example, the consistency of format across help topics as one index of Task four—the ease of searching a topic to find the needed information).

The system yields scores that can range between 0 and 100 for each user task as well as for the system overall. Currently, the evaluation system is in the final stages of development. Two reviewers are evaluating 25 help systems for commercially available software. This data will provide reliability information as well as a database of scores that can be used in comparing other help systems. The validity of the system is difficult to assess empirically. We have already mentioned the limitations of user performance data; it cannot, therefore, serve as a criterion for the validity of the rating system. We argue that the validity of our system depends on

- the degree to which the evaluation is based on a conceptually sound task analysis of "usability" and

- the degree to which the particular items comprise the concept of usability and sample the full range of usability factors.

Assessing usability: accuracy and completeness.

Access and comprehensibility are features of the help system that can be evaluated independently of the application software. In addressing accuracy and completeness, we must focus on the link between the help system and the application being helped. This discussion reflects our initial thinking on the issues involved in assessing accuracy and completeness.

Let us begin by relating the issues of accuracy and completeness to our analysis of the tasks of the user entering a help system. We see three of those tasks as being relevant to the evaluation of accuracy and completeness.

Represent the Problem

Are the tasks the user needs help on represented in the help system? The issue for evaluating access and comprehensibility is whether the topics are framed in the user's terms. Here we are concerned with the number of tasks covered. How comprehensively does the help system address the use of the application program? Is the user's goal represented at all?

Select Needed Information

Is the information on a task accurate and complete? Here we are concerned with the completeness of the coverage of any one topic or task. A complete coverage of the procedure for executing a task would list each action the user should take and describe the consequence of each of those actions. The clarity of the description and the availability of graphics which help the user to locate key information are all issues of comprehensibility; that the steps are present is the requirement for completeness. Complete procedural coverage is usually provided only for novice tasks or startup tasks (for example, booting the system). For some reason, it is assumed that users do not need this procedural support for more advanced functions—an assumption we take strong exception to. Complete coverage of a topic (depth) also means complete description of functions and complete coverage of all "relevant" technical data.

Navigate to New Topics

Is information relevant to the user's goal identified with that goal and co-located or clearly linked? It does little good if the relevant information is in the help system but the user will never find it because it is linked to a different task (from the point of view of the user) or the bits of necessary information are in different places with no cross referencing. In evaluating comprehensibility and access we focus on general navigation aids—aids to permit easy navigation and prevent getting lost. Here the concern is the linkage between specific chunks of information required to complete a task in the application.

Before considering methodologies for evaluating each of these issues, let us consider some of the problems we face in the evaluation of accuracy and completeness. We have defined the breadth of tasks covered—the issue of problem representation—in terms of the users' tasks. The first issue to address is whether or not this is the correct unit of analysis. Should everything be cast in terms of user tasks? We think so. But while we can argue for task orientation in defining a user's needs, we face a second problem, that of defining a task. At what level should a task be conceptualized? In part this is an issue of grain size—is the task cutting, cutting and pasting, or revising. In part it is also a matter of domain representation—are we talking about computing tasks or real-world tasks (Shneiderman, 1987)? There are no ready answers to this issue. However, movement towards an answer must be based on an analysis of how users conceptualize their task or goal in the application.

A third issue involves how well the help system covers the breadth of tasks which the application supports. Even if we agree to represent tasks in the help system, and even if the tasks are defined in terms of grain size and domain, we still must recognize that there are an infinite number of tasks. That is, the application will always be used in new and unanticipated ways by the end users and thus we can never specify all of the possible user tasks. How are we to evaluate the adequacy of the help system for unanticipated tasks?

In part the evaluation can address the wide variety of possible tasks by sampling rather than exhaustively enumerating tasks. That is, we must sample a range of potential tasks in the application and then determine the proportion of those tasks addressed in the help system. Of course the sampling strategy will be critical here. However, this still does not help us evaluate the adequacy of the help system for aiding the user in new, innovative tasks.

Online help systems address the problem of unanticipated tasks by providing reference information on each command in the application. The evaluation of this reference information must be in terms of how well it supports the users needs. This requires identifying the kinds of reference information that must be provided. Of course the designers should also have addressed this issue, but too often this is not done in a systematic fashion. Indeed, the very fact that reference information is organized around commands rather than around the categories of knowledge the user requires in these innovative tasks is an indication of the lack of systematic attention to this issue. What is required is a theoretical and empirical analysis of the categories of knowledge required of the user. This analysis would then serve as the basis for evaluating completeness.

We have been focusing on completeness in terms of the breadth of coverage in the help system. However, there are also methodological issues in evaluating accuracy and completeness of the content provided on any one topic. Given a task in the application program, we now need a method for evaluating the accuracy and completeness of the information on that task. A straight forward procedure would be to simply test the ability (speed and accuracy) of users to perform a task in the application with only the help system available as a source of information. However, there are two problems with this approach. First, the speed and accuracy data will reflect the effects of the comprehensibility and accessibility of the information as well as the accuracy and completeness. Indeed, a user may take a long time or never complete the task simply because he or she cannot locate (access) the relevant information.

One might argue that this approach, while not distinguishing between the components of usability, does, in fact, index the overall usability of the help system and that this, after all, is our goal. However, our goal is not just to assess usability but to assess it in such a way that we can compare help systems. This leads us to the second problem with the use of speed and accuracy in using the help system: these measures will be dependent on the complexity of the application program. The more complex the application program, the longer it will take to perform a task and the more likely that there will be an error in that performance. Thus the overall indices of speed and accuracy cannot be compared across help systems.

We do not think that the evaluation needs to be, or even should be, performance based. Rather, for each task we abstract all relevant information from the help system. We then want to assess the completeness and accuracy of the procedural and conceptual information. Procedural accuracy and completeness can be assessed by comparing the steps required to perform a task with the steps provided in the help system: what proportion of the steps are presented? Conceptual accuracy and completeness can be assessed by identifying the concepts required to perform the procedure and checking the proportion that are "explained" in the help system.

Finally, the assessment of the information and of the navigation proceeds by identifying the proportion of information required for a task that is linked either through co-location or through explicit cross-referencing. Note, however, that the analysis of navigation requires the specification of a user's goal as the primary mechanism for defining a domain of information. Clearly, we recognize that the development of a system for evaluating accuracy and completeness holds more difficult issues—both conceptual and practical—than the evaluation of access and comprehensibility. However, we feel that the focus on the user in terms of user tasks and user knowledge requirements is the key to developing an effective evaluation tool. Also, we should note that the evaluation instrument will not work in isolation; its success will depend on the availability of expert users of the application, on detailed assessment of tasks, and on the use of the help information in the application program.

4. Conclusions

Our goal in this paper has been to review some of the problems posed by online training and assistance and to provide a conceptual model for understanding online help systems. In describing our framework, we have categorized various types of electronic documentation and restricted our definition of online help to systems that are performance-oriented rather than learning-oriented. Performance-oriented information, we have suggested, has two primary functions: to provide information based on the types of impasses users encounter and to provide users with one (or more) repair strategies. We have not denied the constraints presented by the new medium—that is, considerations of screen size, access mechanisms, memory limitations, and lack of context—but rather, we have stressed that online help systems should be viewed as a mixture of content (knowledge required by the user) and constraints imposed by online presentation.

Because we believe that, when talking about online help systems, the focus should be on the user's tasks, we similarly maintain that evaluation should emphasize how effectively the system reduces the user's motor, perceptual, and cognitive demands. With this task-oriented perspective in mind, we have surveyed various evaluation techniques—for example, PAR and benchmarking—and found that a more comprehensive methodology is required. That is, existing methods of evaluation do not capture the elements of a help system that we have suggested make it "usable." A comprehensive evaluation of online help must account for the system's effectiveness in providing users with information that is accurate, complete, easy to access and easy to understand.

Finally, we believe that our model, which is based on an analysis of users' cognitive tasks while accessing an online help system, gives both researchers and practitioners a theoretical understanding that can potentially be used to guide both the design and the evaluation of online help systems.

[1] This work was funded in part by the United States Army Human Engineering Laboratory, Aberdeen Proving Grounds, MD under contract DAAA1–86–K–0019. Maureen Larkin was the contract monitor. The work was also funded by Learning Resources, Indiana University. The views expressed in this paper are those of the authors and do not necessarily reflect the views of the United States Army.

[2] An application interface is itself a species of online communication, including its menu design, the system and error messages, and its other user dialogs. In addition, there are intelligent interfaces, which attempt to integrate help into the interface rather than provide access to information. Our emphasis upon user-accessed information, therefore, is an important one: an extended treatment of online communication in general is beyond the scope of this essay (but see, for example, Brueker & De Greef, 1985).

[3] Clearly error messages, which are not under the users' direct control, are an integral part of the diagnosis stage. That error messages often do not help users indicates that professional writers desperately need to claim error messages as their domain.

References

Bethke, F., Dean, P., Kaiser, E., Ort, E. & Pessin, F. (1981). Improving the usability of programming publications. *IBM Systems Journal*, 20 (3), 306-320.

Borenstein, N. (1985a). *The design and evaluation of on-line help systems.* Unpublished Doctoral Dissertation. Pittsburgh, PA: Carnegie Mellon University.

Borenstein, N. (1985b). The evaluation of text editors: A critical review of the Roberts and Moran methodology based on new experiments. In *Computer-human interaction (CHI) '85 proceedings.* New York, NY: Association for Computing Machinery.

Brockmann, R. J. (1986). *Writing Better Computer User Documentation: From Paper to Online.* NY: John Wiley & Sons.

Brown, J. S. & VanLehn, K. (1980). Repair theory: A generative theory of bugs in procedural skills. *Cognitive Science, 4,* 379-415.

Breuker, J. & de Greef, P. (1985). *Information Processing Systems and Teaching & Coaching in HELP Systems.* Deliverable 12.1, ESPRIT Project P280 (EUROHELP), Amsterdam: Department of Social Science Informatics, University of Amsterdam.

Card, S. K., Moran, T. P., & Newell, A. (1983). *The psychology of human-computer interaction* Hillsdale, NJ: Lawrence Erlbaum Associates.

Carroll, J. M. & Mazur, S. A. (1985). *Lisa learning.* (Tech Report RC 11427). Yorktown, NY: T. J. Watson Research Center.

Duffy, T.M. (1985a). Readability formulas: What is the use? In T.M. Duffy and R. Waller (Eds.), *Designing Usable Texts.* New York: Academic Press.

Duffy, T.M. (1985b). Controlling the usability of technical text: Specifications and guidelines. In D.H. Jonassen (Ed.), *The Technology of Text. Vol. 2.*

Duffy, T.M. & Kabance, P. (1982). Testing a readable writing approach to text revision. *Journal of Educational Psychology, 74,* 733-748.

Duffy, T., Palmer, J., & Mehlenbacher, B. (in preparation). *Online help systems: Design and evaluation.*

Duffy, T., Gomoll, T., Gomoll, K., Palmer, J., & Aaron, A. (1988). *Writing online information: Expert strategies (interviews with professional writers).* Pittsburgh, PA: Communications Design Center.

Elm, W. & Woods, D. (1985, October). Getting lost: a case study in interface design. *Proceedings of Human Factors Society.* Westinghouse Scientific Paper: 85-1C60-CONRM-P2.

Haas, C. & Hayes, J. R. (1987). *Effects of Text Display Variables on Reading Tasks: Computer Screen vs. Hard Copy.* Technical Report CDC-3 (ERIC # 260 387), Pittsburgh, PA, Communications Design Center, Carnegie Mellon.

James, G.. (1985). *Document Databases: The New Publications Methodology.* New York, NY: Van Nostrand Reinhold.

Kearsley, G. (1988). *Online help: Design and implementation.* Menlo Park, CA: Addison-Wesley Publishing Co.

Kieras, D. E. & Polson, P. G. (1985). An approach to the formal analysis of user complexity. *International Journal of Man-Machine Studies, 22,* 365-394.

Kinneavy, J. L. (1970). *A theory of discourse.* Englewood Cliffs, NJ: Prentice-Hall.

Kruk, R. & Muter, P. (1984). Reading of continuous text on video screens. *Human Factors, 26* (3), 339-345.

Lewis, B. & Crews, A. (1985, March). The Evolution of Benchmarking as a Computer Performance Evaluation Technique. MIS Quarterly, 7-16.

Marshall, C., Nelson, C., & Gardiner, M. (1987). Design guidelines. In M. M. Gardiner and B. Christie (Eds.), *Applying cognitive psychology to user-interface design.* New York, NY: John Wiley and Sons.

Meyhew, D. (in preparation). *Principles and methods of interactive system design.*

Moran, T. P. (1983). Getting into a system: External-internal task mapping analysis.. A. Janda (Ed.), *Proceedings of the CHI '83 Conference on Human Factors in Computing Systems* (pp. 45-49). New York: ACM.

Mosier, J. and Smith, S. (1986). Application of guidelines for designing user interface software. *Behaviour and Information Technology, 5,* 39-46.

Muter, P., Latremouille, S.A., Treurniet, W.C., & Beam, P. (1982). Extended reading of continuous text on television screens. *Human Factors, 24,* 401-414.

Ong, W. (1982). *Orality and literacy: The technologizing of the word.* London: Methuen.

Payne, S. & Greene, T. (1986). Task-action grammars: A model of the mental representation of task languages. *Human-Computer Interaction, 2,* 93-133.

Roberts, T. and Moran, T. P. (1983). The evaluation of text editors: Methodology and empirical results. *Communications of the ACM, 26,* 265-283.

Robertson, C.K. and Akscyn, R. (1982). *Experimental evaluation of tools for teaching the ZOG frame editor.* Technical Report. Pittsburgh, PA: Carnegie Mellon University.

Schriver, K. (1988). *Teaching writers to anticipate the readers needs: Empirically based instruction.* Unpublished PhD dissertation. Pittsburgh, PA: Carnegie Mellon University.

Shirk, H. N. (1988). Technical writers as computer scientists: The challenges of online help. In E. Barrett (Ed.), *Text, ConText, and HyperText: Writing with and for the computer* (pp. 311-27). Cambridge, MA: MIT Press.

Shneiderman, B. (1987). *Designing the user interface: Strategies for effective human-computer interaction.* Reading, MA: Addison-Wesley.

Smith, S. and Mosier, J. (1986). *Guidelines for designing user interface software*. (ESD-Technical Report TR-86-278). Hanscom Air Force Base, MA: Electronic Systems Division, United States Air Force.

Walker, J. (1987). Issues and strategies for online documentation. *IEEE Transactions on Professional Communication, PC 30*, 235-248.

Winograd, T. & Flores, F. (1986). *Understanding computers and cognition: A new foundation for design*. Norwood, NJ: Ablex.

Escher Effects in On-Line Text

Judith Ramey

STC, Engineering, FH-40
University of Washington
Seattle, WA 98195

Escher effects are ambiguities or other anomalies in on-line text that force the reader to study the text as text. *On-line text consists of instrumental text (commands, menu items) and commentary (system messages, Help); simple Escher effects result from stylistic strategies used to compress on-line text, tangles of instrumental text and commentary, weak formatting, and home-grown terminology. Complex Escher effects result from deeper rhetorical or structural problems; they interfere with our ability to build a rhetorical contract with the writer/designer and our ability to build a useful mental model of the system.*

What are Escher Effects?

In almost all current commercially-available computer systems, users get work done by understanding and manipulating *text* -- language displayed on the computer screen. Even systems that are partially or essentially "graphics" systems rely to one degree or another on on-line text. This on-line text takes two main forms (although the text involved can vary in complexity from single words to complex narratives): "instrumental" text (text that does work -- for instance, commands in the form in which they are displayed on the screen, menu choices, and dialog-box choices) and commentary (system messages and on-line help, for example).

In designing or writing this text, most writers are severely constrained by limitations on the amount of space that their text can take up; computer screens can display only so much information at once. They therefore condense their text into the physically smallest presentation that they can devise -- the presentation that uses the least number of character spaces.

Unfortunately, the process of condensing text often introduces ambiguities that can cause Escher effects: demands that the on-line text receive attention *as* text (rather than as meaning) -- demands that therefore divert the reader's attention from the content to the syntactic or semantic peculiarities of the text structure. Escher effects are created in on-line text by words, phrases, sentence fragments, sentences, and even topical treatments or discourse structures that can be read equally well with at least two different, but mutually exclusive, meanings.

Escher the artist created drawings that break two kinds of rules: the rules governing the relationships between objects rendered on the same field, and the rules governing the relationship between the creator and the thing created. By doing so, he demands that we contemplate the nature of artifice. Escher effects in on-line text, however, demand that we participate in a less salutary exercise -- or at least a poorly-timed one.

With text that is displayed on-line, the relationship between reading and doing is particularly intimate, because both occur in the same medium and as part of the same broader task. In a well-oiled performance on the computer, in fact, the user may not even be aware of a distinction between the two. Escher effects, however, require the user to stop and unravel the syntactic or semantic "fields" of chunks of text, or even force the user into the role of "creator" of meaning instead of "user" of meaning. By diverting the user's energies to dissecting ambiguities, these effects disrupt the integrity of the user's process of gathering and using information to do the task at hand.

Later in this discussion we will look at some complex Escher effects that create "tangled hierarchies" or "strange loops," to use the language developed by Douglas Hofstadter in *Godel, Escher, Bach* (Hofstadter, 1979). But first, we need to define and illustrate simple Escher effects in on-line text.

Simple Escher Effects

Simple Escher effects result from ambiguities:

- Ordinary ambiguities, created or exaggerated by the stylistic strategies frequently used in on-line text.

- Ambiguities caused by tangling up the discourse of the human-computer interface (the "instrumental" text) with the discourse of the commentary on it.

Users frequently cannot avoid perceiving these ambiguities and have trouble resolving them correctly because of phenomena associated with on-line reading: the user may be suffering confusion, uncertainty, or frustration that reduces his or her reading skill; or the screen on which the text occurs may not provide a context sufficiently rich to cue the correct reading.

Ordinary ambiguities are of course at least as common in on-line text as they are in any other text. For example, the phrase "programming error messages" is typical of the kind of phrase one might encounter in on-line text; let's look more closely at this phrase. It can be read as "programming-error messages," a noun stack describing the kind of messages that result from errors in programming; or, it can be read as "programming error-messages," a gerund phrase describing the activity of programming the computer to display error messages.

If the context in which the phrase occurs is not ambiguous, the reader probably understands the phrase correctly at first reading. Otherwise, the reader may discover that he or she has to stop reading (that is, has to suspend the processing of information), discard the first interpretation, back up, and re-read to discover another meaning. If the material is difficult, once the reader has discovered the alternative meaning, he or she may have to re-read a third time to fit the newly acquired second meaning into the context of the full discourse. All of this interpretive work displaces the user's real work of using the computer to do a task.

To illustrate the impact of Escher effects on the actual process of using the computer, let me describe a simple experience reported to me by one of my colleagues who was learning a computer operating system new to him. In starting the computer's line editor for the first time, he encountered the words "input mode" displayed on the screen. He explains that "when looking at the line editor for the first time, I saw "input mode" and read "input" as a verb. I assumed I had to select some kind of mode before I could begin editing. I did not realize that I was already in the editing mode and that "input" was being used as a noun" (Farkas). That is, the phrase that he took to be "instrumental" (a prompt to enter the name of a mode) was in fact commentary (it told him what mode he was already in).

Thus an ambiguity in the system's text diverted him from proceeding directly to the actual steps in the task sequence and misled him into trying to figure out how to do a nonexistent or "phantom" first step. He then stepped out of his direct interaction with the system and studied the *text* "input mode" to find another reading of it. In extreme cases, such Escher effects can slow down the user's learning of the system or undermine the user's sense of the "frankness" of the system. As a result, the user can come to view system text as "tricky" or "oracular" and thus in need of constant study and interpretation *as a text*.

Sources of Simple Escher Effects

There are a number of sources of these simple Escher effects in on-line text:

- Stylistic strategies that are frequently used to compress on-line text

- Tangles of instrumental text structures and commentary text structures

- Weak formatting that doesn't distinguish clearly between commentary and references to instrumental text

- Home-grown terminology (shorthand terminology used during system development that carries over into the released system) that fosters ambiguities

Users' susceptibility to these ambiguities is increased by the impoverished rhetorical context of the computer screen. The fact that they can see only the "slice" of their interaction with the computer represented by what is on the screen at the moment they encounter an ambiguity may both increase the likelihood that they will perceive the ambiguity and reduce the likelihood that they will be able to resolve it with only an instant's reflection.

When users have to spend any substantial time sharing attention between the task and the rhetorical analysis required to resolve ambiguities in the text that supports the task, their performance can suffer in *both* areas. This susceptibility to the perception of possible ambiguity, and the resulting damage to the quality of performance, is especially evident with two types of user: the naive or beginning user and the frustrated, distracted user. Thus the two kinds of user who are already most likely to have trouble understanding or remembering how to use the system are the ones who are most undermined by the effects of ambiguity.

The four most common sources of ambiguity listed above -- stylistic strategies that are frequently used to compress on-line text, tangles of instrumental text structures and commentary text structures, weak formatting, and home-grown terminology -- frequently occur together, but for the sake of simplicity they be discussed separately below.

Stylistic Strategies Used to Compress Text

The writer of on-line text tries very hard to save space on-screen by compressing the text that must be displayed. This effort frequently results in a style that is to one degree or another "telegraphic" -- that compresses or omits one or more of the parts of a fully formed, fully punctuated English sentence. Such a style relies on the use of one or more of the following stylistic possibilities: sentence fragments, open punctuation style, suppression of subordinating conjunctions and other connectives, and the more extreme characteristics of telegraphic style: suppression of articles, suppression of parts of verbs, and long noun stacks.

Sentence Fragments. The use of sentence fragments does not in and of itself create ambiguities that produce Escher effects -- sentence fragments and phrases can be very useful in saving space in the constricted world of on-line text. For instance, in Help, phrases can appear in text tables where the user's goals appear in the left column and the actions that accomplish the goals appear in the right column ("To do x" on the left, "Choose this command" on the right). But writers must carefully avoid two possible problems with ambiguity in sentence fragments:

- Some fragments can be interpreted as either predicate phrases or imperative sentences, which can force the user to stop and analyze the likelihood that action is really being called for.

- If the first word of a phrase in a set of phrases is not grammatically parallel with the first words of the others, it can force the user to stop and analyze the lack of parallelism and its possible meaning.

Users who are reading on-line commentary are generally in the middle of a task that they have temporarily suspended in order to gather information; that is to say, they are poised ready to act. When they encounter a text string that has a verb in the first position, they are therefore predisposed to take it as an imperative. For this reason, they are particularly susceptible to misinterpreting sentence fragments that are verb phrases.

When users encounter several phrases presented as a set (items in a bulleted list, for instance), they assume that the phrases are interchangeable -- that is, they can interchangeably be plugged into a given slot in an explicit or assumed "frame" sentence. Thus users can achieve an efficiency in their processing of text, by re-using the parsing strategy that they worked out for the first item of the given type. If the first word of a phrase in a set of phrases is not grammatically parallel with the others, users cannot parse that phrase in the same way that they have the others; they have to stop and either resolve the syntactic block to doing so, or come up with a new parsing strategy that works for the odd item. The problem is particularly bad in English because so many of our words (more and more, in fact) can be used as either a noun or a verb ("drive," "input," and now even "edit").

The informative power of parallelism is great enough to have caused the authors of a well-known guideline to caution designers to use consistent grammatical structure. They argue that "consistent grammatical construction may help a user resolve an ambiguous message (e.g., 'Numeric entry') to understand whether it recommends an action ('You should enter a number') or indicates an error condition ('You entered a number when you shouldn't have')" (Smith and Mosier, p. 305).

They offer the following further example of the problem:

Example:

(Good)   (Bad)

Options: Options:
s = Select data   s = Select data
e = Erase display   e = Erasure function
w = Write file   w = Write file

In their comments following this example, they point out that "even minor inconsistencies can distract a user and delay comprehension as the user wonders momentarily whether some apparent difference represents a real difference." This momentary attention to the implications of the structure of the *text* is an Escher effect.

A further example illustrates the process by which users can be misled by their own parsing efficiencies to assign the part of speech of words earlier in a list to a word that breaks the pattern:

Example:

"Edit Folio" Tasks:

Add . . .
Alternate . . .
Create . . .
Format . . .
Title . . .

After realizing that "title" is not quite as likely as a verb, the user then may be uneasy enough to go back and look again at the other words in the list that suddenly do not seem so univocal: "format," probably, and possibly "alternate." The need to reexamine these textual issues is an Escher effect.

Open Punctuation Style. Open punctuation style allows the writer to leave out punctuation that is not absolutely required. In using an open punctuation style, a writer can leave out the comma that might appear after an opening phrase in a sentence ("For instance I will leave out the comma in this example"), but would include commas to separate all but the last two items in a series ("apples, oranges, lemons and pears").

The opposite of "open" punctuation is "closed" punctuation -- using a punctuation mark everywhere that the rules allow it. Writers of on-line text prefer open to closed punctuation for the obvious reason: punctuation marks are characters, so using an open punctuation style means using fewer characters, which means using less space on the screen. But open punctuation can lead to problems of interpretation for users.

Long unpunctuated phrases can exceed the short-term memory capacity of users (especially naive or frustrated users), and they can be hard to "chunk" into pieces of more manageable length. In both cases, users have to stop their routine processing of information and devote some attention to textual analysis.

Unpunctuated phrases can also lead to incorrect parsings: "At prompt key in value." These incorrect parsings also require users to divert their energies to textual analysis.

Suppression of Subordinating Conjunctions and Other Connectives. In informal writing and spoken language, we frequently suppress subordinating conjunctions and other connectives: "the movie I saw" (not "the movie *that* I saw"), "the course I want's Tuesday-Thursdays" (not "the course *that* I want *is taught on* Tuesdays *and* Thursdays").

Again, writers of on-line text use the suppression of subordinating conjunctions and other connectives because it saves them space. The problem is, however, that these connectives help reduce the possibility of ambiguity. Phrases that are not explicitly subordinated can be incorrectly parsed; main subjects and predicates can be confused with the subjects and predicates of subordinate clauses.

For instance, study this example: "In the dialog box options you choose values are decimal." There are three ways to set up an initial parsing strategy -- the first two of which fall apart as you progress through the sentence:

> In the dialog box, options you choose . . .
> In the dialog box options, you choose values . . .
> In the dialog box options you choose, . . .

The two false starts can be avoided by including the subordinating conjunction (and, while we are at it, opting for a closed-punctuation style): "In the dialog-box options *that* you choose, values are decimal."

More Extreme Characteristics of Telegraphic Style. Extreme telegraphic style omits all but the key words, mostly nouns and verbs, in a statement or phrase ("Empty trash." "File open."). On-line text often has these characteristics of extreme telegraphic style:

- Suppression of articles

- Suppression of verb parts

- Noun stacks

The words that get thrown out of a phrase or sentence first are the articles ("a," "an," and "the"); next to go are the copulatives and the forms of "to be" that occur in verb tenses. But because so many words in English can be either nouns or verbs ("drive"), or either adjectives or verbs ("rejected"), we rely on these "little words" to cue us as to the part of speech of a given occurrence of a word. Deleting these word in telegraphic style leads to excessive ambiguity.

Noun stacks are phrases created by juxtaposing nouns (or nouns plus adjectives) in a string without including any words that provide cues about the pattern of modification that exists between any adjacent pair of nouns or among all the pairs or sets of nouns in the stack ("operating system file specification rules"). They are frequently created by compressing a noun phrase that contains prepositional phrases ("rules for the specification of files that are requirements of the operating system").

Noun stacks of limited size are permitted in Standard English ("cough syrup," "book report"); again, they are widely used in on-line text because they save space. Noun stacks create ambiguity when users do not know enough about the subject under discussion to be able to see immediately what the pattern of modification is within the phrase.

People who use this kind of telegraphic style defend it on the grounds that readers want their information short and direct, so that they can read it as fast as possible. But this point of view ignores a basic characteristic of reading -- we don't read word by word, but phrase by phrase, and we use markers that we find in the phrase to reduce the number of possible interpretations that we must maintain in order to reach a successful interpretation of the phrase. Eliminating articles and other markers actually makes us read more slowly, because we have to keep up with more possibilities of meaning until we encounter a clue that enables us to choose the correct one. Once we hit upon the right reading, we frequently have to re-read in order to compose the whole piece of discourse into meaning -- another instance of an Escher effect.

Telegraphic style creates Escher effects both by virtue of its own characteristics and because of the characteristics of what it is being used to describe -- the compressed, elliptical linguistic structure of computer commands and terminology. That is, telegraphic style frequently is used in descriptions of commands or command strings that themselves are sentence fragments written in telegraphic style. This phenomenon creates *tangles*, described below.

Tangles

Tangles of <u>commentary</u> text structures and <u>instrumental</u> text structures usually result from telegraphic style being used at two levels in the on-line text:

- The on-line <u>commentary</u> relies on telegraphic style.

- What is being described in the telegraphic phrases of the commentary -- that is to say, the <u>"instrumental" text</u> that provides instructions to a computer -- itself usually is a telegraphic text, with its own syntax.

Telegraphic style in on-line commentary, discussed above, is generally a stylistic choice that has been made in preparing text that is added to a system at a fairly late stage in its development; it is a characteristic that can be fairly readily changed if the people on the design project are moved to do so. Telegraphic style in the instrumental text of the system, however, is a phenomenon that occurs at a much deeper level in the system.

Command verbs, with arguments and qualifiers, amount to telegraphically presented imperative sentences, or even larger blocks of discourse (for instance, a complex command string might amount to an imperative "paragraph"). The "pieces" of this discourse are assembled as you build the command, either by typing it or by progressively making menu or option selections. Selections from menus and submenus, or from menus and dialog boxes, work the same way linguistically. Naturally, the assembled pieces are not supplemented by articles, copulatives, or other "small" words -- that is, they are in telegraphic style.

These instrumental sentence strings or larger units of discourse are also frequently syntactically different from Standard English. The structure of progressive disclosure (commands that lead to prompts for further input, or menus that progressively lead to sub-menus and sub-sub-menus), for instance, frequently forces us into a reversal of our usual syntactic patterns: instead of "save file" (Verb-Object order, the natural order of English), we select "file save" (Object-Verb order). The progress from menu-pick to dialog box can build similar "non-English" structures.

Furthermore, syntactic structures are often inconsistently implemented across the set of choices. For instance, on the main menu bar of a popular word processing program, the choices are "File, Edit, Search, Character, Paragraph, Document." These words are all labels for sets of actions in broad areas of functionality, under which one can select among related actions; in that sense, they are consistent. But two of them are verbs ("edit, search") and the rest are nouns (even though two of them can be used as verbs -- "file" and, these days, "document").

To complicate matters further, the choices subsumed under a given "heading" (menu title) do not always have a parallel relationship with the heading. For instance, under "edit," one encounters the choices "paste" and "undo typing." In trying to build the discourse structure for this area of functionality, then, users end up with "edit paste" and "edit undo typing." Thus the instrumental text, in addition to being telegraphic, is also inconsistent syntactically.

When this profusion of syntactic possibilities, rendered (by virtue of the structure of issuing commands) in telegraphic style, is then described in a commentary that is itself written in telegraphic style, it is not surprising that the two get tangled up. What is more, untangling the two can be complicated by the fact that the composite text is displayed on a computer screen, which means that the formatting tricks used to set off the text of the command from the descriptive phrase about it are not as simple and well-understood as the formatting tricks we use on the printed page. (On-line formatting problems are discussed below.)

Weak On-Line Formatting

When references to commands and other instrumental text are not formatted strongly enough in the on-line commentary to set them off from the phrase or sentence in which they occur, their syntax gets tangled up with the syntax of the sentence as a whole, which leads to another instance of Escher effects.

The following examples are modeled on text like the text that appears in the Help commentary provided for several popular Apple Macintosh applications. These text strings have no formatting attributes at all. For most readers of Help commentary, it would be very difficult to tell where the instrumental text -- the command -- ends and the commentary begins. To decide what is command and what is commentary, users would have to either do some research -- leave Help and go back to the program to check -- or would have to do a rhetorical analysis. In either case, the ambiguities of the text would have caused Escher effects -- requirements that the on-line information be studied first as a text.

        Examples:

        Phrase:
        macro assign to key

        Possible Meanings:
        "macro assign to" key OR "macro assign to key"?

        Phrase:
        from left indents paragraph

        Possible Meanings:
        "'from left' indents paragraph" OR "'from left indents' paragraph"?

        Phrase:
        move to the appropriate distance to edge

        Possible Meanings:
        "move to the appropriate 'distance to edge'" OR "move to the appropriate distance to edge"?

Writers of commentary on this kind of instrumental text face some difficulties in trying to devise formatting rules that work well on-screen, take up the minimum of space, and at the same time provide the user with sufficiently strong cues to parse the text correctly at first reading.

They want to avoid formatting cues that are characters (like quotation marks) to save space. Some formatting devices to set special usages apart from the syntax of the frame sentence don't work well on the screen (italics is hard to read; high-intensity is subject to the user's settings). Initial capital letters alone can be used to mark off the instrumental terms; however, when this technique is used, small words in command strings (like "to") are frequently not capitalized, apparently in a misplaced application of the rules of capitalization that apply to titles. Thus the technique as used is frequently not successful at marking off the boundaries of the command.

The most successful solutions to the formatting problem use multiple cueing (for instance, the use of initial capitals, quotation marks, and high intensity).

Home-Grown Terminology

Home-grown terminology is a kind of shorthand that embeds command and menu-pick terms in longer phrases. It evolves during the development of a product as the people involved in design or documentation find ways to talk efficiently about the product and its features; it therefore often reflects the product conceptualizations of the designers, sets up contrasts between one function and a second one that did not survive the design triage, etc. On its own terms, home-grown terminology is useful and interesting; it becomes a problem only when it is inappropriately shared with users by being incorporated into the text of the released system.

This kind of terminology gets incorporated into the system partly because the developers have become so familiar with it that they can no longer see the ambiguities in the sentences in which it is used. A person new to the system, however, can be seriously misled by it:

> Example of home-grown terminology:
>
> Phrase: "record ____ to a macro"
>
> Sentence: "You can record editing changes to a macro."
>
> Ambiguity: what is being edited? -- at first reading, it appears to be the macro, but in fact it is editing changes that have been made in some other piece of text that are being "recorded to a macro."

Complex Escher Effects

So far, we have looked at the sources of simple Escher effects -- demands made by ambiguities in on-line text that the text be studied, at least momentarily, as *text* rather than as information. Simple Escher effects are generally limited in impact; they force us to decompose and analyze a particular phrase or a particular sentence, but do not undermine our sense of larger informational chunks.

Complex Escher effects, on the other hand, interfere with our ability to perform higher-order interpretive activities: they prevent our building a sense of the rules of the rhetorical world we are working in, and they prevent us from trusting our ability to build a mental model of the system (Grice).

In an Escher drawing, what is of interest? Escher's drawings break the rules governing the relationships between objects rendered on the same field. If you see a white goose it is flying down, but if you see a black goose it is flying up. Or, you can see the staircase curve toward you as it descends -- or you can see it curve away from you as it ascends. But you cannot see both at once -- even though they are drawn as if they occupy the same space at the same time. Thus, in looking at an Escher drawing, we are led by these visual tricks to think about the rules that govern artifice; we look at our own process of perceiving, rather than at the object being perceived. Because the picture breaks the rules, it cannot function for us *as* a picture.

Complex Escher effects in computer systems break similar sets of rules -- rhetorical rules and cognitive rules. These rules govern the relationships of *ideas* presented on the same "field" -- the same topical space, the same logical framework. Thus they disrupt our ability to build a rhetorical contract with the writer of the text, and to build a mental model of the system being described.

Building a Rhetorical Contract

Computer systems are rhetorical entities; their design results from strategies that are intended to communicate information to the user that the user can rely on and use. The communicative aspects of a computer system (the human-computer interface, including all text presented to the user) therefore ought to follow the ordinary rules of rhetoric.

When the on-line instrumental text and commentary that we find in a computer system presents information to us, we get a sense of who the writer of that text believes the reader is. We can then, to the best of our abilities, take on the role of the reader that the writer has defined for us. This is the essence of the rhetorical contract between the writer and the reader. We have expectations about the way that the writer can reasonably treat us within the confines of the roles that we are playing, and we have a sense of the ways that those roles can evolve logically over the life of our use of the system (Coney).

As we alternate, in using the computer, between reading text and doing tasks, we come to rely on the stability of our relationship with the writer; we don't think about it as a part of the interaction in need of attention. Even when we encounter a simple Escher effect in the text, our attention is only momentarily focused on the potential precariousness of our relationship with the writer. But when we encounter a complex Escher effect, our full attention is required, and the problem does not have to do with understanding information so much as it is explicitly that of our relationship to the writer.

The effect is rather like that of a play in which actors suddenly rise up from audience; the sense of artifice and questions about the appropriateness of the apparatus and mechanics of the artifice intrude on the transaction.

For example, in using the Apple Macintosh, one can develop a sense of the writer of the instrumental text -- a young, unpretentious, no-nonsense sort of person who understands the reader and the reader's needs and isn't going to bully or betray the reader. The instrumental text, for instance, uses words like "goodies" and continually waits for the reader to say "okay." Then the user loses a file that may represent hours of work, and the instrumental text breezily presents a message that a "system bomb" has occurred -- and forces the reader to say "okay!" The psychopathic imperturbability of the writer in this exchange can effect a permanent unwillingness on the reader's part to trust the rhetorical stance that the whole tone of the system text is built on.

The fragility of the rhetorical contract is also threatened by the complexity of the activities that make up on-line reading (a massive parallel-processing activity). We have to control and manipulate the following systems:

- Orthographics, executed in points of light

- Vocabulary and its recognition

- Syntax and semantics of word strings

- Discourse structures

At any point, problems in one of these systems can break into our consciousness and demand our attention. If problems occur in two or more systems at once, the disruption is of course greater. Or if the medium is unfamiliar (with naive users, for instance), any anomalies at all can make the cognitive work underlying computer use the focus of primary attention. When the reader's attention is diverted in this way, the reader can lose the information structure he or she has been building, and perhaps even the task structure itself.

Building Mental Models

Text that is displayed on the computer screen is part of the software that it is describing, and can thus be said to be explaining itself. It succeeds best when it supports the user in building an accurate mental model of the software.

Mental models of computer systems are constructs that users build in their own heads. Part of the material that they can use to build their mental model is the conceptual model, to the extent that the users perceive it, that the designers of the system devised. This conceptual model of the system is the *designers'* idea of the system. Ideally, the on-line information should give users a conceptual model of the system as robust as possible to aid them in building and using a reasonable mental model.

In a series of studies reported by Kieras and Bovair, the experimental groups that learned from a model learned procedures faster, retained them more accurately, executed them faster, and simplified inefficient procedures far more often. They could infer the procedures much more easily, which would lead to more rapid learning and better recall performance (Kieras and Bovair, p. 255).

Users create mental models of a system from their perception of what happens in direct use of the system, or from whatever presentation of system concepts is made available to them by the designers, or from both. But the process of creating mental models is not tidy, and it is not a discrete preliminary stage in system use; it is ongoing and dynamic across the life of the user's experience with the system. In fact, the model itself can be imprecise, messy, superstitious, and even inaccurate. In addition, a human mind maintains a complex interpenetrating tangle of models that are constantly in a state of being refined, revised, tested, or otherwise manipulated (Norman, p. 8).

It is in light of this complexity of model-using and model-revising that complex Escher effects can be seen to undermine the development of a robust mental model of a given computer system.

When faced with a complex Escher effect in a computer system, you can believe one idea, or you can believe the other idea, but you cannot believe both, because each contains a rule that negates the existence of the other. For instance, you can believe that a shape in a computer graphics package is an "object," or you can believe that it is a "bitmap," but you cannot believe both, because objects and bitmaps are mutually exclusive. Nevertheless, some graphics programs allow you to use what is apparently the identical icon -- say, a "triangle" -- to create a shape that is in one case an object (because it can be moved) and in another case a bitmap (because only its composite dots can be moved).

When we encounter these kinds of ambiguities in the concepts of a computer system, the resulting Escher effect leads us to wrestle with the incongruity itself rather than with the operation of the system. We discover our own process of relying on following rules; we devote our energy to figuring out how our rules have been broken, rather than developing a mental model that we trust of the system. While we are engaged in this activity, we suspend our use of the computer.

An even more complex kind of Escher effect results from instances where the computer system apparently turns back on itself -- where the software apparently violates its own rules of what level governs what. Hofstadter in *Gödel, Escher, Bach* explains that in any system there is always some protected level which is unassailable by the rules on other levels, no matter how tangled their interaction may be among themselves. A "tangled hierarchy" or "strange loop" occurs when what you presume are clean hierarchical levels take you by surprise and fold back in a hierarchy-violating way. In this situation, the inviolate level that contains the rules for doing or interpreting things is mixed up with the acts or things being interpreted (Hofstadter, pp. 688-691).

To illustrate an apparent "strange loop" in a computer system that may interfere with the user's ability to form a clear-cut mental model of system use, let me use another example, brought to my attention by a colleague, that occurs in using Microsoft Windows, the operating environment for IBM PCs that runs on top of MS-DOS (Haselkorn). In using the Microsoft Windows environment, the key concept is the window; when you want to use an application, you "open" it, and it opens in a window; then when you close the window, you in effect close the application that was running in it.

When you are running the Windows environment, you may find that you want to use MS-DOS. To do so, you follow the rules of Windows -- you open a window to run MS-DOS. When you are through using DOS, you may reason that you "close" it by closing the window in which it is running. You cannot do so. Before you can close the window that DOS is running in, you must "exit" DOS by typing a command at the system prompt. You may then close the window that it was running in.

This transaction is a strange loop from the user's point of view for several reasons. It confuses the perceived hierarchy of DOS and Windows; Windows runs on top of DOS, but rather than quitting Windows to use DOS, you can "summon" DOS from within Windows (who is the master and who the slave?). Then, once you have subordinated DOS to Windows by starting it within a window, you find that the DOS rules do in fact have precedence; you cannot use the Windows rule in what seems like the normal way to "close" DOS.

How to Prevent Escher Effects in On-Line Text

To prevent Escher effects in on-line text, it is important to look closely for the characteristic sources of these effects outlined in this paper. You can take steps during both the design phase and the evaluation phase of a product to avoid creating Escher effects.

In the design phase, follow guidelines for avoiding the obvious pitfalls:

- Be careful to avoid the excesses of telegraphic style in trying to compress on-line text.

- Be watchful for possible tangles of instrumental text structures with commentary text structures.

- Formulate and follow effective formatting rules for all on-line text.

- Weed out home-grown terminology that users will not understand.

In the evaluation phase, recognize that, since Escher effects are caused by the perception of ambiguity, and since people who are familiar with text are no longer sensitive to its possibilities for ambiguity, you will need to get outside responses to your text. Ideally, you will get such outside evaluation from both expert evaluators (through editing) and typical users (through usability testing):

- Use the services of a senior editor trained to find subtle problems with text.

- Do usability testing with typical users as subjects.

References

Coney, Mary. Personal communication, 9/88.

Farkas, David. Personal communication, 8/88.

Grice, Roger. I am grateful to Roger Grice for suggesting that my original idea could be extended by using Hofstadter's idea of the "strange loop." The faults of the actual extension of the idea are unfortunately mine. Personal communication, 5/88.

Haselkorn, Mark, personal communication, 10/88.

Hofstadter, Douglas R., *Gödel, Escher, Bach: an Eternal Golden Braid*, Basic Books, Inc., 1979.

Kieras, David E. and Susan Bovair, "The Role of a Mental Model in Learning to Operate a Device," *Cognitive Science* 8, 255-273, 1984.

Norman, Donald A., "Some Observations on Mental Models," in D. Gentner and A. Stevens (eds.), *Mental Models*, Hillsdate, NJ: Erlbaum Associates, 1983.

Smith, Sidney L. and Jane N. Mosier, *Guidelines for Designing User Interface Software*, MITRE Report Number MTR 10090 ESD-TR-86-278, MITRE Corporation, August 1986.

Using "Word-Knowledge" Reasoning for Question Answering

Jill Gaulding
Department of Linguistics
Massachusetts Institute of Technology
Cambridge, MA 02139

Boris Katz
Artificial Intelligence Laboratory
Massachusetts Institute of Technology
Cambridge, MA 02139

What skills does a natural language system need in order to answer questions? At a minimum, it must be able to retrieve information that has been given explicitly. It should also be able to employ some sort of reasoning if explicit information is not available. One form of reasoning relies on information about the world. "World-knowledge" reasoning would allow the system to respond "yes" to the question "Is Tom in Europe?" if it were previously told "Tom is in Paris." Another form of reasoning relies on knowledge about words. "Word-knowledge" reasoning would allow the system to respond "yes" to the question "Could Tom have been in Paris?" if it were previously told "Tom was in Paris." This paper presents a model for a certain type of word-knowledge reasoning which uses information about tense, aspect, modals, negation, and embedding, in order to answer questions accurately and informatively. The model is implemented as part of a larger question-answering system, the START natural language processor, at the MIT Artificial Intelligence Laboratory.

1. Introduction

Computers would become better information-processing systems if they could communicate with us using a natural (human) language. This, of course, is an ambitious goal. Using a natural language requires more than the ability to input and output strings of words. In order to store and retrieve data efficiently, a natural language processing (NLP) system needs to be able to map expressions in a given language onto a representation that captures important elements of language structure. In particular, we believe that NLP systems need to understand the *syntax* of language.

An NLP system with the ability to understand syntax would be quite useful. Suppose, for instance, that such a system had access to the entire text of a history book. It would be able to answer questions such as "Who invented bifocals?"

or "When did Robert E. Lee die?" very quickly, provided that these pieces of information were explicitly contained in the input text. We could imagine many applications for such a system.

We might demand even more of a natural language processing system: we would like it to be able to respond to questions for which the answer is not literally recorded within the database. To operate at this level of sophistication, a system would need to do more than map expressions onto structured internal representations. It would also need the ability to compute over these representations, in order to infer an answer when the requested information has not been explicitly given.

A simple example will make this clear. Suppose there were an NLP system which kept track of various people, their vehicles, destinations, *etc.* A user might ask of the system, "Is Tom driving his car?" If the database did not contain a representation of the exact information, "Tom is driving his car," the system could attempt to infer an answer from other relevant information to which it did have access. This reasoning could take several different forms.

One type of reasoning it could use relies on world knowledge. The system might know, say, that Tom's car engine exploded. It could then derive a response to the question by a series of inferences about driving, cars, engines, and explosions. For example, if Tom is driving his car, then the engine must be operable, but if the engine exploded, it is not operable, and therefore Tom must not be driving his car. The domain of relevant knowledge and the domain of possible inferences are each quite large, if not unbounded, for this type of "world-knowledge" reasoning. As a result, world-knowledge reasoning is extremely powerful. Unfortunately, it is also correspondingly difficult to model on a computer system.

Another type of reasoning a system might use has a more limited domain. Consider the following pairs of statements and questions:

(1) Sue will be hitting Billy.
     Has she been hitting him?

(2) Sue was hitting Billy.
     Has she been hitting him?

(3) Tom should speak French.
     Does he speak French?

(4) Tom cannot speak French.
     Does he speak French?

(5) Ann suspects that Ed cheats.
     Does he cheat?

(6) Ann regrets that Ed cheats.

      Does he cheat?

Now assume that the first sentence in each pair provides the only information available, and attempt to answer each question. For pairs (1), (3), and (5), no definitive answer could be given. The other three pairs, on the other hand, would most likely produce a "yes" answer (for (2) and (6)) and a "no" answer (for (4)). What sort of reasoning allows these responses to be derived? The answers seem to rely on facts about the *words*, rather than facts about the *world*. Tense, aspect, modals, negation, and embedding each contribute to the calculation. We term reasoning of this sort "word-knowledge" reasoning.

Both of these types of reasoning would play a vital role in a complete question-answering system. This paper discusses a system which concentrates on the role of word-knowledge reasoning. In particular, it describes the TEAM model (for *t*ense, *e*mbedding, *a*spect and *m*odals) which uses information from individual sentences to produce accurate, humanlike responses in question situations like (1)–(6). TEAM is implemented as part of a larger question-answering system, the START natural language processor, at the MIT Artificial Intelligence Laboratory. After a brief overview of the START system, a description of TEAM follows, including examples of its performance and some suggestions for possible extensions.

2. An Overview of the START system

The START natural language system (SynTactic Analysis using Reversible Transformations) consists of two modules which share the same grammar (see Katz [1980, 1988], Katz and Winston [1982]). The *understanding* module analyzes English text and stores the information contained within it in a knowledge base. Given an appropriate segment of the knowledge base, the *generating* module produces English sentences. A user can retrieve the information stored in the knowledge base by querying it in English; the system will then produce an English response.

START has been used for constructing and querying knowledge bases in English by researchers at MIT, Stanford University, and the Jet Propulsion Laboratory (see, for example, Winston [1982], [1984], Winston, Binford, Katz, and Lowry [1983], Doyle [1984], Katz and Brooks [1987], McLaughlin [1987; 1988]).

When reading text, START has to *index* new knowledge in its memory. When answering questions, START has to *retrieve* knowledge. Section 2.1 describes the indexing procedure of START. The retrieval task is carried out by a matching procedure described in section 2.2.

2.1. Indexing Knowledge

Suppose we type the following English sentence on a computer terminal:

(7) Jane will meet Paul tomorrow.

Now, there are many things about this sentence that the computer should remember: that *Jane* is the subject of the sentence, *Paul* is the object, that *meet* is the relation between them. There is more to remember: the tense and the aspect of the sentence, its auxiliaries, its adverbs. Was this sentence embedded in a larger sentence? Does it have a relative clause? Was the verb in the active or passive form? All this information about the sentence should be stored in the computer's memory. However, there must also be a way to retrieve this information efficiently.

All these sentence features could be stored in one long list. This approach, however, would not account for the fact that some of the features in a sentence seem more salient than others, and would also fail to capture the structural affinity between sentence (7) and the following two sentences:

(8) Yesterday Jane could have met Paul.

(9) Paul wasn't met by Jane.

Finally, this approach would turn the matching/retrieval task into a computational nightmare.

Alternatively, the representation could emphasize the hierarchical nature of sentences by using parse trees for storage in the knowledge base. However, the complexity of full parse trees would still present computational problems for the matching task.

START's representation provides a balance between these two alternatives. It rearranges the parse tree elements by tying together the three most salient parameters of a sentence: the subject, the object, and the relation between them. These are combined into *ternary expressions (T-expressions)* of the form **<subject relation object>**. All three sentences (7, 8, 9) will yield the same T-expression

(10) **<Jane meet Paul>**

The T-expression representation is recursive. In order to handle embedded sentences, START allows any T-expression to take another T-expression as its subject or object. It can therefore analyze and generate sentences with arbitrarily complex embedded structures. Certain other parameters such as prepositions can also serve as relations in T-expressions.

The remaining parameters (embedding, adverbs and their position, tense, auxiliaries, voice, negation, *etc.*) are recorded in a representational structure called a *history*. The history has a *page* pertaining to each sentence which yields the given T-expression. When we index the T-expression in the knowledge base, we cross-reference its three components and attach the history H to it: **<subject relation**

object$>_H$. For example, a text containing "Miriam might have eaten the donut" and later "Gabriella thought Miriam should eat the donut" would produce the T-expression <**Miriam eat donut**$>_H$, with a two-page history. One page would contain additional information about the first sentence, such as the fact that it used perfective "have" and the modal "might". The second page would show the use of the modal "should" and contain a tie to the embedding T-expression <**Gabriella think** <**Miriam eat donut**$>>_H$. One can thus think of a T-expression as a "digested summary" of the use of a proposition within a text.

The T-expression is the cornerstone of the representational hierarchy of the START system. It is the level of the hierarchy where the understanding and the generating modules meet. The understanding module analyzes English sentences and creates a set of T-expressions. The generating module, in turn, retrieves these T-expressions from the knowledge base and produces English text.

2.2 Retrieving Knowledge

In this section we will concentrate on the task of finding the appropriate T-expressions to answer a question. Suppose the system has analyzed and indexed a text containing the sentence

(11) Jessica wanted the computer to print the message.

The knowledge base now contains the following T-expression:

(12) <**Jessica want** <**computer print message**>>

Suppose now that a user asks:

(13) What did Jessica want the computer to print?

The first step in answering this question is to reverse the effect of the *wh*-movement transformation that is used to create English *wh*-questions. In order to accomplish this, START must find the place in sentence (13) that the *wh*-word *what* came from and then insert the *wh*-word in this position:

(14) Jessica wanted [the computer to print *what*]

Next the language understanding system leads sentence (14) through the same flow of control as any declarative sentence and produces the following T-expression, which serves as a pattern used to query the knowledge base:

(15) <**Jessica want** <**computer print** *what*>>

Treating *what* as a variable, START must determine whether there is anything in the knowledge base that matches T-expression (15). The "matcher" finds the T-expression:

(12) <**Jessica want** <**computer print message**>>

The language generation system could then take this T-expression with its associated history and produce the English response to question (13):

(16) Jessica wanted the computer to print the message.

START treats other types of English questions, including *yes/no*-questions, *when*-questions, *where*-questions, *why*-questions, *etc.* in a similar fashion.

As described the matching task is fairly straightforward. However, in many situations more complex reasoning is required. Consider the following pairs of sentences and their corresponding T-expressions:

(17) Miriam presented Gabriella with a gift.

(18) <<**Miriam present Gabriella> with gift>**

(19) Miriam presented a gift to Gabriella.

(20) <<**Miriam present gift> to Gabriella>**

Speakers of English know that sentences (17) and (19) both describe a transfer of possession: *the gift* is the transferred object and *Gabriella* is the recipient of this object in both sentences despite different syntactic realizations of these arguments. The START system handles these syntactic-semantic correspondences (often termed *lexical alternations*) by defining a set of rules (S-rules) which capture the properties of alternating verb classes in English.

S-rules are implemented as a rule-based system which can operate in both forward and backward modes. When the user queries the knowledge base, the backward mode is employed. Each S-rule is made up of three parts, an antecedent (the IF-clause), a consequent (the THEN-clause), and an optional restriction (the PROVIDED clause). Each of the first two clauses consists of a set of templates for T-expressions, where the template elements are filled by variables or constants. The PROVIDED clause can be used to specify the class of verbs to which the rule applies. For example, here is the rule for the class of verbs which pattern like *present*:

If   <<subject verb object1> **with** object2>
Then   <<subject verb object2> **to** object1>
Provided   verb ∈ *present* class

This rule would allow the system to answer the following question after being told (17):

(21) To whom did Miriam present a gift?

Using S-rules to capture syntactic-semantic correspondences for verb classes is one form of word-knowledge reasoning. S-rules could also provide the START system with a mechanism for world-knowledge reasoning, but this function will not be considered here. S-rules are described more thoroughly in Katz [1988] and Katz and Levin [1988]; see also Levin [1985, 1989], Hale and Keyser [1986], Atkins,

Kegl, and Levin [1986], and others for a more detailed discussion of the linguistic regularities S-rules are used to represent.

3. The TEAM System

Combined with the indexing and generating capabilities of START, and the reasoning capabilities of S-rules, the matcher described in section 2.2 could provide a rudimentary question-answering function. However, the performance of such a system would not be very satisfactory. Suppose it were asked "Did John want the computer to print a message?" and the matcher found in the knowledge base the T-expression <**John want <computer print message>>**. Should the system then respond "yes"? It could easily be in error by doing so. This T-expression could simultaneously represent (via its history) a number of different propositions: "John might have wanted the computer to print the message", or "John will want the computer to print the message", or even "John did not want the computer to print the message." Clearly, it is not enough to find the appropriate T-expression; some further reasoning is required in order to determine the proper response.

One way of thinking about the problem is to divide the question-answering task into two parts: (1) finding relevant information within the knowledge base, and (2) determining the implications of this information. Finding relevant information in this case means retrieving the appropriate T-expression, either through matching alone or with the help of S-rules. The TEAM model is designed to perform the second subtask. Given a question and a matching T-expression, it must use the information contained in the history to calculate the most accurate, helpful response possible.

Because context is not considered, this involves comparing each of the statements represented by a page in the history, to the question. Recall that when START analyzes a question, it reverses the effect of the movement transformation that is used to create English questions and converts it into T-expression form, like any other sentence. We will call the question in the assertional form the *Q-assertion*, so that "John will read" is the Q-assertion for the question "Will John read?" The task for the TEAM system is then to determine whether the known statements (individually) imply the Q-assertion.

The information from histories that TEAM must use to calculate the implications falls roughly into three categories. Ties to embedded or embedding T-expressions give the proposition's *intrasentential context*. Tense and aspect place the proposition in a certain *time frame*. Modals, including negation as a special instance, show the *mood* of the proposition.

TEAM essentially consists of an ordered set of filters, one for each type of information. A statement may receive one of three labels, YES, NO, or UNKNOWN, as it passes through the filter set. The UNKNOWN label is further broken down to show which filter assigned it, so that this information can be used in responding to the question in the most helpful way.

The embedding filter must be considered first. We would like the system to know, for instance, that "Ann regrets that Ed cheats" implies that Ed cheats, while "Ann suspects that Ed cheats" does not. This, unfortunately, is an ambitious goal. There are many complexities involved in determining whether an embedded clause can be assumed true. In order to avoid inaccurate responses, the TEAM system currently assumes the worst: if a proposition is embedded, it receives the label UNKNOWN*(embedding)*, and no further reasoning is performed upon it. Section 7 discusses how the notion of *factivity* introduced by Kiparsky and Kiparsky [1971] may help to find a better solution to this problem.

If a statement is not labeled UNKNOWN by the embedding filter, it is passed to the tense-aspect filter. This determines whether the time frame referred to by the statement matches that given by the question. If they do not match, the statement is labeled UNKNOWN*(time)*. For example, in attempting to answer the question "Has Sue been kissing Billy," this filter would label the statement "Sue will be kissing Billy" UNKNOWN*(time)*. On the other hand, the statement "Sue was kissing Billy" would pass through the time-aspect filter, to be considered by the modal filter. The modal filter compares the modals (including negation) used in the statement and the question. Each combination results in one of the three labels YES, NO, or UNKNOWN*(modals)*.

The following two sections discuss the operation of the tense-aspect and modal filters in more detail.

4. The Tense-Aspect Filter

Determining which time frame a sentence refers to is very straightforward in this system, especially since the temporal references made by adverbs and prepositional phrases (such as "yesterday", or "at 7 pm") are not factored into the time reference of the sentence as a whole. The basic assumption made is that there is a universal time line, and that the position of an event or state referred to by a sentence along this time line is a function of the tense of the sentence. The time line is roughly divided into three parts: past, present, and future. The tense of a sentence places it in some interval (not a point) along this line, in relation to these basic divisions.

The interval could be very narrow, as in "John blinked", or very large, as in "The universe will exist".

The three basic tenses are formed either by the tense of the main verb, for past and present, or by the addition of the modals "will" or "shall", for the future tense. The presence of the perfective "have" additionally constrains the interval referred to. Following Reichenbach [1947], we assume that it introduces a "reference event" at the boundary of the interval defined by the main tense. The new interval referred to covers (some of) the time up to that reference event. Progressive "be", when added to any of these tenses, narrows the given interval by some amount. For the purposes of this model, the progressive form is not labeled separately, in most cases, because it is not usually relevant to the implications being calculated. For example, the interval for the past progressive is contained within that of the simple past, and so the sentence "John slept" implies "John was sleeping" and vice versa. Due to the possibility of a "habitual" reading, the present progressive is an exception: "John reads books" does not necessarily imply "John is reading books," and so it is considered separately.

Sentences which contain a modal (other than "will" or "shall", which form the future tense) are also treated separately. The modal system is a very complex one. Although some of the modals look as if they have a past and present form, this is not really the case. "Might" is not the past of "may", "should" is not the past of "shall" and so on. "Could" does function as the past of "can", but it also has other meanings. For this reason, sentences with a modal are labeled with the tense "modal", which is assumed to be able to relate to any interval along the time line. The important thing to consider about sentences with a modal is what meaning the modal contributes, and this is done later on. However, the addition of the perfective or progressive tense does constrain the interval referred to. Any combination of a modal and "be" (termed "modal progressive") defines the same interval as the present progressive. Any combination of a modal and "have" (termed "modal perfect") defines an interval in the past.

The system first assigns the proper tense to each sentence, including the question, based on the presence of a modal, perfective "have", progressive "be", and/or the tense of the main verb. Now, since the task is to determine whether each sentence implies the truth of the Q-assertion, the system must determine whether the interval referred to by the sentence overlaps with that referred to by the question. This is simple, given the definition of each of the tenses. The only important thing to note is that the reference point introduced by the perfective is fixed only within a sentence, and can shift between two sentences. For example, the sentence "John will love Mary" implies "John will have loved Mary", since the reference point introduced by the second sentence can be placed so that the second interval overlaps the first. The addition of contextual information, temporal adverbs or temporal prepositions would of course provide stricter bounds. Sentences which refer to an irrelevant (i.e., non-overlapping) time interval are labeled UNKNOWN*(time)*. Sentences which do refer to a relevant interval are then further examined for their modal meaning.

5. The Modal Filter

The part of the judgement based on the meaning contributed by the modals is a more complex one in this system. Each of the modals has a certain "sense" which operates on the meaning of the kernel sentence to produce an overall meaning. For the purposes of the modal filter, the modals "will" and "shall" are not considered to be "true" modals, since their meaning contributes only to the time referred to by the sentence. The sense of each remaining modal could be described as follows. The word "can" has the sense of "ability". It is sometimes also used as a synonym for "may", but this usage is not taken into consideration. The word "could" has several different senses. It can be used as the past form of "can". It also has other senses which are closer to the word "might": either "possibility of having the ability", or just "possibility". The word "may" has two distinct senses: one of "permission", and one of "possibility". "Might" is straightforward, having only the sense of "possibility". "Would" is more complicated. It has a sense of "(possibly thwarted) intention", so that given the sentence "John would read books" one might be left with the idea that there was some unstated reason why he doesn't. "Would" can also be used by the speaker to show his attitude toward a topic, as when he says "John would read books" to mean that he was expecting to find that that was the case (based on his knowledge of John). When meant this way, "would" is usually stressed. The word "should" contributes a sense of "moral obligation", or of the "appropriateness" of an action. Finally, the word "must" also has two senses. It can have the sense "legally required", as in "You must do this because I told you to do it". It can also be used to mean that the weight of evidence is for or against something, e.g. if the speaker sees John kissing Mary and then comments, "He must love her."

Given that there are several possible meanings for most of the modals, some method must be employed to choose among them. The particular meaning would usually be determined by contextual information. Since the assumption was made that the input statements are individual pieces of evidence, not parts of a connected text, that information can't be used by this system. Instead, empirical evidence was used to determine which meaning is preferred when the sentence is taken out of context.

Once the modal meaning of each statement is characterized, it can be used to determine whether each statement implies the Q-assertion. For example, would a statement containing the modal "might" imply a Q-assertion containing "should"? Or, in other words, if John might love Mary, does that imply that he should love her? The answer for this case is obviously no. Each of the possible combinations must be considered in this way. The results are given in Table 1.

Table 1: The Modal Filter

		sentence modal							
		none	can	could	may	might	would	should	must
question modal	none	Y/N	U	U	U	U	U	U	U
	can	Y/U	Y/N	U	U	Y/Y	U	U	U
	could	Y/U	U	Y/N	U	Y/Y	U	U	U
	may	U	U	U	Y/N	U	U	U	U
	might	Y/Y	Y/N	Y/N	Y/Y	Y/Y	Y/Y	Y/Y	Y/Y
	would	U	U	U	U	U	Y/N	U	U
	should	U	U	U	U	U	U	Y/N	U
	must	U	U	U	U	U	U	U	Y/N

key

Y/N (for *Yes-No*-questions) = *YES* if sentence is affirmative, *NO* if negative

Y/N (for *Wh*-questions) = *YES* (only sentence/question pairs with matching negation values are considered by TEAM)

Y/U = *YES* if sentence is affirmative, *UNKNOWN* if negative

Y/Y = *YES* either way   *U* = *UNKNOWN* either way

Each combination produces a judgement consisting of two parts: what answer is implied if the statement is affirmative, and what answer is implied if the statement is negative. Note that for *yes/no*-questions negation of the question doesn't affect the response. The system will reply "Yes - John is tall" whether asked "Is John tall?" or "Isn't John tall?" This is not true for *wh*-questions — the system would reply "John is tall" if asked "Who is tall?" but not if asked "Who is not tall?"

A discussion of some of the more interesting results follows. First, note that the majority of combinations produce the judgement UNKNOWN. This seems like an unfortunate feature at first, since a "yes/no" response is more satisfying than an "unknown" one. What it means, however, is that the modal meanings are fairly independent. Given the fact that the sentences are to be considered individually, out of context, these "unknown" judgements actually correspond to people's intuitions.

TEAM gives an accurate, informative response by generating statements that have been labeled UNKNOWN, with the disclaimer that they did not allow a definitive answer, and a brief description of the reason that they failed to do so.

It should also be noted that the preferred sense for a modal is not constant, but rather can change as a result of whether it is in a question or a statement, and also with each particular combination. For example, "may" is always assumed to have the "permission" sense when used in a question. This is probably because it is most often used in this way when in question form. When in statement form, the two senses weigh equally. "Could" when combined with "can" is always presumed to have the "past of 'can'" sense, so the combination of these two always results in the "unknown" judgement, since the sentences then refer to different time intervals. "Must" is always assumed to have a "legal obligation" sense, rather than a "weight of evidence suggests" sense. This doesn't necessarily mean that it is used in this way more often. More likely, this preference is a result of the fact that the first interpretation stands alone easily, while the second interpretation makes more sense when the sentence is in context. Another interesting point is that the various combinations are not necessarily reflexive: *might-could* does not equal *could-might*, for example.

As one would expect, the exact-match combinations (down the diagonal) always produce the judgement "yes/no", since for these combinations the proposition made by the Q-assertion is exactly that made by the input statement (with the possible addition of negation). The one exception is for "might". If the question is asked, "Might John love Mary?" the answer is "yes", given either the input sentence "John might love Mary" or "John might not love Mary." In other words, "might not" never precludes "might". "Might" is always assumed to be true, since anything is possible. The only exception occurs if one is told explicitly that something "cannot" or "could not" be the case: for the combinations *might-can* and *might-could*, the judgement is "yes/no", not "yes/yes".

Finally, many of the judgements seem to depend on the speaker's notion of the world. Take the *must-none* combination as an example. If John must love Mary, does that imply that he does? Assume that the "legally required" sense of "must" is the one meant. The intuition is that "John must love Mary" does not necessarily imply "John does love Mary." In other words, the speaker assumes that the freedom to disregard authority exists. The intuition for the *must-should* combination is that "must" does not necessarily imply "should". The "legal" authority of "must" is not the same as the "moral" authority or indicator of appropriateness suggested by "should". Another intuition is that "should" does not necessarily imply "can", i.e. some acts may be morally obligatory, or appropriate, yet not within one's ability.

6. Putting It All Together

At the end of the first stage of the reasoning process, each of the statements from the history has been labeled by one of the filters. Some further computation must occur for those statements which were labeled either YES or NO. If such a statement has internal embeddings, the reasoning process is repeated for each T-expression involved, producing a decision at each level of embedding. These decisions are then arbitrated in the following manner. If at any point the time frame referred to is inappropriate, or the modal combination is inconclusive, the entire statement is labeled UNKNOWN*(time)* or UNKNOWN*(modals)*. Otherwise the logical combination of affirmative and negative responses is calculated, and the overall statement is labeled with the result. For example, suppose the system had indexed the statement "John wishes that Mary had won a race" and were asked "Does John wish that Mary will win a race?" The outer clause would receive the label YES. The inner clause, though, would not pass the tense-aspect filter, and as a result the entire statement would be relabeled UNKNOWN*(time)*. This solution gives the correct label for many internal-embedding situations. However, it seems that the general case requires more complex reasoning. Section 7 describes the problems that arise and suggests possible approaches to them.

Once a final label has been calculated for each statement contained in the history, TEAM must decide upon the final response. The set of statements might have resulted in any combination of YES's, NO's, or UNKNOWN's. These must be arbitrated in some manner. TEAM assumes that definitive information outweighs uncertain information. Thus for *yes/no*-questions it uses the following strategy: if there were any number of UNKNOWN contributions, and some number of YES contributions, then the reply to the question is "yes", and similarly for "no". If there were both "yes" and "no" contributions, in addition to any number of "unknown"s, then the response is that there exists conflicting information. Finally, if all the contributions were "unknown", then that is the final response. Because the overall goal is to be as informative as possible, the response does not consist merely of a "yes", "no", or "unknown". All the statements contained in the matching T-expression are generated for the user, and the reasoning for the response is made clear.

The process for *wh*-questions is identical except for two details: there would never be statements leading to a "no" contribution (negative statements aren't selected by the matcher) and "yes" responses are merely generated in English. The final responses which TEAM produces are faithful to human intuition.

The following short dialogues show how the TEAM system functions within START. We assume that the sentences shown in each interchange represent the only relevant information available to the reasoning system. Inputs to START are given to the prompt "==)". Note that English responses generated by START may differ syntactically from the original text.

- These interactions demonstrate the embedding filter:

==⟩ John wanted Ann to arrest the spy.
==⟩ Was the spy arrested?
I don't know. However, I do have some information:
John wanted Ann to arrest the spy.
(*The proposition* 'Ann arrests the spy' *was embedded within this sentence.*)

This is an example of one-level embedding. The T-expression representation captures the fact that the proposition "Ann arrests the spy" is embedded within the larger sentence. The system responds correctly, because John's wanting Ann to do something is not an absolute guarantee that she will do it.

==⟩ Bill thought that Susan should convince Mary that Tom is in class.
==⟩ Where is Tom?
I don't know. However, I do have some information:
Bill thought that Susan should convince Mary that Tom is in the class.
(*The proposition* 'Tom is in the class' *was embedded within this sentence.*)

Here the requested information is embedded several levels deep. The TEAM system is unable to say where Tom actually is, but it does provide the user with the embedding sentence, since this sentence itself carries information relevant to the question asked.

==⟩ Was Mary convinced?
I don't know. However, I do have some information:
Bill thought that Susan should convince Mary that Tom is in the class.
(*The proposition* 'Susan convinces Mary' *was embedded within this sentence.*)

TEAM can match a centrally embedded sentence as well. Here the fact that Bill thought Susan should convince Mary is useful, but not conclusive, evidence that she was convinced.

==⟩ What did Bill think?
Bill thought that Susan should convince Mary that Tom is in the class.

Here at last the system can give a conclusive answer.

- The interactions below demonstrate the tense/aspect filter:

==⟩ John loved Mary.
==⟩ Does John love Mary?
I don't know. However, I do have some information:
John loved Mary.
(*This sentence did not refer to the time interval about which you asked.*)

The question "Does John love Mary" asks about John's current feelings, but TEAM only has information about his feelings in the past. The fact that he did love her is provided as possibly relevant information.

==⟩ Tom will have seen the test before the exam.
==⟩ Who will see the test?
Tom will have seen the test before the exam.

This is an example of a reference point shift. The statement and the question refer to overlapping intervals in the future.

- These interactions demonstrate the modal filter:

==⟩ Mary might draw the picture.
==⟩ What should Mary draw?
I don't know. However, I do have some information:
Mary might draw the picture.
(*This sentence did not allow a definitive answer*)

The sense of possibility invoked by "might" does not allow the system to conclude that Mary is under obligation to draw the picture. Therefore, it doesn't give a definitive answer.

==⟩ John knits sweaters.
==⟩ Who can knit sweaters?
John knits the sweaters.

TEAM assumes that the performance of an action implies the ability to perform the action.

==⟩ Ed cannot waltz.
==⟩ Might Ed waltz?
No, Ed can't waltz.

Most questions with "might" are answered affirmatively. This interchange demonstrates a situation in which it is answered negatively. The system would also reply negatively if it knew that Ed could not waltz.

- The following interactions show how TEAM handles different combinations of labels:

==⟩ Ann had been dancing.
==⟩ Ann cannot dance.
==⟩ Might she dance?
I don't know - you've given me conflicting information:
Ann had been dancing.
Ann can't dance.

Notice that the START system accepts seemingly contradictory information dutifully recording it in the history of the T-expression ⟨**Ann dance**⟩$_H$. Only after a question is asked does TEAM report that a conflict has been encountered and provides the user with relevant data.

==⟩ Ed expects to like rock music, but he does not like it now.
==⟩ Mom hopes Ed will not like it.
==⟩ Will Ed like rock music?
I don't know. However, I do have some information:
Ed expects to like rock music.
Mom hopes that Ed will not like rock music.
(*The proposition* 'Ed likes rock music' *was embedded within these sentences.*)
Ed doesn't like rock music now.
(*This sentence did not refer to the time interval about which you asked.*)

This interchange shows how in the question-answering process the TEAM system employs every piece of information relevant to the question and displays separately the reasons for its responses.

7. Possible Extensions

Although the system described seems to work well, its task domain is somewhat narrow. Extensions of the domain would make the system both more interesting and more useful. There are many possible ways of doing this. One way would be to use the information provided by temporal adjectives, prepositions and connectives to further restrict the time interval referred to by a sentence. With this type of information, it would be possible to calculate an appropriate response to the question "Will John ride horses next week?" given the statement "John will ride horses tomorrow." Harper and Charniak [1986] discuss a method of incorporating these additional sources of information into the time line representation. See also Allen [1981], Hinrichs [1988], and Moens and Steedman [1988] for additional approaches to representing and reasoning about temporal and aspectual knowledge.

Another limitation which could possibly be eliminated is the assumption that the statements are not part of a larger text. Contextual information would allow the exact determination of the meaning of the modal, and therefore a more sensitive judgement of implication. Of course, discovering the way in which this occurs would not be a trivial problem. On a simpler level, if the statements were considered to have been made in a certain order, then that information could be used to disambiguate the response given when there is conflicting information.

Allowing embedded sentences to contribute more than an "unknown" response to the reply would also expand the task domain. Here, however, the situation is quite complicated. If an embedded sentence is to be treated in the very same way as a normal one, then it must be presupposed to be true in the context of its embedding sentence. When is this the case? Kiparsky and Kiparsky [1971] proposed a distinction between "factive" and "nonfactive" predicates. Factive predicates such as "regret" presuppose the truth of their complement, and nonfactive ones such as "suspect" do not.

Such a distinction would seem to solve this difficulty, but unfortunately it is not so simple. There is no clear definition of just what constitutes a factive predicate. For instance, are "convince" or "force" instances of factive verbs? One would certainly be more likely to believe that Mary kissed Tom, if one were told "John forced Mary to kiss Tom" or "John convinced Mary to kiss Tom," and yet still be reluctant to assert that these verbs always presuppose the truth of their complement. Declaring "convince" to be a factive verb would definitely be problematic, because "John convinced Mary that Tom drives trucks" does not imply that Tom actually does (John could be trying to fool Mary). The syntactic form of the complement is therefore also a factor in the decision. Another factor would be negation. Assume that "force" is factive. Then should "John did not force Mary to kiss Tom" imply that Mary kissed Tom? Obviously not. Nor does it imply that Mary didn't kiss Tom; by the addition of negation the verb has lost any factive aspect. Yet for other factives such as "regret", negation has no effect.

If a class of verbs were determined to be factive (in some constructions), then TEAM could handle the embedded complements of these verbs in the same way as unembedded sentences. This would allow the system to answer questions quite cleverly. For example, suppose that the system was asked:

(22) Did George win the contest?

after being told that

(23) George regretted winning the contest.

Knowing (23) TEAM would respond "yes". On the other hand, TEAM's answer would be "no" if it knew that

(24) George fancied that he won the contest.

Some verbs are not factive, yet assign certain likelihood to their complements. It could also be argued that such verbs form a continuous spectrum, so that "believe" would be more factive than "suspect" which would be more factive than "wonder" and so on. Although this notion is intuitive, it would be very difficult to formalize. And finally, even if it were possible to determine the factivity of predicates, the methods developed here for simple sentences would need to be applied in some upwardly recursive manner, in order to respond appropriately to sentences such as "John might regret that ..."

When examined carefully, reasoning about *internal* embeddings turns out to be equally complex for the general case. Suppose for instance that the user asked "Does John believe that Mary might love Tom?" and the knowledge base had indexed the statement "John believes that Mary should love Tom." The outer clause would be labeled YES, because the question and statement match exactly. The inner clause would also be labeled YES, because "x *should* do y" normally allows the system to reply "yes" when asked "*Might* x do y?". It is not clear, however, that if John believes that Mary should love Tom, he also believes that Mary might love Tom. It seems that the standard modal judgements can be overridden when one or more of the clauses being compared is embedded. In fact, the meaning of a verb can affect modal implications within its own clause: if John loved Mary, then he might love Mary, but if John died, we would not want to say that John might die!

Solving these puzzles will require a better understanding of the inter-relationships among verb meaning, factivity, and the time and modal filters. All in all, the expansion of the task domain to include embedded sentences promises to be a worthwhile but difficult project.

8.   Conclusion

The TEAM model was designed to perform word-knowledge reasoning for question-answering. Although the implemented system does not begin to account for all the complexities involved, within its limited task domain it has proven quite successful. As part of the larger START question-answering system, including the matcher, S-rules, and generator, it produces responses that are informative and echo human judgements closely. If the suggested extensions were incorporated, the performance would improve even further. In any case, it is hoped that the reasoning strategies described here will form part of a more generalized model for successful question answering.

Acknowledgments

I am grateful to Robert Frank, Michael Kashket, Mikhail Katz, Beth Levin, Jeff Palmucci, and Thomas Marill for their helpful suggestions concerning this work.

This paper describes research done at the Artificial Intelligence Laboratory of the Massachusetts Institute of Technology. Support for the Laboratory's Artificial Intelligence research is provided in part by the Advanced Research Projects Agency under Office of Naval Research contract N0014-85-K-0124.

References

1.   J. Allen, "Towards a General Theory of Action and Time," *Artificial Intelligence*, Vol. 23, No. 2, 1984.

2.   B.T. Atkins, J. Kegl, and B. Levin, "Explicit and Implicit Information in Dictionaries," Lexicon Project Working Papers 12, Center for Cognitive Science, MIT, Cambridge, MA, 1986.

3.   E. Charniak and M. Harper, "Time and Tense in English," *Proceedings of the 24th Annual Meeting of the ACL*, Columbia University, New York, NY, 1986.

4.   R.J. Doyle, "Hypothesizing and Refining Causal Models," M.I.T. Artificial Intelligence Laboratory Memo No. 811, December 1984.

5.   K.L. Hale and S.J. Keyser, "Some Transitivity Alternations in English," Lexicon Project Working Papers 7, Center for Cognitive Science, MIT, Cambridge, MA, 1986.

6.   E.W. Hinrichs, "Tense, Quantifiers, and Contexts," *Computational Linguistics*, Vol. 14, No. 2, 1988.

7. B. Katz, "A Three-step Procedure for Language Generation," M.I.T. Artificial Intelligence Laboratory Memo No. 599, December 1980.

8. B. Katz, "Using English for Indexing and Retrieving," *Proceedings of the Conference on User-oriented Content-based Text and Image Handling, RIAO '88*, Cambridge, MA, 1988. (A version of this paper also appears as MIT Artificial Intelligence Laboratory Memo No. 1096, November 1988.)

9. B. Katz and R.N. Brooks, "Understanding Natural Language for Spacecraft Sequencing," *Journal of the British Interplanetary Society*, Vol. 40, No. 10, 1987.

10. B. Katz and B. Levin, "Exploiting Lexical Regularities in Designing Natural Language Systems," *Proceedings of the 12th International Conference on Computational Linguistics, COLING '88*, Budapest, Hungary, 1988. (A version of this paper also appears as Lexicon Project Working Papers 22, MIT Center for Cognitive Science, and as MIT Artificial Intelligence Laboratory Memo No. 1041, April 1988.)

11. B. Katz and P.H. Winston, "A Two-way Natural Language Interface," in *Integrated Interactive Computing Systems*, edited by P. Degano and E. Sandewall, North-Holland, Amsterdam, 1982.

12. P. Kiparsky and C. Kiparsky, "Fact," in *Semantics*, edited by D. Steinberg and L. Jakobovits, Cambridge University Press, London, 1971.

13. B. Levin, "Introduction," in *Lexical Semantics in Review*, edited by B. Levin, Lexicon Project Working Papers 1, Center for Cognitive Science, MIT, Cambridge, MA, 1985.

14. B. Levin, "Approaches to Lexical Semantic Representation," in *Automating the Lexicon*, edited by D. Walker, A. Zampolli, and N. Calzolari, MIT Press, Cambridge, MA, to appear, 1989.

15. W.I. McLaughlin, "Automated Sequencing," *Spaceflight*, Vol. 29, No. 1, January 1987.

16. W.I. McLaughlin, "Computers and Language," *Spaceflight*, Vol. 30, No. 8, August 1988.

17. M. Moens and M. Steedman, "Temporal Ontology and Temporal Reference," *Computational Linguistics*, Vol. 14, No. 2, 1988.

18. H. Reichenbach, *Elements of Symbolic Logic*, Free Press, New York, 1966.

19. P.H. Winston, *Artificial Intelligence*, Addison-Wesley, Reading, MA, 1984.

20. P.H. Winston, "Learning New Principles from Precedents and Exercises," *Artificial Intelligence*, Vol. 19, No. 3, 1982.

21. P.H. Winston, T.O. Binford, B. Katz, M.R. Lowry, "Learning Physical Descriptions from Functional Definitions, Examples, and Precedents," *National Conference on Artificial Intelligence*, Washington, D.C., 1983.

Learning by Doing with Simulated Intelligent Help

John M. Carroll
IBM Thomas J. Watson Research Center

Amy P. Aaronson
IBM US Marketing and Services Group

Intelligent advisory interfaces will afford new approaches to help and training problems. Though there is a considerable base of research literature and engineering practice with prototype systems, little is known about the usability of intelligent advisory facilities. We simulated an intelligent help facility for a PC database and report application, yoking two workstations and allowing an unseen experimenter to play the part of the help system. While there were indeed specific ways that this intelligent help facility supported users, there were also specific problems with the help provided. Implications for further research on the usability of intelligent advisory facilities and for the design of intelligent help systems are discussed.

One of the most important means for facilitating the usability of computer systems is the "advisory interface", the training, reference material, on-line help, and other advisory support available to users. Not surprisingly, this is one of the most active research areas in human-computer interaction. However, a daunting problem inheres in advisory interfaces: this work is governed by advances in information management and user interaction techniques with respect to both the user problems that require help and training support, and the means to deliver help and training to the user (Carroll, 1987). Put another way, studying advisory problems and developing advisory solutions for the "leading edge" of human-computer interaction is hampered by the fact that the leading edge *must have already been codified and deployed* before advisory problems can even exist. One can get the impression that research and development of advisory interfaces *necessarily* lags other research on human-computer interaction.

Intelligent advisory interfaces provide a current example of this. How can we meaningfully analyze the usability problems of intelligent advisory facilities when, for the most part, such facilities only exist as demonstration systems (Carroll and McKendree, 1987)? Several investigators have analyzed naturally occurring advisory interaction between humans as a model intelligent help situation (Aaronson and Carroll, 1987a, 1987b, 1987c; Coombs and Alty, 1980; Kidd, 1985; McKendree and Carroll, 1986; Pollock, 1985). This work has identified a variety of patterns in how people ask other people for help and how advice is provided. Some of these patterns challenge commonsense views of what giving and taking advice is like. For example, seeking advice often is not a matter of question-answer dialog. People frequently make specific claims about the answer to their *own* query; the advisor's role is to verify these claims (Aaronson and Carroll, 1987a).

One limitation in using human consultants as a model for an on-line intelligent help facility is that they often provide advice in an *off-line* situation; the client has brought a problem to a consultant's office for discussion. Another limitation is that the client's actual implementation of the advice usually occurs outside of the purview of the interaction, and hence is not available for analysis. In this study, we simulated an on-line intelligent help facility in a learning by doing task environment: participants learned to use an interactive application by performing several tasks with it.

We had two goals. First, we wanted to define usability issues for intelligent help as a new advisory interface technology, and thereby to be able to contribute to the development and deployment of the technology. Second, we wanted to explore the use of interface simulation as a technique for investigating issues in intelligent help.

1. Methodological preliminaries

We inventoried typical user errors with a popular PC application and designed error recovery help for them. We then remotely monitored users' console activity and provided error recovery help using an apparatus called SmartHelp (Checco and Carroll, 1986).

1.1 Understanding user tasks and user errors

Our starting point was to define the basic application tasks for the commercial PC database and report application we worked with. These canonical tasks include setting up a simple database (including the design of forms for entering names, addresses and other data fields), producing formatted output from the database (e.g., lists of mailing labels), and producing summary reports (e.g., a salary report for a subset of entries). The second stage in our research was to develop an empirically derived inventory of the most common and serious user errors that occur within the canonical task scenarios (typos are of course quite common, but we did not include them in this taxonomy).

The application we studied is a menu-driven system in which the user first designs a "form" and then uses it in a variety of ways, entering data, specifying subsets of data for printing, querying the database, formatting output, etc. The form is created by entering field labels (e.g., Salary, First Name, Street Address) and explicit blanks (e.g., for data fields). A typical user problem we observed was that people did not respect the distinction between the operations of designing the form and entering data into it: they frequently entered data values in fields *as they were creating the form itself*. The correct procedure is to design and save the form (with blanks where data will later be entered) and then subsequently to select Add Data to *re*present the form as a template for data entry.

Our understanding of the basic application tasks and typical user errors was based upon a prior study of 6 users. Based on this study, we designed a suite of three task scenarios, described in Table 1. These tasks were designed to provide opportunities for users to make 13 basic errors we had inventoried in our prior study (e.g., entering data while creating a form design). Table 1 also indicates points in the task scenarios at which each of these user errors are likely to occur.

1.2 SmartHelp

The database and report application we studied includes a contextual "passive" help system; from any application menu, the F1 function key displays a panel of reference information pertaining to that menu. We added to this facility a simulated "active" help system. one that provided error recovery information when the user made an error *without* requiring an explicit help request on the part of the user (see Fischer, Lemke and Schwab, 1985, for discussion of "active" and "passive" help). We used an apparatus called SmartHelp (Checco and Carroll, 1986; Aaronson, Carroll, Kelley and Canetti, 1988), consisting of two workstations yoked in a master/slave relationship. The master workstation has the capability of monitoring the slave, and of taking control of the slave's keyboard and display. We conducted the study with two experimenters: one sat with the participant, observing behavior and nondirectively prompting the participant to "think aloud" while working. Our notes and the videotape record of events and think aloud commentaries are the principal source of data we will discuss (see Carroll and Mazur, 1986; Mack, Lewis and Carroll, 1983, for other examples of our use of the "thinking aloud" technique).

The second experimenter operated the master workstation monitoring the participant's activity on the slave workstation. When an error was recognized, the experimenter operating the master workstation took control of the keyboard and display of the slave workstation and send a SmartHelp message. The message appeared in a separate window on the display; its arrival was accompanied by a beep. If the error was one of those we had inventoried and for which we had stored messages, response time was a few seconds. If the error was not one in our inventory, a message was created on the fly. In these cases, response times were longer, ranging up to 30 seconds. If an error was left uncorrected after three successive SmartHelp messages, we stopped advising on it for that episode, and waited for a subsequent opportunity to provide more help. This technique of simulating an advanced interface technology with an unseen human performing some of the functions is sometimes called the "Wizard of Oz" technique (see Gould, Conti and Hovanyecz, 1983; Kelley, 1983; Malhotra and Sheridan, 1976).

Table 1: Task Scenarios and Typical User Errors

Three basic database and report tasks were suggested to participants. Within these tasks were opportunities for making the 13 typical user errors we inventoried. (The numbers referencing these errors correspond to those in Table 2, which presents the help messages designed for each error.)

Task 1

The first task was to "set up a new file to keep track of information for three employees. Limit the number of characters that can be typed for State to 2." The participants were initially positioned at the Main Menu, from which they needed to select File. A key subtask was naming the file they were creating. Many failed to do this (1). After successfully entering a filename, they would see a nearly blank screen on which they were to design their forms, laying out field labels, such as Salary, followed by colons and blank space for data. They were not to enter data at this point, but sometimes did so (2). Some were unsure what to do and hesitated (3). Participants often typed only a Name field rather than separate First Name and Last Name fields (4). It was common to misposition the field delimiter > in restricting the size of the State field for two-letter postal abbreviations (5).

After the form was laid out, the system prompted the user to specify a data type for each field by entering a code. Participants sometimes hesitated, or entered incorrect codes (6). Once the form was designed, the user needed to select Add Data from the File menu to obtain a blank form template on which to enter data. After filling in the form for one employee, name, address, salary, etc., the user needed to press F10 to get another blank form and enter data for the second, and so on for the third. After filling in the third form, the user was to press Shift-F10 to save and quit, however, many continued to use F10 instead, erroneously adding blank forms to the file (7).

Task 2

The next task was printing a mailing list, the employee names and addresses in alphabetical order on a single page. The participants needed to select Print, and then Design/Redesign a Print Spec, which prompted them to name the print specification. Participants sometimes hesitated at this point or tried a series of abortive gambits (8). At the Retrieve Spec screen, they needed to specify which forms would contribute data to the the listing they were trying to create. Again, participants sometimes hesitated at this step (9). Some thought they should be specifying the *fields* they wanted to print and entered the wrong information.

The participants needed to press F6 to alphabetically sort the list. At the Field spec screen, participants were to enter codes to control which fields would print and in what order. Some bypassed this screen, confusing it with the Retrieve spec screen they had just used (10). Others entered incorrect codes (11). At the Print Options screen, participants needed to alter the default (of 1) for forms per page in order to print all sets of names and addresses on one page. Some neglected to change this (12).

Task 3

The final task was to print a Report, with headings and totals. Participants needed to return to the Main menu and select Report. Participants often tried instead to adapt the Print function they had used for the mailing list (13). At the Column Spec screen, participants needed to fill in sort codes and specify which fields should appear in columns and which should be summed to produce totals. They needed to pick the PF key Define Page to get a report heading.

1.3 How-to-do-it versus How-it-works help

For each of the 13 errors in our inventory, we designed two "intelligent" help texts, a how-it-works text and a how-to-do-it text. The how-it-works messages were intended to provide model-based explanations of errors (Halasz, 1984;

Mayer, 1981). In designing how-it-works messages we avoided mentioning names of specific commands or keys. However, we stressed ultimate objectives and goal-based rationales, metaphors for interface objects (e.g., a blank tax form metaphor for the application's form design), and the system-state consequences of user actions. The how-to-do-it messages were intended to be strictly procedural. Our design rules for them were *not* to give goal-based rationales for procedures, *not* to use metaphors or other model-constructs, but to stress immediate procedural prerequisites and specific sequences of keypresses.

Our interest in this contrast for intelligent help dialogs was to explore impacts on user's learning strategies in the context of error recovery. How-it-works help requires the user to discover the procedural details from information about underlying causal relationships. How-to-do-it help requires the user to infer underlying causal explanations from the results of executing procedures. Our study was *not* designed to make a simple experimental contrast of two help styles. We included two styles to afford a broader, albeit preliminary, exploration of potential problems and possibilities.

We cannot of course be sure that we adequately understand how to design advisory information for SmartHelp interactions, where traditional techniques like making eye contact are just not available. In the absence of pedagogical theories, we took an empirical design approach, re-iteratively shaping our help messages through the course of our prior study of six users. The how-it-works and how-to-do-it messages we ultimately designed for the user errors we inventoried are displayed in Table 2 (on-the-fly messages were created according to the same design rules as those used for the 13 inventoried errors, using the message library as a source of prototypes).

We deliberately *bounded* SmartHelp's intelligence, as projected to the user. SmartHelp knew about the task domain (for example, that state abbreviations are two letters, that NY is one such but that XY is not, the people's names consist of a first name and a last name, that zip codes consist of five digits). But we *avoided* incorporating knowledge of the *particular* task instances users performed into the help messages. For example, if a participant entered data while creating a form (error 2 in Tables 1 and 2), SmartHelp tried to clarify the distinction between field labels and data, but did not take the further step of providing *specific* field labels to the participant. In other work, we have studied training environments that do refer to knowledge about specific user tasks (Carroll and Kay, 1987; McKendree and Carroll, 1987). This technique, however, creates a rather rigid task environment for the user, perhaps more generally appropriate for training than for help. In the present study, we wanted to examine a more flexible advisory facility; one that allows, for example, the freedom to eschew our suggested tasks or to perform them in a different order.

Table 2: Messages Designed for Inventoried Typical Errors

Numbering of errors is the same as in Table 1.

(1) Not knowing what to put for a file name

How-it-works: Before create a file, you must name it. This is a list of files that already exist. You must choose a different name of up to eight characters. The first part of the filename has been filled in for you.

How-to-do-it: Type a new filename (of up to 8 characters) where it says: "Drive (or path) or file name:"

(2) Entering data while creating a form

How-it-works: You are entering data along with your field labels. You should be creating a blank form (like an income tax form that hasn't been filled in yet.) Later, you can use copies of this form to store and retrieve data.

How-to-do-it: Erase the information that you just entered, using the backspace key. Type each field label (e.g. Salary), followed by a colon, followed by enough blank space for the form field.

(3) Hesitating at blank screen to set up form

How-it-works: In (the application) you must first create a blank form (like an income tax form that hasn't been filled in yet.) This form is used for all subsequent operations. (e.g., Adding Data, specifying what fields to print etc.).

How-to-do-it: Type each field label (e.g. Salary) followed by enough blank spaces to hold the information in the field.

(4) Putting first and last name in one field

How-it-works: The field label you just created includes more than one type of information. Later, you will enter codes in the individual fields to indicate what you want to print. You can't refer to parts of a single field. Therefore, if do not distinguish First and Last Name as separate fields, you cannot print a report showing just the last name.

How-to-do-it: Erase the field you just created by using the backspace key. Create two fields, one with the label First Name: the other with the label Last Name: If you have address information, create four fields called Address: City: State: and Zip Code:

(5) State field too short

How-it-works: When you enter data later, (the application) will position the cursor two spaces to the right of the colon. (The application) will not let you type in the position that has the > in it. You must leave more space for State to be entered.

How-to-do-it: Move the > one space to the right.

(6) Confusion on the Format screen

How-it-works: You need to specify the type of data that will appear in each field. (The application) uses this information to treat different data types appropriately (e.g. it automatically formats dates and money amounts).

How-to-do-it: Put an M in the Salary field, a D in the Date field and an N in fields that are included in calculations. Leave a T in fields that contain text.

(7) Not knowing how to stop (entering blank forms as a result)

How-it-works: When adding data, pressing F10 adds the current form to the file and gives you a blank form. Pressing Shift-F10 adds the current form to the file and exits. You pressed F10 before when you should have pressed Shift F10, and a blank form has been added to your file. Blank forms cause gaps in reports and should be removed.

How-to-do-it: Before, you pressed F10 when you should have pressed Shift F10. Choose Remove, and, on the next screen, put an = sign in any field and press F10. Then respond Y.

(8) **Hesitating on the Print Spec screen**
How-it-works: Before you specify what fields to print from what forms, (The application) asks for a name that will be associated with this information. This avoids having to respecify the information later if you want to print the same list.
How-to-do-it: Type a name (of 20 characters or less) at the prompt: Print Spec name.

(9) **Hesitation at Retrieve screen**
How-it-works: You might not want all forms to print on a list or report. Here is where you specify what forms to retrieve. You enter something in the field, and (the application) checks for forms that match what you enter. On the next screen, you will indicate what fields to print.
How-to-do-it: You can leave the fields blank, or optionally, put a name in the Last Name field, or a dollar amount with a < or > in the Salary field, etc. (e.g. typing Jones retrieves forms with Jones).

(10) **Skipping over the Field Spec screen**
How-it-works: It appears that either (1) you wanted to print your entire form but forgot to print field labels, or (2) you wanted to print only certain fields, but neglected to specify this. Start over and specify what you want to do.
How-to-do-it: Choose Design/Redesign Print Spec. Enter the Print Spec name you just created. When you get to the Field Spec screen, enter a sequence number, followed by a + or x in each field you want to print (e.g. Salary: 4x). To print an entire form, leave the Field Spec blank and change the print option.

(11) **Entering wrong information in Field Spec**
How-it-works: You might not want to print all fields, or you may want to print fields in a different order than the way they appear on the form. You put codes in fields you want to print, indicating the sequence and whether to skip a line or a space before printing the next field.
How-to-do-it: Enter a sequence number followed by a + or x in each field you want to print or leave all fields blank.

(12) **Failure to specify more than one label per page**
How-it-works: Since your forms are so small, you might want to save paper by printing several forms on a standard page, redefining the page length to make it smaller.
How-to-do-it: Choose Design/Redesign a print spec. Proceed as before, but, when you get to the Print Options screen, change the Number of forms per page.

(13) **Using the print module to produce a report**
How-it-works: You cannot print out data summaries with column headings and totals using the Print function. For these features, you need to use the Report function.
How-to-do-it: Hit the Esc key enough times to return to the Main Menu, then select the Report function.

1.4 Participants and procedure

The study we report here included 8 people drawn from the working population of the IBM Watson Research Center, selected as having had little prior experience with business professional software. Three participants had limited computing experience (1-3 years) focused principally on document editing and electronic mail (P4, P5 and P8). Three other participants had more extensive computing experience (6-8 years) including statistical packages, computer aided design, and publishing (P3, P6, P7). The other two participants had professional programming backgrounds, though their recent experience consisted only of using statistics and text-processing applications (P1 and P2). We organized two groups of 4 participants each to be roughly balanced with respect to computing experience: P1, P3, P6 and P8 received how-to-do-it SmartHelp messages; P2, P4, P5, and P7 received how-it-works messages.

We explained to participants at the outset that our research interest was new approaches to on-line help. They were told that "a prototype help facility was running on top of" the PC application they would be using. We provided them with a single quick-reference card. This card contained some basic getting started information, stressing the availability of both a passive, or user-initiated help, and an active, or system-initiated help. Participants could refer to the card throughout the work session. We suggested that they undertake the task scenarios described in Table 1. All participants followed the suggested scenarios, but with a variety of small departures. Many of these seemed deliberate. For example, one participant cautiously copied his work, even though this was not suggested in the scenarios. Another browsed her forms before printing them to verify that everything was in order. A third proceeded with the task having filled out only the first two fields of his form, saying that he wanted to see how things worked before bothering to add all his data. Other departures were inadvertent: several participants forgot aspects of the scenarios and then ended up performing some of the tasks in a different order (e.g., sorting the mailing list *after* an unsorted print). Average time on task was 103 minutes (1 hr. 43 min.; the range was 69-134 minutes).

As a check on learning achievement, we asked each participant to perform three transfer tasks and to complete a brief systems concepts test at the end of the work session. The first transfer task consisted of creating a database of names and salaries. This is simpler variant of the first task in Table 1. The second task consisted of printing a list of names and addresses of employees living in Oregon and earning over 20,000. This is similar to tasks 2 and 3 in Table 1. The third task consisted of altering a data record in the file created earlier. This is unlike any of the training tasks (although some participants had had some experience with it in correcting errors). Seven of 8 participants (all but P8) were able to complete tasks 1 and 2, although four of them (P2, P3, P6, and P7) had some difficulty with task 2. Only four of 8 (P1, P3, P4, and P7) successfully completed task 3. On average, participants scored 4 right out of 5 on a brief systems concept test (in which basic application procedures were described and participants were asked to predict the result, or functions were named and participants were asked to describe them).

In the study, we sent 164 SmartHelp messages; 73 of these were drawn from our prepared inventory of messages, and 91 were created on the fly. The majority of errors provoking on-the-fly messages were made in the context of recovery from a prior error. Note that one participant (P8) received 57 messages (39 on-the-fly). For the other seven participants, the proportion of libraried and on-the-fly messages was about even.

1.5 How well did the simulation work?

SmartHelp was convincing to users as a simulation of intelligent help. In our introductory remarks to participants, we referred to it as a "facility", deliberately equivocating as to whether it was purely software. However, none of the participants "unmasked" the Wizard in their thinking aloud protocols, or even voiced suspicions. Indeed, their occasional complaints about system response times were articulated as if the help facility was purely software. At the end of the experiment, when the apparatus was described in detail to participants, they were all mildly surprised to find it was a simulation -- but only mildly surprised. It seemed to us that expectations about intelligence in software are very labile.

Nevertheless, there were several methodological problems with SmartHelp. As mentioned above, the majority of the SmartHelp messages we sent had to be generated on the fly. People are incredibly creative at generating errors and misconceptions, and incredibly fast. The pressure of having to quickly generate the messages sometimes led to messages we would have liked to have done differently. For example, the distinction between how-it-works and how-to-do-it sometimes blurred. P4, in the how-it-works group, received a SmartHelp message telling him to go to the Report function: "If you are trying to create a report you should use the Report Function." We worried later that this was too procedural for the "How it Works" condition; that something like "Report and Print are different. Report does ... Print does ..." might have been better.

Though we selected our database and report application on the grounds of its popularity and excellence (gleaned from reviews), its interface includes several idiosyncratic features that were difficult to advise on. For example, the commands to set headings and titles for reports are "hidden functions". They are not mentioned in the application's help panels and can only be accessed via function keys in particular menus -- which themselves do not provide hints (e.g., headings are set using the "define page" function key which is accessible only in the menu whose main purpose is to change default print options). In one case, P4 was trying to add a header to his report. He was browsing systematically, but making no progress in finding the hidden function. Although he was in our how-it-works group, SmartHelp became more directive, telling him to look at the bottom line of the screen for functions that he might not see on help screens. He happened to be on the screen where the function could be found, looked down and saw the function. We faced the dilemma of letting the user languish in an interface glitch or compromising the rules that SmartHelp should not "know" about the user's specific current task and that how-it-works help should not include procedural details.

2. Being smart can help

Our simulated intelligent help facility did seem to help the participants use the database application. In some cases, the user seemed to be wondering how the system worked at *just* the moment that a pertinent how-it-works message was sent. The user might have just tried an incorrect method, and while pondering what to try next, received a how-to-do-it message. Indeed, users even seemed to appreciate the "companionship" of SmartHelp as they worked out the consequences of their errors, as P5 put it, "The little help system makes me feel like someone is going to come and answer my question".

2.1. Finding out how-to-do-it

Particularly with how-to-do-it messages, success could be gratifyingly simple. P1 was trying to print a report with column headings and totals. To do this, she needed to use the Report function, but she was instead exploring the Print function which does not support headings and totals. She received a how-to-do-it message advising her to access the Report function via the Main Menu. She went directly to the Main Menu, selected Report, and completed the task.

P6 was trying to create a print specification, without having first entered a data set. SmartHelp intervened and suggested he Escape and choose Add Data. At first, he wondered if he should follow this advice, but then, he said, "OK, that does make sense, I mean, since I haven't entered any data, I can see why it might have a point, so I'm going to try to do that." This is a nice example of getting how-to-do-it help and then generating a how-it-works rationale.

2.2 Needing confirmation of a plan

Sometimes the participant seemed to have a specific plan in mind and SmartHelp, by independently suggesting that plan, provided confirmation and therefore encouragement. P6 had earlier made an error in specifying the field length for the state field (error 5 in Tables 1 and 2). As he added data to a form, he found that indeed he could only enter one character for state abbreviation. He laughed, recalling earlier SmartHelp advice on this error, "OK, I can only put in one letter for state." He decided to redesign the file, but was unsure whether to use F10 (Continue) or Escape in order to proceed. He did not want to lose the data he had already entered, and so was worried about trying Escape. He reasoned that F10 would just give him a new blank form, and was thus still inclined towards trying Escape. Since he had hesitated for several seconds, SmartHelp intervened: "Hit Escape and choose Design a File. Then redesign the file and move the cursor to the left in the State field." P6 seemed happy that the message provided confirmation. "OK, its telling me to go back and do what I want to do. That's what I would have done."

2.3 Wondering how-it-works

As participants were sometimes perfectly primed to receive "how to do it" help, they also were sometimes ready to receive how-it-works help. After typing her field labels, P7 commented "I just realized that I made all these things (field labels), and now I have to go back and fill them in... I wish I knew if there was some way to repeat this format instead of having to type it in every time." She began to type in the data for her first form, and received a message telling her that forms and the data they contain are entered separately (see error 2 in Table 2). "There's the answer!" she exclaimed.

P5 was trying to use the Print function to produce a Report with headings. She had just printed her data, noted that there were no headings, and was retracing her steps in search of clues as to how to get headings. She selected the Expand Field function, which presented a prompt labelled "Long Value:". She commented "I have no idea what this is.", but haltingly began to type a heading anyway. This field takes a formula, not a text string. Hence, SmartHelp was able to diagnose Error 13 and sent the library how-it-works message. P5 immediately exited Print, and correctly accessed the Report function.

2.4 Previewing consequences of an action.

Some how-it-works messages presented causal consequences of action sequences. This in effect allowed the user to preview possible courses of action. P4 was specifying the size of the state field, leaving it too short to enter two characters for state (error 5). He got a how-it-works message telling him how the system positions the cursor in a field: "When you enter data later, the cursor will be two spaces to the right of the colon." Even though he was somewhat annoyed to have his work interrupted, he exclaimed that this was a good message and immediately moved the field delimiter to allow the right amount of space for the date. Moreover, he avoided making the analogous mistake in subsequently defining the zip code field.

Later, P4 too literally followed an example in the application's passive help system. In the example, he had been shown that to retrieve all forms with x in a given field, one should put an x in the field specification. P4 typed xNY in the state field specification -- to retrieve all forms with NY in the state field, thinking that the x in the example was required. He got the how-it-works message: "Putting xNY in the state field will retrieve all forms with xNY in the state field." He immediately saw the consequences of his mistaken action and eliminated the x.

2.5 Taking advice "anyway"

Perhaps a mixture of failure and success were cases in which a user balked at a SmartHelp message, but then successfully followed the advice anyway. P7 was specifying the data types for fields and put an N (for a numeric field) in the date field (which should been a D). There was no system error message, and P7 had not expressed uncertainty about her action. Indeed, she did not appreciate the relevance of the SmartHelp message explaining that specifying the type of data allowed the application to automatically format date and money amounts (see error 6 in Table 2). "I'm already doing that!" However, moments later she did go back to change the N to a D, anyway.

Though our SmartHelp simulation did help users recover from errors and use the system, there were instances in which it failed to help, provided help awkwardly, or even precipitated further problems. Users often preferred to pursue their own goals and chains of reasoning over following advice. Their goals were sometimes difficult to diagnose, and routinely became tangled with errors and changes in the system state, which made problems difficult to unstack and advise on. Despite this complexity, users often expected too much of SmartHelp and were both distracted and disappointed by its bounded intelligence. We sort these incidents for discussion, but in the situations we describe it was often the case that multiple factors were involved. We note that nearly all of the user problems we describe below were eventually resolved, usually by way of "on the fly" SmartHelp messages in concert with user problem solving. We focus principal concern here on the types of problems that arose, as opposed to their solutions.

3. The clash of intelligence

People are ineluctably active in learning and using computing systems (Carroll and Rosson, 1987). They are initiative-takers. They have unique personal histories that shape their expectations and goals. Based on this background, they take action. Their personal agenda of goals and concerns focuses their attention on only a subset of the objects and events they could potentially notice. They tend not to notice things irrelevant to their current analysis of a situation (Mack et al., 1983). Faced with incomplete and conflicting information, they make assumptions -- again based on their own expectations and goals -- and take further actions on an as-if basis. Addressing goals and guiding attention with intelligent help may ameliorate these problems, but the user's own knowledge and initiative can always preempt or distort the advice.

3.1 Relying on prior experience

All of the participants had some experience with computers. A few had tried applications similar to the one we studied. This specific prior experience understandably could predispose a user to particular expectations about what should happen or how to do something. In the opening phases of the session, P4 kept trying to modify an existing form, adding data and redesigning it, rather than setting up one of his own. This approach stemmed from his experiences with a similar product in which creating a new form design was accomplished by editing a pre-stored template form design. In the application we studied, modifying an existent form destroyed the prior contents. SmartHelp explained this to P4, who commented, "Why should I design a new form? This is a great form." After two further messages from SmartHelp, P4 did choose to design a new form, although in a later comment, he still regretted not having found an existing form that he could edit. We speculate that the help messages might have been more effective if they had directly addressed P4's prior experience (e.g., differentiating copying and creation).

In another example, P6 was having trouble copying a data set. Suddenly, he broke out of the application to perform the copy using the operating system commands. This is a challenge for an application-bound help system, but it makes perfect sense from P6's perspective: he already *knew* how to do the copy there. The problem he traded was that now he had to start the application up!

3.2 Pursuing personal goals

Often the sequence of goals prescribed by the application mismatched those on the user's personal agenda. In Section **2.4**, we referred to P4's annoyance at having his work interrupted, even by help messages he acknowledged were useful. We wanted our participants to be engaged by realistic tasks, and not just waiting for SmartHelp messages. But this meant that they had their own goals and that SmartHelp messages were often seen, at least initially, as distractions.

In some cases, goal mismatches led participants to ignore the messages. P8 hesitated at the Retrieve screen (error 9) and got a SmartHelp message telling her what operations she could perform. However, P8 had a specific goal in mind; she wanted to print mailing labels for all her forms. She could not make sense of the message (see Table 2) in the context of this goal: "If I'm supposed to define a print spec and tell it where I'm supposed to print the characters on the page, this doesn't help me at all." Rather than taking an action on the Retrieve screen, she exited and started the task over, concluding that she had missed something along the way. In fact, her goal would have been appropriate on the immediately following screen; she was unaware that she needed to first define what forms to select (on the Retrieve screen) in order to print. Table 3 presents a further example.

Table 3: The user's own goals can outweigh how-it-works explanations

After making an error in adding data into his form, P4 decided to delete the form and start over. He selected Remove, specified that he wanted to remove all forms, and started to design a new form, using his old filename. He was surprised to see that a file with that name still existed. He tried Remove again, and got a SmartHelp message: "Remove is used to remove data once it has been entered. You don't have any data in your file." The form itself was correct, and he could have continued by adding data into it. P4 did not, however, give up his stated goal of erasing the old form: "Well, obviously I'm going to have a tough time removing that file, so maybe I should just redesign the file. I should be able to erase it, though." He chose Redesign and then deleted *every field* in the design, field by field. "I'm going back to delete everything and start with a clear form anyway." Merely clarifying how Remove works was not enough in this case to help P4 determine what goal was appropriate.

P5 wanted to sort her forms by last name and to print the last name as the second field (following the first name). She was trying to do both using the Field Spec screen, which in fact could only used for the second goal. When she entered both a sort code and a print sequence code, she got a SmartHelp message (error 11 in Table 2) explaining how fields are selected and sequenced for printing. However, since the message did not explicitly say *not* to enter the sort code, she persisted with that goal. In this case, explaining how things worked was not enough, since P5's goal could only be addressed by explaining how they did not work.

3.3 Noticing selectively

Users do not always notice everything they do or everything that appears on the system display (Mack et al., 1983). Not knowing exactly what was noticed by the user, makes it difficult for an advisor to provide help that is appropriate. P4 was at the File menu, where one selects a function category by typing an id letter, and then enters the name of a file. P4 wasn't looking at the screen. By mistake, he typed the name of the file he had just created, without first indicating a function category. He also happened to make a typo on the last letter of the filename, typing Employa, instead of Employe1. The E of Employa had no effect, since there was no menu item with this letter. This should have evoked a SmartHelp message, explaining how the File menu works. However, since the e was typed as part of continuous string, we missed the error.

The next letter in the string, m, selected the Mass Update function. The string ploya was then interpreted by the application as a filename, and evoked a system error message: "file not found." Apparently not noticing that Mass Update had been selected, P4 quickly corrected the filename, and the application put up the Mass Update screen. Here P4 hesitated. SmartHelp was able to catch up and provided a message explaining how Mass Update works. P4 was confused by this. "I guess I had it on the wrong thing, Mass Update. I thought I had it on Add Data." However, the message did help him notice what had happened, and he returned to the File menu to try again.

P3 was adding data. He entered an H instead of a Y when typing NY in the state field. "If I try another letter, let's see what it does." SmartHelp did not intervene, of course, because NH is in fact a state abbreviation, but P3 seemed to have hoped for a SmartHelp response. He went on to add data in the zip code field, which he had initially defined with field length 4, instead of 5. (He had earlier received SmartHelp messages about this, but had ignored them.) Now he commented, without surprise, that the field was too short. Since he was cursoring the zip code field, a SmartHelp message was sent (similar to that for error 5 in Table 2), suggesting he select Design/Redesign to move the field delimiter (>) to the right. P3, however, was still focussed on the NH-for-NY substitution, he interpreted the message as pertaining to *that* error and complained about the extent of the help procedure: "I haven't done THAT much wrong."

3.4 Making assumptions

In understanding SmartHelp messages, users had to make inferences. P1 had neglected to specify that she wanted to print more than one form on a page (error 12). As she was about to print, she received a SmartHelp message telling her to "proceed as before, ... but change the Number of forms per page". This was specific advice, but she had trouble interpreting it because she was not aware that she had done anything wrong. She made a series of assumptions in order to understand this message. "I assume this is a change in instructions, not a help message." P1 searched for a possible correspondence between the message and prior actions. She noticed that she had not alphabetized her list of mailing labels, and speculated that the message might have been a result of this error. She spent time looking for a way to alphabetize the list. Finally, she made a further assumption about how the system works that allowed her to make progress: "each one of these things [the mailing labels] is a form, maybe?"

P8 selected Report before choosing File to create a file. When SmartHelp advised her to Escape and select File, she assumed that this was because she had mis-specified a filename in Report, and not because files cannot be created at all in Report: "[The help message] should tell me if I need a specific suffix. DTF was what the other files were called. I just want to name a file... It just told me to go back to the beginning, so I'm going back again." This incorrect assumption about how the system worked did not prevent her from following the how-to-do-it help message, but it did obscure the correct inference for her.

Participants sometimes made very specific, and quite wishful, assumptions. After receiving a message explaining that she needed to use the Report function instead of Print (error 13), P2 paraphrased what she had to do: "Ah, so I'll go all the way back and find the Report function." She pressed Escape, and got to the File menu, where she had found the Print function. Report does not appear on the File menu, it appears on the Main menu which is one level further back. P2 exclaimed "but nothing here says Report!" She had imposed the constraint that Report would appear in the same menu as Print. She incorrectly chose Print again.

In some cases, users seemed to make the simplifying assumption that only part of what was said in a help message was necessary for them. When creating a form, P8 started to enter data along with field labels (error 2). She received a SmartHelp message suggesting she delete the data she had entered and type each field label (e.g. Salary) followed by a colon, followed by enough blank spaces to hold the data. P8 inserted a colon between a field label and some data she had already entered, but she did not replace the data with blanks. Nevertheless, *she* appeared to think that she had complied with the help message.

4. Coordinating time and sequence

The user's situation and the user's construal of the current situation change very rapidly. Errors are committed, and then further errors are made in the course of error recovery. Goals are rapidly satisfied or given up in favor of other goals. Against this very dynamic background, every user action alters the system state in potentially many ways. The complexity of such circumstances, already a a difficult diagnostic challenge for intelligent help, is greatly exacerbated by their fluidity: a given piece of help may only be pertinent at a single point in time.

4.1 Tangled errors

Users prefer to respond to errors and uncertainties with action, instead of pausing to sort things out. They often defer error correction advice, hoping that a later opportunity will be more convenient. The result is that they often make a series of mistakes before they have corrected the first in the series (e.g., Carroll and Rosson, 1987). It is not always clear how to perspicuously *unstack* errors in providing recovery information for the user.

In Section 3.4 we described the problem P8 had in defining field labels (error 2). She had partially designed a form, but had entered data along with her field labels. After several messages, she succeeded in deleting the data and in creating additional field labels. However, in making this correction she omitted the city, state and zip fields from her form. Perhaps in settling her more long-standing concerns about adding data, she lost her place in the form design task. She went on in spite of this error, but as she began to enter data into her form, she recognized that it was incomplete. She received a SmartHelp message suggesting she select Redesign, and add city, state and zip fields, but decided to instead continue adding what data she could to the incomplete forms.

That done, P8 tried to follow the SmartHelp advice, but was confused by the appearance of the Redesign screen. She exited, and tried Add Data, a more familiar, but in this case irrelevant, function. The Add Data function does not display data that has been previously entered, it just presents blank forms. P8 used the Next Form function several times, searching for her prior work, and inadvertently adding several blank forms to the file (error 7). She had not solved the missing-fields problem, and now faced a blank-forms problem too. In such cases, our strategy was to try to advise on the problem of current interest. The example in Table 4 is a case in which this led to some convolution.

4.2 User goals are dynamic

Telling someone how to do it even a moment after they figure out how to do it can frustrate more than assist. And users' goals are in constant flux; one goal quickly leads to another or the "same" goal is rearticulated in a different vocabulary. When P3 repeatedly accessed the application's passive help without taking action, we assumed he was having trouble and sent a SmartHelp message.

Table 4: Guiding recovery from tangled errors can be problematic

P3 had continuingly postponed correcting his problem with zip code field length (see Section **3.3**). In the context of this uncorrected error, he later made an error with date format. He chose "September 6, 1950" as a format template, not realizing that this was too long to fit in the date field he had specified for his form design (n.b. the format "9/6/50" would have fit). SmartHelp sent a message for this error, but P3 again postponed action. A complication with both of these errors is that the consequence does not become plain until later when the user attempts to add data to the form. (How-it-works help, in fact, is directed at explaining these subsequent effects). P3 continued on to the stage of adding data, though now he faced unravelling a tangle of errors.

When P3 tried to enter data for his first form, he saw that he could only enter a four digit zip code. He got a SmartHelp message describing how to redesign the form; however, he continued to add data. When he attempted to enter the date he got a system error message. He also got another SmartHelp message suggesting he specify another date format, or more space for dates in the form design. He was unhappy and puzzled that so much was being made of "one" error: "What's wrong with my file design? There's only one field that's too short." This comment indicates that he had not noticed all of his errors. He announced that he would go back and change the length of the zip code field, but while deciding this he had paused while cursoring the date field. SmartHelp sent another message on how to correct the date field error, and P3 set about doing this. In the course of this error recovery, he apparently forgot how to correct the zip code error.

He next selected Add Data, perhaps trying to directly alter the zip code field length in his first form (which is not possible). However, in the process of doing a search for the first form, he made yet another error, inadvertently adding blank forms to the file (error 7). Again, there were two tangled errors. SmartHelp advised him to select Remove to correct the latter error. However, P3 was afraid of taking this advice, and instead he tried the Search/Update function to browse his file. This was in fact the correct function for correcting the zip code field length, but he seemed to have forgotten all about that error and instead just confirmed that he indeed had some blank forms in his file. He exited to choose Remove and delete them. He then tried to resume work, only to get yet another message about zip code field length. At this point he was confused enough to insist that he had already corrected that error. He again browsed the file, confirmed that it was still wrong, and (finally) corrected the error, conceding, "Ah, you are right system, I forgot to catch it."

But it turned out that he was merely browsing the help and had already figured out what he wanted to do with respect to his current problem. The message just annoyed him: "Well I've already guessed that!" In another case, he made an error (placing an x where he should have put a +) immediately after checking a help screen. Again, we saw a clear case on which to provide SmartHelp. But again, he complained that he had already recognized the error and set a goal for himself to fix it: "I knew I hadn't specified where the new lines were, and I intended to go back and change it. I would have preferred the system not to have told me that." It is daunting how fine a line there is between annoying the user (as in these examples) and helping the user to confirm or better articulate a plan (as in section **2.2** above).

P1 entered a sequence code without a + or x (error 11). She got a system error message which she interpreted to mean that she should enter an x in *all* fields. As she was doing this, she received a SmartHelp message designed to clarify the system error message. Unfortunately, this message arrived at *just* the moment that P1 had made a typo in adding one of her erroneous x's. She had already switched her attention to correcting the typo; she did not appear to even read the SmartHelp message; she commented that it annoyed her to get help for mere typos.

4.3 The system state changes

Perhaps the harshest timing problem we noted involved episodes in which help was sent to a user whose most recent action before the help had the effect of changing the system state. This is a type of error that can occur anytime a help facility is not fully integrated with its application. SmartHelp, of course, was not integrated with the application we studied, but this is also typical of intelligent help demonstration systems. In one example, P8 happened to press the Escape key immediately after having typed Name as a field label (instead of separate first and last name fields, error 4). Thus, the arrival of the SmartHelp message was immediately preceded by a system confirmation prompt asking whether P8 really wanted to exit without saving. P8 was in the process of reading this prompt when the SmartHelp message arrived, advising her to create separate first and last name fields. The prompt was more salient (clearly more threatening); P8 seemed not even to read the SmartHelp message. She quickly closed the SmartHelp window and responded that she did *not* want to exit without saving her data. The SmartHelp message was effectively lost to her as a consequence of the Escape prompt.

In other cases, the SmartHelp message arrived coincident with an ineluctable state transition (one with no buffering prompt). The user might see the situation, see and understand the help, and even have the intention to follow the advice, but be unable to do so because as soon as the help panel was dismissed (and control returned from SmartHelp to the application) the suspended system state transition would occur. The user would have to try to implement the advice from a *different system state*. When P3 originally made his zip code field too short, SmartHelp was a moment too slow in intervening. P3 had already made the keypress to save his form design and proceed to the next screen when a SmartHelp message arrived. The action suggested in the message to correct the zip code field length was to be accomplished on the screen that was about to disappear. When P3 closed the SmartHelp window, the system presented the next screen (the Format screen), and the advice no longer applied.

5. Expectations and bounded intelligence

We deliberately bounded SmartHelp's "intelligence" in what we thought was a reasonable way: it knew about the application function and the user task domain but *not* about the specific tasks we had suggested to our participants or about a given participant's knowledge and skill. Our participants, however, were both distracted and disappointed by the limitations of SmartHelp's intelligence.

5.1 Meta-dialogs

Generally, our participants did maintain a task focus, that is, they were engaged by creating database reports. In some cases, they became distracted by SmartHelp itself though, directing their attention to it, rather than using it as a task-transparent tool (see Winograd and Flores', 1986, discussion of "ready to hand"). For example, there were a few comments that SmartHelp was inconsistent; some errors caused the system to intervene, while others (those we considered mere typos) did not. In a few cases, participants appeared to be "testing" the system. P6 designed a state field that was too short (error 5). The consequence of this error is only apparent at a later point when data is entered. Therefore, when P6 received a message suggesting he move the field delimiter one space to the right, he wondered why. Two spaces seemed to be there and that was enough. He ignored the advice and continued to the next field. He got the same message a second time. At this point, he correctly deduced that the space immediately after the field label was a nondata region. However, the how-to-do-it message had not given him this explanation, and he decided to test it further by flouting the advice once again. When another message did not arrive (SmartHelp had already given him the same advice three times), he exclaimed, "I got away with it!"

5.2 Problems with intention

Participants sometimes acted as if in principle *anything* could be done by SmartHelp, that what it did not do was simply not implemented (yet). P2 was entering data into a form and making a routine typo: she was typing both first and last names into the last name field. She noticed this very quickly and corrected herself. However, she appeared to be surprised that the system didn't "notice" this problem and offer help: "obviously there are no messages for that error ... the system isn't set up for that". The messages she received earlier gave her an expectation that the system was smart, but not a clear expectation about its specific limitations.

In several troubling cases, users seemed to expect that SmartHelp could, or perhaps should accurately discern their *intentions*, regardless of how indeterminately these were reflected in their actions. Table 5 presents an example of a user who expected the system to recognize what she meant to happen when she made an error. In another example, P3 was experimenting with upper versus lower case letters in the state field. He got a SmartHelp message, and while waiting for it, speculated that it was due to his experiment. "Maybe it's complaining because I messed around in the Oregon [State] field. That would be interesting because I intended to mess around. I really didn't want to get a message." The user seemed to think that the system should be able to distinguish "messing around" from genuine error.

Table 5: Users may expect their intentions to be obvious

Sometimes SmartHelp would have had to be omniscient to satisfy users' expectations. P7 accidentally added a blank form to her file (error 7) just before exiting. When she received a SmartHelp message explaining how adding data works, and that the blank form she just entered should be removed, she seemed annoyed. "I wish I knew this before. This is a really snotty message. It's telling me that I did something wrong when I didn't know what I was supposed to do. What I did was, I entered my last form and I didn't know how to get out. I pressed F10 and nothing happened, so I pressed help and it told me what to do. So then I pressed Shift F10 to get out, and it comes back and tells me 'you pressed F10 - you shouldn't have done that. You should have pressed Shift - F10,' which I eventually did." However, SmartHelp could not diagnose the error *until* she had exited since she might have added data to the blank form (before exiting). She expected SmartHelp to recognize what she *intended to do* when she pressed F10.

5.3 Fragile credibility

The upshot of the various problems our participants experienced in interpreting and using SmartHelp advice led some of them to seriously question its advisory competence. P2 tried to create and format a report using the Print function instead of the Report function (error 13). SmartHelp eventually diagnosed this error from a series of inappropriate codes and a lengthy hesitation. When a message was sent P2 expressed relief, but also frustration: "Finally, a message that tells me something useful!" It was difficult to diagnose this error, but P2 couldn't know this. What was salient to her was that the process was halting and misleading.

The problem of credibility was especially poignant in cases where SmartHelp provided apparently correct and appropriate advice, that was not followed, after which SmartHelp was blamed for whatever unfortunate outcome ensued. P6 had inadvertently stored a blank form (error 7), and SmartHelp advised him to choose the Remove function. P6 thought the advice sounded "arbitrary", but started to carry it out. However, he did not follow the instruction to put an = in the Retrieve Spec, but instead pressed F10, which selected all his forms for deletion. A confirmation prompt appeared, asking whether he was sure that he wanted to delete all his data. He sarcastically said, "Thanks!" Had he in fact followed the help, he would never have faced this confirmation prompt. Nevertheless, even much later in his work session, P6 still mistrusted SmartHelp: "I don't believe it. I don't trust it."

6. How-it-works and How-to-do-it help

Our contrast of how-to-do-it and how-it-works styles of help was very exploratory (we only studied 4 users in each style). Moreover, as mentioned earlier, we found that operationalizing the distinction in practice is difficult (though it sounds so clear in principle). Error (9), as described in Tables 1 and 2, involved retrieval. The how-to-do-it message we developed contained some how-it-works information (the material in parenthesis).

> You can leave the fields blank, or optionally, put a name in the Last Name field, or a dollar amount with a < or > in the Salary field, etc. (e.g. typing Jones retrieves forms with Jones).

The mere list of procedural options did not seem to be coherent without *some* overall example, but giving the overall example compromised our design rule by implying *why* the procedural steps might be useful. Despite our reservations about such compromises, we included the contrast to try to begin to understand the qualitative consequences of different advisory strategies. To that end, we have classified the how-it-works and how-to-do-it patterns we noticed in our protocols.

6.1 Managing procedural details

The how-to-do-it variant of SmartHelp provided users with step-by-step procedures. Sometimes the suggested procedures involved too many steps for the participant to keep in mind. When the SmartHelp window was closed (to return control to the application), the steps were no longer in view and participants began to forget the details. SmartHelp advised P3 to separate last and first name fields and to type separate fields for address, city and state (error 4). By the time he had finished typing the last and first name field labels, he had forgotten the rest of the advice: "Now I've forgotten what the instructions were... something about city and state."

In other how-to-do-it cases, some procedural details were left to be inferred by the participant, but sometimes were not correctly inferred. P3 was entering blank forms (error 7). Our message suggested the Remove function, but did not explicitly remind the user that pressing Escape was a prerequisite. P3 took the help literally and was stymied. P6 was following SmartHelp advice, using Escape as a preliminary to redesigning his form. SmartHelp omitted specifying how P6 should respond to a system prompt asking if he wanted to exit without saving. Confused by this prompt, he became snarled in a loop, answering "no" to the prompt and then keying Escape again, getting the prompt again, and so forth.

Our intent in providing how-it-works help was to give the user a rationale and let the user generate procedural details. This clearly did not always work (though in several cases this seemed to stem from inconsistencies in the application itself). In the course of printing mailing labels, P2 hesitated at the option field for indicating number of forms per page. The default was set at 1, but she wanted to print all her labels (forms) on one page: "I'm not sure if they're counting each one of these as a form or not, if each one of these is a form, or all together it is a form." She incorrectly left the default at 1, exiting from the Print Options screen (error 12). She received the how-it-works message for this error but it didn't seem to help: "I would like to print more than one on a page, but

I'm not quite sure how to do that. I'm wondering if I have to go all the way backwards."

P5 had inadvertently added a blank form to her file (error 7) and had selected Remove to recover. This brought up the Retrieve screen, which looked like a blank copy of the form. P5 was unsure what to do and ultimately went on with the Remove operation without taking any action on the Retrieve screen -- thereby specifying that *all* forms were to be removed. She got yet another explanation of how Remove works (i.e., that it would remove all her data): "I was surprised that all four forms were going to be removed, because I was on a blank form and I was assuming I was going to delete that one ... So maybe I want Search and Update because Remove did not work." Indeed, P5 discovered a method to remove blank forms using Search/Update, but she had to do this because she could not reason from the how-it-works help on Remove to a procedure for using Remove.

6.2 Users need rationales

Despite some problems getting from a how-it-works rationale to a procedure, our participants seemed to want to know *why* they were doing what they were doing. This unfulfilled need was quite salient to us with the how-to-do-it participants. Recall how P6 was led to "test" SmartHelp because he could not see the reason for the advice he was given (section **5.1**). P3 typed Name as a field label (error 4), and was advised to delete that field label and to type two separate fields for first and last name. He seemed annoyed, "Well, it's very fussy, insisting that I type in first name and last name." He was unaware that he needed a separate field for items that he might want to list separately on reports, and the how-to-do-it message did not help him see this rationale. P3 evidenced a similar reaction later when he had accidentally added blank forms to his data (error 7) and was advised on how to remove them. He examined the description of Remove in the application's passive help system. "I don't want to delete them. Why should I want to delete them [the forms]?" It seemed too severe a remedy without more rationale.

Without an explicit rationale, participants sometimes generated their own incorrect explanations. In section **4.1** we described P3's problem with date format. SmartHelp advised him: "Pick a different date format or make the field larger." P3 paraphrased this: "I see, it didn't like my date field." He picked a shorter format for the date (i.e., "9/6/50" instead of "September 6, 1950), commenting: "This is easier for me to remember." His problem was fixed, but the rationale he generated indicates that he didn't understand *why* it was fixed. The date format refers to how the application displays the dates, not to how it accepts them as input. It seemed that following how-to-do-it help without rationales could actually *impair* learning, as illustrated in Table 6.

Table 6: Over-dependence on how-to-do-it help

P8's self-initiative seemed to be undermined by the how-to-do-it help: "I'm thinking now that these help messages are great. When I get stuck I just do something wrong 'cause I know it will come back and help me out." This indeed seemed to be her principal strategy. Through the work session, she became increasingly dependent on SmartHelp -- both in terms of the frequency with which she required help and the level of procedural detail required (i.e., even after 20 very detailed how-to-do-it SmartHelp messages, she still failed to sort her mailing labels; we eventually compromised our no-knowledge-of-task-specifics principle and directed her to "Put 3x in Address, 4 + in City...", but even this to no avail). Especially toward the end of the session, P8 rarely accessed the application's passive help to puzzle out what to do on her own. Perhaps not surprisingly, she was our least successful participant with respect both to progress during the learning phase of the work session and with respect to the three transfer tasks.

7. Usability and intelligent help

It seems paradoxical that while learning to use computing equipment is difficult (Carroll and Mazur, 1986; Mack et al., 1983), computers are seen as having the potential to enable major advances in education (Sleeman and Brown, 1982). How can one learn with a tool that is itself hard to learn? A resolution of this puzzle may reside in the application of artificial intelligence techniques to education and assistance (e.g., Jackson and LaFrere, 1984). Intelligent training and help might ease the difficulties of learning to use computing equipment and at the same time pioneer new educational technology.

Our study shows how it is possible to help people by providing "intelligent" help. This may seem curiously understated. But it must be taken in context: our study also shows how it is possible to frustrate and annoy people by providing intelligent help. This range of possibilities is important since current research on intelligent advisory facilities has not adequately addressed their utility and usability as a research issue (Carroll and McKendree, 1987). Our study urges reconceptualizing intelligent interface services as being simultaneously usability *problems* as well as usability *solutions*.

7.1 Lessons from simulated intelligent help

Our simulation of intelligent help in fact helped people in a diversity of ways. In some cases, SmartHelp seemed to be "answering the unasked question". Just as the user became aware of a concern, SmartHelp provided the right insight. In other cases, users were interested in pursuing a particular plan. When SmartHelp suggested that plan to them, they had the encouragement they needed to try it out. Some success cases were more marginal: the user followed SmartHelp's advice on an "anyway" basis, that is, without clearly coming to an understanding of why the help had suggested what it had. In this description, we have focused most attention on the *problems* we noted with SmartHelp, both because they were more salient to us and because we expect that at this point in the development of the technology more can be learned from the problems. There was a great variety of problems.

Our participants had diverse prior experience with systems; they generated their own goals, and bridged between goals in unique and creative ways. Recognizing and tracking goals was difficult, as was interpreting errors in terms of user goals. The users' prior knowledge and experience routinely preempted and distorted their use of SmartHelp. SmartHelp messages that arrived a split second after the user had come to a conclusion about a problem were regarded as annoyances. Errors were frequently tangled with other errors, increasing the chance that SmartHelp messages could be misattributed by mere coincidence. The non-integration of the help facility and the application itself allowed help messages to sometimes arrive coincident with system state changes, which rendered the help inapplicable and difficult to interpret.

SmartHelp lost credibility with users for even small deficiencies. In some cases the root cause of the deficiency was the user's misinterpretation or misexecution of the advice. There may be a rather high cost to systems in projecting "intelligence" to users. Intelligent entities are expected to be responsible; they can be "blamed" for troubles with greater impunity. Intelligent help systems can be experienced by users as *making commitments* to render assistance (Winograd and Flores, 1986). This is qualitatively different than the experience of using traditional panel-based help. Failing to find some relevant information in a book or panel-based help is frustrating but familiar, failing to get help from an intelligent help system is a case of interaction breakdown without further arenas of discourse on which to fall back (Winograd and Flores, 1986).

In sum, the development of intelligent help systems faces serious usability challenges. Systems may eventually do a better job of recognizing users goals' and expectations; of representing, diagnosing and using the user's prior knowledge and experience in designing help; of answering current, but unasked, questions more frequently than currently irrelevant questions; of sorting out and advising on tangles of user errors. But how good a job is good enough? Even human advisors, advising in face-to-face interactions, succeed only moderately in providing appropriate advice -- and they often attain this level of success by adjusting strategies and trying again and again (Aaronson and Carroll, 1987a, 1987b, 1987c; Coombs and Alty, 1980). In both cases the real question is how to deploy a less than perfect advisory capability. In the area of intelligent help, this has not yet been seriously articulated as a research concern.

7.2 Directions for further research and development

In the immediate future we are concerned with making the SmartHelp simulation a more usable delivery vehicle for intelligent help. The simulation was compelling to our participants, and this encourages us to want to carry this work forward. In using Wizard of Oz simulations to study new user interface technology, there is always a question of how far the simulation can be pushed. For example, the listening typewriter studies of Gould, Conti and Hovanyecz (1985) examined behavioral issues for a speech recognition application before that technology was able to actually support such applications. Gould et al. were able to usefully simulate recognition failures in their study, but not false positives (i.e., cases in which the recognition device mistakenly recognizes a word in its vocabulary). We do not as yet understand what all the limitations of the SmartHelp simulation are, but this seems like an important area to push on.

One area we would like to address is that of providing a communication "backchannel" (Krauss and Glucksberg, 1977). SmartHelp did not allow participants to respond to the help it provided or to initiate requests for SmartHelp. Indeed, this limitation may have aggravated the problem of interaction breakdown: if the help was not adequate, there was nothing the user could do but ignore it, only a further or persisting error would trigger further SmartHelp. Our participants did sometimes express a desire for more or less help to the Experimenter, but the comments could not be directed to SmartHelp. We are experimenting with approaches to providing a backchannel. In one the user can request additional help as an option when closing a SmartHelp message window. In another, the user can open a dialog window and send a natural language request to SmartHelp. These techniques may increase the user's sense of being in control of interactions with the help system.

More generally, we need to gain experience with providing advice through vehicles like SmartHelp. Existing pedagogical theory and expertise overwhelmingly pertains to interactions with human advisors or with books. We tried to exert control on help dialogs by creating a library of prototypes to cover common cases and to guide on-the-fly design. But we had to do this by empirical trial-and-error. Studies focussing on how people advise others when they are interacting via limited channels like SmartHelp can complement our work (see for example, Aaronson and Carroll, 1987b; Hill and Miller, 1988).

We deliberately bounded SmartHelp with respect to task-specific knowledge. We wanted to provide help for system problems and for general task planning, but not for the specific intentions and plans of given users. Yet, as we have observed, some of the problems people had with SmartHelp devolved from its lack of specific knowledge about what they were trying to do. In some of these cases, it was really unclear that we even *could* have accurately diagnosed intentions and plans from user actions. One direction in which to develop our SmartHelp work is to expand the bounds of SmartHelp's intelligence in the direction of supporting more detailed plan and goal inferencing, perhaps allowing the system to pose questions to the user in cases for which no confident analysis can be made.

We also decided to advise only on overt serious errors (i.e., not typos) and lengthy pauses in user activity that suggested incipient errors. Errors are extremely important user interaction events, both as potential disasters and as potential learning opportunities. However, there are other important interaction events, for example, entering a new arena of system function for the first time. SmartHelp could provide conceptual or procedural guidance to new function when it is first accessed, and in doing so control user errors.

SmartHelp treated nonadjacent errors as independent events. If a user was snarled in a tangle of errors, making the same error repeatedly, we treated the episode as a whole (for example, shifting from prepared messages to on-the-fly messages). But if the same error were repeated at distinct points in the work session, SmartHelp gave the same advice both times. We had no articulate strategy for altering the content of messages on the basis of what system function the user had already explored or what messages the user had already seen. There are many approaches to analyzing sequences of error instances into patterns (Coombs and Alty, 1984) or bugs (Burton and Brown, 1982; Reiser, Anderson, and Farrell, 1985; Spohrer, Soloway and Pope, 1985). Another direction in which to develop this work is to incorporate this kind of more abstract behavior analysis into diagnoses the simulation makes.

The present project also examined only simple advisory strategies, how-to-do-it and how-it-works, and made only a very preliminary analysis of these. We have, for example, remarked on the problem of providing compelling how-to-do-it help for errors that only have manifest effects later (Section **4.1**). The simulation technique seems robust enough to encourage further examination of the how-to-do-it versus how-it-works contrast, but also to consider compound advisory strategies. We have considered investigating how-to-do-it help as a backup for how-it-works, for example. Both styles seemed to have weaknesses and strengths, and might in fact complement each other. We also see the possibility to incorporate further styles of help into the SmartHelp simulation (e.g., example-based help, Rissland, Valcarce and Ashley, 1983; demonstration-based help, Lewis, 1986; Kirson, Carroll, Eckhoff, Kelley and Canetti, 1988).

Entering into a simulated coaching dialog with users is very delicate. Brown, Burton and deKleer (1982) note that good coaches don't break in every time *they* could have done it better. But whatever it is that guides them is pretty much an art. We were naturally constrained in that we only provided advice on diagnosable errors and long pauses, but we still sometimes felt the need for better guidance in deciding whether to intervene. Our approach of ceasing advice after three attempts within a single episode is similar to the "time out" approach of Fischer, Lemke and Schwab (1985) in which the frequency of advice is bounded for specified temporal envelopes. Both of these techniques are heuristic though, and somewhat arbitrary. We need a more explicit understanding of coaching intervention (e.g., with respect to issues like task interruption).

We also noticed some details in the implementation of the SmartHelp simulation that suggest further work. SmartHelp takes control of the keyboard and display of the user's "slave" workstation when it presents help windows (Checco and Carroll, 1986). In our system, the user regains control by a keypress which, as a side effect, closes the SmartHelp window and restores the display. This is a neat interaction with respect to managing the display, but it exacerbated the problem of confusing and misexecuting advice. After all, the advice was no longer there when the user went to apply it. (This is similar to the problem of switching screens in full-screen presentations of on-line help; Clark, 1981). Thus, we are considering approaches to maintaining SmartHelp windows while the user continues with the application, though this raises the question of how to control explicit closing of the help windows.

We mentioned at the outset that we carefully selected the database and report application we used with SmartHelp for its popularity and excellence as reported in the trade literature. Nevertheless, we ended up doing considerable advising on what could be called glitches in its interface. We are still confident that we selected a good application with respect to the state of the art; we are less confident that the state of the art in user interfaces is "clean" enough to provide the kind of testbed we wanted. This is an aspect of what we call the Advisory Interface Dilemma (Carroll, 1987): advances in advisory techniques are constrained by advances in information management and user interaction techniques. One solution to this problem, for us, is to work in the context of joint development of an application and its advisory facilities (though such joint development is not typical in current practice).

We are also examining approaches to obtaining a better library of prepared SmartHelp messages. As noted, most of the messages we provided were created on the fly, placing a great burden on the Experimenter operating SmartHelp. Perhaps we can improve our coverage by doubling or tripling the number of errors categorized (e.g., in previous work, an analysis of 6885 observed word processing error tokens into 40 types left only 250 in the Miscellaneous category; Carroll, Smith-Kerker, Ford and Mazur, 1986). A complicating factor in the present case is that most of our on-the-fly messages were evoked by errors committed while recovering from a prior error.

A final issue we are facing is that our simulation addressed intelligent help issues *only* in the context of people *learning* to use an application. Learning is a relevant task, but it is not the only task. An important aspect of the usability of any help facility is its use over time, and this must be assessed in a longitudinal investigation. This would be an extremely expensive and tedious kind of study for us to conduct (involving as it would round-the-clock human SmartHelp). Nevertheless, this kind of study may expose issues in the use of intelligent help systems that are not apparent when users are learning by doing instead of just doing (Campbell, 1988).

Current demonstration systems are being developed into tomorrow's intelligent help facilities. It is now truly a practical question to ask how this technology can be deployed in real application environments. The issues raised by our SmartHelp simulation and the possibilities we are investigating for enhancing the simulation are issues and possibilities for user interface presentations of real intelligent help facilities. Of course, we cannot know in advance how far we can push SmartHelp as a tool for articulating interface designs for intelligent help and anticipating problems and strengths in these designs. But we feel that this approach is a practical alternative to fully implementing an intelligent help facility in order to learn anything about its usability.

Acknowledgements

This paper originally appeared in *Communications of the ACM, 31,* 1064-1079. We thank R.B. Bhaskar, R.L. Campbell, R.L. Mack and M.B. Rosson for comments on earlier drafts of this paper. We also got many useful comments from presentations to the Yale University Artificial Intelligence group and the Software Development Technology Department at the Watson Research Center.

References

Aaronson, A.P. and Carroll, J.M. (1987a). The answer is in the question: A protocol study of intelligent help. *Behaviour and Information Technology, 6*, 393-402.

Aaronson, A.P. and Carroll, J.M. (1987b). Intelligent help in a one-shot dialog: A protocol study. In J.M. Carroll and P.P. Tanner (Eds.), *Proceedings of CHI + GI'87 Human Factors in Computing Systems and Graphics Interface.* (Toronto, April 5-9) ACM, New York.

Aaronson, A.P. and Carroll, J.M. (1987c). Understanding intelligent help: A protocol analysis of advisory interactions. IBM Research Report RC 13059.

Aaronson, A.P., Carroll, J.M., Kelley, J.F. and Canetti, S. 1988. SmartHelp: A dynamic prototyping tool for intelligent advisory dialog. Videotape demonstration, CHI'88 Human Factors in Computer Systems (Washington, D.C., 15-17 May).

Alty, J.L. and Coombs, M.J. 1980. University computing advisory services: the study of the man-computer interface. *Software -- Practice and Experience, 10,* 919-934.

Brown, J.S., Burton, R.R. and de Kleer, J. 1982. Pedagogical, natural language and knowledge engineering techniques in SOPHIE I, II, and III. In D. Sleeman and J.S. Brown (Eds.) *Intelligent tutoring systems.* New York: Academic Press.

Burton, R.R. 1982. Diagnosing bugs in a simple procedural skill. In D. Sleeman and J.S. Brown (Eds.) *Intelligent tutoring systems.* New York: Academic Press.

Campbell, R.L. 1988. Evaluating online assistance empirically. *IBM Research Report*, RC 13410.

Carroll, J.M. (1984). Minimalist training. *Datamation, 30/18* (November 1, 1984), 125-136.

Carroll, J.M. (1987). Five gambits for the Advisory Interface Dilemma. In U. Ulich, W. Dzida, and M. Frese (Eds.), *Psychological issues of human computer interaction in the work place*. Amsterdam: North Holland.

Carroll, J.M. and Kay, D.S. (1987). Prompting, feedback and error correction in the design of a Scenario Machine. *International Journal of Man-Machine Studies*, in press

Carroll, J.M. and Mazur, S.A. (1986). LisaLearning. *IEEE Computer, 19/11*, 35-49.

Carroll, J.M. and McKendree, J. (1987). Interface design issues for advice-giving expert systems. *Communications of the ACM, 30*, 14-31.

Carroll, J.M., Smith-Kerker, P.A., Ford, J.R., Mazur, S.A.. (1986). The minimal manual. *IBM Research Report 11637*.

Checco, J.C. and Carroll, J.M. (1986). SmartHelp. *IBM Research Report*, RC 12371.

Clark, I.A. 1981. Software simulation as a tool for usable product design. *IBM Systems Journal, 20/3*, 272-293.

Coombs, M.J. and Alty, J.L. (1980). Face-to-face guidance of university computer users--II: Characterizing advisory interactions. *International Journal of Man-Machine Studies, 12*, 407-429.

Coombs, M.J. and Alty, J.L. 1984. Expert systems: An alternate paradigm. *International Journal of Man-Machine Studies, 20*, 21-43.

Fischer, G., Lemke, A., and Schwab, T. 1985. Knowledge-based help systems. In L. Borman and B. Curtis (Eds.), *Proceedings of CHI'85 Human Factors in Computing Systems* (San Francisco, April 14-17), ACM, New York, 161-167.

Gould, J.D., Conti, J., and Hovanyecz, T. 1983. Composing letters with a simulated listening typewriter. *Communications of the ACM, 26/4*, 295-308.

Halasz, F.G. 1984. *Mental models and problem solving in using a calculator*. PhD Dissertation, Stanford University.

Hill, W.C. and Miller, J.R. 1988. Justified advice: A semi-naturalistic study of advisory strategies. MCC Technical Report.

Jackson, P. and LaFrere, P. 1984. On the application of rule-based techniques to the design of advice-giving systems. *International Journal of Man-Machine Studies, 20*, 63-86.

Kelley, J.F. 1983. An empirical methodology for writing user-friendly natural language computer applications. In A. Janda (Ed.), *Proceedings of CHI'83 Human Factors in Computing Systems*. (Boston, December 12-15) ACM, New York.

Kirson, D.A., Carroll, J.M., Eckhoff, R., Kelley, J.F., and Canetti, S. 1988. Specialist help using multiple media. Videotape demonstration, CHI'88 Human Factors in Computer Systems (Washington, D.C., 15-17 May).

Krauss, R.M. and Glucksberg, S. 1977. Social and nonsocial speech. *Scientific American, 236,* 100-105.

Lewis, C.H. 1986. Understanding what's happening in system interactions. In D.A. Norman and S.W. Draper (Eds.) *User-centered system design: New perspectives on human computer interaction.* Hillsdale, NJ: Erlbaum, pp. 171-185.

Mack, R.L., Lewis, C.H., and Carroll, J.M. 1983. Learning to use office systems: Problems and prospects. *ACM Transactions on Office Information Systems, 1,* 254-271.

Malhotra, A. and Sheridan, P.S. 1976. Experimental determination of design requirements for a program explanation system. *IBM Research Report,* RC 5831.

Mayer, R.E. 1981. The psychology of how novices learn computer programming. *Computing Surveys, 13,* 121-141.

McKendree, J., and Carroll, J.M. 1986. Advising roles of a computer consultant. In M. Mantei and P. Orbeton (Eds.), *Proceedings of CHI'86 Human Factors in Computing Systems* (Boston, April 13-17), ACM, New York, 35-40.

McKendree, J. and Carroll, J.M. (1987). Impact of feedback content on initial learning of an office system. In H. Bullinger and B. Schakel (Eds.), *Proceedings of Interact'87* (Stuttgart, September).

Pollack, M.E. 1985. Information sought and information provided: An empirical study of user/expert dialogues. In L. Borman and B. Curtis (Eds.), *Proceedings of CHI'85 Human Factors in Computing Systems* (San Francisco, April 14-17), ACM, New York, 155-159.

Reiser, B.J., Anderson, J.R., and Farrell, R.G. 1985. Dynamic student modelling in an intelligent tutor for Lisp programming. IJCAI *Proceedings,* pages.

Rissland, E.L., Valcarce, E. and Ashley, K. 1983. Explaining and arguing with examples. *Proceedings of the National Computer Conference.* Los Altos, CA: Morgan Kaufman.

Sleeman, D. and Brown, J.S. 1982. *Intelligent tutoring systems.* New York: Academic Press.

Spohrer, J.C., Soloway, E., and Pope, E. 1985. A goal/plan analysis of buggy Pascal programs. *Human Computer Interaction, 1,* 163-207.

Winograd, T. and Flores, F. (1986.) *Understanding computers and cognition.* Ablex, Norwood, NJ.

Index

The MIT Press, with Peter Denning, general consulting editor, and Brian Randall, European consulting editor, publishes computer science books in the following series:

ACM Doctoral Dissertation Award and Distinguished Dissertation Series

Artificial Intelligence, J. Michael Brady, Daniel G. Bobrow, and Randall Davis, editors

Charles Babbage Institute Reprint Series for the History of Computing, Martin Campbell-Kelly, editor

Computer Systems, Herb Schwetman, editor

Exploring with Logo, E. Paul Goldenberg, editor

Foundations of Computing, Michael Garey and Albert Meyer, editors

History of Computing, I. Bernard Cohen and William Aspray, editors

Information Systems, Michael Lesk, editor

Logic Programming, Ehud Shapiro, editor; Fernando Pereira, Koichi Furukawa, and D. H. D. Warren, associate editors

The MIT Electrical Engineering and Computer Science Series

Research Monographs in Parallel and Distributed Processing, Christopher Jesshope and David Klappholz, editors

Scientific Computation, Dennis Gannon, editor